JEWISH
HISTORY
—— IN ——
100 NUTSHELLS

JEWISH HISTORY
IN
100 NUTSHELLS

Naomi Pasachoff
Robert J. Littman

JASON ARONSON INC.
Northvale, New Jersey
London

This book was set in 10 pt. Times Roman by Alpha Graphics, Pittsfield, New Hampshire, and printed by Haddon Craftsmen of Scranton, Pennsylvania.

Library of Congress Cataloging-in-Publication Data

Pasachoff, Naomi E.
    Jewish history in 100 nutshells / Naomi Pasachoff, Robert J.
  Littman.
      p. cm.
    Includes bibliographical references and index.
    ISBN 1-56821-179-1
    1. Jews—History. 2. Judaism—History. I. Littman, Robert J.,
  1943– . II. Title. III. Title: Jewish history in one hundred
  nutshells.
  DS118.P335 1995
  909'.04924—dc 20   94-19020

Manufactured in the United States of America. Jason Aronson Inc. offers books and cassettes. For information and catalog, write to Jason Aronson Inc., 230 Livingston Street, Northvale, New Jersey 07647.

To our respective children,
the next generation:
Eloise and Deborah
Adam, Emma, and Tish

CONTENTS

PREFACE

Why have we chosen to write another history of the Jews? Many excellent one-volume histories have been written this century, such as Margolis and Marx's *History of the Jewish People*; Paul Johnson's best-seller *A History of the Jews*; and the highly scholarly work *A History of the Jewish People*, edited by H. H. Ben-Sasson. This book does not attempt to compete with these, but rather to fill a different need. Because the history of the Jews covers such a long period, over 3,500 years, and so many lands, it is a microcosm of the history of the West. Consequently, even a one-volume work is difficult to read from beginning to end to gain the sweep of Jewish history. We have therefore chosen to write a review, about half to a third the size of other one-volume histories, which the reader can more easily digest. We recognize, too, that many readers will not want to begin on page 1 and read through to the end, but are interested in individual topics or periods in Jewish history. To fill this need, we have broken the book into 100 "nutshells," individual topics that stand on their own, that can be understood without reading what has come before. At the same time, to make events more comprehensible, these nutshells, if read from beginning to end, or in sections, will provide a history of the Jews in chronological order.

The choice of topics has been difficult. Some major individuals and events have been omitted. Other authors might have made other choices. For those who want to fill in the gaps, we suggest they consult the history by Ben-Sasson and other works cited in the bibliography. To denote the period before the birth of Jesus, we use B.C.E. (before the Common Era) and after Jesus, C.E. (Common Era), rather than B.C. and A.D., respectively.

We are indebted to various scholars who have read all or part of our manuscript. They gave valuable guidance and in many cases they saved us from error. However, all errors and omissions remain our own. These scholars include Professor Yehuda Bauer, Hebrew University of Jerusalem; Professor Shaye Cohen, Brown University; Professor Cyrus Gordon, New York University; and Professor Paula Hyman, Yale University. We are also indebted to Rabbi Morris Goldfarb for his translation of *Love* (see nutshell #43). Our respective spouses, Jay and Bernice, aided and encouraged us and mediated any disputes between us.

Naomi Pasachoff wrote nutshells 39, 40, 42 and 53 through 100. Robert Littman wrote 1 through 38, 41, and 43 through 52. We, however, are both responsible for the whole.

Williamstown, Massachusetts, and Honolulu, Hawaii

CHRONOLOGY

1600 B.C.E.	Abraham and the first patriarchs
1200–1300	Moses
1200	Joshua and the early settlement of Israel
1050	Saul and the establishment of the monarchy
1000	King David
970	King Solomon
928	Split of the kingdom into Israel and Judah
720	Sargon conquers and destroys northern kingdom of Israel and transports the population to Assyria
586	Destruction of the First Temple; fall of Jerusalem to Nebuchadnezzar and the Babylonians; population transported to Babylon
538	Jews allowed to return to Jerusalem by Persian king Cyrus. Building of the Second Temple
458	Ezra leads second wave of returnees from Babylon
330–323	Alexander the Great conquers the Near East
167	Revolt of the Maccabees begins
37	Herod becomes king of Judea with Roman support
4	Birth of Jesus
66–70 C.E.	Jewish War
70	Destruction of Second Temple
132–135	Bar Kokhba revolt
200	Redaction of the Mishnah

337	Constantine dies and the Roman Empire becomes Christian
350–450	The Talmud edited
572	The birth of Mohammed
1200	Maimonides
1492	Expulsion of Jews from Spain
1800–1900	Emancipation of Jews
1881	Pogroms in Russia and beginning of *aliyah* to Israel and immigration to the United States
1897	Theodor Herzl and First Zionist Congress
1914–1918	World War I
1917	Balfour Declaration
1939–1945	World War II and the Holocaust—6 million Jews murdered
1948	Birth of State of Israel
1956	Sinai campaign
1967	Six-Day War
1973	Yom Kippur War
1977	Peace with Egypt
1985	Falashas arrive in Israel
1992–1993	Mass immigration of Russian Jews to Israel

1

ABRAHAM AND THE PATRIARCHS

Abraham is the first Jew, from whom all Jews trace their descent. According to the Bible, the God of Israel appeared to him and chose him to father a great nation. Abraham originated in Babylon or Mesopotamia and settled in Canaan. The biblical chronology dates him to about 1600 B.C.E.

Every group of humans creates a myth to explain its foundation and origins and how it came to be in its present state. Groups that practice a religion formulate such myths as part of their sacred history, that is, a history that links them with a god or gods, and details their origins from the beginning of the world to the present, intertwining their historic relationship with that deity or deities. Societies that trace their descent from a common ancestor use this sacred history to show the kinship links that join all the population.

The sacred history of the Jews is embodied in the Hebrew Bible, which consists of three sections: the Torah (see nutshell #4), or Five Books of Moses; the Prophets; and the Writings. The Torah recounts the origins of the Jewish people, all of whom share common ancestors, Abraham and Sarah. The first event in the sacred history of the Jews is God's creation of the world and of the first man, Adam, and the first woman, Eve. There follows a genealogy that traces Adam's descendants patrilineally, that is, through the male line, to Abraham, the son of Terah. In addition to the myth of their foundation from Mesopotamia through Abraham, the Israelites had a second foundation myth, from Egypt through Moses. These separate foundation myths were integrated with the settlement of the descendants of Abraham in Egypt and the return of the Israelite people to Canaan from Egypt under the leadership of Moses 400 years later.

God appeared to Abraham, who lived in a town called Ur of the Chaldees by the Bible. This city has been variously identified, including the Sumerian royal town of Ur or a town in northern Mesopotamia in Aram. God told Abraham that He would make him a great nation and instructed Abraham to leave his country and go to the land He would show him. Abraham obeyed God. Taking his wife, Sarah, who was his paternal half sister, and his brother's son, Lot, he went to Canaan. Having settled in Canaan as a seminomad,

1

Abraham was driven by famine to Egypt, but later returned to Canaan. Abraham fathered Ishmael by Sarah's handmaiden Hagar. Through the intervention of Sarah, Hagar and Ishmael were later driven off. It is from Ishmael that the Arabs trace their descent. God had promised Abraham abundant offspring, and finally in her old age Sarah conceived and gave birth to Isaac. Circumcision was introduced as a mark of God's covenant with Abraham and his descendants.

After some years had passed, God decided to test Abraham. He ordered him to sacrifice his son Isaac on Mount Moriah. Abraham went to obey, but God provided a ram for sacrifice in Isaac's place. This incident sets apart the God of Israel, who did not demand human sacrifice, from the god of the Canaanites. The general picture of Abraham in the Torah is that of a wealthy patriarch, head of a large clan that consisted of relatives, children, wives, and retainers. In his attack on Sodom, for example, Abraham had 318 men under his command. He made military alliances, dealt with kings, and established various altars and places of worship. He worshiped God, obeyed Him, and was a righteous man, a fitting father of his people.

The genealogy continues with Abraham's son Isaac, who does little of distinction, but who fathers Jacob and Esau. Jacob was later named Israel; from him the Jews take their name b'nei Yisrael, or "sons of Israel." Jacob had twelve sons, whose descendants became the twelve tribes of Israel, known collectively as the people of Israel. One of them, Joseph, was sold into slavery by his brothers. He was taken to Egypt, where he rose to a position of prominence. He was reunited with his family when, as governor of Egypt, he helped them during a famine that devastated the area. His family then settled in Egypt, but over a period of several generations, the Egyptians enslaved the Israelites.

Except for the Torah, no account exists of the early history of the Jews. Archaeological material gives us information on settlement and conquest, patterns of trade, and monumental architecture, but relates little specific historical information about individuals or events, at least until the first half of the first millennium B.C.E. Even in that period, except for archaeological confirmation of some historical events, such as the Assyrian invasion of Palestine, we must rely largely on the Torah and the Prophets for our history of the period. In evaluating this earlier material, all we can say is that the ancient Israelites believed these stories to be a true account of their origins.

While archaeological evidence is at variance with many of the early foundation myths, especially regarding a large-scale conquest of Canaan by the Israelites after they left Egypt, it is compatible with other aspects. Canaan in the second millennium was inhabited by one of a group of people, named Semites from their common language group. The Semites included many of the peoples of the Middle East, such as the Babylonians, Canaanites, Israelites, and Aramaeans. The major non-Semitic groups were the Hittites and the Egyptians. Canaan was under the control of Egypt for much of the latter half of the second millennium. Pharaoh Thutmose III in 1459 B.C.E. conquered it, garrisoned cities with soldiers, and collected tribute. Native rulers were left in their positions as clients. The Israelites grew as a distinct group in Canaan around the 13th century. Egyptian influence was strong in Palestine, both in politics and in commerce. Many foreign groups lived and worked in Egypt, particularly as mercenaries in their wars with the Hittites in the early 13th century. Thus, the existence of people of Babylonian or Mesopotamian origins settling in Palestine and later Egypt is consistent with archaeological material and historical sources other than the Torah.

2

MOSES

Moses is the single most important figure in Jewish history and religion. He led the Israelites out of Egypt and gave them the Ten Commandments at Mount Sinai. The story of Moses is contained in the Torah, also known as the Pentateuch (from the Greek "five books"), or the Five Books of Moses.

Many generations after Joseph there arose in Egypt a pharaoh who "knew not Joseph" and his good works for Egypt, and oppressed and enslaved the Israelites. Pharaoh ordered all newborn Hebrew males to be thrown into the river to drown. The parents of one Hebrew infant placed their baby in a basket and set it adrift in the Nile, in an effort to save the child. The daughter of Pharaoh discovered the infant among the bulrushes. She named him Moses and raised him as her own, an Egyptian prince. When he reached adulthood, Moses saw an Egyptian overseer beating a Hebrew slave. Angered, he killed the overseer. To avoid the consequences of this act, he fled to Midian, which is probably in the Sinai (or possibly in present-day Saudi Arabia). There he married Zipporah, the daughter of a Midianite priest. One day while tending his father-in-law's sheep, by the mountain that was God's abode, he beheld a burning bush that was not consumed by the fire. Moses heard a voice calling from the bush, identifying Himself as YHVH, the God of Abraham, and using a new name: I AM THAT I AM. God revealed that He was always with His people and would be their helper and savior. He vowed to free the people of Israel from Egypt, with Moses as his messenger. Moses claimed to be an inadequate spokesman, not a man of words but one possessed of a slow tongue. God then assigned Aaron, Moses' brother, to aid him.

Moses returned to Egypt and demanded that Pharaoh free the Israelites, but God hardened Pharaoh's heart. Only after ten plagues struck Egypt, the last of which was the smiting of the firstborn in the homes of the Egyptians, did Pharaoh let the Israelites leave. Under Moses' leadership they fled as far as the Red Sea. Pharaoh changed his mind again and sent troops to kill the Israelites. God parted the sea and Moses led his people safely across. When the Egyptians tried to follow, the sea closed on them and drowned them.

The Israelites marched to Mount Sinai. While Moses ascended the mountain and communed with YHVH, the people under Aaron reverted to their idolatrous ways and fashioned a golden calf. When Moses descended, he smashed the tablets of the law that had been given to him by YHVH. Assisted by the sons of Levi, he then slaughtered 3,000 of the Israelites who had worshiped the golden calf. The people repented. The Israelites then wandered in the desert for forty years before reaching the land promised to them by YHVH. Just before they entered the land of Israel, Moses died.

There is no reason to doubt the historicity of Moses. He probably lived in the 13th century B.C.E., and the Pharaoh of the Exodus was most likely Ramses the Great (reigned 1292–1225 B.C.E.) or his son Merneptah (reigned 1225–1215 B.C.E.). From archaeological and extrabiblical sources, we know that Egyptians dominated Palestine in this era. Many foreign groups settled in Egypt, as did Jews throughout their history, including the prophet Jeremiah many centuries later. The earliest layers of the Torah were written by the 11th century B.C.E., at most 200 or 250 years after the migration from Egypt. In such a short period, it is likely that major events, such as a period of dwelling in Egypt, would be preserved. Moreover, Moses and other personages in the account, especially Levites, the members of Moses' tribe, bear Egyptian names. These include Phinehas, Merari, Hophni, and possibly Aaron and Miriam. Although the Torah gives a folk etymology, connecting the name Moses with the word *mashah*, meaning "draw forth," it probably derives from the Egyptian word for "born from" or "is born" and occurs in many Egyptian names, such as Ra-mose (Ramses) and Ptahmose.

Circumcision, adopted by the Hebrews, or Israelites, was an Egyptian custom. The Egyptian historian Manetho, who wrote a history of Egypt in the 3rd century B.C.E., described Moses as a disaffected Egyptian prince who led a slave revolt. Given our general knowledge of what Egyptian sources included in their records, it is most likely that Manetho did not obtain his material on this event from those sources, but from the Pentateuch, which he would have known from the many Jews who were living in Egypt at this period.

The most important element with possible Egyptian antecedents in the Moses story is the introduction of monotheism. This religious belief made the Jews unique in the ancient world, until it infiltrated the Roman Empire under Christianity. The text of Exodus indicates that in its earlier phases, Judaism acknowledged the supremacy of the One God, but also the existence of other gods. This is evident in victory hymns to YHVH, in such phrases as "who is like you among the gods." The first two commandments do not say that YHVH is the only god, but rather "You shall have no other god before my face." Monotheism was only fully developed and totally victorious among the Jews by the time of the Book of Deuteronomy. In its present form this text was written or at least revised substantially in the 7th century B.C.E., and there we find the central monotheistic prayer, *Shema*: "Hear, O Israel, YHVH is our God, YHVH alone." Since new concepts in all areas, including religion, do not originate ex nihilo, but develop out of existing trends, and since the Egyptian Moses was credited with the introduction of monotheism, Egyptian origins of this belief may exist. While Egyptian society was polytheistic, the Pharaoh Akhenaten (Amenhotep IV) (reigned 1367–1350 B.C.E.) tried to break the power of the priesthood by encouraging and elevating the worship of Amon Ra, thus creating a system that was monolatrous (worshiping a central god). After the death of Akhenaten, the power of the priesthood was revitalized and the city Amarna, built by Akhenaten, was destroyed and its very stones shattered. However, the monotheistic leanings, encouraged by Akhenaten, may have already entered the general belief system in Egypt. Whatever the Egyptian antecedents, it was the Israelites who took the creative step of developing monotheism and an invisible God.

Jewish tradition has Moses as an Egyptian nobleman, of the royal house, who is at the same time an Israelite. Ultimately, there is sufficient historical evidence to say that Moses was a Hebrew living in Egypt, who introduced the worship of YHVH, an all-seeing, invisible God who required no idols, and led his followers out of Egypt proper to the edges of Egyptian territory, where they lived for a long period of time. This group eventually entered Palestine, also under Egyptian influence. For the Jewish people, while Abraham was the first Jew and their ancestor, Moses was the founder of the Law and the religion.

3

THE TEN COMMANDMENTS AND THE REVELATION AT SINAI

According to the Bible, the Ten Words or Commandments—also called the Decalogue (from the Greek deka, "ten," and logos, "word")—were given by God on Mount Sinai and contain the central concepts of Judaism as a monotheistic religion. They have become the basic moral creed of Western civilization, first for Jews, then for Christians.

According to the Pentateuch, God came to Moses on Mount Sinai, amid thunder and lightning and fire. By His own finger He wrote the Ten Commandments on two stone tablets and gave them to Moses to convey to the people of Israel. But because Moses was so long on the mountain, the people reverted to their pagan ways and constructed a golden calf as an idol, under the direction of Aaron. When Moses descended from the mountain and saw the idolatry, he shattered the tablets. A battle ensued, and Moses and his forces slew the idolaters. At God's instruction, Moses then hewed two more tablets, which God reinscribed.

Christianity, which grew out of Judaism, adopted these commandments as the heart of the Law. The Protestant reformer Martin Luther wrote in the 16th century, "Never will there be found a precept comparable or preferable to these commands, for they are so sublime that no man could attain to them by his own power." Throughout Western culture they have been central not only to religious law but also to civil law and ethical behavior.

The Ten Commandments have been interpreted in various ways throughout history to suit the values of society of a particular time and various religious viewpoints. The commandments, slightly abbreviated, are as follows:

1. I am YHVH your God, who brought you forth from Egypt.
2. You shall have no other gods before Me. You shall not make for yourself a graven image, or any manner of likeness.
3. You shall not take the name of the Lord your God in vain.
4. Remember the Sabbath day, to keep it holy.

7

5. Honor your father and your mother.
6. You shall not murder.
7. You shall not commit adultery.
8. You shall not steal.
9. You shall not bear false witness.
10. You shall not covet.

In the first commandment God identifies who He is by His name, YHVH. This name was never pronounced, except by the high priest at Jerusalem on Yom Kippur in the sanctuary known as the Holy of Holies. In the sacred history of the Jews, as presented in the Torah, it is clear that ancient Israelite society was not consistently monotheistic, but rather began with YHVH as its God, the one who was superior to the gods of the neighboring people. We find much evidence of this in the text of the Torah. During the majority of the period of the First Temple, idols were present in the sanctuary and there was worship in part of other gods besides YHVH. Only through a long process, which concluded in the late 5th century B.C.E., did a unique concept in the ancient world emerge triumphant.

The second commandment forbids the making of graven images, that is, of representations. Judaism was alone in the ancient world in this doctrine. No ancient or primitive peoples believed that the images they fashioned were themselves gods. Rather, idols were like electric plugs, through which one could tap into the power of the gods. Thus, if one wished to become pregnant, one would pray to the image of the goddess of fertility and through this image would reach the power of the goddess. The use of images to focus the power of the gods was universal.

Even among the ancient Israelites the use of idols was difficult to eradicate. They remained a major part of the religion, at times sanctioned by the central worship at the Temple in Jerusalem. We find, for example, that during the First Temple period (10th to 6th centuries B.C.E.), idols of Asherah were present at the Temple and officially recognized for the majority of the period that the Temple stood. Various kings would throw out the idols, or readmit them at other periods. However, excavations almost without exception have unearthed large numbers of fertility idols in Israel, belonging to every biblical period. Judaism did not rid itself completely of idols until well into the rabbinic period in the first several centuries of the Common Era.

The remaining commandments were not unique to the Jews. Like many other elements in early Israelite culture, there is Egyptian influence. We find in the Egyptian document *The Protestation of Guiltlessness* from the *Book of the Dead* (18th to 21st dynasties, 1550–950 B.C.E.) a negative confession, including:

I have not blasphemed the god.
I have not killed.
I have not committed adultery.
I have not stolen.
I have not told lies.
I have not been covetous.

Except for the prohibition against graven images, all the negative charges from the Ten Commandments forbidding certain behaviors are contained in this Egyptian funerary text. The positive commandments—graven images, remembering the Sabbath day, honoring father and mother—are not there. However, similar sentiments are expressed in Egyptian wisdom literature. In *The Instruction of the Mayor ànd Vizier Ptahhotep* we find the following: "How good it is when a son accepts what his father says!" The observance of the Sabbath, however, does not appear in the small number of surviving Egyptian texts.

Although the Ten Commandments had their antecedents in Egypt, the unique features—the invisible God and the primacy of YHVH—developed over the course of the first millennium B.C.E. into the unique concept of monotheism, the major theological contribution of Judaism to religion and theology.

4

THE HEBREW BIBLE

The Hebrew Bible contains the history of the Jews, their religion, and their law codes. It reports historical events from the middle of the 2nd millennium B.C.E. to the 2nd century B.C.E. The different sections of the Bible were composed and put in written form over a 900-year period, from the 11th to the 2nd century B.C.E.

The Hebrew Bible is the sacred history of the Jews. It is sacred because it recounts the encounter of Jews with God and prescribes His worship, rules, and regulations between both God and man and man and man. It is a history because it explains how the Jews came to be at a particular time. The account begins with the creation of the world, the first man, and the genealogical links to Abraham, the first Jew, then proceeds to the historical events of the 5th century B.C.E. The noncanonical portions of the Bible, the Apocrypha, relate historical material as late as the 2nd century B.C.E.

The Hebrew Bible consists of three parts: the Torah (also known as the Five Books of Moses, or the Pentateuch), the Prophets (*Neviim*), and the Writings (*Ketuvim*). An acronym formed by the first letters of the Hebrew words (*T*)*orah*, (*N*)*eviim*, (*K*)*etuvim—Tanach—*is used for the Hebrew Bible.

The Torah is made up of five books—Genesis, Exodus, Leviticus, Numbers, and Deuteronomy. These names are derived from the Septuagint, the Greek translation of the Hebrew Bible developed in the 3rd to 1st century B.C.E. in Alexandria, Egypt. These books contain the sacred history of the Jewish people from the origin of the world to the death of Moses, just before the Israelites enter the land of Israel. As well as a narrative of events, the books contain the law code of the Jews and rules and regulations of the Temple, as practiced during the first millennium B.C.E. The Torah is the core of Jewish religious practice and worship. Since at least as early as the 5th century B.C.E. part of Jewish worship involved the public reading of the Torah. For the Jews of the Diaspora, and for the Jews of Israel after the destruction of the Second Temple by the Romans in 70 C.E., the public reading of the Torah in the synagogue was the key to worship and study, indeed to the religion itself. The Torah reached its present literary form about the 5th century B.C.E., although many sections of it were probably given their present form as early as the 9th century B.C.E. However, most Orthodox Jews and all ultra-Orthodox Jews believe that the entire Torah, along with the Oral Law, was given to Moses on Mount Sinai and contains the immutable word of God.

The second section, the Prophets, tells the story of the Israelites from Joshua, who leads the children of Israel into the Promised Land in the 12th century B.C.E., to the destruction of the Temple in 586 B.C.E. by the Babylonians, to the return to Israel under the Persians in 538 B.C.E. It comprises twenty-two books that bear the names of individual prophets. These books were considered divinely inspired. With the last prophet, Malachi, in the late 6th century, the divine spirit ceased to be active in Israel, according to tradition, but was preserved in rabbinic sources.

The third section, the Writings, was grouped together as works that seemed to be of human rather than divine inspiration. For example, in the Book of Esther the name of God does not appear. Not until the 2nd century C.E. was this section finally canonized.

There are also two other sections of writings not considered part of the official canon. These were composed in the Second Temple period (538 B.C.E.– 70 C.E.) and are referred to by the Greek names *Apocrypha* ("hidden") and *Pseudepigrapha* ("false writings"). The Talmud refers to them as *Sefarim Hizonim* ("extraneous books"). The Apocrypha are anonymous historical works, such as the Book of Maccabees, which is not included in the Jewish canon but is accepted by the Roman Catholic and Greek Orthodox churches. The Pseudepigrapha, which include often visionary texts, such as the Book of Enoch, are not accepted as a whole by any church. The Apocrypha were at times part of the Jewish canon, as evidenced by their appearance in the Septuagint, but did not become canonical. On the other hand, the Pseudepigrapha are not considered canonical by any religion.

Taken together, the Hebrew Bible tells the sacred history of the Jews from Abraham in the late second millennium B.C.E. until the 2nd century B.C.E.

The ancient Israelites considered their Bible to be an absolutely true account of their history and their encounter with God in an ongoing relationship. Historically until the Enlightenment of the 18th century most religious Jews have believed that the account in the Hebrew Bible is true and immutable, although not necessarily literal. The Jewish philosopher Maimonides (12th century C.E.) spoke of the allegorical nature of biblical language, and Rashi (11th century C.E.) asserted that the biblical story of creation was not meant to be taken literally. Since then less fundamentalist views of religion and secularism have developed. Beginning in the mid-19th century, the Hebrew Bible has been subjected to historical and textual analysis. The father of this critical approach to the Bible, Julius Wellhausen, a non-Jew, and his followers postulated different hands who edited the Bible in various centuries from the 9th to the 5th century B.C.E.

From internal evidence alone, there are clearly other texts, no longer extant, on which parts of the Bible were based. The Prophets and the Writings, for example, refer to other literary sources that have not survived. In the ancient Near East kings kept chronicles and accounts of their reign, which were often inscribed on monuments. Given the general literacy of ancient Israel, we can assume that the kings of Israel followed similar practices. The texts themselves suggest that rewriting for theological and political reasons went on. From the Prophets we learn that a lost book of the Bible, most likely Deuteronomy, was rediscovered in the reign of Josiah in 622 B.C.E. It presumably was extensively rewritten before release to foster that king's monotheistic, anti-idolatrous policies. Deuteronomy was given its title, which means "second law," in the 3rd century B.C.E. because it was even then considered an obvious restatement of events and laws.

Can we believe the historical material in the Bible, and if so, to what extent? Archaeological information (see nutshell #5) confirms the broad outlines of the account and some specific events. From the period of the establishment of the kingdom onward, certainly from the kingdom of David in the 11th century B.C.E., all the material in the Bible was based on documents that were at one time contemporary to the events. Thus events that were described before the settlement of Jews in Israel, that is, the stories of Abraham and the patriarchs Moses and Joshua, have much less historical probability than those afterwards. During the 3rd century B.C.E. advances in editing and assembling texts were occurring throughout the empire of Alexander, under Greek influence. Hence, the works of the late prophets, such as Ezra and Nehemiah, are considered more reliable, since there was a relatively short lapse between their lives and the recording of events. In contrast, the works of the earlier prophets, like Samuel, had a history of transmission of 600 years or more before the very accurate texts of the Hellenistic period were written. The long political and religious struggles that went on in the First Temple period, so well described in the Prophets, suggest that much of the legal material in the Torah could have been edited, interpreted, and even changed. Consequently, we can be fairly certain that the historical events described in the Prophets, particularly after the establishment of the monarchy, really occurred, though our accounts might be biased and incomplete. However, the historical information in the Torah, while possibly based on real figures and events, must be considered very unreliable.

5

ARCHAEOLOGY AND THE BIBLE

Archaeology can tell us many things about the Bible, but little about biblical events. We can learn from it when the Israelites entered Canaan and where they settled. But unless we can find an inscription, we do not know whether their leader was called Moses. Archaeology can tell us about the material culture of ancient history but can only confirm the general background of biblical events.

Archaeology is the study of the material remains of human cultures. It usually entails the excavation of historic sites. Over time ancient areas of civilization became buried because of the way people settled and built in the particular location and through the patterns of nature. People throughout history have chosen their places of habitation based on standard criteria. Most important are the availability of water, food, and defense. Consequently, whenever a favorable location is developed, it often remains a site for human settlement for hundreds, if not thousands of years. If the existing population is killed, conquered, dies out, or leaves, the next group of inhabitants will settle on the same site. In a typical site in the Near East, especially Israel, we find a Neolithic layer replaced by a Bronze Age layer, then Canaanite, Israelite, Persian, Greek, Roman, and Byzantine. The city of Jerusalem has been settled continuously, for example, from at least 1100 B.C.E. to the present, the city of Damascus even longer. New settlements replace existing ones, often built after older settlements are destroyed, and often the materials from previous building are reused. This creates an artificial hill, called a tel, with each level belonging to a different period, the top of the hill or tel being the most recent settlement. Another factor that results in the burial of the past is the dust in the air. If a site is abandoned, dirt will settle at varying rates, but typical might be one foot per century. Consequently, the relics of previous civilizations are often buried in the earth.

Archaeologists systematically dig up and analyze these past cities and civilizations. In the course of excavating, material remains are found, including monumental works, such as temples; remains of walls, statues, coins, and pottery; inscriptions on stone; and occasionally written records, such as the scrolls made of papyrus found at ancient sites in Egypt.

13

Archaeology can give us information on general patterns of settlement, events of daily life, water supplies, population changes, and trends in art and architecture. But because we are examining physical remains, it gives us little information about specific events. For example, suppose a thousand years from now the White House was excavated. Much could be learned about the living patterns of the presidents, but little about events during the life of a particular president, unless documents were found. We can look to archaeology to confirm the broad strokes of biblical history, rather than specific events, though at times we do find confirmation even of these.

Archaeological evidence tells us little about the origins of the Hebrews, but it does give us background information that is consistent with biblical accounts. Through excavations we have learned that the area of Palestine was under Egyptian domination in the late second millennium B.C.E., as seen in Egyptian remains found at sites in southern Palestine. The Torah gives an account of the Jews settling in Egypt. Although there is no direct evidence to confirm this settlement, we have evidence of the arrival in Egypt as immigrants and conquerors of other Semites, the group to which the Jews belonged. In the tomb (1890 B.C.E.) of Khnum-hotep III at Bani Hasan, Egyptian wall painting depicts a Semitic clan arriving in Egypt. In the 18th century B.C.E. Egypt was vanquished by a Semitic group called the Hyksos, who included such Semitic forms of their names as Jacob-el.

In Egypt and other Near Eastern cultures, we find records of a group called the Habiru, who some scholars believe were Jews. The Habiru appear to have been a group of wanderers or brigands, not only in Canaan but in other areas of the Near East. The word appears in Hittite documents of the middle second millennium B.C.E. and in the El-Amarna letters written in Egypt during the reign of Akhenaten in the 14th century. We find in these letters the account of the capture of Sechem in Canaan by a Habiru named Lab'ayyu. By this period the Habiru were probably hired agricultural workers, mercenaries, and migrants, outside the normal structure of Canaanite society. The word *Hebrew* or *Ivri* tends to be used only occasionally in the Pentateuch, and Israelites are usually called "children of Israel." While the Habiru may have some connection to the Israelites, it is clear that the term had a general usage in Near Eastern languages. It is equally possible that there is no connection except a late application of the name, or a linguistic coincidence only.

The only reference in Egyptian documents to Israel, but not necessarily the Hebrews, is found inscribed on a stele from the reign of Merneptah (reigned 1225–1215 B.C.E.), who may have been the Pharaoh of the Exodus. The inscription reads: ". . . carried off is Ashkelon; seized upon is Gezer; Yanoam is made as that which does not exist; Israel is laid waste, his seed is not. . . ."

The Bible describes the entrance of the Israelites into Palestine as a conquest of various cities, including Jericho. While archaeological evidence shows

Late Bronze Age destruction of such cities as Lachish, Beth-El, Tell Beit Mirsim, and Hazor in the mid-13th century B.C.E., in Jericho and Ai, primary targets for Joshua, there is no evidence of destruction. The biblical account of an all-encompassing military conquest of Canaan is distorted and must be tempered by a more complex view, although the archaeological evidence indicates some warfare. Archaeological remains suggest that the hill country of central Canaan was only sparsely inhabited before the Jews. Possibly Israelite elements of nomadic pastoralists gradually settled this area in the 13th and 12th century B.C.E. The physical remains of widespread destruction in Canaan at the end of the Bronze Age are consistent with conquest. Some recent scholars have argued that Israel arose as a result of a social revolution of an indigenous population. To argue this, however, these scholars must reject the biblical account and attribute the destruction in Canaan to non-Israelites.

In summary, the archaeological evidence confirms the destruction of some of the cities said by the Bible to have been destroyed. However, in other cases the archaeological evidence shows that the destruction described in the Bible did not occur. Our conclusion on this early material, then, is that the biblical account is at least partially correct. It presents a one-sided, and probably incomplete, picture of the settlement of Canaan.

As we move on to the periods of the kingdom of Israel, we find material remains that confirm certain events described in biblical history. For example, the water tunnel cut by order of Hezekiah, king of Judah, to bring water from the Gihon spring into Jerusalem (2 Chronicles 32:30) has been excavated, together with inscriptions. A frieze from the palace of King Sennacherib at Nineveh depicts the Assyrian campaign against Hezekiah and the siege of Lachish in 701 B.C.E. (2 Kings 18:13–15; 2 Chronicles 32:9, 21; Isaiah 36, 37). A stele found near Amman, Jordan, relates that Mesha, king of Moab, freed his kingdom from the rule of Israel (2 Kings 3), and that Moab was victorious over Jehoram and Jehosaphat (c. 850 B.C.E.). However, another inscription from the reign of Shalmaneser III of Assyria in Nimrud in the 9th century B.C.E. records King Jehu, son of Omri, prostrated before Shalmaneser, paying tribute. This event is not described in the Bible, but the archaeological material supplements the biblical account. As an example from the New Testament period, an inscription was found in Caesarea, where a building was dedicated by Pontius Pilate, procurator of Judea, in honor of Tiberius Caesar, although nothing specific was noted about the events surrounding Jesus' death. The best-known example of material remaining today is the Western or Wailing Wall, a section of the western supporting wall of the Second Temple Mount at Jerusalem that has become a historic shrine for Jews. The remains of this wall, along with other excavations in the area, confirm much of the physical description of the Second Temple in the biblical sources.

The evidence of pottery and of coinage shows a cultural climate and foreign influences in Israel that are reflected in the Bible's rendition of history. For example, in the 5th century B.C.E., Jewish coinage imitated that of Athens, and at the same time we can see the beginnings of influence of Greek culture in Jewish writings, especially in Ecclesiastes.

Archaeology tells us much about the life and customs of the Israelites. In some cases, there is broad confirmation of events in the Bible, especially in the First and Second Temple periods. In other cases, it supplements details found in the Bible. Since about 50 of over 200 sites in Israel have been excavated, the future holds bright promises of further discovery about biblical history.

6

SAUL AND THE ESTABLISHMENT OF THE KINGDOM

The prophet Samuel in the 11th century B.C.E. was instrumental in welding a loose-knit group of Israelite tribes into a monarchy under the leadership of Saul. This unification of the tribes of Israel was in response to their conquest by the Philistines. Saul spent most of his reign fighting the enemies of Israel, the Moabites, Ammonites, Edomites, and particularly the Philistines, and died in battle against the Philistines in 1005 B.C.E.

King David wrote this epitaph for Saul, his predecessor and the first king of Israel, and for Saul's son Jonathan:

> Saul and Jonathan, the lovely and the pleasant;
> In their lives, even in their death they were not divided.
> I am distressed for thee, my brother Jonathan;
> Very pleasant hast thou been unto me;
> Wonderful was thy love to me,
> Passing the love of women.
> How are the mighty fallen,
> And the weapons of war perished!

After a lifetime of fighting, Saul came to a gruesome end at the hands of the Philistines, who cut off his head and hung his body on the wall of Beth-shan, then dedicated his armor as an offering in the temple of Astarte.

Political changes in Palestine spurred the development of the Israelite state. During the 15th and 14th centuries the Egyptians had dominated Palestine, but after the battle of Kadesh in Syria in 1286 B.C.E. between the Egyptian Empire, moving north, and the Hittite Empire, moving south from Turkey, the power of Egypt was waning. Pharaoh Ramses III brought in many Greeks, from a group called the Sea Peoples, to fight as mercenaries. One of these Sea Peoples, the Philistines, settled in southern Palestine in the late 12th and 11th century and became a formidable military power. The Philistines began to extend their

17

power north, and near Eben-ezer in 1080 B.C.E. they decisively defeated the Israelites. According to the Book of Samuel 30,000 Israelites were killed and the Philistines captured the Ark of the Covenant. The Philistines inexorably advanced, and they burned to the ground the sanctuary at Shiloh, the center of worship of YHVH.

Amid this turmoil arose the figure of Samuel, the prophet. As a young man he was initiated by the prophet Eli into the priesthood at the sanctuary at Shiloh. Samuel was called a *ro'eh*, or a seer. His charismatic personality and his use of prophecy added a certain mysticism to the religion.

The Israelites at this time were organized into groups of clans and tribes, which served both as legal and social entities and the basis of military organization. Samuel saw that these independent tribes in a loose confederacy were no match for the power of the Philistines and that a centralized leadership was required. Since the militarily stronger nations around Israel were monarchies, kingship seemed to Samuel the answer. Samuel recruited as king Saul, son of Kish of the tribe of Benjamin, from Gibeah, a member of his religious following. The neighboring Ammonites at this time invaded and attacked the city of Jabesh in Gilead, which appealed to Gibeah for help. Saul seized an ox, cut it into pieces, and sent the pieces to all the tribes of Israel, threatening that whoever did not send help would receive the same treatment for their oxen. The tribes obeyed, and after the Israelites assembled, under Saul's leadership they marched to Jabesh to relieve the siege.

Saul was proclaimed king, and warfare broke out against the Philistines. Jonathan, Saul's son, slew the Philistine governor of Gibeah. After an initial victory over the Philistines, the Israelites regained control of the territory of Benjamin and most likely Judah. The Ammonites, Moabites, and Arameans were driven back across the Jordan. Saul then mounted an expedition against the Amalekites, to secure Judah from raids. He defeated the enemy and captured Agag, king of the Amalekites.

This campaign led to a break between Samuel and Saul. Saul had chosen to spare Agag against Samuel's wishes. Infuriated, Samuel had Agag brought in chains to him, then hacked him to pieces. Saul would not tolerate this challenge to his authority and dismissed Samuel, never to look on his face again. Samuel faded into obscurity.

Once king, Saul broke away from the influence of Samuel and strengthened the hold of his tribe, Benjamin, on the kingship. He recruited into his military structure other members of his tribe, particularly David, his son Jonathan's friend. Saul gave David the position of his attendant and armor bearer. Warfare continued with the Philistines, and in one encounter, David used a sling to kill the huge Philistine Goliath. Goliath may have been exceptionally tall, or possibly suffered from a glandular condition called acromegaly, which gave him his stature. David commanded a division in the army and had many successes.

David's popularity increased, and the women sang that "Saul hath slain his thousands, And David his ten thousands." Saul seemed to have been afflicted with a mental illness at this time, perhaps manic-depressive syndrome or mild schizophrenia. The illness, however, did not progress enough to prevent him from ruling. According to the Book of Samuel, Saul became jealous and attacked David, first with a spear, then ordered guards to seize him. This motivation sounds like an excuse by later writers who favored David. Saul most likely had a justified fear of a distinguished military leader, who was developing a loyal following among the army and might eventually try to usurp the throne. According to the Book of Samuel, at some point Samuel, opposed to Saul, anointed David as the new king, chosen by God.

David fled to the south, first to Nob, where the priesthood of Shiloh had settled after its destruction. This place of flight suggests that David was allying himself with the opponents of Saul and was taking advantage of the split between the priests and Samuel on the one hand, and Saul on the other. From here David went farther south to Adullam, where he collected a force of about 600 dissidents. Fearing a coalition between David and the priests, Saul killed all the priests and their retainers at Nob. David continued to harass the Philistines, and when the town of Keilah was attacked, soundly defeated the invaders. David was becoming a power in the southern region, and cemented this power by a marriage alliance with Abigail, of the Calebite clan.

Finally, David, continually harassed by Saul's troops, quit Israelite territory and fled to the domain of the Philistine Achish, king of Gath, where he allied himself with the Philistines. In 1013 B.C.E., perhaps at David's urging, the Philistines mounted a major expedition against Saul, but they refused to allow David to join them because they questioned his loyalty. The Philistine armies poured into Israel through Sharon, into the Plain of Jezreel. At Mount Gilboa, Saul encountered them. The Philistines overwhelmed the Israelite forces. Rather than become a prisoner of the enemy, Saul fell on his sword. His three sons perished in battle with him.

7

KING DAVID

David unified Israel under his 40-year rule and established the Davidic dynasty, which was to rule Israel for 500 years. He captured Jerusalem and made it the capital of the kingdom and the center for the worship of YHVH, the God of Israel. The Bible attributes to him the authorship of many of the psalms, which even today inspire and comfort by their beauty and sentiments.

David, the shepherd boy, stood in the valley of Elah, watching the Israelites fighting the Philistines. He had come to bring ten loaves of bread to his brother. Suddenly he saw emerging from the line of the Philistines a giant of a man, Goliath, who slew the Israelites on every side. Goliath taunted the Israelites to send a champion against him, but none would come. David volunteered. But King Saul would not consent to let him fight because he was a mere youth. David recounted how he had slain a lion that was preying on his flocks, and Saul relented. First Saul decked David out in heavy armor, but David cast it aside. He took only his staff, five smooth stones, and his sling. Goliath laughed when he saw the boy. But David replied, "This day will the Lord deliver you into my hand; and I will smite you, and cut off your head, and give your corpse to the birds of the air and the beasts of the earth, so that all will know that there is a God in Israel" (1 Samuel 17:46). As Goliath charged, David reached into his bag for a stone, and whirling the sling round his head, threw the stone and struck Goliath in the forehead. David ran up and took Goliath's sword and used it to cut off the Philistine's head. This is the account in the Book of Samuel of how David began his military career, eventually becoming king of Israel.

David was the greatest ruler in the history of the Jews. After many military adventures and civil war, he went on to conquer Jerusalem and make it his capital. This city became the political and religious center of Judaism. Even today, 3,000 years later, Jews revere this city in their prayers: "If I forget thee, O Jerusalem, let my right hand lose its cunning." "Next year in Jerusalem" has been recited for the past 2,500 years at the Passover meal. The six-pointed star, although it became a Jewish symbol long after King David's time, is called the

"shield of David" and has become the emblem of the state of Israel, the synagogue, and Jews everywhere.

David established his royal line and dynasty from which the kings of Israel
were drawn during the entire First Temple period, from the 11th century until
the destruction of the Temple in 585 B.C.E. The great kings of Israel—Solomon,
Hezekiah, Josiah, and even Zerubabel, the leader of the return from Babylon
in the 6th century—were his descendants.

Even after the fall of King David's dynasty, the messianic fervor of the late
Second Temple period led people to proclaim that the Messiah would come
from the line of David. The followers of Jesus trace his descent from David,
and the Gospel of Matthew, which recounts the life and death of Jesus, begins
with this genealogy.

With his capture of Jerusalem, David centralized the political power of the
state and the religion, with that city superseding Shiloh as the center of worship of YHVH. The construction of the Temple by David's son, Solomon, forever made Jerusalem the religious and spiritual center of Judaism.

"The heavens declare the glory of God; and the firmament proclaims his
handiwork. Day to day utters speech, and night to night expresses knowledge
. . . the judgments of the Lord are true and are righteous altogether. More to be
desired are they than gold, even much fine gold: sweeter also than honey and
the honeycomb" (Psalm 19). "The Lord is my shepherd, I shall not want. He
makes me lie down in green pastures: He leads me beside the still waters. He
restores my soul: He leads me in the paths of righteousness for His name's sake.
Even though I walk through the valley of the shadow of death, I will fear no
evil: for Thou art with me . . ." (Psalm 23). These are but two of the psalms
written by King David, or ascribed to him. They have inspired and comforted
people the world over for three millennia. A poet as well as a warrior, David
played a central role in the poetry of the Bible. He is reputed to have written
many psalms, and these have had a profound effect on the spiritual and aesthetic life of Jews, Muslims, and Christians.

David's victory over Goliath made him a popular figure in King Saul's army.
Ambitious and energetic, he soon became a military leader and married Michal,
Saul's daughter. David's ambition drove him to plot to depose Saul and make
himself king. Saul came to suspect his designs and decided to kill David, who
fled to the southern region of Palestine, where he assembled a motley crew of
mercenaries and dissidents, which he welded into an effective fighting force
in the southern region of Palestine.

When Saul was killed in battle against the Philistines at Mount Gilboa, his
fourth son, Ishbaal, succeeded to the throne. David continued to solidify his
power in the south and transferred his troops and harem to Hebron, then the
chief city of Judah. He was proclaimed king of Judah (1013 B.C.E.) and began
to plot to take control of all Israel. Civil war broke out near Gibeon, in the ter-

ritory of the Benjamites, Saul's tribe, between Ishbaal and David. The war dragged on, with David gradually growing stronger. Eventually several of Ishbaal's ministers, including Abner, went over to David. Abner was soon murdered by Joab, one of David's generals. Ishbaal was then assassinated by two of his captains, who brought his head to David. With the death of Ishbaal, Israel and Judah both were now in David's hands, and he was anointed and proclaimed king (1006 B.C.E.).

The Philistines saw David and his military prowess as a threat. Soon after he was made king, they invaded again and captured Bethlehem. After several years of warfare, David finally captured the Philistine city of Gath and was able to confine the power of the Philistines to the coastal areas.

Now in command of the entire country and his enemies at bay, David saw that he needed a new capital, one that might not favor either Israel or Judah, or any particular tribe. In a similar way in the United States, in order not to favor any of the states, Washington, a city not in any state, was chosen as the capital. The ideal spot was Jerusalem, which commanded the inland route between Israel and Judah and was located in the center of the two regions. Jerusalem was well located for trade and commerce and was easily fortified, since it was located in the hills with one side inaccessible and impregnable. It also boasted a good water supply in case of siege. One problem, however, existed: Jerusalem was controlled not by the Israelites, but by the Jebusites, who had maintained their power for 200 years. David besieged the city without success, until his general, Joab, discovered a water tunnel from the spring of Gihon into the city. He and his soldiers climbed through the tunnel, entered the city, and opened it to the Israelite troops.

David understood the interplay of religion and politics, which he had seen in the relationship of Saul and Samuel. In a bold step he refounded Jerusalem, not only as a political center, but also as a religious center to replace Shiloh. The Ark of the Covenant was transported to Jerusalem in solemn procession, with David dressed in the linen garments worn by priests and leading the dancing of the marchers.

Like the emperor Augustus, who found himself ruler of Rome, and unlike Alexander, who died shortly after establishing his empire, David was to have a long rule, for forty years (1013–973 B.C.E.), which gave him time to build a kingdom and a dynasty that was to last five centuries. Egypt was in decline and Assyria was not yet a major power, which allowed the development of this small, but strategic and powerful kingdom. Much of David's reign was taken up with consolidating his power through wars with his neighbors and suppressing revolts within Israel. First the Ammonites attacked, and David beat them back and under the leadership of Joab conquered and sacked their capital, Rammah (modern Amman). David next attacked the Moabites because they had helped the Ammonites. He swiftly defeated them, then executed two thirds of their population. Moab and Ammon were now subject to Israel. Next King Hadadezer of Zobah was conquered, and Damascus in Syria. David turned to the south and defeated the Amalekites, near Beer-sheba, which gave David ports on the Gulf of Akabah, Ezion-geber, and Elath. David's realm now extended to Lebanon in the north, to Damascus and the Euphrates in the northeast, and to the Red Sea in the south.

David had similar troubles with his families and succession, another parallel with the Roman emperor Augustus. He became intoxicated with Bath-sheba, the wife of Uriah, one of his mercenary captains. As related in the Bible, David was walking on the roof of his palace one day, when he looked down and saw a woman bathing. Sexually aroused by the sight, he sent his guards to bring her to him, and he immediately slept with her. From this one incident, she became pregnant, and sent a messenger to David to tell him. David was anxious to cover up the fact that the child she bore was his, and not her husband's, Uriah the Hittite, who was away fighting. He devised a plan: Uriah was recalled so that while on leave he might have intercourse with his wife, and the pregnancy be explained. But Uriah failed to sleep with his wife that night, perhaps through Bath-sheba's own connivance. Consequently, David sent Uriah back to battle, with a secret communique telling the troops to abandon Uriah in an exposed position. This they did, and Uriah died in battle. David now added Bath-sheba to his harem, and another to the list of those he had killed.

David's son Absalom was ambitious to replace his father as king. Drawing on discontent from northern Israel, Absalom led one of many revolts against David. The rebels were defeated and Absalom was killed. David lamented, perhaps hypocritically, "Would I had died in thy stead, O Absalom, my son, my son!"

In 973 B.C.E., shortly before his death and after a long and glorious reign, David had Solomon, his son by Bath-sheba, proclaimed king. He made Solomon promise that as his first act he would kill Joab, David's friend and general, who had been at his side for four decades. Joab supported another of David's sons, and David feared civil war.

David's foundation of Jerusalem as the religious and political center of Judaism, and the establishment of the Davidic dynasty that was to persist for so long, gave David the foremost place in Jewish history and religion after Abraham and Moses. A great military leader and conqueror with the skill of an Alexander the Great or the Roman emperor, Augustus, he built a secular dynasty that was to last as long as that of the Roman emperors, and a religious heritage that will survive as long as there are Jews.

8

SOLOMON AND THE FIRST TEMPLE

Succeeding his father, David, to the throne of Judah and Israel, Solomon centralized the kingdom, brought it much prosperity, and increased its political and military power in the region. He built the First Temple at Jerusalem, which survived until the 6th century B.C.E. Renowned for his wisdom, his wealth, and his many wives, he died in 928 B.C.E., after a reign of forty years.

While King David was famous for his psalms, Solomon was known for his proverbs and wisdom. The Bible says: "And God gave Solomon very much wisdom and understanding, and largeness of heart, like the sand that is on the sea shore . . . and Solomon's wisdom excelled the wisdom of all the children of the east country, and all the wisdom of Egypt. For he was wiser than all men" (1 Kings 5:9–11). A story is related about two women who came to court, each claiming the same baby. They were both prostitutes who lived together. They gave birth three days apart, but one child had died. One woman claimed the other had substituted her dead child for the living one. Since there were no witnesses, Solomon found a unique solution. He ordered the baby to be cut in two and divided. One woman agreed, but the other said she would rather give up the baby than have it killed. Solomon decided that woman must be the true mother, and gave her the baby. Solomon's reputation for wisdom grew as time passed, and even late works of the Bible, such as Ecclesiastes, were attributed to his authorship. Throughout the Middle Ages and the Renaissance in art and literature he was depicted as the man of wisdom.

Solomon, like his father, David, was a talented poet and skillful ruler. His major achievement was the building of the First Temple in Jerusalem. Despite the division of the kingdom upon his death, his development of the military and economic power of Judah and Israel was so successful that at least the southern kingdom of Judah would continue as an independent or quasi-independent kingdom in the Middle East for almost a thousand years, until the destruction of the Second Temple by the Romans in 70 C.E. The combination of two exceptional monarchs, David and Solomon, who together ruled for eighty years, gave Judah and Israel the stability and opportunity to develop and become a major power in the region, a factor that allowed Judaism and the people of Israel to maintain their identity, particularly in the southern kingdom of Judah.

Solomon, as a younger son of David, had to fight for the succession. His older brother, Adonijah, who was supported by David's general, Joab, declared himself king when David was in failing health. Bath-sheba persuaded David to recognize Solomon as king. Whether he believed that Solomon would make the better king, or was persuaded by the entreaties of his wife or by the fact that his own mercenary troops supported Solomon, David in 967 B.C.E. made Solomon his coruler. On David's death in 965 B.C.E. Solomon succeeded his father. Constant revolts had been a major problem, and David was ever vigilant to threats to the throne. Since David saw Joab as an ally to Adonijah, he instructed Solomon to execute Joab upon ascending the throne. This Solomon did, and for good measure executed Adonijah and other possible claimants to the throne.

Mercenary troops had formed the basis of David's power, augmented with tribal levies from Judah. The northern tribes had provided military levies, but David had not relied on them. Like his father, Solomon was faced with revolts, both in the north and in the south. Since the union of the two kingdoms was still weak, and the northern kingdom resented being ruled from the southern kingdom, Solomon went one step further and excluded the north entirely from levies and military service. Instead he instituted a kind of forced labor for the tribes, exempting only Judah. Furthermore, he divided Israel into twelve administrative units, along lines different from the twelve tribal units, possibly to curtail further the powers of the tribes. Judah was exempt from this organization and remained a special political unit.

Solomon attempted to solidify his power by constructing royal fortresses at strategic locations throughout the country, at Hazor, Megiddo, and Gezer. These became the center of Solomon's new army, which consisted of 1,500 chariots and 4,000 horses. Since iron and the chariot were becoming important military weapons, and because Solomon seized upon the new technology, he became a military force in the region.

Few kings in history wed as many women for strategic purposes as Solomon, or had as many wives and concubines. If the Bible is to be believed, Solomon wed 700 princesses and had an additional 300 concubines. To consolidate his throne, he began to contract alliances with the most powerful rulers in the region. His greatest success was his marriage to the daughter of the Pharaoh of Egypt. This brought him into an important alliance with that country and eliminated a potential military threat on his southern border. The Book of Kings recounts that he also wed Moabites, Ammonites, Edomites, Sidonians, and Hittites. He also entered into close alliance with the powerful Phoenician kingdom to the north, ruled by Hiram of Tyre.

Like his father, Solomon saw the strategic importance of Jerusalem, and there tried to unite the country further by the construction of a magnificent Temple to YHVH, as well as a munificent royal palace. The Temple was adorned with much gold, which reflected the great wealth of the king.

Under Solomon Judah and Israel prospered, as at no other time in history. The routes for the newly developed spice trade from southern Arabia and East Africa came through the country. Solomon's control of these routes gave him great economic power and prosperity. He mounted trading expeditions to East Africa, and in addition to spices, traded in gold, sandalwood, ivory, and rare animals and birds. Even the famous queen of Sheba (from southern Arabia or East Africa) visited him, bearing spices, gold, and precious gems, on either a political or a trading mission. Solomon even became an arms dealer. He purchased horses in Anatolia to the north and sold them to Egypt, where he bought chariots for resale to the Aramaeans and neo-Hittites. He imported iron and copper from Lebanon and Anatolia and processed and smelted them for reexport.

Building on the successes of his father, Solomon turned Judah and Israel into a major power in the region. His kingdom split apart on his death, not because of his failure, but because his son Rehoboam was not astute or strong enough to quell the revolts from the northern kingdom of Israel. Both David and Solomon fought against and suppressed many revolts throughout their reigns, but managed to maintain a united kingdom by military force. However, their efforts were not sufficient to weld the countries into one entity. Despite the division of the kingdom, Solomon's legacy was a powerful Judah and Israel. The kingdom of Judah, except for the period of the Babylonian captivity in the 6th century, was to last a thousand years in various forms, while the northern Kingdom of Israel survived for another 200 years.

Solomon's legacy on the religious side were the writings attributed to him and the foundation of the Temple at Jerusalem, which, with its successor, was to be the focus of Jewish worship for a thousand years, its site a spiritual center to this day.

9

THE DIVIDED KINGDOM

With the death of Solomon, the kingdom of Judah and Israel split apart, with Israel in the north and Judah in the south. David's dynasty continued to rule in the south until the destruction of the Temple in Jerusalem by the Babylonians in 586 B.C.E., while the northern kingdom under various dynasties lasted only until 720 B.C.E., destroyed by the Assyrians. The kingdom of Judah was revived in 538 B.C.E., when the Jews returned from exile, and lasted to 70 C.E. The kingdom of Israel never revived, but the Jewish identity of the inhabitants survived to this day as a small sect, the Samaritans.

King Rehoboam succeeded two very successful leaders, his grandfather, David, and his father, Solomon. He did not match up. David had quelled revolts with his mercenaries and levies, Solomon with his armies and strategic cities. Rehoboam failed from the outset. Upon ascending the throne, Rehoboam went to Shechem, the center of the northern tribes. A delegation of the northerners under Jeroboam announced that they would serve Rehoboam if he decreased the levies. Instead of negotiating and defusing the situation as David or Solomon would have done and Rehoboam's senior advisers suggested, the new king followed the impetuous advice of the young men with whom he surrounded himself. He replied to Jeroboam, "My father made your yoke heavy, and I will add to your yoke: my father chastised you with whips, but I will chastise you with scorpions." Inflamed by his reply, the Israelites stoned to death Adoram, chief of the levy. Rehoboam ran for his life, mounted his chariot, and fled to Jerusalem. The north seceded and Jeroboam was made king.

For a variety of reasons, the southern kingdom of Judah was more stable and its legacy emerged as the mainstream of Judaism. Judah had a larger area and a more homogenous population of Israelites, while Israel had many more foreign elements. Israel's geographical situation made it a target for expansion by surrounding kingdoms, such as Aram-Damascus and later Assyria. Judah had Israel as a buffer on the north and the relatively stable Egypt on the south, with which it was generally allied.

The monarchy in the north, unlike the south, was unstable and passed through many dynasties, first of Jeroboam and his son, then of Baasa, then Omri, and the longest, that of Jehu and his descendants (reigned 842–744 B.C.E.). Besides the political and ethnic differences between Israel and Judah there were religious ones. Israel, with its more diverse population and ties with neighboring Tyre, tended toward the worship of Baal, alongside that of YHVH, while Judah remained closer to YHVH.

The northern kingdom of Israel was torn by religious strife between the Canaanite Baal and the God of Moses for its first hundred years. The reign of Ahab (875–853 B.C.E.) and his notorious queen, Jezebel, who was the daughter of Ethbaal, king of Tyre, marked the most violent, bloodthirsty period. Jezebel was a worshiper of Baal, although as a polytheist, she saw no difficulty with the worship of YHVH. The prophets of YHVH, on the other hand, were violently opposed to the worship of other gods. To please his wife, Ahab built a temple to Baal Melkarth, the god of Tyre. When the priests of YHVH objected, Jezebel ordered the execution of a hundred of them. But Obadiah, the minister of the household, warned the priests and they escaped. The tension continued between the worship of Baal and YHVH until the emergence of Elijah, the prophet. Miraculous cures were ascribed to him, including the revival of a dying child. Finally, in the face of a drought throughout the country, a contest was held. On Mount Carmel the prophets of Baal put an offering on the altar to their god, with prayers to bring down fire from heaven. But fire from heaven came down and consumed Elijah's offering. Elijah ordered the people to seize the 450 prophets of Baal and march them down to the river Kishon, where they were massacred. Then the rains began and the drought was ended.

Incensed at the loss of her prophets, Jezebel determined to kill Elijah. He fled to the south to Mount Horeb, where he urged the overthrow of the house of Omri. In the Jordan valley he found a disciple for this purpose, Elisha. Elijah, reaching the end of his life, according to the biblical account, miraculously ascended to heaven in a chariot of fire, drawn by horses of fire.

During this period the Assyrians began their expansion into Israel. They were a Semitic people, who had been a major power in Mesopotamia since the 14th century B.C.E. Ahab joined with Osorkon II of Egypt, as well as with the kingdoms of Damascus and Tyre, to fight the new threat. A battle was fought at Karkar in 854 B.C.E., which stopped the Assyrian advance (although the Assyrian records, which never admit a defeat, proclaimed Assyria the winner). Ahab, with the alliance of Judah, then attacked the kingdom of Damascus, but died in the fighting.

In 843 B.C.E. Elisha finally had the political opportunity to restore the worship of YHVH. Jehoram (reigned 852–843 B.C.E.), the son of Ahab who had succeeded his brother to the throne, was wounded in the siege of Ramoth. Elisha seized the moment and anointed the ruthless and bloodthirsty general Jehu as king. Jehu made war on both the rulers of Israel and Judah. First he killed King Jehoram, then Azariah, the king of Judah. Victorious, Jehu was now bent on murdering all his previous opponents. He marched to Jezreel, where Jezebel was holding her court. With nowhere to run, she bedecked herself in her finest robes to meet her executioner. Jehu ordered her own palace eunuchs to throw her out the palace window, and her blood was sprinkled on the walls and on the horses. To remove further claimants, Jehu had the surviving seventy children of Jehoram decapitated and their heads delivered to him in baskets. To eliminate opposition from Judah, he massacred forty-two princes of Judah, who had come as an embassy to inquire about the welfare of the royal family of Israel. Jehu entered Samaria, where he continued his butchery. He massacred the worshipers of Baal and tore down their temple stone by stone, destroying forever the cult of Baal in Israel. Jehu and his descendants were to rule in Israel for almost a hundred years until 744 B.C.E., when the kingdom of Israel was nearing its last days under the impending onslaught of Assyria.

In the mid-8th century B.C.E. the power of Assyria increased rapidly. The great Assyrian king Tiglath-pileser IV (reigned 745–727 B.C.E.) subdued Syria, Damascus, and Tyre. Although under the threat of Assyria, during this period Israel and Judah experienced renewed prosperity and power under the reigns of Jeroboam II (reigned 784–748 B.C.E.) in Israel and Uzziah, or Azariah (reigned 785/4–734/3 B.C.E.), in Judah. But Israel could not hold out against Assyria's growing power, and within the next twenty years the Assyrians annexed Galilee and about two thirds of the territory of Israel.

On the death of Tiglath-pileser of Assyria in 727/6 B.C.E. his son, Shalmaneser V, became king. Believing that with the transition of rulers the time was ripe, Israel under King Hoshea ben Elah revolted again. This time Shalmaneser captured Hoshea and exiled him to Assyria, then besieged Samaria, which he captured in 722/1 B.C.E. But Shalmaneser died about this time and a new ruler, Sargon, took the throne, which led to more revolts in Israel. Finally in 720 B.C.E., Sargon defeated Samaria and made it an Assyrian province. His own annals record this conquest: "I captured Samaria, 27,290 people dwelling in it I took as spoil, 50 chariots I requisitioned from within it, and the rest of them I settled in Assyria. I rebuilt the city of Samaria and made it bigger than it was. People from the land which I had conquered I settled in it and directed them in their own particular skill. I placed over it my palace-official as governor and imposed upon them a tax payment as on the citizens of Assyria."

The Assyrian Sargon adopted a practice of breaking the power of conquered peoples by transporting the nobles and elite of those countries to other parts of the Assyrian Empire. This deprived those who were transported of their economic, military, and political base, and deprived those left behind of leadership and organization. Some of the descendants of the 30,000 Jews transported to Assyria may have been among those who returned from Babylon in 538 B.C.E., but the vast majority were simply absorbed into the Assyrian Empire. In turn, the Assyrians transported to Israel large numbers of settlers who mixed with the local population and brought about the end of Israel as an independent people.

10

AMOS AND HOSEA

Amos and Hosea were the two great prophets during the decline of the northern kingdom in the 8th century B.C.E. Amos preached that the pursuit of social justice was the primary action for pleasing YHVH, while Hosea saw Israel as the bride of YHVH, and exclusive love of YHVH as the basis for Israelite behavior and belief. While neither prophet had much effect in his own time, both became major influences in the history of Judaism and Western religious and political thought, Hosea for the concept of the love relationship between God and humanity, and Amos for justice as the basis of all societies.

Hosea was ordered by YHVH to marry Gomer, a prostitute, by whom he had three children. He used his personal experience to bring a message to Israel of love for YHVH. Amos began his prophecies against the injustice of foreign nations, but when a major earthquake struck Israel, he turned his prophecies toward justice within his own land. Both men were influenced in their views by the threat of Assyria, which hung like a sword over the nation.

Neither Amos nor Hosea had much influence in his own time, but their words and prophetic messages had a profound effect on the history and theology of the Jewish religion. Amos prophesied during the reign of Jeroboam II (reigned 784–748 B.C.E.), but his exact dates are unknown. By profession a herdsman and a dresser of sycamore trees, he was possibly from Judah, and prophesied only in the northern kingdom. His prophecies, recorded in the Book of Amos, take place over a long period of time. His chief theme was justice. He saw that there was prosperity in Israel: the palaces were decorated with ivory, the rich had lavish feasts and used expensive oils to anoint themselves, and the wine flowed. But despite this plenty, the rich "trample[d] the head of the poor into the dust of the earth" and sold them into slavery, and the judges were corrupt. YHVH was not interested in burnt offerings and fatted beasts, as the priests offered, but rather justice.

Amos prophesied that if the people of Israel did not turn to justice, the king of Israel would be killed by the sword and the people of Israel would be taken into exile. Either Amos was basing his prophecies of the fall of northern Israel on analogies with the Assyrian policy of conquest and deportation and resettlement, or else these verses belong to a period when the Book of Amos was compiled, after the fall of Israel in 722/1 B.C.E.

To Amos, justice was a divine requirement. The Book of Amos begins with a warning to do justice or face death, exile, and God's displeasure. It ends with a prophecy of comfort. God will scatter the people of Israel, but will later gather in the dispersed, and the people of Israel will inherit the land of Edom. Most scholars view this last section as a later addition to the book. Amos did not reject the Temple and organized sacrifice, but rather believed that these rituals were empty if practiced without justice in the land. Unlike the prophets Samuel and Elisha, who made and unmade kings, Amos's message had little effect that we know of during his life. But the message of Amos has become an essential part of Jewish consciousness throughout history.

While Amos preached justice, Hosea preached spiritual love. Both prophesied during the reign of Jeroboam II, but Hosea most likely continued his mission much longer and may have been active as late as the fall of Samaria in 722 B.C.E. Little is known about his life, and even some of the biographical details from the Book of Hosea may be allegorical and not represent actual events.

Hosea saw the relationship of Israel and YHVH as that of husband and wife, YHVH the groom and Israel the bride. Israel had forsaken YHVH and worshiped foreign gods, and by this act had become morally corrupt. He warned that YHVH would punish Israel, as a man punishes an adulterous wife by expelling her from the home. Israel would be destroyed and sent into exile. Despite this, YHVH would forgive the harlot Israel if she underwent expiation; when Israel stopped whoring after other gods, then YHVH would take her back: "O Ephraim, you have played the harlot, Israel is defiled" (Hosea 5:3). Israel had forgotten YHVH and for this she must be reminded: "She did not know/ That it was I Who gave her/The grain, the wine, and the oil,/and Who lavished upon her silver/And gold which they used for Baal" (Hosea 2:8). To Hosea, the people of Israel did not "know" YHVH. In Hebrew the verb meaning "to know" covers both intellectual and carnal knowledge, which continues the sexual image that runs through the Book of Hosea.

These sexual images are made concrete when YHVH tells Hosea to marry a prostitute, who bore him three children. The names of two, Loruhama, "Not-Pitied," and Loammi, "Not-My-People," were signs that YHVH had rejected Israel. Although most modern scholars have taken Hosea's marriage as historical, many medieval scholars, including Ibn Ezra, Maimonides, Kimchi, and Rashi, believed that this description was a vision, or a parable, and not actual fact. Temple prostitution was often part of the worship of Baal, as well as YHVH, both in Israel and Judah and throughout the Near East. Since polytheistic societies saw that sexual union was the creative force of the universe, the analogy of YHVH as the husband and Israel as the bride was consistent with other cultural approaches. For example, the Greeks saw erotic love as the motive force behind the creation of the world. There is no need to assume, as do some scholars, that Hosea was simply oversexed or preoccupied with sex.

Hosea's message was that of love for YHVH: "For I desire love and not sacrifice, and the knowledge of God more than burnt offerings" (Hosea 6:6). Hosea saw what Israel lacked: "There is no loyalty, no love, and no knowledge of God in the land" (Hosea 4:1). Amos, on the other hand, condemned not lack of love for YHVH, but the lack of justice in the land. Just as Amos's concept of justice was to permeate Jewish thought, so Hosea's idea of love of God was to permeate the spiritual and mystical side of Judaism, even to this day.

11

ISAIAH AND HEZEKIAH

The prophet Isaiah began his activities at the end of the reign of Uzziah of Judah in 735 B.C.E. Like Hosea, his message was one of social justice and his vision was of an idealized time in the future when peace would reign and war would be no more. Like Samuel and Elisha, he took an active role in politics and was particularly influential during the reign of Hezekiah (reigned 727–698 B.C.E.). Hezekiah managed to develop the power and wealth of Judah and still withstand the advance of Assyria, even the siege of Jerusalem by King Sennacherib (reigned 705–681 B.C.E.) of Assyria in 701 B.C.E.

A political gadfly, Isaiah walked through Jerusalem naked and barefoot, like a slave, to show what would happen to those who would oppose Assyria. He unsuccessfully advised Hezekiah not to take this course of action, and he was to prove correct. Isaiah also prophesied the downfall of Assyria:

> Assyria shall fall by a sword, not of man:
> A sword, not of man, shall devour him; . . .
> His rock shall pass away through terror
> And his princes in panic shall desert the standard,
> Says the Lord Whose fire is in Zion,
> and Whose furnace is in Jerusalem. (Isaiah 31:8–9)

Isaiah, who began his prophecies in the last year of the reign of Uzziah (734 B.C.E.), had three agendas. First, he preached concerning political involvement with Assyria and Egypt, and warned of disaster and deportations for the people of Judah. Second, he was a prophet of eschatology, an idealized time in the future when peace would reign. Third, like Amos in the northern kingdom, he preached social justice.

He foretold a time when the "wolf shall dwell with the lamb, and the leopard shall lie down with the kid," when men would "beat swords into ploughshares and not know war anymore." This eschatological vision of ultimate peace made Isaiah a prophet who captured humanity's hopes and desires. Another of his prophecies, that of a messiah who will usher in a reign of everlasting peace and justice, was used by Christians to foretell the coming of Jesus. But if one examines this prophecy closely, it is clear that Isaiah was talking, not about some event in the future, but of an event that had just occurred, most likely the birth of Hezekiah, who like the previous kings of Judah was of the line of David. Isaiah announced that a son would be born to a young woman and would be called Immanuel ("God is with us"), and that before the child was two or three years old the allied kings would depart and evil days would be visited on Judah, which would be laid waste by Egypt and Assyria. A remnant of the people would eventually return, and a reign of everlasting peace and justice would prevail in the land. This messiah ("anointed one") would come from the line of Jesse, a descendant of David.

Isaiah saw corruption and social inequality in Judah. It flourished in the palaces (Isaiah 1:23); the guilty were released through bribes and the innocent refused justice (Isaiah 3:14). The peasants lost their lands to the rich (Isaiah 5:8), and the rich women of Jerusalem and their opulence were a disgrace and portended doom for the state. If God's demands "to seek justice, relieve the oppressed, judge the fatherless, plead for the widow" (Isaiah 1:17) were met, the country would prosper. If not, God would come and punish Judah. Isaiah had a vision of the ideal state, ruled with justice and without war. Although God dwelt in Zion and spoke from the Temple, sacrifice and the rites of the Temple at Jerusalem were secondary. Influenced by Isaiah, Hezekiah closed many sanctuaries outside Jerusalem and rid the Temple of many idols, including the Brazen Serpent set up by Moses. Hezekiah, however, did not remove the Assyrian sun horses, lest he offend Assyria.

Like his fellow countrymen, Isaiah was affected by the political events of the time, particularly the oppressive imperialistic Assyrian Empire to which Judah had become a vassal. He had seen the deportations of the Israelites of the northern kingdom in 733/2 B.C.E. and those that occurred after the destruction of Samaria in 722/1 B.C.E. Furthermore, toward the end of his life, a large percentage of the population was deported when Assyria attacked Judah. Isaiah viewed these deportations as YHVH's punishment for improper and unjust behavior. But he also saw a time when the remnant would return (Isaiah 8:18, 10:21), and the world would be transformed and peace reign.

Isaiah was a political figure in his time, intimately involved with King Hezekiah. When Hezekiah came to the throne in 727 B.C.E., Judah was a subject of Assyria. As at so many points in history, Judah was in the middle of the struggle between Egypt in the south and Syria in the north. The Assyrians kept expanding southward, and in 716 B.C.E. they established a military garrison on the "Brook of Egypt" (wadi El-Arish). The Pharaoh sent gifts to Sargon of Assyria, but Egypt still tried to foment revolt among the Assyrian vassal states. Although several states revolted in 712 B.C.E., Hezekiah remained loyal, although he allied himself with Merodach-baladan, the king of Babylon. Once the great Assyrian king Sargon died in 705 B.C.E, however, Hezekiah joined in the revolt against Assyria to reestablish the independence of Judah.

In preparation for his revolt, Hezekiah secured a water supply with a tunnel from the Upper Gihon spring into the city, the Siloam Tunnel, which was rediscovered in 1880 with an accompanying inscription describing its building. Sennacherib (reigned 705–681) was an effective military leader. First he reestablished control of Babylon in 702 B.C.E. In the spring of 701 B.C.E. he set out with a large army along the Phoenician coast. His *Annals*, perhaps the only detailed surviving extrabiblical contemporary historical documents, describe this campaign and the siege of Jerusalem. He reconquered many of his vassal states, although he fought an inconclusive battle against Egypt at Eltekeh. Sennacherib took forty-six of Hezekiah's walled cities, as well as several smaller cities. Surviving to this day is a depiction on the walls of Sennacherib's palace of the assault of one of these cities, Lachish, and its capture.

Sennacherib next demanded the surrender of Jerusalem. Isaiah prophesied to Hezekiah and the people of the city that Sennacherib would never capture Jerusalem. Sennacherib besieged the city and sealed it off completely, "like a bird in a cage." The *Annals* indicate that although Jerusalem was not captured, Hezekiah decided to submit, become a vassal again, and send tribute:

> Thirty talents of gold, 800 talents of silver, choice antimony, large blocks of carnelian, beds of ivory, chairs of ivory, elephant hides, ivory, ebonywood, garments with multi-colored trim, linen, wool dyed purple, copper vessels, iron bronze, tin, chariots, slings, lances, armor, dagger, arrows, implements of war, with his daughter, his palace women, his male and female musicians he had sent after me to Nineveh, my royal city, and he dispatched his personal messenger to deliver the tribute and to do obeisance. (Rassam Cylinder of Sennacherib, trans. H. Tadmor)

Sennacherib's *Annals* give no reason why he failed to take the city, but the biblical account gives the victory to Hezekiah. According to 2 Kings 19:35, "[T]he angel of the Lord went out, and smote in the camp of the Assyrians a hundred fourscore and five thousand: and when they arose early in the morning behold, they were all dead corpses." During the siege Isaiah told Hezekiah to have faith and the city would be delivered. Another section (2 Kings 19:7) notes: "Behold I will send a blast upon him, and he shall hear a rumor, and shall return to his own land; and I will cause him to fall by the sword in his own land." Indeed Sennacherib was assassinated by his sons (2 Kings 19:36–37). While Sennacherib's *Annals* claim victory for Assyria and the Bible claims victory for Hezekiah, the truth of the outcome lies probably in between. The besiegers of a city are only successful if they succeed in taking the site.

Sennacherib was unable to do this. Whether he broke off the siege because of events at home, the cost of the siege, or Hezekiah's agreement to return to his vassal state is uncertain. To Isaiah and the people of Jerusalem, Sennacherib's failure to take the city was a tremendous victory.

However, while Jerusalem survived with its reputation as a sacred city enhanced, the countryside was devastated. Assyria had conquered most of the area except for Jerusalem and, in its usual fashion, had deported many of the inhabitants (the *Annals* claim 200,150 people). Part of Judah was annexed by the Philistines. When Hezekiah died in 698 B.C.E., he left Judah smaller and poorer than he had found it. However, Hezekiah's resistance to the might of Assyria gave Jerusalem a new spiritual position as the unconquerable city of David.

12

THE FALL OF JERUSALEM

*The power of Assyria reached its zenith in the 7th century B.C.E. King
Manasseh of Judah was a faithful ally and encouraged foreign cultic
practices. His son Josiah introduced reforms and centralized the religious power of Jerusalem. The influence of Assyria began to wane and
toward the end of the century, the Medes and the Babylonians replaced
them as the major power in the Middle East. Nebuchadnezzar, the
Babylonian king, expanded his power into Syria and Palestine, and in
586 B.C.E. captured and sacked Jerusalem, destroyed the Temple, and
transported much of the population to Babylon.*

Isaiah prophesied the fall of Jerusalem and the destruction of the Assyrian
Empire. His prophecy took a hundred years to come true. Isaiah met his death
violently at the hands of Manasseh, the son of Hezekiah. Manasseh jettisoned
his father's reforms and brought the worship of foreign gods into the Temple,
even that of Molech and child sacrifice. His fifty-year reign allowed many of
these practices to become firmly entrenched. Contrary to Isaiah's predictions,
the reign of Manasseh saw Assyrian influence in Judah at its height. Manasseh
was succeeded by his sons, first Amon, then Josiah. Although Josiah was not
particularly a good military or political ruler, his reign marked an important
stage in the development of Judaism.

Josiah turned against the polytheism of Manasseh and sought to cleanse the
country of his father's foreign cultic practices. According to 2 Kings and
Chronicles, in 628 B.C.E. Josiah began his reforms. He removed the Assyrian
chariots of the sun from the Temple, as well as cultic items of Baal and Asherah.
The "high places," cultic sites in the countryside, were destroyed, as was the
cultic center at Bethel. The priests of the "high places" were removed to Jerusalem, but prevented from engaging in sacrifice. These moves centralized the
religious power in Jerusalem. In 622 B.C.E., while the Temple was undergoing
some renovations, a "book of the law" was discovered. This book was
Deuteronomy. It was probably extensively rewritten by Josiah and his followers to restate the laws of Moses and to reinterpret them in line with Josiah's
reforms. Emphasis was placed on the prayer known as the *Shema*, "Hear O

Israel, YHVH is our God, YHVH alone," which said that no gods other than YHVH should be worshiped. Furthermore, the Book of Deuteronomy (12:5) prohibited worship anywhere except Jerusalem. Deuteronomy is constructed in the form of a treaty, a covenant between the Jews and God, similar to a Near Eastern treaty of vassalage. The treaty is enforced by a list of curses that will fall upon the vassals if they fail to obey. The Book of Deuteronomy gave religious sanction to eliminating all foreign cults and gods. It became a new Covenant, to reaffirm the Covenant at Mount Sinai between God and the Jewish people through his agent, Moses.

During the 7th century Assyria continued to expand its power into Egypt. The Assyrian king Esarhaddon (reigned 681–669 B.C.E.) conquered the Delta in 671 B.C.E. and died in 669 B.C.E. while fighting in Egypt. His son Ashurbanipal pursued these policies and conquered and sacked Thebes, the capital of lower Egypt. The forces of Manasseh fought alongside Ashurbanipal in Egypt.

The might of Assyria, however, faced serious challenges, particularly with the emergence of a new power, the Medes. With the death of Ashurbanipal in 627 B.C.E., the Assyrian Empire began to crumble. Babylon revolted and established itself as an independent entity; at the same time, a war of succession broke out between the sons of Ashurbanipal, with the result that the empire was divided into two sections. The Assyrian Empire was pressed by the Cimmerians in the northwest. Egypt's power began to rise again, and in 616 B.C.E. Egyptians were found fighting beside the Assyrians against the Medes. But in 614 B.C.E. the city of Asshur was captured by the Medes, and in 612 B.C.E. Nineveh, the great Assyrian capital, was sacked and destroyed. The Medes made an alliance with Babylon, but the fighting continued. The Assyrians withdrew to Carchemish, where they awaited help from Egypt. Josiah tried to block the Egyptian forces, but he was killed. With his death, Egypt gained control over Judah through the use of Josiah's children as puppet rulers.

In 605 B.C.E. at Carchemish, the Babylonian Nebuchadnezzar defeated the Egyptians and later that year became king of Babylon. After taking control of Philistia, in the winter of 598/97 B.C.E. he invaded Judah and captured Jerusalem for the first time. The Babylonian account of this capture has survived in the *Chronicle of Nebuchadnezzar*: "In the seventh year, the month of *Kislev*, the king of Akkad mustered his troops, marched to the Hatti-land, and encamped against the city of Judah, on the second day of the month of Adar he seized the city and captured the king. He appointed there a king of his own choice, received its heavy tribute and sent [them] to Babylon." Nebuchadnezzar plundered the city and transported 10,000 troops and craftsmen to Babylon. He designated Zedekiah as king of Judah and made the state a vassal of Babylon. Zedekiah played a double game: he conspired with Egypt and Pharaoh Psammetichus and entered into a secret treaty to revolt from Babylon. The death of Psammetichus in 589 B.C.E. prompted Nebuchadnezzar to strengthen his hold on Judah and forestall Egyptian expansion in Palestine. In the winter of 587 B.C.E. he again invaded Judah and besieged Jerusalem. Zedekiah managed to survive as king for another decade until the second capture of Jerusalem in 586 B.C.E., when the city, short of water and food, fell.

King Zedekiah escaped through a gate in his garden. But the Babylonian armies pursued him and captured him in the plains of Jericho. Brought before Nebuchadnezzar, he watched as his sons were slaughtered. It was the last thing he saw. Nebuchadnezzar put out his eyes, bound him in chains, took him to Babylon, and imprisoned him until the day of his death.

This time Nebuchadnezzar treated the city much more harshly. He took as spoils the king's treasury and the Temple vessels, then set the city ablaze, destroying and burning the Temple and all the houses of Jerusalem. He transported much of the population to Babylon, especially the upper classes, though he left behind the poor and the peasants to farm the land. The city of David, the fortress that had withstood enemies for 400 years, was no more.

13

JEREMIAH

Jeremiah prophesied in the 7th century B.C.E. during the reigns of kings Josiah, Jehoiakin, and Zedekiah. The extensive reforms that King Josiah made were not enough for Jeremiah, and he continued to be a prophet of doom. He insisted that God was not bound to one place, and he and his philosophy influenced the universalization of God and the development of monotheism. After the fall of Jerusalem in 586 B.C.E., he went into exile in Egypt.

Jeremiah died at Daphne in Egypt, an old man in his sixties, in an exile that he himself had prophesied would come to the Jews, along with the destruction of Jerusalem. Born of a priestly family in 645 B.C.E., Jeremiah began to preach in the thirteenth year of the reign of Josiah (627 B.C.E.). He was only eighteen at the time, but he could not abide the apostasy and paganism that was upon the land. King Manasseh, the son of Hezekiah, had left a legacy of child sacrifice and idol worship. The young king Josiah had begun some feeble reforms, but not enough. In the year that Jeremiah began to preach, the Book of the Law, or Deuteronomy, was rediscovered. With this new document as a stimulus, and under the leadership of Josiah and the high priest Hilkiah, reforms were intensified. For five years the reforms were carried out, reestablishing the Mosaic Covenant. Jeremiah wanted to see the people of northern Israel associate themselves with the religious life of Jerusalem. Most important of all, he wanted Israel to be united at the national sanctuary in Jerusalem. He told the people that they owed everything to the God of Israel, who was unique, whose divine love had brought Israel into being and without it, Israel could not continue. Israel and God were like husband and wife. Israel, like a loving wife, had to love and submit and give loyalty to God. But Israel, like an unfaithful wife, had betrayed Him by being unfaithful and lusting after pagan ways.

The reforms of Josiah restored the Covenant, but Josiah and his followers had made the Temple, with its sacrifices, the only access to God. According to Jeremiah, they neglected the moral principles of the Covenant and kept the people away from direct communication with God. When Josiah died in 609

B.C.E., Jehoiakin succeeded him to the throne. The Temple priests and their opponents grew more and more at odds. Then Jeremiah delivered his famous "Temple sermon," in which he indicted the policy of the king and attacked the priests. Uriah of Kiriat-Yearim, another prophet, joined him in his attack. No one heeded Jeremiah; instead, he was barred from entering the Temple, and his own family and the villagers from his hometown of Anathoth conspired to kill him for his words. He continued to preach, even at the cost of his own life. Somehow, he survived. No one killed him, whether out of respect for the word of God, or lack of courage.

Jeremiah warned of the impending doom, that they would all be destroyed. After Nebuchadnezzar was victorious at the battle of Carchemish in 605 B.C.E., he was even more convinced that the "Foe from the North" would do God's work and bring destruction to the people of Judah. He tried to warn them, but they would not listen. Finally, since he could not enter the Temple on pain of death, he dictated a message to his friend Baruch, who recorded his words on a scroll. When Baruch began to read Jeremiah's warning, King Jehoiakin snatched the scroll from his hands and threw it into the fire. Jehoiakin was angered and ready to execute Jeremiah, but Jeremiah went into hiding and dictated the scroll again.

The Babylonians captured Jerusalem in 597 B.C.E. and deported the king and the leading citizens. How great was the suffering of the young king, a victim of his father's folly. But God had spoken. God had shown that He was too great to be worshiped in the Temple of Jerusalem. Other prophets were trying to make one shrine essential to the true religion, but Jeremiah prophesied that this was wrong. Israel was set apart for God and His property, His bride. The worship of God was therefore not tied to one location or outer circumstances. His word was everywhere and needed prayer and obedience, not a shrine. Resistance to Babylon was resistance to Divine Will. The armies of Babylon were God's instrument to punish a guilty nation.

When vassals of Nebuchadnezzar sent to King Zedekiah to talk rebellion, Jeremiah opposed it. He appeared before the conspirators, having put on a yoke, and exhorted them to wear the yoke of Babylon. In 587 B.C.E. the Babylonians moved against Jerusalem, and King Zedekiah sent to Jeremiah and asked him for the word of the Lord. Jeremiah told him that God Himself was fighting on the side of Babylon. The leaders of Judah arrested him for saying this, and he remained in custody until the city fell. After the conquest of the city, the Babylonians allowed Jeremiah to live with the new governor, Gedaliah, at Mizpah. But when Gedaliah was murdered, his followers forced Jeremiah against his will to flee to Egypt with them. Jeremiah believed that the sinfulness of Israel would not be forgiven until an entire generation of seventy years had passed. Then God would contract a new Covenant with the people and restore the Temple.

Jeremiah died in Egypt, in exile, his prophecies of destruction fulfilled. His prophecies of return were to prove correct, but earlier than he had predicted. In 538 B.C.E., almost 60 years after the first deportation of Jews from Judah to Babylon in 597 B.C.E., the Persian ruler Cyrus restored the Jews to Jerusalem, and the Temple was rebuilt in the 520s B.C.E., 65 years after the destruction of the First Temple.

14

THE BABYLONIAN EXILE
AND THE RETURN

The Jews transported to Babylon developed a prosperous life in exile. The Persians conquered the Babylonians and pursued a policy of religious tolerance. In 538 B.C.E. the Persian king Cyrus allowed the Jews to rebuild their Temple in Jerusalem. The first wave of returnees journeyed from Babylon to Jerusalem and began to rebuild not only the Temple, but a Jewish province as part of the Persian Empire. During the Babylonian Exile Jews transformed themselves into an ethno-religious group that could exist without a central Temple. This adaptation contributed to the survival of Judaism.

In 597 B.C.E. Nebuchadnezzar, king of Babylon, seized Jehoiakin, king of Judah, along with the priests, nobility, and leaders of Jerusalem, and brought them to Babylon. In a single strike he crippled the leadership of Judah. He forcibly settled the captives on the Chepar River, near the city of Nippur. The Jews maintained their family structure and seem to have been absorbed into the culture of Babylon. The prophet Ezekiel, who was among the first wave of exiles, prophesied that the exile would be a long one, while others wrongly predicted the quick destruction of Babylon and the return to Jerusalem. After the destruction of Jerusalem in 586 B.C.E. and a second wave of deportations of Jews to Babylon, the exiles realized that their captivity would be a long one.

The exiles were greatly influenced by Babylonian culture. They adopted Babylonian names, such as Zerubbabel ("seed of Babylon") and Mordechai (man of Marduk). During this period Hebrew began to be written in the alphabet of Aramaic, a lingua franca of Babylon. Names of Babylonian months were adopted, and Hebrew documents, such as the Book of Kings, were reedited according to Babylonian chronicle tradition.

In the middle of the 6th century B.C.E. a new power rose in the Middle East, Persia. Much of modern-day eastern Turkey, Iran, and Kurdistan was ruled by the Medes, an Indo-European–speaking people allied with the Babylonians. The Medes dominated another Indo-European group, the Persians, who were a vassal state. In 550 B.C.E. Cyrus led the Persians in a revolt against the Medes, defeated them, and proclaimed himself king of the Persian Empire. Surrounded by able followers, he quickly expanded his power base and in 546 B.C.E. conquered Lydia, the major power in Asia Minor. This victory provided him with money and an additional territory. He then moved against Babylon and in 539 B.C.E. defeated Nabonidus, king of Babylon. Cyrus proclaimed himself King of the Lands, the legitimate ruler of all Mesopotamia.

Nabonidus had caused dissatisfaction among his subjects by taking the statues of various gods from other cities and transferring them to Babylon. These Cyrus restored. Cyrus seemed to have a policy of religious toleration, whether for political reasons or spiritual ones, and made an effort to restore and rebuild temples in the subject lands. He recorded this in an inscription that still survives:

> From [Nineveh] to the cities of Ashur, Shushan, and Akkad, the Land of Eshnunna and the cities of Zamba, Meturnu, Der and as far as the boundary of the Land of the Gutians, across the Tigris, whose temples were destroyed in the distant past, [to all of these] I have restored and returned their own gods and I have set them up on their eternal seats. I have assembled all their [dispersed] people and restored them to their habitations. (Cyrus Cylinder 22–23, trans. H. Tadmor)

As part of this policy, Cyrus made the decision at the beginning of his reign in 538 B.C.E. to restore the Temple in Jerusalem. Ezra 1:2–3 preserves Cyrus's decree: "Thus said Cyrus, king of Persia, YHVH God of Heaven hath given me all the kingdoms of the earth and he hath charged me to build him an house at Jerusalem which is in Judah. Who is there among you of all his people? His God be with him, and let him go up to Jerusalem, which is in Judah and build the house of the YHVH God of Israel, he is the God, which is in Jerusalem."

With the backing of the state, the Jews in Babylon were eager to return. According to Ezra 2:64, about 50,000 returned over the next half century. The first group was led by Sheshbazzar, probably the son of King Jehoiakin, who had died in Babylon. At this stage Cyrus was interested in rebuilding the Temple, not in restoring the monarchy. The Persian Empire was ruled, not by vassal kings, but by a series of provincial governors. Apparently the Temple and the priest class were exempted from taxes, but not the populace. The rebuilding of the Temple was started in the second year of the return, but was stopped and not resumed until 520 B.C.E., when we find Zerubbabel, the grandson of Jehoiakin, who headed a second wave of returning Jews, with the title of Persian governor. By this time Darius, the successor of Cyrus, was on the throne, and it was at this period that the Temple was completed.

The transportation of the Jews from Judah to Babylon after the destruction of the First Temple in 586 B.C.E. might have spelled the end of the Jewish people except for two factors. One was that the Jews were able to maintain a sense of identity, even without a central religious shrine, through their adherence to the Mosaic laws. In contrast, most of the Jews of the northern kingdom of Israel had come under the influence of the worship of other deities, such as Baal, and when they were transported, they were more easily absorbed into local cultures. The major factor, however, that allowed the survival of Judaism in Babylon was the victory of the Persians over the Babylonians. The Persians pursued a policy of religious tolerance and allowed the Jews to return from Babylon to rebuild the Temple at Jerusalem after a seventy-year exile. Without the ability to maintain their identity, or without the repatriation in such a relatively short time, the Jews of Babylon might have gone the way of the peoples of the northern kingdom, who died out as a group with the exception of a handful of Samaritans, who survive to this day.

The Babylonian Exile, though it lasted only fifty years from the final fall of Jerusalem to the return of the first settlers, had a profound effect on the history of the Jews. Although in the days of Moses the religion had existed in a nomadic fashion, since the time of David and Solomon in the 10th century B.C.E. Judaism was a religion practiced through worship at a central shrine and Temple at Jerusalem. The Jews of the northern kingdom had been unable to preserve their religion in exile with any success. But the Jews of Judah survived as a group, whether because the religion had become more sophisticated and developed through the reforms of Deuteronomy or because they were able to remain a cohesive group in Babylon under the leadership of their nobles and priests, who accompanied them in exile.

The Jews of Babylon managed to preserve their religion and adapt it so that it did not require a central shrine. The observance of the Sabbath became a main focus, and the practice of circumcision was used to separate Jews from the rest of the population. In addition, while the synagogue was primarily a development of the Hellenistic period (3rd century B.C.E. to 1st century C.E.), we have perhaps the first beginnings of local congregations for religious observation. These groups were called by the Babylonian word *kinishtu*, or "assembly," from which the Hebrew word *knesset* derives.

Once Jewish life was reestablished with the Temple in Jerusalem and only part of the Jewish population returned, a symbiosis developed between the Diaspora Jews living in Babylon and those in Jerusalem. Thus the Jews of Judah developed from a national state with a centralized religion to an ethno-religious group living in the Persian Empire. This transformation gave Jews the strength to survive as a people of the Diaspora when the Second Temple was destroyed by the Romans in 70 C.E.

15

EZRA AND NEHEMIAH

Ezra led a second wave of returnees from Babylon in 458 B.C.E. A religious as well as a civil leader, he insisted that the Jews divorce their foreign wives, renew the Covenant, and observe the Torah. He was probably the first to introduce the public reading of the Torah. In 445 B.C.E., a third wave of returnees arrived under Nehemiah, who was appointed the Persian governor of Judah. Nehemiah rebuilt the walls of the city, centralized and increased the power of Jerusalem, and undertook land and economic reforms to alleviate the serfdom that many of the poorer landowners and peasants had fallen into at the hands of the returning nobles.

While the Persian king Cyrus had allowed Jews to return to Judah in the 6th century B.C.E., probably for reasons of toleration, the returns in the 5th century were motivated by political and military considerations of the Persian Empire. While the account of the return in the Book of Ezra does not give us much information about the motives of the Persians, the Greek sources tell us a great deal about the history of Persia, the Near East, and Greece during this period. Of particular importance was the work of the 5th century B.C.E. Greek historian Herodotus, who wrote a history of the war between Greece and Persia, with digressions on the history and customs of Persia and Egypt.

The 5th century ushered in the golden age of Greece, producing great literature, including tragedies by Aeschylus, Sophocles, and Euripides; advances in medicine by Hippocrates; works of philosophy by Socrates and Plato; and history by Thucydides. Greek culture did not have a major impact on Judah during this period, although we find Athenian pottery and the standard Athenian coinage, the owl, stamped with the name Judah, in many archaeological sites in Judah. However, by the end of the 4th century Greece had conquered the Near East, including Judah.

By the beginning of the 5th century B.C.E. Persia had extended its empire throughout the Middle East, from Egypt in the south to the borders of India in the east. Already in control of the Greek settlements along the coast of Asia Minor, Persia tried to expand westward but was defeated by the Greeks, first at Marathon in 490 B.C.E., then at Salamis in 480 B.C.E. Athens headed a coalition of Greek city-states, called the Delian League, which by mid-century had been transformed into the Athenian Empire. In 460 B.C.E. the Athenians encouraged and aided an Egyptian revolt from Persia, which was not suppressed until 454 B.C.E. Since Palestine, Judah, and Samaria were at a crossroads between Egypt and the rest of the Persian Empire, and perhaps wishing to strengthen Judah as a defense against Athens' expansion in the eastern Mediterranean and the revolt in Egypt, the Persian king Artaxerxes sent a new wave of settlers from Babylon to Judah in 458 B.C.E.

This wave of returnees was led by Ezra, with government authority that authorized him to appoint judges and rule in accord with the law of the God of Heaven. At this time Judah was part of the Persian satrapy (province) of Trans-Euphrates, and it is unclear whether Ezra had authority over both religious and civil affairs. Ezra was accompanied by 1,500 people, who were exempted from taxes. In the Book of Ezra his genealogy, which extends back to Aaron, may indicate that he was a religious leader of the Babylonian community.

From the Book of Ezra we learn that Ezra saw himself as the leader of "the people of the exile" as opposed to the "people of the land," presumably the Jewish peasant population that had not been transported to Babylon. He insisted that those who had taken foreign wives, particularly those from the leading families, should divorce them. Ezra 10:44 lists the Levites who had taken foreign wives and agreed to leave them. The narrative of Ezra abruptly ends here. He is mentioned briefly in the Book of Nehemiah, some fourteen years later.

We know little of what happened during the next decade, except that some unsuccessful attempts were made to rebuild the walls of Jerusalem. However, in 445 B.C.E. Nehemiah, son of Hachaliah, was appointed governor of Judah. We learn the details of his life from his memoirs, called the Book of Nehemiah, which seems to be a firsthand account. Nehemiah describes how he was courtier to King Artaxerxes, when he was visited in Susa by Jews from Jerusalem who told him of the sorry state of the city and its walls. He approached Artaxerxes and was given permission to go to Jerusalem and rebuild the walls, as the governor of Judah.

When Nehemiah arrived in Jerusalem, he found severe social and economic problems. The chasm between the indigenous peasant Judeans and small landowners and the noble returnees had grown. Many peasants were enslaved or in bondage for debt: "We have mortgaged our lands, vineyards, and houses, that we might buy corn, because of the famine. . . . And we bring into bondage our sons and daughters" (Nehemiah 5:3–5). Nehemiah, following the same course as Solon of Athens did under similar circumstances in the 6th century B.C.E., canceled debts, removed mortgages, and redistributed the land. He persuaded the nobles to acquiesce by convening an assembly in which he brought moral pressure for them to agree, with the unspoken threat that if they did not, he would impose the reform with the might of Persia.

Nehemiah next set about to strengthen the position of Jerusalem in Judah. Besides the rebuilding and enlargement of the walls, he required 10 percent of the population to settle in the city. He then instituted a tithe to be paid to the Temple in Jerusalem. Furthermore, he restructured the way allotments were made to the Levites, the Temple assistants, who had lost control of their income, to guarantee their maintenance. To them also he entrusted the strict enforcement of the laws of the Sabbath, and even had the gates of the city closed during the Sabbath.

Nehemiah met opposition to his measures from Samaria, particularly the governor Sanballat, who was a follower of the Temple at Jerusalem and YHVH. Sanballat had married his daughter to the grandson of the high priest in Jerusalem, Eliashib, who was a political opponent. Nehemiah followed Ezra's idea of purification of the people of Judah from foreign wives, and among other moves, banished Eliashib's grandson, Manasseh. Manasseh went to Samaria, where he built a rival Temple on Mount Gerizim. This marked the permanent religious division between the Jews of Judah and those of the northern kingdom, who became the Samaritan sect.

Nehemiah eventually returned to Persia, probably in 433 B.C.E., but left his brother Hanani in charge of Jerusalem and perhaps Judah. We find Hanani mentioned in the year 419 B.C.E. in a letter from the Jewish community in Elephantine, Egypt.

Ezra and Nehemiah were major rebuilders of Jerusalem. Ezra influenced the religious revival, introducing perhaps the first public reading of the Books of Moses and fighting against intermarriage. Nehemiah followed in Ezra's footsteps, extending reform to civil matters. The two stand as the major figures in the resettlement of Jerusalem and the rebuilding of the Temple and the homeland of the Jews.

16

HELLENISM

Alexander the Great, king of Macedon, conquered the Persian Empire, and with it Palestine and Jerusalem. After his death, his generals created independent kingdoms in Egypt and Syria, which fought continually for control of Palestine. During this period, Greek culture and language, known as Hellenism, were superimposed on the region. The Bible was translated into Greek (the Septuagint), the language of most Jews outside Palestine, and Jews grappled with the benefits and threats of the influences of this foreign culture. Large numbers of Jews, either by force or by choice, settled in Alexandria, Egypt, and in many cities in Greece and the Mediterranean, which resulted in a diaspora.

Judah settled into a quiet province of the Persian Empire, with a growing and stable population, in the 4th century B.C.E. But at the end of the 4th century the Mediterranean world was thrown into turmoil by the rise of one of the world's greatest military leaders, Alexander the Great, who was to change the face of Greece and the Near East. For the next 300 years, Jews were to fall under Greek influence.

In 336 B.C.E. Alexander the Great assumed the throne of Macedon in northern Greece. Raised in a militaristic state and in command of the finest fighting force in the world, he embarked on a journey of conquest that was to lead him to the gardens of Babylon and as far as the Indus River in India. He conquered not only countries, but also their cultures. His legacy was the hellenization of much of the eastern Mediterranean and the Near East, including Judah. This legacy has lasted even into the modern Western world, which is culturally, intellectually, and spiritually a Greco-Roman civilization.

Alexander crossed the Hellespont (the Dardanelles) in 334 B.C.E. with 40,000 troops and engaged the Persian forces. Inspired by the tales of Homer about Greek conquests of Asia Minor and, like Achilles of Homer's *Iliad*, seeking glory, he set about to conquer Persia. At the battle of Issus (333 B.C.E.) in Asia Minor he overwhelmed the forces of King Darius III. Turning southward after a difficult siege, he took the walled city of Tyre, then conquered Judea in 332 B.C.E. Egypt soon fell. Alexander next marched into the heart of the Persian

Empire and decisively defeated its armies in 331 B.C.E. to make himself the new Great King of Persia. He continued his conquests as far as India. On his return to Babylon, he died of a fever in 323 B.C.E. at the age of thirty-three. Although he died too soon to consolidate his new empire, he did try to spread Greek culture, to unite the Greeks with the conquered peoples by marrying a Persian woman, and by having many of his troops and generals do the same.

An apocryphal story relates that on his deathbed he was asked to whom he willed his kingdom. His reply was that it would be left "to the strongest." With his death, his generals fought for control of the empire. After many years of warfare three distinct kingdoms emerged: Egypt under Ptolemy, the Near East under Seleucus, and Greece and Macedon.

The Greek rulers imposed not only Greek power on the conquered peoples, but also the Greek language and culture. In Egypt, for example, Greek became one of the official languages of the country. The Jews who lived in Alexandria learned to speak Greek in place of Aramaic and Hebrew. We find this evidenced in the 3rd century B.C.E. when the Hebrew Bible was translated into Greek. This translation, known as the Septuagint, was designed for the Jewish population, who spoke Greek as their primary language. Ptolemy II is reputed to have encouraged this translation, possibly because he wished to procure a translation of the document for his library.

Not only did the Greek language and rule influence the cultures of the eastern Mediterranean, but also Greek philosophy, particularly that of Plato and Aristotle. The concept of YHVH as the God of the Jews first was that of monolatry rather than monotheism, the worship of one deity in preference to all others. While from an early time Judaism was aniconic, that is, forbidding the worship of idols and representations of a god, its development into monotheism was gradual. The reforms of Josiah emphasized YHVH as the only Supreme Being for the Jews. But it was the Babylonian captivity and Persian influences, particularly with the exposure to Zoroastrianism, with its universal concepts, that accelerated the process toward an omnipotent, omnipresent, omniscient, invisible deity. The loss of the Temple as a central religious shrine perhaps encouraged this development. The encounter with Greek philosophy, particularly that of Plato, with his "idea of the good," brought monotheism to the form as we know it. Judaism became an amalgamation of a Semitic religion, originating under Egyptian influences, and the universalizing forces of Persian Zoroastrianism and Greek philosophy.

The encounter with Greek culture presented another chapter in the struggle of Jews to assimilate. The lure of the worship of Baal, Astarte, and other foreign gods had always been strong to the Jews. Now the lure of the Greek secular humanistic intellectual culture became a threat. But Jews survived this threat to their culture, despite a civil war during the Maccabean period that resulted from this issue.

Under the Hellenistic monarchies Judah came to be called Judea, from its Greek spelling, and the larger region, Syria and Phoenicia. As it had for the past 2,000 years, and as it would for its future history, this area stood at a crossroads between the powers of Egypt in the south and Syria in the north. Ptolemy I in 320 B.C.E. took Jerusalem and incorporated it into the Egyptian kingdom. In reaction, when the Seleucids gained control in Syria and Babylon, they attempted to take Judea. Wars continued and in 249 B.C.E. Ptolemy II married his daughter Berenice to Antiochus II, and with her the rights to Judea went from Egypt to Syria. This union did not settle the issue, and the area was a battleground until the year 200, when the Seleucid Antiochus took firm control.

Judea continued much the same, despite its rulers. Though it had no independence, it had its own language, religion, and semiautonomous government. The high priest was the head of the government and was responsible to the foreign overlords for the collection of taxes and revenues. He was assisted by a senate of elders and priests, much on the Greek model. But the Babylonian Exile had changed religious life for Jews, both in Judea and in the Diaspora. Since in the 6th century Jews had to learn to practice their religion without a central shrine, the synagogue developed, along with the codification of the Torah. Thus, even when a central shrine was reinstituted, it had less importance in the religious life of Jews than previously. The populace might come to the Temple at Jerusalem on the pilgrimage festivals of Passover, Sukkot, and Shavuot, as well as on the Day of Atonement, but the daily practice of their religion came to be the observance of the Mosaic code wherever they lived.

The conquest of Judea by the Greeks and the influence of Greek culture did much to universalize the religious concepts of Judaism, but it also brought a great threat, that of assimilation and loss of identity. Beginning with the Babylonian Exile, Jews started to live abroad in greater numbers. Even after the return to Judea under the Persians, more Jews lived abroad than in Judea. This tendency was increased in the Hellenistic period by the development of centers such as Alexandria in Egypt and Jewish settlements in other parts of Greece, such as in Rhodes. Fortunately for the survival of the Jewish people, the Diaspora developed great strength during this period, so that when finally the Second Temple was destroyed, Jews managed to survive as a people and a religion.

17

JUDAH MACCABEE

Judea stood between the powers of Egypt in the south and the Seleucids in the north. As a reaction to the hellenizing influences of the Judeans who supported the Seleucids, a revolt broke out among the Hasidim (the Pious), under Mattathias and his son Judah in 168 B.C.E. After years of fighting, Judah Maccabee molded the Jews of Judea into an effective fighting force and laid the foundation for the country to become an independent kingdom before his death in battle against the Seleucids in 160 B.C.E.

Soldiers came to Modiin, a small town near Jerusalem, in 167 B.C.E. to force local Jews to sacrifice pigs. The priest Mattathias was ordered to conduct the sacrifice. He refused to obey, but another Jew standing nearby came forward to perform the sacrifice. Enraged at this desecration, Mattathias killed the Jew and the government official who had given the order. "Everyone of you who is zealous for the law and strives to maintain the covenant, follow me" (1 Maccabees 2:27), he shouted. With this event the revolt of Judea from the Syrian Greeks began.

By the 2nd century Judea fell into the hands of the Seleucid Greek Empire. Hellenism, that is, Greek culture and language, was spreading throughout the Near East, particularly in the cities. The Greek concept of politics saw the *polis*, or city-state, as the center of life. The Greek philosopher Aristotle wrote in the 4th century that "man is a political animal," by which he meant that man's nature was to live in a *polis* or city. Greek became the official language of politics and administration, though Aramaic and Hebrew were still spoken. Central to the Greek *polis* were several institutions, found in every city—the *agora*, or marketplace, the theater, and the gymnasium. Under the rule of the high priest Jason the gymnasium was introduced into Jerusalem in the first quarter of the 2nd century B.C.E. There Jewish youths, naked or wearing only a strip of cloth and a Greek-style hat, wrestled and competed in athletic events. Some men even tried to have their circumcisions reversed by an operation that was perfected in Egypt, so they could appear naked without "bodily mutilation" in the Greek games. The social and political center of life became the gymnasium instead of the Temple. The author of 2 Maccabees 4:14 complains that the priests themselves left the Temple and went to watch games in the gymnasium. The high priest Jason even sent delegations to the pagan games of Heracles in Syria and Phoenicia. The populace resented the Temple officials, since the Seleucids used them to collect taxes. Now, when Greek customs, which seemed to undermine the Laws of Moses, were introduced, religious hatred was added to the hatred of taxation.

The country split into two factions. The hellenizers, who represented the upper class, lived in the cities and looked to the Seleucids as their rulers. The antihellenizers, called the *Hasidim*, or "the pious" (not to be confused with the Hasidim of today), wanted to remove the sacrilegious hellenizing institutions and restore the pure worship of the Laws of Moses. They looked to Egypt for help, since they saw that the Jews of Alexandria were left alone to practice their religion without Greek culture being forced upon them.

When Antiochus IV Epiphanes ascended the throne in 175 B.C.E., he looked to expand southward against Egypt. Judea and Palestine were a strategic buffer region between the Seleucids and Egypt. Finally, in 168 B.C.E. Antiochus took an army into Egypt and was on the point of capturing Alexandria and defeating the Ptolemaic Empire, when the Romans entered upon the scene. The Romans had expanded into Asia Minor and had decisively defeated Antiochus's father twenty years before, although they did not take any significant territory as a result of their victory. The Romans possessed the greatest fighting machine in the Mediterranean, and when they cautioned Antiochus to end his siege of Alexandria and withdraw, he obeyed.

Antiochus deposed Jason as high priest and put in his own candidate, Menelaus. He later came back through Judea from an expedition against Egypt and called on Menelaus to help him steal part of the Temple treasury to pay for his military adventures. The people of Judea felt this was an insult to their autonomy and their God. In 168 B.C.E. a rumor that Antiochus died in Egypt in the middle of a military campaign ran through Jerusalem. This was a signal for revolt. Jason, the deposed high priest, seized control of Jerusalem. But Antiochus was not dead, and he swiftly took back the city and butchered many men, women, and children. He tore down part of the city walls. To eliminate resistance and secure his position, he settled a foreign colony on the citadel of the city. Menelaus and the hellenizers helped him do this. The foreign settlers brought in their pagan gods and worshiped them in view of the Temple.

To strike against the Jewish population in 167 B.C.E., Antiochus passed a decree forbidding the practice of the Jewish religion, with the death penalty for anyone who circumcised his sons or observed the Sabbath. As the final outrage, Jews were forced to eat pork and join in pagan rites. These edicts caused a revolt in the countryside led by Mattathias and his sons, whose families are known as the Hasmoneans. However, Antiochus's actions seem strange compared with his relatively tolerant policies elsewhere in the empire. Some scholars suggest that Antiochus would not have known or cared enough to pass such a decree, and that the timing be reversed. First came the revolt; Menelaus and the hellenizers, loyal to Antiochus, masterminded the decree to strike at the Hasidim. The decree backfired and inflamed the population to join the revolt.

Mattathias, with his sons and supporters, took to the countryside and emerged as the leader of the Hasidim. One of his first innovations was to allow fighting on the Sabbath. Mattathias fought a guerrilla war in the countryside. After he was killed during fighting in 166 B.C.E., his son Judah, a brilliant general, took command and brought the revolt to Jerusalem. Judah won a decisive victory at Mizpeh, north of Jerusalem, and marched on the city. A Seleucid army under Lysias, Antiochus's lieutenant, attacked. Again Judah was victorious and marched on Jerusalem. The Romans negotiated a settlement between the Seleucids and the Jews, but the compromise was short-lived. Antiochus died within a few months, and Judah used the opportunity to attack Jerusalem in December 164 B.C.E. and take the city. Judah purified the Temple, demolished pagan altars and buildings, and put priests from the Hasmonean faction in charge. According to legend, when the sacred oil was to be relit in the Temple, the supply was only enough for one day, but by a miracle, it burned for eight days. The festival of Hanukkah was inaugurated to commemorate the rededication.

The Seleucids could not tolerate this revolt. Antiochus V invaded Judea and besieged Jerusalem. Unable to take the city, he was forced to negotiate a peace. The decrees against the practice of the Jewish religion were annulled. Menelaus was executed, a moderate hellenizer was named high priest, and Judah Maccabee was left as military leader.

The peace lasted only until 162 B.C.E., when Demetrius I succeeded to the throne of Macedon and tried to retake Jerusalem. Judah was forced to flee and leave the Seleucids in charge of the city. But their oppressive behavior fanned another revolt in the countryside. Judah mobilized his army and again went to war. The price was personal this time. In the fighting near Beth-zechariah the Seleucid forces brought their elephants into battle. They had given them the juice of grapes and mulberries to madden them and make them rampage through the Jewish battle lines. Eleazar, Judah's brother, saw that one of the elephants was equipped with royal armor, and he thought that the Seleucid king was on it. He ran into the middle of the battle, got under the elephant, and stabbed it from underneath. The elephant fell dead, but toppled right on top of Eleazar and crushed him to death. The Jews fled. However, Judah regrouped and within a year defeated the Seleucids and killed their general, Nicanor, in 161 B.C.E. on the 13th of *Adar* (Nicanor's Day).

Judah astutely saw the rising power of Rome in the region, and realized the path to real independence lay through Rome. In 161 B.C.E. he concluded a treaty of neutrality and mutual defense with Rome. This treaty gave Judea some claim to independence, but Demetrius ignored it and sent another army into Judea in 160 B.C.E. and Judah Maccabee, like his father before him, died fighting the Seleucids. Judah had welded the people of Judea into an effective fighting force. The successful revolt and the subsequent establishment of the Hasmonean dynasty in large part was a result of his leadership, as well as that of his brothers, Simon and Jonathan, who took command on his death.

18

THE HASMONEAN STATE

Under the able leadership of Judah Maccabee's brothers, first Jonathan and then Simon, Judea was established as an independent kingdom under the Maccabees, called the Hasmonean dynasty. This was the first independent Jewish state since Nebuchadnezzar destroyed and captured Jerusalem 440 years before in 586 B.C.E. The Hasmonean kingdom lasted until 37 B.C.E., when it came under the control of King Herod and the Romans. Jews were not to have another independent nation for 2,000 years, until the establishment of the state of Israel in 1948.

An accident of history allowed the development of the Hasmonean state as an independent entity. Four factors contributed to this. First, Rome was extending its empire into the Near East. Although the Romans defeated the Seleucids at Magnesia in 189 B.C.E., they did not follow up their conquests by seizing extensive territory. Rather, they maintained a sphere of influence. As such they did not allow the Seleucids to defeat Egypt, which prevented the latter from subduing all of the Near East. When Judah Maccabee made overtures of friendship, the Romans signed treaties. Although they did not come to the aid of the Judeans in their fight with the Seleucids, the knowledge of the Seleucids that Rome would allow them to go so far and no further may have inhibited their conduct.

The second factor was the breakup of the Seleucid Empire into warring factions. This gave an opportunity for the Judeans to establish their independence.

The third factor was twenty-five years of superb leadership by the Maccabees. Mattathias was a first-rate leader who inspired his followers. Though he was killed two years after the revolt broke out, he was succeeded by the most able of his sons, the charismatic Judah. In turn Judah was succeeded by Jonathan, who was to show himself equal to his brother. Following Jonathan's murder, Simon, the youngest of Mattathias's sons, assumed control. He too was extremely able and finished the work of his brothers and father.

The fourth factor was that the growing population of Judea allowed the Maccabees to field large armies, perhaps 40,000 at the largest. In contrast, the Seleucid army comprised perhaps 70,000, but not all of these troops could be brought to bear at once in Judea.

In 160 B.C.E. Jonathan succeeded Judah as the head of the Jewish forces. By this time the Seleucids had retained Jerusalem, and the Maccabees returned to their guerrilla tactics in the countryside, which they controlled. They were unable to make much headway against the Seleucids until, at last, an opportunity presented itself with a struggle over the Seleucid throne. Alexander Balas challenged Demetrius I for the throne. Both sides were of approximately equal power, but Alexander Balas had his capital in nearby Acco. Consequently, in an effort to induce Jonathan to join his cause, Demetrius allowed him to regain Jerusalem. Jonathan negotiated with both sides, and when Alexander Balas offered to make Jonathan the high priest, Jonathan joined him. With the office of high priest Jonathan now was the official Seleucid secular and religious head of Judea. From 152 until 37 B.C.E., a Hasmonean held the office of high priest and through this office the role of ruler of Judea. Jonathan remained a loyal ally of Alexander Balas, until the latter was killed by Demetrius in 145 B.C.E. Because Jonathan had solidified his military might, he became the most powerful political figure in Judea. Demetrius opted to make peace with him, reaffirm him as high priest, and approve the annexation of parts of southern Samaria.

The civil wars of the Seleucids continued, and Jonathan deserted Demetrius for Tryphon, who was acting on behalf of Antiochus VI, Alexander Balas's son. However, as Jonathan's power grew through a treaty with Rome, Tryphon murdered Jonathan.

Jonathan had consolidated the power of Judea both militarily and diplomatically. He managed to choose the right side in the civil wars and established Judea as the dominant power of southern Syria. He not only extended the territory of Judea to southern Samaria, but also acquired the port of Jaffa and some Greek cities along the coast of Palestine. Most important, as the first high priest he established the Hasmonean dynasty over Judea.

Simon succeeded his brother and fought against Tryphon and Antiochus VI. Consequently, he allied himself with Demetrius II. As a result, Demetrius II waived taxes for Judea, and Judea thus became an independent kingdom in 142 B.C.E. After a revolt and warfare that lasted over twenty-five years, what had started as another small revolt against the authority of the Seleucids resulted in the reestablishment of an independent Judea, the first independent kingdom for over 440 years, since the destruction of the Temple and the conquest of Jerusalem by Nebuchadnezzer.

Simon renewed the treaty with Rome, and also made treaties with Sparta and other cities in the Mediterranean. He continued to consolidate Judean military power and beat off the last great attack by the Seleucids. Antiochus VII Sidetes, the successor of Demetrius, first confirmed Simon in office in 138 B.C.E. But when Antiochus VII grew more powerful, he decided to attack Judea. Simon, with an army of 20,000, engaged the Seleucid forces near Ashdod, where he overwhelmed them.

In 140 B.C.E. Simon had been confirmed by the Great Assembly as ethnarch (leader of the people), high priest, and supreme commander. These offices were declared hereditary until a true prophet should arise and became the constitutional basis of the Hasmonean dynasty.

The Hasmoneans continued in charge of an independent Judea until the Roman general Pompey took Jerusalem in 63 B.C.E. and slaughtered 12,000. Jerusalem and Judea were made tributaries of Rome. Pompey installed the Hasmonean Hyrcanus II (reigned 63–40 B.C.E.) as high priest, without the title of king. Judea was now under Roman domination. Crassus, the Roman general, plundered the Temple treasury in 54 B.C.E. In 40 B.C.E. the Parthians, a Persian tribe who had long fought the Romans, invaded Syria and Palestine. The Hasmonean Antigonus joined with the Parthians, and Hyrcanus II was defeated and replaced by Antigonus. Finally, in 37 B.C.E. the Romans retook Jerusalem and captured and beheaded Antigonus. Thus ended the Hasmonean dynasty, and Herod of Galilee became king of Judea.

19

HEROD THE GREAT

Herod seized the throne of Judea from the Hasmoneans with the support of Roman troops in 37 B.C.E. He was a vicious and cruel tyrant, but he politically extended the borders of Judea and increased its prosperity. His greatest achievement was his vast building programs, both the renovated and enlarged Second Temple and the new cities and fortresses throughout Judea and Samaria. He was a patron of the Jews of the Diaspora in political and economic matters, and they looked upon him as a great king. With his death the kingdom of Judea was not to survive, but quickly became a Roman province.

"It is better to be Herod's pig than his son," said the Roman emperor Augustus, when he heard that King Herod had executed his own son, Antipater. Herod behaved like many oriental despots and ruthlessly murdered all enemies and potential rivals, particularly in his own family. Most rulers in antiquity lived a precarious existence, and it was common for a new king to kill his relatives who might plot against him. On defeating Antony and Cleopatra, Augustus executed their three children, along with the son of Caesar and Cleopatra, to eliminate future claimants to the throne. When Tiberius became emperor of Rome, he murdered his relative Agrippa Postumus as a potential rival.

Herod particularly seemed to single out members of his own family. He started with forty-five out of the seventy members of the Sanhedrin, the Jewish religious court, who had supported the Hasmoneans. Then he murdered Aristobulus, a Hasmonean who was the brother of his wife Mariamne. Next Herod killed Hyrcanus II, the former Hasmonean king, who was his wife's grandfather. His mother-in-law Alexandra, and even his wife Mariamne, followed. Herod's two sons by Mariamne lasted longer and were not executed until late in Herod's reign, in 7 B.C.E. This left only Herod's son, Antipater, by another wife. Antipater understandably feared for his own life and began plotting against his father. Herod discovered the plot and had Antipater executed.

Based on Herod's reputation for murdering rivals, the New Testament presents an apocryphal story that Herod attempted to have Jesus killed. According to Matthew, chapter 2, wise men came from the east to Jerusalem to worship the king of the Jews, who was just born. Herod tried to trick the wise men into revealing Jesus' location in Bethlehem. He ordered all the male children two years old or younger in the region of Bethlehem to be put to death, but an angel appeared to Joseph and told him to take Jesus and Mary and flee to Egypt.

Herod the Great brought an end to the Hasmonean dynasty and made himself king of Judea. Though a Jew, he was hated by many of the Jews of Judea because he ruled so harshly. Those who favored the Hasmonean dynasty also despised him. The Talmud reviled him as a cruel and bloodthirsty tyrant. However, to the Jews of the Diaspora in the 1st century B.C.E. he was a popular king, and the Romans saw him as an able leader. He was an ally of many Roman nobles, especially Agrippa, a general and close friend of Augustus and the second most powerful figure in the Roman Empire.

The reality of Herod's reign falls between these extremes. He was the greatest builder in the history of Judea, surpassing even King Solomon. He enlarged and rebuilt the Temple at Jerusalem, founded new cities, and undertook a massive building program. A skillful political leader, he preserved semi-autonomy for Judea as a vassal kingdom of the Romans for his long reign. Under his rule peace and prosperity came to Judea, and the country flourished. Herod was one of Judea's most able and successful kings. The negative portrait of him comes from several factors: his vicious personal behavior, especially his wholesale executions of his close relatives; his replacement of religious authority by a civil authority as the ruler of the country; and his close association with the Roman overlords. He even built temples in the Roman emperor's honor. He ruled Judea with an iron fist, prohibiting assemblies and associations in an effort to reduce potential challenges to his rule. Although these measures stabilized his rule, they alienated him from much of the Jewish population within Judea.

Herod was the son of Antipater, who had been governor of Edom and whose family had embraced Judaism in the late 2nd century B.C.E. Antipater had aligned himself with Julius Caesar and later Cassius. Before he was poisoned to death by his enemies in 43 B.C.E., Antipater had appointed Herod as governor of Galilee. Two Hasmonean brothers, Hyrcanus II and Antigonus II, were struggling for the throne. Herod used their quarrel as an opportunity to seize power. First he married Mariamne, the granddaughter of Hyrcanus II, to give him a claim to the Hasmonean succession. Next he turned to the Romans.

Throughout his career Herod acquired and maintained power by allying himself with the winning Roman faction. When he saw that the Roman faction he supported was about to lose, he invariably changed sides at the crucial moment and gained the support of the victors. He first became tetrarch of Judea by bribing Mark Antony in 41 B.C.E. When the Hasmonean Antigonus allied himself with Rome's enemies, the Parthians, and invaded and captured Jerusalem, Herod escaped and went to Rome. There he asked Antony to make him king of Judea. The Romans were interested in stabilizing their empire, and hence loyal vassal kings were highly prized. Herod had already shown his loyalty to Rome, and the present king, Antigonus, was siding with Rome's enemy. Thus the Roman senate proclaimed him king of Judea. Herod returned to Judea with mercenaries, but was unable to conquer the country until Antony supplied him with Roman troops. In the summer of 37 B.C.E., Herod took Jerusalem and established himself as king. After Antony was defeated at Actium (30 B.C.E.), Herod promptly switched his allegiance to Augustus.

Despite his despotic and murderous nature and behavior, Herod was a successful king. The resentment of the religious Jews arose from Herod's secularizing policies and attitudes, although Herod himself generally observed Jewish practices. While the Hasmonean kings held their power through the roles of high priest and ethnarch, Herod was not eligible by birth for these offices. His authority as king came from the might of Rome. He downgraded the importance of the role of high priest and filled the office with Jews from the Diaspora, whose loyalty he could command. Herod tried to bring in Roman and hellenized elements. He surrounded himself with Greeks and foreigners. His court attracted Greek scholars, such as the famous historian Nicolaus of Damascus, as well as Greek poets, musicians, and athletes. A lover of sports, he built a hippodrome and a theater in Jerusalem. The Olympic games in Greece were in decline at this period, and through his funding he reinvigorated them, for which he received the honorary title of president for life.

However, his building programs were his great monument. He rebuilt the city of Jerusalem, particularly an opulent expansion of the Temple. He founded new cities, including Caesarea along the coast and Sebaste on the old site of Samaria, which he settled with Greeks and foreigners. He founded and expanded other cities and built a system of forts throughout the country. Although the general economy benefited from trade, commerce, and the vast building programs, the population was heavily taxed to pay for these monuments to Herod's ego. Josephus, the Jewish general and historian of the 1st century C.E., commented, "[S]ince he was involved in expenses greater than his means, he was compelled to be harsh to his subjects . . . since he was unable to mend his evil ways without harming his revenues, he exploited the ill will of the people to enrich himself privately" (*Antiquities* 16:154–155).

The Jews of the Diaspora regarded Herod as a hero. He often took their side and used his influence with Rome on their behalf. He was their patron and provided monies for the building of synagogues, for libraries, baths, and welfare needs. He encouraged many Diaspora Jews, especially from Babylon, to migrate to Jerusalem. To the Jews of the Diaspora, Herod was a ruler who protected them and gave them pride through his political connections with Rome and his magnificent building programs, especially those of the Temple at Jerusalem.

Herod died of natural causes in 4 B.C.E. Because his power rested on his relations with Rome, his kingdom barely outlasted him, and by 6 C.E. Judea became a Roman province. Herod attempted to bring the Jewish population into the mainstream of Hellenism, but failed. His legacy was his great building program, especially the Temple. Today Jews regard as the most holy of sites the Western Wall, which is a supporting wall of the Temple Mount, built by Herod.

20

THE PHARISEES AND SADDUCEES AND HILLEL AND SHAMMAI

The Pharisees and the Sadducees were two competing religious groups from the 2nd century B.C.E. until the destruction of the Temple in 70 C.E. The Sadducees were fundamentalists; they believed only in the Written Law and saw the Temple and animal sacrifice as the center of Judaism. The Pharisees believed in the Oral Law to interpret and update the Written Law, and saw the synagogue as the basis of Jewish religious observance. Diaspora Jews favored the Pharisees, and after the destruction of the Temple the Sadducees died out, leaving the Pharisees. The greatest of these Pharisees was Hillel, who founded a dynasty of religious scholars that lasted 400 years.

In the 2nd century B.C.E. two distinct religious factions arose, the Sadducees and the Pharisees, which were to have a profound effect on the future of Judaism. The Sadducees took their name from Zadok, the high priest at the time of King David. They were the officials of the Temple and dominated the Sanhedrin (the religious court). The Sadducees comprised the wealthier elements of the state, including the priests, merchants, and aristocrats. They represented the entrenched religious hierarchy who controlled the practice of the religion through their role as Temple officials and priests of the Temple.

The Sadducees saw as central to their beliefs the Laws of Moses, or the Pentateuch. Temple sacrifice was an integral part of their practices. They were conservative, bordering on fundamentalist, were strict observers of the letter of the law, and opposed change and innovation. For example, the biblical law of "an eye for an eye, and a tooth for a tooth" was literally enforced by the Sadducees. The Sadducees were more like the priests of the First Temple period, while the Pharisees were influenced more by the prophets.

The Pharisees emerged as a distinct group in the same period. Several factors prompted their development. First, while Jews were in exile in Babylon, since they had no Temple, the synagogue and the observance of the Laws of the Torah developed as the vehicle for religious practice. When Jews returned from

Babylon they brought this tradition with them, and the rebuilding of the Temple at Jerusalem did not bring an end to this familiar practice. In Judea, with the discouragement of altars and places for sacrifice and the centralization of the cult in Jerusalem, the people outside the city had no daily vehicle for the practice of their religion. Three times a year they might make a pilgrimage to Jerusalem, but otherwise the Temple was not part of their program of worship. Consequently, the idea of the local synagogue and individual study took root. During this period a large proportion of Jews lived in the Diaspora. For such Jews, distant from the Temple, Pharisaic ideas, particularly with the focus on the synagogue, were particularly appealing.

A second major factor was greater emphasis on literacy that followed in the wake of the Greek conquest of the Near East. Great libraries developed in such cities as Alexandria and Pergamum. Because of the increased demand for writing materials, the output of papyrus increased and its price fell, as did the price of parchment. While in the First Temple period the reading and knowledge of the Laws of Moses tended to be confined to the scribe class, by the 2nd century B.C.E., general literacy was widespread. Furthermore, Ezra started a tradition in the 5th century of public reading of the Law of Moses. The many manuscripts recovered from the Dead Sea Scrolls (see nutshell #24), the earliest of which date from the 3rd century B.C.E., confirm the growth of available texts and general literacy. By the same token, the translation of the Torah into Greek, the Septuagint, as well as Aramaic translations of this period, showed an increasing literacy. The Pharisee Hillel urged people to study the Torah. He went so far as to say that "he who does not study, deserves to die." This study presumes literacy and the reading of texts. Once the sacred texts of the Torah were available on a widespread basis, the monopoly of the religion passed out of the hands of the Sadducees, and the texts became available for interpretation by non-Temple priests. Thus the Pharisaic movement arose.

The Pharisees probably took their name from the Hebrew word *parash*, which means "to be separated." Thus *Pharisee* may mean those separated from the impure or the heathen. The Pharisees developed a theology and religious practice at variance with the Sadducees. Their concept was a double law. They believed that Moses received from God not only the Written Law on Mount Sinai, but also simultaneously the Oral Law, which had the same validity as the Written. The Torah ought to be interpreted in every generation through the Oral Law by the agency of the rabbis of that generation. If the spirit of the law was in conflict with the letter of the law, then Oral Law allowed a new interpretation. An example is the *lex talionis*, "an eye for an eye." The Pharisees, unlike the Sadducees, believed that the law need not be taken literally, but that a monetary payment of an equivalent value of the damage could be substituted. Through this notion of Oral Law, Pharisaic Judaism was able to adapt to changing social and intellectual ideas and to become the dominant force in Judaism.

Thus, by a process of interpretation of written texts by each generation, the Jewish law code developed much in the same way that U.S. constitutional law has emerged by the interpretation of the Constitution by each new Supreme Court.

The Pharisaic concept of God became the bedrock of Judaism. For the Pharisees, God was omnipotent, omniscient, all-just, and all-merciful. God gave individuals free will to choose between good and evil, with the Torah as a guide for behavior. The Pharisees believed in the bodily resurrection of the dead and immortality of the soul, while the Sadducees did not. Again, these beliefs entered Judaism from Greek and Persian influences, especially Platonism and Zoroastrianism. Most important, the Pharisees saw God as omnipresent, and therefore he could be worshiped everywhere, not just in the Temple and by animal sacrifices. This belief not only reinforced the importance of the synagogue, but also gave a legitimacy to worship and prayer by Jews of the Diaspora. Once the Temple was destroyed in 70 C.E., the Sadducees, lacking their center of worship, faded, while the Pharisees became the dominant force in Jewish life.

The major Pharisaic figures of the 1st century B.C.E. were the sages Hillel and Shammai. Shammai (c. 50 B.C.E.–30 C.E.) was one of the leaders of the Sanhedrin. Little is known about his life, except that he was a builder by trade. Within the Pharisaic tradition Shammai and his school tended to take the more stringent line of interpretation of Jewish law (*halakhah*), as compared with Hillel. One explanation of their differences is that Shammai was in favor of a strict interpretation of rituals, no matter what hardships or social price their observance entailed. Hillel saw a rigid interpretation at times excessively burdensome to the poor, and so looked liberally on any observance of the law that could be performed for less money or with minimal economic hardship. An example can be seen on their ruling on the permissibility of using olive oil or mustard seed oil for the Sabbath lights. Hillel argued that either oil could be used, while Shammai insisted on olive oil only. Olive oil was much more expensive than mustard seed oil, and hence Hillel's decision may have been motivated by his desire to make things easier for the poor. Like Hillel, Shammai viewed the study of the Torah as of primary importance: "Make your study of the Torah a matter of established regularity, say little and do much, and receive all men with a friendly countenance" (*Avot* 1:15).

Hillel was from Babylon and was active during Herod's reign, from about 10 B.C.E. to 10 C.E. He came to Jerusalem, where he became a member of the Sanhedrin because of his wide learning. Hillel inaugurated a dynasty of Pharisaic religious leaders, many of whom bore the title *nasi*, or prince. His descendants for 400 years occupied the position as spiritual leaders and experts on Jewish law.

Many of Hillel's teachings are preserved in the form of proverbs. One of the best known is the story of a gentile who, after being rebuffed by Shammai, came to him and agreed that he would convert to Judaism if Hillel could teach him the entire Torah while standing on one foot. Hillel answered, "What is hateful to you, do not unto your neighbor; this is the entire Torah, all the rest is commentary. Now go and study!"

Hillel was a man of humility, simplicity, and compassion. He became a model for behavior and action for future rabbis. While David established a dynasty of kings that was to last for 400 years, Hillel established a dynasty of religious leaders that was to last until the death of his descendant Hillel II in 365 C.E. These leaders were in the forefront of developing the Mishnah and Talmud, the basis of Jewish law from the time of Hillel onward.

21

THE DIASPORA DURING THE ROMAN EMPIRE

By the end of the 1st century C.E., Jews were settled in almost every corner of the Roman Empire and comprised perhaps 10 percent of the total population. More than half the Jewish population lived outside Judea, particularly in Egypt, Syria, Greece, and Rome itself. The Roman government gave religious freedom to the Jews and treated them with tolerance. During this period another million Jews lived in Babylon and elsewhere in the Parthian Empire. This large Diaspora gave the Jews strength, cohesiveness, and independence, and was able to ensure the survival of the Jewish people after the destruction of the Temple at Jerusalem and their national homeland.

The geographer Strabo wrote in the 1st century B.C.E. that in the entire civilized world, hardly a place could be found where the influence of Jews was not felt (Josephus, *Antiquities* 14:115). A Roman seer, known as the sibyl, said: "Every land is full of you, every sea." By the 1st century C.E. perhaps 10 percent of the Roman Empire, or about 7 million people, were Jews, with about 2.5 million in Palestine. These population figures are very unreliable, but they are probably fairly accurate in regard to percentages. Such an explosion in population could not have been caused entirely by natural birthrate, but conversion must have played an important part. In Babylon, which had become part of the Parthian Empire, there were perhaps another million.

Jews could be found everywhere within the Roman Empire, in Palestine, Syria, Egypt, North Africa, Greece, Italy, even Spain and Gaul, as well as throughout the Parthian Empire, including Babylon, and the cities of Nehardea and Nisibis, Persia, Media, Elam, Seleucia on the Tigris River, and other surrounding countries.

The Diaspora of the Jews was caused by several factors. It was not a unique dispersal, since other peoples settled by choice or by force far from their native lands. However, the Jews were one of the few groups that managed to maintain their distinct identity, and with that identity to survive. This happened largely because of the unique religious system of the Jews, which kept them separated from their neighbors and preserved their identity.

Jews lived in Egypt from the beginning of their history. The Bible tells us that Joseph and his brothers settled in Egypt and that Moses led the Jewish people from Egypt to Israel. It must be remembered that many times during the first two millennia B.C.E., Palestine was part of Egypt, or under its influence. We know that after the fall of Jerusalem Jews settled in Egypt, including the prophet Jeremiah. A military colony settled in Elephantine near Aswan in the 5th century B.C.E., from which many original documents have survived, including wedding contracts. After Alexander the Great conquered the Near East and Egypt, he founded Alexandria. His successors, the Ptolemies, encouraged Jews to settle in the new city, and soon they comprised perhaps as much as 25 percent of the population of the Ptolemaic capital. Jews spread from Alexandria to Cyrenaica in North Africa, as well as all over Egypt, as far south as Syene in Upper Egypt, including most cities and districts such as the Fayyum, Edfu (Apollinopolis Magna), and Oxyrhyncus, and the old Egyptian capital of Thebes. Perhaps as many as a million Jews lived in Egypt.

The Jewish population of Syria was also considerable. The 1st-century C.E. Jewish historian Josephus (*Jewish War* 7:43) noted that Syria had the largest Jewish population of any nation outside Judea, which presumably included Egypt. A large Jewish population existed in Antioch, Damascus, and Apamea. In Asia Minor there were many prosperous Jewish communities, including Ephesus, Pergamum, Miletus, and Sardis. Indeed, in recent years the remains of a large synagogue have been excavated in Sardis.

During the Hellenistic period, when Judea was under a united rule with much of Greece, migration to that area was fairly easy. Large communities developed on the Greek islands, including Rhodes, Cyprus, Crete, Delos, and Melos. On the mainland as well by the 1st century C.E. we find large numbers in Athens and Corinth, in the Peloponnesus in the south, and in the northern part of the country in Thessaly and Thessalonica, as well as northward into the Balkans.

Jews were found in Rome as early as the 2nd century B.C.E. They probably first came as slaves under the Roman conquests of the Near East at the beginning of the 2nd century. The first real mention occurs in 139 B.C.E., when we find an expulsion of Jews from Rome because they were converting non-Jews to Judaism. More Jews came in, probably some as slaves, after the conquest of Jerusalem by Pompey (63 B.C.E.), and by 59 B.C.E. the Roman orator and statesman Cicero was complaining of their excessive influence in the Roman assemblies. The number of Jews grew rapidly, particularly since Julius Caesar and the Emperor Augustus both treated them well. Although later emperors Tiberius and Claudius tried to stop the growth of the Jewish population, their number increased, and they were an important part of the population of the city. From Rome, Jews spread south to Pompeii and Sicily, as well as into northern Italy.

Also coming from Italy, Jewish settlers moved to other provinces of Rome in the west, including Gaul, Spain, and Germany.

Since the Roman Empire had so many Jews living in its borders, it developed a uniform policy toward them and showed particular toleration of Judaism. Manifold reasons prompted this, including general religious tolerance by the Romans, the Roman tendency to follow local administrative practices, the loyalty of one Jewish community to another, and the loyalty to the Temple in Jerusalem.

The Romans had been able to expand from a small city in Italy to a power that controlled all of the Mediterranean through an astute policy of conquer and absorb. Absorbing conquered peoples did not mean replacing their native culture with Roman culture, but rather absorbing them by granting citizenship rights and tolerating their customs and religion. The Romans tended to follow the administrative practices of areas they conquered. Consequently, when they conquered the Hellenistic Near East, Judea was a defined entity and Jews were allowed self-government. Jews were unified in their communities, and showed allegiance to other Jewish communities. An attack on a community in one part of the empire would have reverberations in other parts. The large number of Jews in the empire and their important role in commerce, especially in the eastern part of the empire, made the Romans wary of doing anything that would offend them. Jews were very loyal to their religion and looked at the Temple of Jerusalem as their center. Any attack on the religion would be met with protests and hostility, not only in Jerusalem but also throughout the empire. Indeed, some historians argue that the Jewish revolt of 66–70 C.E., and later the Bar Kokhba revolt of 135 C.E., came close to toppling the eastern Roman Empire.

The existence of a large Diaspora, spread from Spain in the west to India in the east and southern Egypt in the south, created a strong Jewish religion and ethnic group. The geographical distribution of the Jewish population necessitated the development of the synagogue, or some other vehicle, as a means of practicing Judaism. The result of the Diaspora was that the Jewish community was no longer dependent on a national homeland for its survival. Indeed, after the destruction of the Temple in 70 C.E. and the sack of Jerusalem, Jews existed without a national homeland for 1,900 years, until the foundation of modern Israel. The existence and the strength of the Diaspora preserved the Jewish people and religion. An essential part of Judaism came to be that no intermediary was needed between the individual and God. God is everywhere, and hence one did not need to be in Jerusalem to pray to him. God's laws could be carried in the Ark of the Covenant, then in scrolls and books. Without the development of the Diaspora, Judaism might have ended with the destruction of the Temple in 70 C.E.

22

JESUS

Jesus lived in the first quarter of the 1st century C.E. in Judea and Galilee and was believed by his followers to be the messiah, who would restore the rule of David. He was crucified in 30 C.E. by Pontius Pilate and the Romans. Jews believed him to be a false prophet, while his followers saw him as God and the fountainhead of a new religion, Christianity.

Jesus, the founder of Christianity and its godhead, was a Jew who lived in the first quarter of the 1st century C.E. in Judea and Galilee and was crucified by the Romans probably in 30 C.E. He was believed by his followers to be in the line of prophets, like Elijah, Hosea, and Isaiah. Indeed, the Ebionites and the Nazarenes, early Jewish-Christian sects, considered him to be a prophet. In the 1st century B.C.E. and in the 1st century C.E., many other religious figures existed in Judea and Galilee. One of them, Theudas, made various messianic claims. Like Jesus, he died without proving his claims, but he did not have the impact on his followers that Jesus had. The Jews might have recognized Jesus as a miracle worker, magician, healer, or prophet. But when his followers proclaimed him the messiah, the son of God, and started a new sect of Judaism, which became a separate religion, Jews completely rejected Jesus and considered him a false messiah and false prophet.

In the 3rd century C.E. the church father Origen said that the exact details of the life of Jesus were irrelevant. What was relevant was his message. Jesus, son of Joseph and Mary, was considered to be the son of God and God incarnate by the members of the religion that grew after his death on the cross. If Jesus were to return to earth today, he would not recognize the religion of Christianity and its doctrines. Two separate questions exist: First, what was the historical Jesus really like? Second, what was done to that historical Jesus to transform him into the God of the Christians?

The only near-contemporary sources we have on the life and death of Jesus are the Gospels of Matthew, Mark, Luke, and John. These works were written in the last quarter of the 1st century. They may have been based on earlier written sources. However, by the time they reached their present form, they had been heavily influenced by the developing Christian theology.

Certain basic historical details about Jesus can be believed from the Gospels. Jesus was the son of Mary and Joseph of Nazareth; he lived and preached in Galilee and Jerusalem; he cured people of illness, especially possession by demons; he had a large following; he disputed over details of the Law of Moses, and he was crucified by the Romans at the hands of Pontius Pilate, the governor of Judea. He had a brother, James, who became head of the Christian church in Jerusalem and who was murdered in 62 C.E. by a Sadducean priest because of his belief in Jesus. A cousin, Simon, succeeded James. Jesus had other brothers, including Judah, whose grandchildren were leaders of the Christian churches in Galilee in the first quarter of the 2nd century C.E.

Virtually nothing is known about Jesus' life, except for the last few years. His first appearance, agreed on by the Gospels, was his baptism by John the Baptist, about a year before his crucifixion. He then went to the area near the Sea of Galilee, where he preached, then to Capernaum, where he performed miraculous healings. He appointed twelve apostles to be the judges of the twelve tribes of Israel at the Last Judgment. Herod Antipas wished to kill Jesus, whom he feared would become the heir of John the Baptist. Jesus came to Jerusalem at the time of the Passover, where he predicted the destruction of the Temple. He took the Passover meal, which was to become the Eucharist. He was betrayed by Judas Iscariot, arrested, and turned over to the Romans for execution.

In the 1st century B.C.E. and the 1st century C.E., with the fall of the Hasmoneans and later the death of Herod and the loss of independence for Judea, the Jewish idea of the messiah became very prominent. The idea of the messiah can be traced to the fall of the First Temple. The kingdom of Judea had been ruled by the line of David from its inception until its destruction at the hands of Babylon. The Davidic dynasty based its legitimacy on the fact that its kings were "anointed" by God through a prophet or priest. The word for "anointed" in Hebrew is *mashiah*, in Greek, *christos*. By the 1st century B.C.E. the concept of the messiah had become universalized with apocalyptic views, particularly based on the Books of Enoch and Isaiah. We can see that Jesus' followers in the Gospels tried to strengthen his ties with King David. The Gospel of Matthew opens with a genealogy connecting Jesus' father, Joseph, to the line of David. His birth is moved from Nazareth in two of the Gospels, to Bethlehem, the home of David. Generally, the messiah was believed to be an earthly ruler of the line of David who would restore the political rule of Israel and extend it over all nations. Jesus did not seek to assume worldly rule, but he did follow the beliefs of John the Baptist, who was teaching about the messiah at this time, concerning repentance and rebirth.

Jesus' followers proclaimed him the messiah, and he probably thought of himself as such. However, once Jesus died, his followers were left in a quandary. The messiah was supposed to restore the rule of the line of David. If Jesus were dead, he obviously could not be the messiah. The answer was to change Jesus from an earthly messiah to one who would be reborn and come again to restore the kingdom of David; to transform the concept of the messiah from that of a mortal being to that of an immortal one; to transform Jesus from a man to a miraculous being who would return, from a man to a god, the son of God.

Jesus' theology and philosophy were apparently rooted in Pharisaic Judaism, with some influence from the Essenes, an ascetic Jewish sect, and John the Baptist, especially regarding baptism and eschatology. The Pharisees believed in bodily resurrection. Jesus apparently was influenced by the teachings of Hillel, and it is possible that he might have studied with him. The Golden Rule—"What is hateful to you, do not unto your neighbor"—is prominent in the school of Hillel and in Jesus' teachings. Like Hillel, Jesus believed that the spirit of the law was more important than the letter of the law. He opposed the Sadducees and the Temple as an intermediary between man and God. However, the portrait of Jesus in the Gospels suggests that Jesus himself was selectively observant of the Torah and Jewish law.

This much of Jesus' theology can be reconstructed from the Gospels. However, this view may be entirely false. For the Gospels are not the myth or story of Jesus as written by Jesus and the Jews who followed him, but the writings of Christians, the successors of Paul. As a result, virtually nothing that is ascribed to Jesus can with certainty be attributed to him. In historical writing in the ancient world, let alone mythic historical religious writing, it was considered proper to put fictitious speeches in the mouths of the characters of history. In the 5th century B.C.E., the great Greek historians Herodotus and Thucydides admitted that they made up the speeches of their characters according to what they thought those characters would have said appropriate to the occasion. Historiography in the middle to late 1st century C.E. exhibited the same tendency. Another element was at work: Christian doctrine was fast developing and trying to separate itself from Jewish Christianity and Judaism. Hence, this goal would influence the portrayal of Jesus. Consequently, although the Gospels might preserve some of the flavor of Jesus and his words, their accuracy is questionable.

If we assume that Jesus' theology was as it is portrayed in the Gospels, we can understand why the Pharisees joined with the Sadducees in opposing him. While the Pharisees wanted to broaden the interpretation of the law, they still placed the role of the law as central to Judaism. Thus they joined with the Sadducees in opposing Jesus. Jesus was seized by the Temple authorities, who handed him over to Pontius Pilate and the Roman authorities, who executed him on the grounds of sedition, that is, his claims to be the messiah.

Although Jesus himself lost his faith on the cross and cried out in Aramaic, *Eli, Eli, lama sabakhtani*—"My God, my God, why have you forsaken me?"—

his followers reported that on the third day his tomb was found empty. They claimed he had risen from the dead. The Gospel of Mark reports that an angel revealed that Jesus had risen, while the other Gospels relate that after his death Jesus appeared to his followers. By this resurrection he was proclaimed a spiritual messiah, the son of God and God incarnate.

Jesus was born a Jew and died a Jew with Pharisaic philosophy and messianic beliefs in resurrection and eschatology. It was left to his followers, particularly Paul, to invent the Christian religion.

23

PETER, PAUL, AND EARLY CHRISTIANITY

The early Christian church was dominated by two figures, the apostles Peter and Paul. Peter believed that to be a Christian, one had to follow Jewish Law, including circumcision and dietary practices. Paul, who began as a Pharisaic Jew and persecutor of Christians, had a vision of Christ and became a convert to Christianity. He believed that the future of Christianity lay with gentile Christians, who need not observe Jewish Law. Paul's beliefs and theology formed the basis of normative Christianity, while the Jewish Christians, rejected by both Jews and Christians, withered away.

Paul was the founder of normative Christianity. He was born a Jew in Tarsus and had the distinction of being a Roman citizen. His Hebrew name was Saul, and he later used the Roman cognomen Paul. At an early age he went to Jerusalem and there studied under the eminent rabbi Gamaliel. Like Gamaliel, he was an ardent Pharisee. He came to hate and persecute the new sect of Christians and was involved in the stoning of Stephen at Jerusalem. But in 35 C.E. on the road to Damascus, where he was going to persecute Christians, Paul claimed to have seen Jesus in a vision. On the spot he converted from a persecutor and hater of Christians to a Christian. Paul began to preach that Jesus was the messiah. When he arrived in Damascus, some of his fellow Jews turned on him and plotted to kill him. But he escaped, lowered from the city walls in a basket. Returning to Jerusalem, he met with the apostles Peter and James for two weeks, then left Jerusalem and spent the next thirteen years (35–48 C.E.) in missionary works.

The rise of Christianity is one of the most important events in the history of Judaism. Christianity began as a sect of Judaism, and shortly amalgamated Greco-Roman religious elements into it. By the 4th century C.E. it was to become the official religion of the Roman Empire, and the dominant religion of Western culture to this day. Christianity became the vehicle for Jewish history and religion to be universalized. Christians adopted the Jewish Bible, which they called the Old Testament, as their own. They considered this book a pre-history to the New Testament, the story of Jesus Christ. With the universal spread of Christianity, the Old Testament moved from a religious-historical text of a small group of people to the religious text for most of humanity. The Bible (both New and Old Testaments) has become the best-selling book in all of human history. The Jewish concept of monotheism, which was unique to the Jews, was taken up by the Christians, and hence monotheism came to be almost universally accepted. Another important aspect of Christianity is that after the 4th century c.e., the majority of Jews lived in Christian lands, though after the 7th century a large number lived under Islam. Consequently, the history of Judaism is interwoven with the history of Christianity, as well as of Islam. Even today, despite the existence of an independent Jewish state, the majority of Jews in the world live in countries that are essentially Christian.

The first Christians did not consider themselves anything but Jews. They worshiped in the Temple at Jerusalem and scrupulously obeyed the Laws of Moses. They maintained that Jesus had come, not to end the Law, but to fulfill it; heaven and earth would pass away before a letter, or even part of a letter, of the Law would cease. They followed the Pharisaic interpretation of scriptures, with the added belief that Jesus had come as a spiritual messiah and would reappear. Ritual bathing was a religious rite among Jews at this period and before. Among the Christians this practice was adopted as the initiation rite of baptism in the name of Jesus. The leadership of the early church at Jerusalem fell to James, Jesus' brother, and a group of elders. The twelve apostles played a role in the early Church, particularly Peter and John, son of Zebedee. James, Peter, and John became the pillars of the church, and what they decided was binding.

The early Christian church had a missionary vision. Proselytizing was first done among Jews in Palestine and in the Diaspora. Soon Jews from the Diaspora who were more assimilated into Greek culture began to be attracted to Christianity. This group, particularly under Stephen, had little regard for Temple worship and the rigors of Jewish rituals. This led to their persecution by the Sanhedrin in Jerusalem, and a split in the early church between the Jewish elements and the hellenizing elements of the early church. The hellenized elements began to proselytize outside Palestine, in Phoenicia, Cyprus, and Antioch, usually among Jews. But in Antioch a few missionaries began to preach to the gentiles, with enormous success.

It was not the beliefs and practices of Jewish-Christians under James and Peter, nor those of the hellenized Jewish-Christians, that became normative Christianity, but rather the sect that depended on the teachings of Paul, the gentile Christians, that won out. With this victory the Jewish-Christian sects, such as the Nazarenes, Ebionites, and Elchasaites, shunned by both Jews and Christians, ultimately disappeared.

The growing strength of the hellenized Jewish-Christians and the increasing number of converts from the gentiles created a new problem. Paul believed that the message of Jesus was for all, Jew and gentile alike, and the requirement to observe Jewish law, particularly that of circumcision and dietary practices, was a great detriment to gentile converts. Basing his arguments on passages in the Hebrew Bible, he argued that circumcision of the body was not required, but "circumcision of the heart," that the spirit of the law was preached by Jesus, not the letter of the law, and that the logical conclusion was "freedom from the law." Paul had advocated this interpretation in his missions, particularly to the gentiles. Finally, probably in about 47/48 C.E., he returned to Jerusalem and negotiated the matter with James, Peter, and John. Henceforth the gentile mission was free from Jewish Law: baptized pagans did not require circumcision and were free from dietary restrictions. The church at Jerusalem declared that it would confine its mission to Jews only. The gentile church would look to Jerusalem as its spiritual head and continue to send financial support.

The new compromise soon ran into problems, particularly over dietary laws when gentile Christians and Jewish Christians celebrated the Lord's Supper together. Peter attempted to keep the compromise, when he came to Antioch, the center of the gentile Christians, and dined without regard to the dietary laws. But James was more conservative, and Peter retreated from this position. This led to a confrontation in Antioch. Paul verbally attacked Peter in front of the assembled church in Antioch. Peter would not retreat from his position. Henceforth, Jewish Christians and gentile Christians could not share the Lord's Supper, and the bitterness and anger of Paul led him to a separate path. Peter and James drew up an "apostolic decree" stating that gentile Christians were not required to practice circumcision, but that they must not engage in illicit sexual intercourse and must use only *kosher* meat at meals.

Paul, a charismatic figure, continued his missionary work, particularly in Asia Minor and Greece. He returned to Jerusalem, and there was seized by Jewish authorities for bringing a non-Jew into the Temple. The Romans took custody and imprisoned him. Rather than be tried by the Sanhedrin, Paul fell back on his status as a Roman citizen and demanded to be sent to Rome for trial. He was sent there and spent two years under house arrest, but was free to attend the church in Rome and to preach. He disappears from history at this point. One tradition says he was killed in the persecutions of the Christians by Nero.

Paul had a missionary belief and vision that Christianity could not spread as a universal religion unless it was made acceptable to the gentiles and freed from Jewish law. He was proved right by history. The Jewish Christians withered away, and the gentile Christians became normative Christianity, which spread over the Roman Empire until it became its official religion in the 4th century C.E. Paul strove to free Christianity from Judaism, but he did not reject his race and religion. Rather, he made Judaism the basis for gentile Christianity—Judaism the Old Covenant with God, Christianity the New Covenant. Paul asserted that God had hardened the Jews to deny Christ only temporarily, and in the end, Israel would throw aside its blindness and turn to Christ. This doctrine meant that the Christian church needed to tolerate Jews within their countries, so they would be available to return to Christ when he reappeared.

Christianity gradually absorbed many pagan religious and mythic ideas into its system. Christ was elevated from a messiah to the son of God, and became the dying god reborn, so common in Greco-Roman and Near Eastern myth. Mary became transformed into a virgin mother goddess, who, impregnated by God, gave birth to Jesus. To fit Jesus as a god into a monotheistic system, the idea of the Trinity was developed, whereby Jesus, God, and the Holy Ghost were viewed as one.

While at the time of Christ, 10 percent of the Roman Empire was Jewish, it took several centuries before Christians expanded to anywhere near this number, not before the 3rd century C.E. However, Christianity, with its doctrine of resurrection and reward in the next life and with its only requirement of baptism and faith, made a particularly appealing religion, especially in times of turmoil and distress. Indeed, Christianity spread most rapidly in the Roman Empire in the 3rd century C.E., amid terrible civil disruption and war.

The spread of Christianity throughout the Roman Empire meant the triumph of Jewish monotheism, although in an altered form. The Christian belief that Jews were their foundation gave a permanent place to the Jewish Bible and Jewish concepts of monotheism. However, the indomitable belief of Jews in their own religion over thousands of years, their adamant refusal to convert to Christianity, as well as their claim that God's Covenant is with them, and by implication not the Christians, as well as the accusations of deicide, have instilled a distrust and hatred for Jews throughout Christian history, forming the basis of antisemitism.

24

THE DEAD SEA SCROLLS

The Dead Sea Scrolls are a collection of manuscripts discovered in caves near the Dead Sea. These documents date from the 2nd century B.C.E. to the 1st century C.E. and contain books of the Hebrew Bible, including the Apocrypha and Pseudepigrapha. There are also many documents of the Essene sect of Judaism, which tell of their origins, beliefs, and social organizations. These documents are the earliest biblical manuscripts in existence and are of monumental importance in the study of early Christianity and Judaism, as well as the history of biblical texts.

In March 1947 Muhammad adh-Dhib, a fifteen-year-old boy of the Ta'amirah tribe, chased a goat he was herding into a cave near the Dead Sea, about a mile from a ruin called Khirbet Qumran. Inside the cave he found a cache of manuscripts in pottery jars. Muhammad and his friends took the manuscripts to a Muslim sheikh in Bethlehem. The sheikh did not recognize the writing, and thinking that the documents were in Syriac, sent the manuscripts to a merchant who was a member of the Syrian Orthodox community in Bethlehem. The manuscripts then found their way to the Syrian Orthodox Monastery of St. Mark in the Old City of Jerusalem. The archbishop negotiated a purchase of most of the scrolls, but one of the Bedouins took his scroll elsewhere, and it was purchased by the noted archaeologist E. L. Sukenik for Hebrew University. The scrolls that had been acquired by the Syrian Orthodox church were offered for sale, but because of the political situation not to the government of Israel. The archbishop came to the United States in 1953 to sell the scrolls, but had little success. Finally, he placed an advertisement in the *Wall Street Journal*. Fortunately, Yigael Yadin, the son of Professor E. L. Sukenik, who was also an archaeologist, as well as a distinguished general, saw the ad. Yadin realized that the archbishop would not sell to an Israeli, and negotiated through intermediaries. He raised $250,000 from the Gottesman Foundation in New York and purchased the scrolls for the Hebrew University.

Meanwhile, after the 1948 War of Independence, on the Jordanian side, Roland de Vaux, a French priest and archaeologist, organized a systematic excavation of forty other caves in the area of Khirbet Qumran. Thousands of fragments were discovered, which ended up in the Rockefeller Museum on the Jordanian side of Jerusalem. When Israel conquered all of Jerusalem and the West Bank in 1967, the museum, and with it the rest of the Dead Sea documents, fell into Israeli hands.

The Dead Sea Scrolls were hailed as the most important discovery of the century because of their contents. They contain the oldest extant manuscripts of the Hebrew Bible. A few books, such as the Book of Isaiah, are complete, and there are fragments from all the books of the Bible, except the Book of Esther. Among the scrolls were works of the Apocrypha and Pseudepigrapha, noncanonical books of the Bible, including unknown texts that had disappeared 2,000 years ago, such as an unknown psalm. These works are in Hebrew, Aramaic, and Greek. Also found were documents of the Essene sect, which had a center at Qumran.

The importance of the Scrolls is in four areas: (1) The manuscripts tell us much about the history of the text of the Hebrew Bible, including the Apocrypha and Pseudepigrapha. (2) The scrolls tell us much about the Essene sect, which until now was known only from a few passages in the Jewish historian Josephus. He wrote that they were one of the four major sects of Jews. (3) Christianity developed in the 1st century C.E., just at the time when the Qumran community was flourishing. The Essene influence, particularly with its messianic ideas and notions of eschatology, can be seen in early Christianity. The scrolls reveal much about the religious climate that resulted in the development of Christianity. (4) Information about the Essenes and the textual history of the Bible tell us much about the development of rabbinic Judaism, which coalesced during this period.

Before the discovery of the Dead Sea Scrolls, no text existed of the Hebrew Bible older than the Masoretic text of the 9th century C.E. The canon of the Hebrew Bible was fixed in the late 1st century C.E. At that time new attention was paid to the texts themselves, with great detail given to minute points of grammar and language. Once canonization of books of the Bible occurred, noncanonical books ceased to be copied and transmitted, and many of these disappeared. There was a greater tendency to standardize the text of the Bible, and by the 6th century C.E. one main tradition resulted, that of the Masoretic text. Once this text reached its final form in the 9th century C.E., other manuscript traditions became religiously unacceptable and died out. Consequently, all Hebrew texts are virtually identical. Other sources for biblical text existed, among them the Septuagint in Greek, the Samaritan Pentateuch in Hebrew, and the Latin translations of the Bible. When we compare these with the Masoretic text, we find literally thousands of small differences, and some major ones. For example, in the Septuagint Esther, the name of the Persian king is different. Whole sections have been added or deleted. The Dead Sea Scrolls contain Hebrew texts that are in many places closer to the Septuagint readings than to the Masoretic text. However, the general agreement of the Masoretic text with those of the Dead Sea texts shows that the current version of the Hebrew Bible is essentially accurate and correct, and virtually the same as that used by Jews in the 1st century C.E. Aramaic translations of such books as Job and Leviticus also were found, which give us more information on the nature of translation during this period.

Many apocryphal and pseudepigraphal works are represented among the scrolls, including fragments from the Book of Tobit, Ecclesiasticus, Book of Jubilees, and Book of Enoch. Other apocryphal works that show the presence of Christian influence include the Testament of Levi in Aramaic and the Testament of Naphtali in Hebrew, from the apocryphal collection entitled the Testaments of the Twelve Patriarchs. Unknown pseudepigrapha discovered at Qumran include the Sayings of Moses, the Vision of Amram, the Psalms of Joshua, the Prayer of Nabonidus, and some sections of a Daniel cycle.

The Dead Sea Scrolls contain much Essene material, which tells of their sect, its origins and history, the rules that governed them, and its eschatology. These works include the Manual of Discipline, the Damascus Document, the Thanksgiving Psalms, and the War Scroll. There are manuscripts about angels, known as the Angelic Liturgy, which show a well-developed belief in such beings, including the angel Melchizedek, who leads the struggle against Belial. These documents reveal that the Essene sect was an apocalyptic movement that expected the end of days imminently. History and its epochs had been preordained by God. When the end of days came, evil would cease, the wicked would perish, and Israel would be freed. Until then man was partially under the influence of Belial. God would create an elect to be saved. God split men into two camps, the Sons of Light against the Sons of Darkness, each of which was led by a superhuman figure. The founder of the sect was called the Teacher of Righteousness, the spiritual as well as the social leader.

Many similarities exist between early Christian doctrine and that of the Essenes, particularly in their apocalyptic vision and eschatology and their views of the elect. Some scholars have argued that John the Baptist was an Essene, or at least associated with and was influenced by them, and by inference, then, so might Jesus have been. More recently, scholars argue from the Dead Sea material that many of these Essene views had entered the mainstream of 1st-century C.E. Judaism. The similarity of early Christianity to some of the Essene doctrine might thus reflect Jewish rather than Essene influences. That is, Christianity may come somewhat more out of the mainstream of Judaism than we had previously believed.

The Dead Sea Scrolls have already told us much about the history of biblical text, early Christianity, Judaism of the 1st century C.E., and the Essenes. Many of the texts, even after forty-five years, still have not been edited and translated because of academic disputes over who has the right to publish the material. This controversy has resulted in several lawsuits, and finally in a photo facsimile publication of all the texts. Now that this logjam has been broken, the next several decades should see the publication, editing, and translation of all the material, together with new and important insights into the foundations of Christianity and Judaism.

25

THE JEWISH WAR (66–70 C.E.)

After a period of sixty years as a Roman province, Judea revolted from Rome in 66 C.E. The uprising was caused by many factors, including the rise of concepts of freedom, mismanagement by Rome, and strife between Jewish and non-Jewish inhabitants. The result was a long and bitter war, which lasted until 70 C.E. The war was a disaster for the Jewish people. An enormous number of Jews were killed, and a national state for Jews disappeared for 2,000 years.

The spark that set off the Jewish revolt was the seizure of money from the Temple treasury by the procurator Florus in 66 C.E. A riot broke out and Florus allowed his troops to loot the Upper Market. Two cohorts of soldiers from Caesarea arrived and the bloodshed continued. The Jews seized control of the Temple hill, cutting the connections between the Temple Mount and the Antonia fortress, which held the Roman garrison. Florus fled the city. Agrippa II, the son of Herod Agrippa, was in Jerusalem at the time, and he tried to restore peace. However, the extremists prevailed and it was agreed to stop the sacrifices in honor of the emperor. The moderates, helped by 3,000 cavalry of Agrippa II, tried to regain control and seized the upper city, while the extremists controlled the Temple Mount and the lower city. Agrippa's troops were vanquished, but were allowed to leave the city. The Roman cohort surrendered, but as they walked out, the extremists massacred them.

The underlying causes of the Jewish War stretched back to the beginning of the 1st century C.E. When Judea became a Roman province in 6 C.E., the population at first welcomed the change of rule from Herod and his heirs. The Romans chose Caesarea over Jerusalem as the administrative center of the province. As was the case in all Rome's provinces, the Romans taxed Judea, with a levy on land, as well as a type of poll tax. Troops were based in the province of two types: legions, which were composed of Roman citizens, and auxiliaries, made up of people usually from the provinces. In the case of the auxiliaries in Judea, these were recruited from the non-Jewish population of Samaria and Caesarea. The Romans stationed a regiment of infantry in Jerusalem to keep order, particularly during the pilgrimage festivals, and this proved a source of irritation between the Romans and the Jewish population.

Although the early governors had relatively peaceful administrations, by the time of Pontius Pilate (governed 26–36 C.E.) relations began to deteriorate. Many factors contributed to this, particularly the development of a revolutionary ideology that said Jews should not be subject to any king, since they were servants of God alone. Judaism had grown increasingly monotheistic and free of idol worship, and the Roman governors often sowed unrest by inadvertently treading on Jewish sensibilities. Pontius Pilate, like many Roman provincial administrators, was harsh and stubborn. He brought the banners of the army, bearing the picture of the emperor, into Jerusalem, contrary to the practice of previous governors. This provocation outraged the population, many of whom gathered at Caesarea to protest peacefully. Pilate relented this time. Next, he took money from the Temple treasury to improve the water supply. This action, too, offended the Jews. Then he brought shields dedicated to the emperor into Jerusalem, which created such a reaction and resistance, that the emperor himself intervened to reverse Pilate. Pilate put cultic emblems on his coins, contrary to the practice of previous governors, and this offended the religious sensibilities of the population.

Real trouble, however, began in the reign of the emperor Caligula (37–41 C.E.). The non-Jewish minority of the town of Yavneh set up an altar to the emperor to provoke their Jewish townsmen. The tactic worked. When the Jews of Yavneh destroyed the altar, Caligula as punishment ordered a golden statue of himself to be erected in the Temple at Jerusalem, and the Roman governor of Syria to enforce this with two legions. The population was outraged, and mass demonstrations followed. Herod Agrippa, the grandson of Herod, who had been raised at Rome and was a friend of Caligula, went to the emperor and persuaded him to reverse this policy.

The assassination of Caligula in 41 C.E. prevented an escalation of the tension and led to the reestablishment of a Jewish king. Agrippa, who happened also to be friendly to Claudius, the new emperor, was in Rome at the time of Caligula's death. He proved a skillful intermediator between Claudius and the Roman Senate, and thereby helped solidify Claudius's position. As a reward, Claudius appointed Agrippa king of Palestine, including Judea and Samaria. Judea temporarily ceased to be a province and became a subject kingdom. Agrippa proved an able ruler, sensitive to religious issues, and like his grandfather, Herod, was a patron to the Jews of the Diaspora. He came to be regarded as a lawful successor to the Hasmoneans. Unfortunately, his rule was very short, and he died in 44 C.E., after which Judea reverted to a Roman province.

The next twenty-two years saw a succession of Roman procurators, some of whom were sensitive to the religious sensibilities of the Jewish population, while others were not. Clashes continued between the Jewish and non-Jewish elements of the population, and by the administration of Felix (governed 52–60 C.E.) a group of extremist freedom fighters had emerged, encouraged by the ideology so prevalent in the country, that a messiah of the line of David would emerge and throw off foreign rule. By the end of Felix's term, these rebels had spread discontent throughout rural Judea, and even attacked Jews who did not cooperate with them. They oppressed the countryside, in some ways more than the Romans did with their taxation and rule. By the eve of the Jewish revolt in 66 C.E., the extremists operated almost unhindered in the villages and country-side, while the upper classes in Jerusalem had recruited their own armed fol-lowers.

The main driving force of the revolt was the group known as the Zealots. This group, who were Pharisees in their outlook, had as the basis of their phi-losophy the idea of freedom and a boundless love of liberty. Only God was their master, and they would suffer death before bowing to any mortal. Once the abstract idea of freedom was raised to the level of a religious tenet, it gave a philosophical and religious justification to resistance to Rome. The center of this movement was in Galilee, and it had been active since the time of Herod. Its leader at the outbreak of the revolt was a man named Menahem, who tried to become king and proclaimed himself the messiah. But this Menahem was murdered by the leader of the Jewish rebels in Jerusalem.

Finally, in 66 C.E. Judea broke out in full revolt from Rome. There were several causes of the uprising. One was the growing movement of the Zealots, who were ideologically opposed to Roman rule. The population as a whole resented Roman control of the Temple and the Temple cult, as well as the vari-ous taxes that had been imposed. However, a major source of anger was the tension between the Jewish and Greco-Syrian elements in the province. The Roman auxiliaries were composed almost entirely of local Greco-Syrian re-cruits. The Jewish population was resentful at having this group be militarily dominant over them. Roman provincial administration in Judea was flounder-ing. The situation in Judea was not helped by the appointment of Florus as procurator (governed 64–66 C.E.), who was corrupt and plundered the prov-ince. The procurators could barely keep order in the province; the Zealots domi-nated the countryside and banditry was everywhere. Jerusalem was practically in anarchy. Much of the impetus for the revolt came from the lower classes, who resented the wealthy Jews, as well as the Romans. One of the first acts of the revolutionaries was the destruction of the municipal archives at Jerusalem, which kept a record of debts.

When the revolt broke out, Gallus, the Roman governor of Syria, marched into Judea with the 12th Legion. After some initial success at the outskirts of the city, he ordered a retreat, because he lacked the forces to take the city. The extremists pursued them and routed them at Beth-horon. With the defeat of a Roman legion, the peace party's voice was silenced.

The Roman emperor Nero saw a great danger in the revolt. Rome and Parthia had engaged in a desultory war for control of Armenia. A possibility existed that Parthia might try to extend its influence into Palestine. Nero reacted swiftly. He sent Vespasian, one of his most experienced generals, into Galilee with an army of 60,000. At the same time, he entered into negotiations for peace with Parthia, which shortly came about. The Jews were no match for the Romans in the field, and all they could do was to hold out in their fortresses. In 67 C.E. Vespasian captured the fortress of Jotapata in Galilee, which was under the command of Josephus. Josephus was of the priest class, and a moderate. When his men decided on suicide rather than surrender, Josephus contrived to be the last to die, and when it came his turn, surrendered to the Romans. He became a confidant of Vespasian and wrote an extensive history of the Jewish War, which survives today.

The Romans fairly swiftly conquered the rest of the country, including Jewish Trans-Jordan. Vespasian was on the point of attacking Jerusalem when Nero died in June 68 C.E. Vespasian turned toward politics, and by July 69 C.E. was proclaimed emperor. He left it to his son Titus to finish the campaign against Jerusalem.

Finally, in 70 C.E. Jerusalem fell and the revolt was finished, although some fortresses held out, particularly Masada, which fell in 73 or 74 C.E. (see nutshell #27). Hundreds of thousands of Jews lost their lives, and Judea had received a crippling blow from which it would never recover. Henceforth, Rome exercised greater control over Judea. Jewish nationalism was to make one last attempt with the Bar Kokhba revolt in the 2nd century (see nutshell #29). But the Jewish War and the Bar Kokhba revolt started the Jews on a downward spiral of rapidly decreasing population, from 7 to 8 million before the revolt to under 2 million by the 3rd century C.E. While some of this spiral may have been caused by a falling birthrate, much was due to conversion to Christianity, assimilation, and abandonment of Judaism. These two wars rank with the Holocaust as the greatest catastrophes in the history of the Jewish people.

26

THE DESTRUCTION OF THE TEMPLE

The Romans captured Jerusalem in 70 C.E. and burned the Second Temple to the ground. It had stood for 600 years. Now, for the first time in a thousand years, except for an interval in the 6th century B.C.E., the Jews had no Temple. The loss of a central shrine changed the nature of the religion and ushered in rabbinic Judaism.

Flavius Josephus watched the flames burn the Temple to the ground. He wrote an account of this catastrophe, which survives to this day. Josephus was appointed commander of the Jewish forces in Galilee in 66 C.E. at the outbreak of the Jewish War. When the Romans attacked Josephus and his men at Jotapata, the city was swiftly taken. Josephus and forty of his men fled and barricaded themselves in a cave. During the Jewish War, when defeat and capture were inevitable, Jews often chose death. Suicide was forbidden by Jewish law, but "assisted suicide" was permissible. The leaders would stab to death the men under them, and then only the last man left would have to commit the sin of suicide. Josephus and one other man aided their troops in taking their lives, but when the time came to kill himself, Josephus could not bring himself to do it. So he surrendered and joined the Romans. He became an adviser to Titus, the Roman general, whose father, Vespasian, would become Roman emperor in 69 C.E. Josephus participated on the Roman side in the Jewish War and was present at the siege of Jerusalem, even being wounded by the defenders. He wrote an account of the Jewish War with the thesis that no power or people, even a people as committed as the Jews, could withstand the might of Rome. He relates in books 5 and 6 of his *Jewish War* in great detail the siege and capture of Jerusalem.

The Roman general Titus had four legions under his command for the siege. While the Romans were attacking the city, the Jewish defenders inside were busy fighting each other as well as the Romans. There were 23,400 defenders divided into various factions: Simon bar Giora, the leader of the lower classes, controlled the largest force, including 5,000 Idumeans (from Edom, which had been converted to Judaism in the 2nd century B.C.E.); John of Giscala, who had led the revolt in Galilee, with 6,000; and Eleazer ben Simon, with 2,400 Zealots.

The defenders divided into main two factions, Simon and the Idumeans versus John of Giscala and the Zealots. John of Giscala and his faction occupied the Temple, while Simon held the lower city. As the Romans tightened the siege, the two factions fought one another, and at one time Eleazer ben Simon and John of Giscala were fighting. Josephus portrays the situation in Jerusalem as one of anarchy with complete disregard for human life.

After months of siege, food began to run out and the defenders were reduced to eating grass and straw. Josephus describes the scene:

> The roofs were thronged with women and babes, completely exhausted, the alleys with corpses of the aged; children and youths, with swollen figures, roamed like phantoms through the marketplaces and collapsed wherever their doom overtook them. As for burying their relatives, the sick had not the strength. For many fell dead while carrying others, and many went forth to their tombs ere fate was upon them. And amidst these calamities there was neither lamentation nor wailing: families stifled the emotions, and with dry eyes and grinning mouths these slowly dying victims looked on those who had gone to their rest before them. The city was wrapped in profound silence and night laden with death. (*Jewish War* 5:513–515)

The famine grew so bad that one woman killed her baby and ate it (*Jewish War* 5:201–219).

Finally on the 9th day of the Jewish month of *Av*, the anniversary of the destruction of the First Temple by the Babylonians in 586 B.C.E., the Jews were forced by a Roman assault to barricade themselves in the inner precincts of the Temple. A soldier threw a burning brand into the chambers of the sanctuary, and flames broke out; soon the sanctuary was engulfed. The Romans slaughtered the Jewish population throughout the city: "No pity was shown for age, no reverence for rank; children and graybeards, laity and priests alike were massacred" (*Jewish War* 6:271). Six thousand people were trapped within the Temple court, and all perished in the fire. Not one building within the Temple precincts was left standing. The fire next spread to the lower city. Thousands more perished. The Temple fell for the second and final time in history.

Titus seized cultic objects from the Temple, including the table of shewbread and seven-branched *menorah*, and brought them to Rome for his triumphal procession. Simon bar Giora was dragged in chains to Rome, where he was executed. To commemorate this victory, Titus commissioned the construction of the famous Arch of Titus, showing his triumphal procession, including these cultic objects. It can still be seen in the Forum in Rome, and even today Jews will not walk under the arch, which would be a sign of submission.

The Temple was of profound importance to Jews. Israel from its very inception had been a theocratic state. The kings of Israel drew their authority from God; they were God's anointed ones. The Temple was the center of the religious life of the state. The political center of the state was at Jerusalem, and the center of Jerusalem was the Temple. The Temple was more than a national religious shrine. It also was a main economic center of the state. Taxes were levied and collected by the Temple officials, and its resources were enormous, since all Jews throughout Palestine and the Diaspora were required to pay a half shekel tax to the Temple. When the Roman general Crassus came through Jerusalem in the 1st century B.C.E., he plundered the treasury of the Temple of over 2,000 talents of silver, an enormous sum.

When Judea fell under the influence of Greek rulers and culture in the 3rd and 2nd centuries B.C.E., the Temple became the civil center of the state. Since the Law of Moses was the governing code of the country, and the priests at Jerusalem interpreted that Law, they controlled the legal system. Assemblies of the people took place there. At the head of the Temple was the high priest, who was not only an important religious but also a political figure.

The Temple was the center of the priesthood, which exercised control over the religious life of the land. Daily animal sacrifices were conducted. Incense was burned, and the lamp was lit in the sanctuary. A large staff of priests officiated and were chosen by lot to offer the daily burnt offerings. Three times a year Jews from all over the country came on pilgrimage to Jerusalem, on Shavuot, Sukkot, and Passover. The pilgrims brought their own sacrifices, which were made in addition to the regular daily sacrifices. On the festivals the Temple gates stood open and the curtain that hung in front of the Holy of Holies was parted, allowing the pilgrims to see within. The services were filled with music, vocal selections accompanied by trumpets, as well as lutes, lyres, and cymbals, with flutes added on festivals.

With the destruction of the Temple, the nature of Judaism changed. For over a thousand years the worship of God was centered in the Temple. When other religions lost their central shrine, the religion usually was irreparably damaged. This was not the case with the Jews. Two factors enabled Judaism to survive. One was the development of monotheism, with an invisible God who was omnipotent and omnipresent. This meant that although the Temple was the center of the worship of God, He could be worshiped everywhere without a shrine. The second factor was the development of the Diaspora. Once Jews began to settle throughout the Roman Empire and throughout Babylon, they needed to adapt their religion to life without a temple where they lived. This they did through the synagogue. While the Temple stood, Jews throughout the Diaspora looked to Jerusalem and the Temple, and remitted their annual taxes. But once the Temple was destroyed, they carried on their religion much as before, except now they mourned for the Temple and paid their annual tax to the Roman government.

The year 70 C.E. marks the end of the Temple at Jerusalem, and the end of a Jewish state. Henceforth Jerusalem became transformed into a spiritual center. But always in the minds and hearts of the Jewish people was the yearning for the restoration of a Jewish state. This desire persisted for close to two thousand years, amidst life in the Diaspora. Finally, the tenacity of the Jewish people resulted in the reestablishment of the state of Israel in 1948. However, the religion was too long adapted to a structure that functioned without a Temple and without animal sacrifice, and consequently the Temple has not been rebuilt. Some religious Jews argue that the Temple can be restored only by the messiah, while a few are encouraging its rebuilding. But for most Jews today the issue is irrelevant.

27

THE FALL OF MASADA

After the fall of Jerusalem in 70 C.E., the Zealots held out against the Romans at the fortress of Masada for three more years. It took the efforts of the Roman governor Flavius Silva and an entire legion to conquer the fortress, protected by only 960 men, women, and children. The defenders, however, preferred mass suicide to capture and enslavement by the Romans. In modern Israel, Masada has become the symbol of resistance to the enemies of Israel.

"Masada shall not fall again" is the oath sworn by recruits of the Israeli Armored Corps on the top of the fortress of Masada. Masada has caught the popular imagination of Israel and has become a symbol of the country's willingness to fight to the death to preserve its freedom. Yigael Yadin, who had been one of the leaders of Israel's war of independence in 1948 and the chief of staff of the Israel Defense Force, was one of Israel's foremost archaeologists. In 1963 he became interested in excavating the fortress of Masada, partially because he saw the defiance of the defenders of Masada as a symbol for modern Israel. Because Masada did not have many layers of settlement, Yadin reasoned that he could use a massive effort of digging, without the usual inch-by-inch removal of dirt required at many sites. Consequently, he assembled a volunteer crew of thousands of people. In response to advertisements placed in such papers as *The Times of London* and *The New York Times*, people came pouring in from all over the world. Through his influence with the army, he managed to recruit off-duty soldiers; schoolchildren, scouts, homemakers, as well as archaeology students flocked to Masada. Yadin managed in two short seasons of eleven months to excavate the site that ordinarily would have taken decades. What he found was startling.

The Jewish general of the Jewish War, Josephus, gives us an account of the siege of Masada. King Herod had fortified Masada between 37 and 31 B.C.E., but after the Romans made Judea a province, they placed a garrison there. When the Jewish War broke out, the Sicarii (who are closely related to the Zealots) under Menahem captured the fortress by a trick. Upon the death of Menahem in Jerusalem, his nephew, Eleazar ben Yair, took command of the fortress.

Although the fall of Jerusalem marked the virtual end of the Jewish War in 70 C.E., Masada continued to hold out against the Romans and served as a place of refuge for another three years.

In 72 C.E. the Roman governor Flavius Silva, with the 10th Legion, marched against Masada. He brought with him thousands of Jewish prisoners of war as slaves to build the siege works. First he sealed off the fortress by encircling it with a siege wall, with towers placed at intervals along the wall. On the western slope he constructed a siege ramp of dirt and stones, and on top of it he erected a tower. In 73 C.E. the final assault began. Silva attacked the fortress with battering rams, catapults, and fire. When the Romans at last broke in, they found the buildings and stores of food burning, and the bodies of 960 men, women, and children, who had committed mass suicide. Seven people survived: two old women, one of whom was a relative of Eleazar ben Yair, and five children. According to Josephus, they recounted what had happened. Seeing that the end of the siege was near, the defenders knew that the Romans would kill all the men and sell the women and children into slavery. Josephus records the final speech of Eleazar ben Yair, which calls for freedom over slavery, death before slavery. Since suicide was not permitted under Jewish law, the onus of suicide was taken on by the leaders. Ten men, including Eleazar ben Yair, were chosen to kill the others, then draw lots among themselves to see who would kill the remaining nine. The lone survivor would then commit suicide. These men were chosen by lot, with their names written on broken pieces of pottery, called ostraka. One of the most stunning discoveries of Yadin was eleven small ostraka, containing names, including ben Yair's.

Masada represented to the Zealots their ultimate resistance to the Roman Empire and the willingness to die and see their children die, rather than to be enslaved. But the example of Masada was but one response to Rome, a response that was devastating to the Jewish people. Perhaps as much as 10 percent of the Jewish population of the Roman Empire perished in the Jewish War. Without this disastrous war, Judaism instead of Christianity might have emerged as the main religion of the Roman Empire. Jewish-Christians, who were centered in Jerusalem, never recovered their influence lost in this war, and they ceased to be a major factor in the development of Christianity.

Had all of the Jewish population chosen the route of Masada, no Jews would have survived. In contrast, Yohanan ben Zakkai and his followers chose another path, to retreat into the religion, which provided the major vehicle for Jewish survival. The Holocaust in the 20th century brought an end to the Jewish tradition of withdrawal and laid the foundation of the state of Israel. With these two events Masada has reemerged as a symbol of a willingness to fight to the death to preserve Jewish freedom and the national homeland of the Jews.

28

YOHANAN BEN ZAKKAI AND THE SANHEDRIN AT YAVNEH

Yohanan ben Zakkai deserted Jerusalem while it was under siege by the Romans and was detained at Yavneh. There he began a religious center to substitute for the Temple at Jerusalem. He and his successors, particularly Rabban Gamaliel ben Simon, laid the foundation for rabbinic Judaism and what was to become the mainstream of Jewish belief and practice from the fall of the Temple to the present.

During the siege of Jerusalem Yohanan ben Zakkai chose to desert the city. The Zealots would not permit defection and guarded the exits to the city. Yohanan ben Zakkai, however, found a way. He faked his own death, then had his followers wrap him in a shroud and take his body out of the city for burial. The Romans, however, captured him and took him to Yavneh, where he was imprisoned. However, he managed to persuade the Roman authorities to allow him to teach there.

While the Zealots believed it was preferable to die rather than submit to the will of Rome, Yohanan ben Zakkai and his followers chose to submit to the Roman authorities and draw inward, toward the religion and away from politics. Yohanan ben Zakkai's position enabled Judaism to adapt and survive without the Temple and a national homeland. Since Jews of the Diaspora had for centuries practiced their religion far removed from the Temple, Judaism itself was easily capable of surviving without the Temple, but the psychological blow of the loss of the Temple was crushing. Judaism had adapted before to existence without the Temple, but political and religious persecution by the Romans in some Diaspora cities, like Antioch, slowed the Jewish recovery.

Judaism's adaptation to a religious system without the Temple was led by Yohanan ben Zakkai, a leading Pharisee, and second in authority to Simon ben Gamaliel, the head of the Sanhedrin. While Simon ben Gamaliel became one of the leaders of the revolt, Yohanan ben Zakkai was at least a moderate, and opposed the extreme positions of the Zealots.

Very shortly thereafter Jerusalem fell and the Temple was destroyed. Yohanan ben Zakkai almost immediately began to replace the religious authority of the Temple with that of his school at Yavneh. The Sanhedrin was reestablished, and the religious calendar was proclaimed from Yavneh, with regard to New Moons and leap years. Yohanan ben Zakkai was not able to gain complete religious control for Yavneh. Many of the sages did not join him there, and resentment undoubtedly existed because of his flight from Jerusalem. Although Yohanan ben Zakkai did much to create substitutes for Temple practice and had high prestige, as soon as political conditions eased, he was forced out of Yavneh by Rabban Gamaliel ben Simon, of the house of Hillel. Gamaliel ben Simon was the son of Simon ben Gamaliel, one of the leaders of the Jewish revolt and head of the Sanhedrin. But it was probably not until the death of Vespasian's second son, Domitian, in 96 C.E. that political conditions would allow the son of a leader of the revolt to resume a conspicuous position of leadership in the Jewish community.

While Yohanan ben Zakkai never had the status of leader of the Jewish people in the eyes of the Romans, his successor, Rabban Gamaliel, did. Gamaliel went to Rome with the Sanhedrin several times and was invested in his position by the Roman governor of Antioch. With the emergence of Rabban Gamaliel, the Jewish Diaspora came to recognize the authority of the Sanhedrin at Yavneh. With Rabban Gamaliel's assumption of control, many other rabbis who had avoided Yavneh because of Yohanan ben Zakkai now came there, and its authority increased even further.

The sages at Yavneh were responsible for laying the foundation of rabbinic Judaism, which was to become the mainstream in Jewish life from 70 C.E. to the present. The achievements of Yavneh were in four main areas: (1) the adaptation of a Temple-based religion to one that functioned without a Temple; (2) the development and consolidation of Jewish law, called *halakhah*; (3) the consolidation of various Jewish sects into one normative group; and (4) the canonization and systematization of religious texts.

The sages at Yavneh created substitute prayers for Temple sacrifices and transformed the pilgrimage festivals into ones that could easily be celebrated in the Diaspora without a Temple. This trend had already been developing among the synagogues in the Jewish Diaspora, but it was regularized and systematized at Yavneh. In particular, the feast of Passover, which required the sacrifice of the paschal lamb, was adapted. Henceforth, the Passover meal, or *seder*, was emphasized. The requirements of unleavened bread and bitter herbs were reinforced, even though there was no sacrificial lamb.

Jewish law, or *halakhah*, which had already been developing during the Second Temple period, was given a theoretical and philosophical basis. Practical applications were emphasized, and the Pharisaic school of Hillel, with its more flexible interpretations, won out over the school of Shammai, with its rigid adherence to rules of purity. This was, of course, to be expected, since Yavneh was controlled by Hillel's descendants.

A rapid process of consolidation of Jewish sects took place. The Sadducees, who were dependent on the Temple and Temple rites, withered away, as did the Essenes. Judeo-Christian sects, which had remained within the orb of Judaism, began to be pushed out. Added to the daily prayer, the *Amidah,* was a 19th benediction, *Birkat Haminim,* or "benediction against heretics." Rejected by the Jews and declared heretics by the Christians, these Judeo-Christian sects soon disappeared completely.

At Yavneh texts were also systematized. The canon of the Hebrew Bible was closed. Certain texts, like the Book of Esther, barely made it into the canon, while others, like the Books of the Maccabees, did not. A new Greek translation of the Bible was undertaken by Aquila of Pontus, who had first converted to Christianity and then to Judaism. The earlier Greek translation, the Septuagint, had been used as a sacred text by the Christians, and hence Jews preferred Aquila's version. His translation was more in keeping with the new halakhic approach, particularly with regard to the exact meaning of words and text.

Because Jews were dispersed throughout the Roman Empire, Jews and Judaism survived the destruction of the Temple. However, the direction that normative Judaism was to take was determined by Yohanan ben Zakkai, Rabban Gamaliel ben Simon, and the sages at Yavneh.

29

BAR KOKHBA

Despite the devastating defeat in the Jewish War (66–70 C.E.), within sixty years the Jewish population had recovered, and again they rebelled against the Romans in 115–117 C.E. This new revolt was centered in Cyrenaica, Egypt, and Cyprus, although there was some involvement in Judea. In 132–135 C.E. a widespread revolt occurred, which spread to the Diaspora. Under the leadership of Bar Kokhba, who was hailed as the Messiah, the Jews defeated several Roman legions and held a dozen others at bay, until they were defeated in 135 C.E.

The Romans led Rabbi Akiba out for execution. His crime was that he was a rebel from Rome. They lacerated his body with combs of iron, then flayed his skin. Nonetheless, Rabbi Akiba, with a peaceful smile on his face, continued to say his prayers. Rufus, the Roman general in charge of the execution, cried out, "Are you a wizard or are you utterly insensible to pain?" Akiba replied, "I am neither. But all my life I have been waiting for the moment when I might truly fulfill this commandment. I have always loved the Lord with all my might, and with all my heart; now I know that I love him with all my soul." Whispering the entire first verse of the *Shema*, he pronounced its last words—"God is One,"—with his dying breath.

Rabbi Akiba was the religious head of the revolt of 132–135 C.E. He hailed Simon bar Kosiba, who came to be referred to as Bar Kokhba (Son of the Star), as the king and the messiah, who would restore the kingdom of Israel. Bar Kokhba was an able military leader and defeated two Roman legions, the 10th and the 6th, that were stationed in Judea. He swiftly gained control of Jerusalem and much of Judea. He issued coins, proclaiming "Year One of the Redemption of Israel" and "For the Freedom of Jerusalem."

Because of the current political situation and the fine generalship of Bar Kokhba, the Jewish revolt had the potential to topple the Roman Empire in the east. Throughout its history the kingdom of the Parthians, who had carved out an empire in the east, fought against Rome. Had Rome not reacted so swiftly and with so much force against the Jewish revolt, the Parthians might have entered the conflict. If they had joined Judea in its revolt, the whole of the eastern empire of Rome might have fallen.

The seeds of the revolt go back to the capture of Jerusalem and the destruction of the Temple in 70 C.E. After that catastrophe, economic recovery had been swift. Although many Jews had been killed in the Jewish War, the population soon began to increase, and by the end of the 1st century C.E., many towns had been rebuilt and Judea had regained much of its prosperity and numbers. Jews of the Diaspora continued to grow in strength and wealth, as did the Roman Empire in general. The half-shekel tax, previously paid to the Temple, was now changed to two drachmas paid to the Roman treasury, a source of resentment and a constant reminder of the destruction of the Temple.

Although Jews were spread throughout the Roman Empire, there was unrest among them. This unrest was brought to a head during the rule of the Roman emperor Trajan (reigned 98–117 C.E.). In an attempt to expand the empire, Trajan became involved in a war with the Parthians, who dominated in Babylon and Persia. At first successful, Trajan expanded the limits of the empire with his conquest of Armenia and northern Mesopotamia, including Adiabene, the rulers of which had converted to Judaism. However, while in the midst of this war, the Jews of Cyrenaica, Egypt, and Cyprus revolted in 115 C.E. This rebellion spread to Judea, particularly to Galilee, but was apparently not too widespread there. The revolt expanded further to Mesopotamia, incorporating not only the Jews but also other elements of the population. Trajan suppressed the revolt very severely. The Jewish populations of Cyprus, Cyrenaica, and Egypt were decimated, as was the Jewish community in Alexandria, Egypt, whose Great Synagogue was destroyed. To deal with the revolts in Mesopotamia and Judea, Trajan appointed his general Lucius Quietus, who so savagely put down the revolt in Mesopotamia and Judea, that on Trajan's death, the new emperor, Hadrian, recalled him to Rome and executed him, possibly for his conduct.

This second Jewish war set the stage for a third rebellion, the revolt of Bar Kokhba in 132–135 C.E. The latter was even more devastating to Judea than the war of 66–70 C.E. and was perhaps the worst single catastrophe for the Jewish people until the Holocaust. When Hadrian succeeded to the throne, he at first pursued a policy of reconciliation and restoration in the provinces. Destroyed cities were rebuilt, and Hadrian even considered allowing the Jews to rebuild the Temple in Jerusalem. However, he soon changed his mind, perhaps because of his tendencies to want to hellenize his empire. He came to hate foreign religions, and went so far as to forbid castration, which was interpreted to include circumcision. This was a strike at the very heart of Jewish identity and religion. It is uncertain whether this decree was made before or after the war. The spark that ignited the revolt was Hadrian's decision in 130 C.E. to build a pagan city, Aelia Capitolina, on the site of Jerusalem.

While Hadrian was active in the east, there was unrest, but no open revolt. But when he left the east for Rome in 132 C.E., the Jews did break into open rebellion. This uprising spread throughout the Diaspora, and even some Samaritans joined it. Hadrian reacted with great force. Publius Marcellus, the governor of Syria, was sent with his armies, reinforced by legions from Egypt and Arabia. Bar Kokhba again showed his able leadership, totally wiping out the 22nd Legion from Egypt and defeating the Syrian army.

Reinforcements were sent for, and Julius Severus, governor of Britain, arrived to take command with his legions. By 134/135 c.e. the Romans had twelve legions or their equivalents. At full strength these legions would number about 120,000 men. The Romans had earlier conquered Galilee and confined Bar Kokhba to Judea. In the face of growing numbers of Roman soldiers, Bar Kokhba was gradually forced back, until in 135 c.e. he was besieged at Betar. In August 135 c.e. Betar fell and Bar Kokhba was killed, according to tradition on the 9th of *Av*, the anniversary of the destruction of the First and Second Temples. Some holdouts in the revolt hid for several years in caves in the Judean desert, where recently actual letters from Bar Kokhba were found.

With the crushing of the revolt, the Romans dealt harshly with the Jewish population. Jews were prohibited from living in Jerusalem. The name of Judea was changed to Syria-Palestina, and religious persecution followed, including the forbidding of circumcision. Many religious figures, particularly those associated with the revolt, were hunted down and executed. The Romans destroyed 50 fortresses and 985 towns and villages. According to the Roman historian Dio Cassius, 580,000 Jews died fighting, and others by fire and sword. Nearly the entire land of Judea was laid waste. The world's slave markets were glutted with Hebrew slaves, whose price fell to less than a horse's feed.

In the aftermath of the revolt the emperor Hadrian began a religious persecution in Judea and outlawed the teaching of the Torah. One of the victims of this persecution was Hananiah ben Teradyon. When arrested Hananiah admitted that he taught the Torah because it was God's will. The Romans sentenced him to be burned at the stake, his wife to be executed, and his daughter to be sold into a brothel. The Romans wrapped him in the scroll of the Torah, which he had with him when he was arrested, and put him on a pyre of green brushwood. His chest was covered with water to slow the burning. According to legend, his pupils watched the flames and asked, "Master, what do you see?" He answered, "I see parchment burning, while the letters of the Torah soar upward." His disciples advised him to open his mouth to let the fire enter and put him out of his misery sooner. He answered, "It is best that He who has given life should also take it away; no one may hasten his own death."

The harsh laws of Hadrian lasted only as long as his reign, which ended in 138 c.e. Under his successor, Antoninus Pius, the Jews were again allowed to practice circumcision. But during the Bar Kokhba revolt hundreds of thousands of Jews had perished, many more than in the Jewish War of 66–70 c.e., and in the aftermath there was less rebuilding in Judea. The center of Jewish life shifted to Galilee.

Despite the devastation in Judea, the Diaspora, which had comprised 60 percent of the Jewish population, continued to thrive under the Roman Empire, as did the Jews of Babylon. However, in Judea the Jewish population never again reached the same level of prosperity as it had in the 1st century C.E. Its numbers never recovered, although by the end of the 2nd century C.E. the Jewish community of Palestine was again affluent and its numbers had grown. The Bar Kokhba revolt was the last resistance to the Roman authorities, and henceforth Jews accepted the rule of Rome.

30

RABBI JUDAH THE PRINCE AND THE REDACTION OF THE MISHNAH

The great tenacity and resilience of the Jewish people were reflected in their swift recovery from the devastating effects of the Bar Kokhba revolt. By the end of the 2nd century C.E. Rabbi Judah the Prince emerged as the leader of the Sanhedrin and the Jewish community. Having established cordial relations with Rome, he embarked on what was a major step in Jewish religion and law, the Mishnah, a codification of previously existing oral law. The Mishnah became one of the three legal codes of Jewish law.

Hailed by his contemporaries as the savior of Israel and even the "anointed" of Israel, Rabbi Judah the Prince was born "on the day Rabbi Akiva died," according to *aggadah*. Though a religious leader, he held court like a secular potentate. By fiat he excused scholars from taxes and in addition fed them at his own table. A great teacher, he said of his students, "Much I learned from my teachers, more from my associates, and most of all from my pupils." He despised ignorance and said, "It is the unlearned who bring trouble into the world."

Despite the devastation of Judea by the Bar Kokhba revolt, by the end of the 2nd century C.E. the Palestine community had reached a high level of prosperity and stability. The center of Jewish religious life ceased to be at Yavneh during the revolt, and moved to Galilee. By this time the head of the Sanhedrin took on the title *nasi*, or prince, and had emerged as the leader of the Jews not only in religious matters, but also in political and legal spheres. The Romans formally recognized the *nasi*, whom they called Patriarch, as the leader of the Jews. At this period Rabbi Judah the Prince ruled as head of the Sanhedrin. The church father Origen, who lived in Israel at this time, wrote that "the Patriarch [*nasi*] is so powerful among the Jews that it seems as if, subject to the Emperor's consent, there is no difference between him and the former kings of the nations, for cases are being tried without official permission, according to Jewish law" (*Epistula ad Africanum* 14).

Rabbi Judah the Prince, like so many heads of the Sanhedrin, was a descendant of Hillel. Although it was not official by Jewish law, the head of the Sanhedrin had become virtually hereditary in the line of Hillel. After the Bar Kokhba revolt Rabbi Judah's father, Rabbi Simon ben Gamaliel, was one of the few survivors of the persecutions. Only after the passage of time was he able to emerge from hiding, becoming head of the Sanhedrin at Usha in Galilee. Because of his absence and the presence of very distinguished scholars, such as Rabbi Meir, he had to struggle to reassert his authority, which he was gradually able to do. Rabbi Judah inherited his father's position, as well as great family wealth that had been accumulated.

Rabbi Judah ruled as Patriarch at the end of the 2nd and beginning of the 3rd century C.E. During this period the relations of Jews with Rome were very amicable, and according to talmudic legend, Rabbi Judah was very friendly with an emperor called Antonine. Since most of the emperors bore this as part of their name, it is uncertain which one was meant. The Roman emperor Septimus Severus seems to have been well disposed toward the Jews. We even find synagogues dedicated to members of the Severan dynasty. Septimus Severus was from the east and inclined toward a religious syncretism, which may have explained some of his goodwill toward the Jews. The Sanhedrin was given additional secular power, including civil and criminal jurisdiction, and the ability to levy taxes. During this period the economic prosperity of Judea and Galilee attracted immigration from the Diaspora, as compared with emigration for the previous seventy-five years.

Rabbi Judah's greatest contribution was in the area of religious law. He was a brilliant scholar and jurist, considered the foremost of his time. His great work was the redaction, or compilation, of oral Jewish law, called the Mishnah, which was to become the foundation of Jewish law to this day.

The code of Jewish law was embodied in the Pentateuch, dating from the first half of the first millennium B.C.E. The Pharisaic movement in Judaism, which began to develop in the 2nd century B.C.E., believed that Moses received two laws at Mount Sinai, written and oral, so that their decisions should have authority. The Oral Law came about through legal decisions and judgments of learned men, such as the Sanhedrin. The major figure in the Pharisaic movement was Rabbi Judah's ancestor, Hillel (see nutshell #20). From the 2nd century B.C.E. until the beginning of the 3rd century C.E., a vast body of oral law had grown. The process was accelerated after the destruction of the Temple in Jerusalem. Sages, such as Yohanan ben Zakkai, adapted to life without a central shrine those parts of Jewish life that were centered on the Temple, including the daily sacrifices, pilgrimages to the Temple, and regulations for priests. Another problem faced by the interpreters of oral law was a changing society. The written code of the Pentateuch fit the requirements of a society of a certain period with a defined political and social structure; it was not designed for a Diaspora community. Consequently, without oral interpretation, it became increasingly difficult to function in a changing world.

Rabbi Judah undertook to produce a compilation of the body of oral law. Others, such as Rabbi Akiba, had previously made collections, but none were very extensive. Rabbi Judah first collected teachings from previous generations, as well as his own generation. He summarized these according to a topical arrangement: Sabbath, divorce, marriage, the Sanhedrin. These sections were organized in a logical sequence, except in those cases where Rabbi Judah was preserving whole previous compendia. The form usually followed was a summary of various opinions, juxtaposed to fixed rulings of previous generations. Specific rules are generally attributed to the person who made the judgment, and if there is a controversy, both sides of the argument are given.

Three types of material are found in the Mishnah: *halakhah,* or legal rulings; *aggadah,* or homilies; and *midrash,* which usually took the form of stories used to interpret or supplement the Pentateuch. *Halakhah,* or the Law, is the heart of the Mishnah, while *midrash* and *aggadah* are used to illustrate or educate about the *halakhah.*

Those familiar with the Passover *seder* song *"Ehad Mi Yodea"* know that the answer to the question "Who knows six?" is "Six are the orders of the Mishnah." A Hebrew acronym serves as a mnemonic device for those six orders, or *sedarim: z'man nakat.* These orders are Seeds (*Zera'im*), Festivals (*Mo'ed*), Women (*Nashim*), Damages (*Nezikin*), Holy Things (*Kodashim*), and Purities (*Tohorot*). Previous legal decisions that were not included in the main body of the Mishnah but were important enough to preserve were called *Tosefta.* Those scholars whose opinions are preserved in the Mishnah are called *tanna'im.* Their successors for the next two or three centuries are labeled *amora'im.*

Rabbi Judah insisted that the language of the Mishnah be Hebrew. Hebrew at this period was dying out as a spoken language in favor of Aramaic and Greek. He even insisted that his servants speak Hebrew, and there is a story that great scholars visiting the house of Rabbi Judah at times learned obscure Hebrew words from talking with the servants.

The Mishnah marks a milestone in the history of Jewish law, as the first major comprehensive written collection of the body of oral law. Oral law did not stop with the Mishnah, but further commentaries developed in the centuries to come, which served the same purpose: the interpretation of written law and previous oral law in light of changing times and circumstances. The Mishnah thus came to be the basis of the next great compendium of oral law, the Talmud, which developed in Jerusalem and Babylon (see nutshell #33). Jewish law thus rests on three legs: the Torah, the Mishnah, and the Talmud.

31

CONSTANTINE AND CHRISTIANITY

The Roman emperor Constantine converted to Christianity on his death-bed in 337 C.E., and within a few decades Christianity was to become the official religion of the Roman Empire. Henceforth, much of the world's Jewish population would live under Christian rule, discriminated against and reviled as a stiff-necked people who were the killers of Christ, yet must be tolerated to bear witness to the truth of Christianity.

The rule of Constantine marked the victory of Christianity over the Roman empire. When Constantine was seeking to control the empire, he fought a great battle at the Milvian Bridge. The story goes that he had a vision of a cross in the sky with the words *in hoc signo vinces* ("in this sign will you conquer"). He had his troops put the sign of the cross on their shields and subsequently was victorious. One of his early acts was the Edict of Milan (313 C.E.), by which all subjects of the empire were allowed to practice their religion. This included the Jews. The Council of Nicaea in 325 C.E. was the first step in establishing Christianity as the official religion of the Roman Empire.

Constantine's mother, Helena, an ardent Christian, used the power of her son to further Christian causes. She traveled to Jerusalem in search of the Holy Sepulchre, which she claimed to have found. On that spot she erected the Church of the Holy Sepulchre, which still stands today. Constantine, however, was not a Christian, but at his death in (337 C.E.) he supposedly converted. This death-bed conversion must be suspect. While it is possible that Constantine did convert, he was surrounded by many Christian advisers, and his son Constantius II (reigned 337–361 C.E.) was a Christian. Consequently, after his death his supporters might simply have circulated this story as Christian propaganda.

The spread of Christianity in the Roman Empire was a slow process until the 3rd century C.E., which was a period of turmoil for Jews and Christians. During the first three centuries Jews, scattered throughout the empire, had learned to adapt to life under Roman rule, despite the devastation in Palestine of the Jewish War and the Bar Kokhba rebellion. The great period of peace, the *Pax Romana*, ended in 235 C.E. The Roman Empire was plunged into fifty years of upheaval, civil war, and destabilization. Various pretenders proclaimed themselves emperor in different regions, some of whose reigns lasted only a few years. Throughout their history, Jews' religious freedom and economic success parallel that of the lands in which they lived. Jews often tended to be more economically successful than the general populace, since they were not primarily agriculturalists. But when times were bad for the general population, so it was for the Jews. This was the case for Jews during the late 3rd century throughout most of the empire, particularly Palestine.

Throughout this period of upheaval, Christianity was spreading. While no accurate figures are available, at the beginning of the 3rd century, it has been estimated that there were perhaps 1.5 million to 2 million Christians in the empire, a far lower number than that of Jews. By the middle of the century their numbers were rising rapidly. When Decius became emperor in 249 c.e., he believed that a return to the worship of the traditional gods would help stabilize the region. Christians thus were enemies to the Roman order, and consequently Decius began to persecute them, particularly their bishops. Toward the end of the century Diocletian assumed control of the empire and did much to stabilize it. The reign of Constantine, which began in 311 c.e., reestablished a strong central rule and brought dominance to Christianity.

With the death of Constantine, the Roman Empire was essentially Christian. Judaism was not outlawed, nor Jews persecuted. But Jews had an ambiguous position. In its outward forms Christianity followed Jewish practice, although it was strongly influenced by pagan religions and practices, particularly with regard to christology, the nature of Christ. The church was equivalent to the synagogue. The priest replaced the rabbi, the Pope became the equivalent of the *nasi*. Passages from the New and Old Testaments were read in church, while in the synagogue the Pentateuch and the Prophets were studied. The church's use of hymns, the communal organization, were all taken from the synagogue. Since Christianity adhered to the monotheism of Judaism, by its very nature it was less tolerant than paganism, which recognized many gods. When Roman rulers persecuted Jews or Christians, it was not for theological reasons, but for political or social purposes; that is, these groups failed to recognize the divinity of the emperor, or showed disloyalty by failing to swear by the gods of the state. Thus, persecutions of Jews and Christians in the Roman Empire occurred rarely, and usually desultorily. Christianity, however, saw in paganism a theological threat. As a result, its practices were not tolerated, and eventually paganism itself was outlawed. At the same time, Christianity had many divergent sects, tolerated while it was not in political control. Once Christianity became the official religion of the empire, it centralized its administration, on the lines of the Roman imperial bureaucracy, and began to coalesce into one sect, Roman Catholicism. Consequently, over the next several hundred years, many divergent sects, such as Manichaeism and Arianism, were labeled heretical, and persecuted.

The position of Jews was different from that of either pagan or Christian heretics. Paul's doctrine that the Jews in the end would recognize Christ, and that they were spiritually blinded only temporarily, meant that the Christian society needed the Jews to remain as witnesses for the second coming of Christ. Christian countries, at least until the Enlightenment in the late 18th century, reviled all those who were not Christian and often did not allow non-Christians to live within their borders. In most cases, the exception was the Jews. Jews were often to be tolerated as necessary for Christian eschatological theory, but as a people who denied Christ, and who had killed Christ, they were to be an object of hatred and mistreatment. Indeed, antisemitic feelings grew so great in England, France, and later Spain, that they completely expelled their Jewish populations.

Thus the Christianization of the Roman Empire had a twofold effect. One was that it spread many Jewish theological and moral principles to the entire world through its daughter religion, Christianity. The Roman Empire extended through France, Spain, Italy, England, North Africa, Greece, the Near East, and most of the Mediterranean. When Christianity became its official religion, it thereby became the dominant religion of Europe and Western society. After the fall of the Roman Empire in the 5th century c.e., the European successors of Rome remained Christian. A second effect was that Judaism was relegated to a persecuted status throughout Western civilization from the 4th century to the present day. Henceforth, the history of the Jews who lived in the western and European part of the Roman Empire became a history under Christianity. In the Near East and North Africa in the 7th century, a new religion emerged, Islam (see nutshell #34), under which the other half of the Jewish world lived until the 20th century, when the rise of the state of Israel led to the expulsion of Jews from Arab lands. Today the bulk of the world's Jews live in either Christian countries or their own state, Israel.

32

THE JEWS OF BABYLON

The Jews of Babylon had a long, prosperous history from the 6th century B.C.E. to the 15th century C.E. and beyond. For most of this period it was the largest, best educated, and most influential of the Diaspora communities. In the 1st century C.E. it probably numbered over a million, compared with 7 million to 8 million in the Roman Empire. After the Bar Kokhba revolt (132–135 C.E.) the community grew in size and influence, and it was there that the Babylonian Talmud was produced. Except for certain periods during the rule of the Sasanids (224–640 C.E.), the Jews of Babylon had religious freedom and were the most flourishing and stable of all Jewish communities.

In 502 C.E. the exilarch, or head of the Babylonian Jewish community, Mar Zutra, along with his grandfather, was beheaded by the Persians. Their bodies were hung on crosses on the bridge at the town of Mahoza. This marked the end of an independent Jewish kingdom that Mar Zutra had established seven years before. In 495 C.E., in the aftermath of revolts in Babylon and elsewhere in the Persian kingdom, King Kabad I was overthrown and imprisoned. Mar Zutra saw these disruptions as an opportunity to establish a Jewish state, with its capital at Mahoza. He raised an army, levied taxes, and consolidated his rule. But King Kabad I was freed from prison and crushed those who had revolted, including Mar Zutra.

This incident is but one in a 2,000-year history of the Jews of Babylon, which represented the most stable and continually prosperous community in all Jewish history. The community fared well, with a few exceptions, from the 6th century B.C.E. until the 15th century C.E., living first under the Babylonians, then the Persians, followed by the Greeks and Seleucids, then the Parthians, and, beginning in the 7th century C.E., the Arabs.

The first wave of Jewish immigration was a deportation from Judea to Babylon by Nebuchadnezzar at the time of the destruction of the First Temple in 586 B.C.E. Although settled in Babylon against their will, they nonetheless prospered and integrated into Babylonian society. When Babylon was captured by the Persians in 538 B.C.E., Jews were allowed to return to Judea. Although many did, a large proportion remained in Babylon. We have virtually no record of the Babylonian Jewish community at this period, except that Ezra and Nehemiah came from Babylon with new returnees to govern Judea in the 5th century B.C.E.

Alexander the Great and his army conquered Babylon in 331 B.C.E. and imposed Greek culture on the area. On Alexander's death, his general Seleucus took over control of the empire in the Middle East and founded a dynasty that was to last 200 years.

In the late 2nd century B.C.E. the Parthians, a Persian tribe from north of the Caspian, gained power. Under the Arsacid dynasty (120 B.C.E.–224 C.E.) founded by the Parthian leader Arsaces, the Jews were well treated and flourished. Close ties existed with Jerusalem, which had always been revered as the center of Jewish life, particularly the Temple. Many Babylonian Jews went to Jerusalem on pilgrimages. The sage Hillel (see nutshell #20) may have come from Babylon. Jewish proselytizing in Babylon in the 1st century C.E. resulted in the royal family of Adiabene, near the Tigris in Babylon, converting to Judaism. While most Babylonian Jews were engaged in agriculture, many became traders. Since the Jews of Babylon were part of the Parthian Empire and those of Judea part of the Roman Empire, they were in a natural position to pursue trade with each other, particularly the trade in silk, which came to Babylon from the Far East, then was sent to Rome.

The Jews of Babylon apparently did not join in the Jewish War (see nutshell #25) or the Bar Kokhba revolt (see nutshell #29); however, the destruction of the Temple and of so many towns and villages of Palestine by the Romans encouraged many Jews to migrate to the area. This brought Pharisaic Judaism to Babylon. As a result of the Bar Kokhba revolt, academies along the lines of Yavneh were established for the first time. The influx of scholars from Palestine was a great stimulus to the Babylonian community, and many Babylonian rabbis in turn went to study in Palestine. One of the luminaries from Babylon was Abba Arkha, known as Rav or Rabbeinu. After studying in Palestine, he returned to Babylon in 219 C.E. and founded a new academy at Sura. A competing center of long standing was at Nehardea, whose head was Samuel. While Rav looked to the religious authorities of Palestine and their decisions on law as binding, Samuel considered himself independent. Rav introduced the newly edited Mishnah into Babylon. These two centers became great rivals as the centers of Jewish life for hundreds of years. The academies at Nehardea and its successor, Pumbedita, along with that of Sura, developed the Babylonian Talmud.

The Jews of Babylon had a great deal of autonomy because the Arsacids presided over a feudal administrative system. The head official of the Jewish community was the exilarch (*resh galuta*, or "head of the exile") who claimed descent from King David. The Talmud records that Rabbi Judah the Prince (see nutshell #30) said he would have to yield his place to the exilarch Rabbi Huna, if he came to Palestine, since Rabbi Huna was descended from King David on the male line, while he was on the female. The exilarchate existed as an institution of Babylonian Jewry until the Mongol Tamerlane ended it in 1401.

Another Persian group, the Sasanids, succeeded the Arsacids in 224 C.E. The new dynasty originated from a priestly family that was particularly devoted to the worship of the gods Ohrmazd, Anahita, and others in the Mazdean religion. Intolerant, they often tried to impose their practices on their subjects, including the Jews. Various rulers promulgated laws making it difficult for Jews to bury the dead because they enforced the principles of the Mazdean religion in which the dead were exposed to be eaten by birds. Persecutions of Christians, Manichaeans, Brahmans, and Jews occurred at the end of the 3rd century. At one point during the reign of Yezdegerd II (reigned 438–457 C.E.) Jews were forbidden to observe the Sabbath. There was some relief in the 6th century under the rule of Chosroes (reigned 531–578 C.E.) and Chosroes Parwez (reigned 590–628 C.E.). But it was not until the Arab conquest of Persia in 640 C.E. that an end was brought to Sasanid rule, and a measure of tolerance and stability was restored to the Jews under the new rulers.

33

THE JERUSALEM AND BABYLONIAN TALMUDS

The Talmud is a collection of oral discussions on the Mishnah and Jewish law, which took place in the academies in Palestine and Babylon from the 3rd to the 5th century C.E. Two Talmuds exist, the Jerusalem and the Babylonian, which represent the scholars of Palestine and Babylon, respectively. The Babylonian Talmud emerged as the dominant work and became the basis of the study for Jewish scholars and rabbis from the Middle Ages to the 18th century. For Orthodox Jews it remains the foundation of their intellectual efforts.

In June 1242 the Inquisition (see nutshell #45) condemned the Talmud to be burned at the stake. In Paris twenty-four wagonloads of books were brought to a public square and burned. Church officials, especially Pope Gregory, saw that Judaism rested on the Bible and the Talmud. If the Talmud and the Oral Law it contained were destroyed, the Jews would be left only with the Bible, and conversion to Christianity would be easier. Despite confiscations and burning by the Church in the 13th and 14th centuries, the Talmud survived and remained fundamental to Judaism.

The Mishnah comprises a codification of the Oral Law that had grown through the works of scholars, called *tanna'im*, from the 2nd century B.C.E. to the beginning of the 3rd century C.E. under the direction of Rabbi Judah the Prince (see nutshell #30). After the close of the Mishnah, the rabbis continued to study and write about the Law. Their results, from the time of Rav until the early 5th century in Israel and the mid-5th century in Babylon, were again codified, this time into two documents known as the Jerusalem and the Babylonian Talmud. The scholars of the period from the end of the Mishnah to the end of the Talmud are called *amora'im*.

The study of Jewish law did not decrease, but rather grew rapidly after the Mishnah was codified. The establishment of a collected text of the Mishnah gave a focus for continued study and exposition. The growth of Pharisaic Judaism, the increase in the number of scholars turned out by the academies in

Galilee in Palestine, and the rapid growth and expansion of centers of learning in Babylon dramatically affected the number of rabbis who were studying Jewish law. At one point in the first quarter of the 3rd century, Rav had 1,200 students at the academy at Sura. At that time the custom of *yarhei kallah* was introduced, by which for two months of the year, *Adar* and *Elul*, work virtually ceased and thousands of Jews gathered at the academies for study. Whether the numbers were as great as the Talmud would have us believe or the practice as widespread, nonetheless this custom indicates that the number of scholars of the Law was increasing. Approximately 2,000 rabbis are mentioned in the Talmud. Once so many scholars were working and the methods of legal exegesis continued, the amount of material grew exponentially.

These scholars used the Mishnah as their basis and discussed the topics raised in it. The Mishnah tends to focus on discussions of Jewish law, while the Talmud contains much anecdotal information about life and customs, both before and after the period of the Mishnah. We find in the Talmud the recording of the discussions concerning various topics. These may include folklore, philosophical questions, *aggadah*, proverbs, humor, as well as detailed legal discussion. These discussions began as oral traditions from the various academies over generations. As the volume of material grew, it became apparent that to preserve and utilize it, it must be compiled, in the same way that Rabbi Judah the Prince had compiled the Mishnah. Two Talmuds were systematized, the Jerusalem Talmud in Palestine in the late 4th century and the Babylonian Talmud about 50 to 100 years later in Babylon. The two Talmuds are similar in organization and design, but the Babylonian is much more extensive.

Little is known about by whom and when the Jerusalem Talmud was compiled. The 12th-century Jewish philosopher and theologian Maimonides attributes its compilation to Rabbi Johanan, in the late 3rd century. But many 4th-century scholars are quoted in the text. The Jerusalem Talmud seems to be an amalgamation of the Palestinian schools located at Tiberias, Caesarea, and Sepphoris.

The editing of the Babylonian Talmud began under Rabbi Ashi, who presided at the academy at Sura (371–427 c.e.), and his contemporary Ravina. Rabbi Ashi collected and edited the material to follow the order and form of the Mishnah. We do not possess the Babylonian Talmud on the entire Mishnah. Some of the missing sections are dealt with in the Jerusalem Talmud, but the Jerusalem Talmud itself also does not preserve a complete commentary on all the orders of the Mishnah, particularly *Kodashim* and *Tohorot*. We have no evidence that these commentaries existed, but it would be reasonable to assume that they once did.

The two Talmuds differ in language, method of analysis, and length. The Mishnah was written in Hebrew, at the insistence of Rabbi Judah the Prince, despite the fact that by the 3rd century c.e. Aramaic had become the major language of Jews in Palestine and Babylon. The two Talmuds, on the other hand, are written in Aramaic, a Semitic language closely related to Hebrew, which had been the lingua franca of the area for a thousand years and had been one of the official languages of the old Persian Empire in the 6th century B.C.E. However, the dialects of Aramaic differed. The Jerusalem Talmud is written in Western Aramaic, with many Greek loan words, while the Babylonian Talmud is composed in Eastern Aramaic, with Persian loan words.

The discussions in the Babylonian Talmud tend to be discursive, almost rambling, full of anecdote and argumentation by syllogism and induction, while the Jerusalem Talmud is more factual, and depends on logical deduction in its argumentation. In both the Babylonian and Jerusalem Talmud, however, we can see the seams caused by the fact that both are compilations from many different schools in Palestine and Babylon. The Babylonian Talmud has more *aggadah*, about a third of its content, while the Jerusalem version accounts for about a sixth. More influenced by its Persian setting, the Babylonian Talmud is filled with angelology and demonology. The Babylonian Talmud is much longer than the Jerusalem, and consists of about 2.5 million words.

The Babylonian Talmud soon became the more accepted version for historical reasons. The influence of the Jerusalem Talmud extended only to Palestine. The Jewish community of Palestine was on the decline, especially after the 4th century, while the Babylonian community continued to prosper and grow. During the Middle Ages, the Babylonian community became the intellectual center for all the Diaspora, and many communities sent their scholars to study in Babylon. Communities as far away as Spain sent to Babylon for legal rulings and questions about ritual. Consequently, since the scholars of the Diaspora were educated in Babylon, or at least under its intellectual influence, the Babylonian Talmud came to be the authoritative and definitive work.

During the Middle Ages the Talmud came under attack by Christian theologians. The Jewish Bible could not be burned, because the Christians had adopted it as their own. Thus the Talmud became the target. In the 13th to 15th century the books of the Talmud were often burned at the urging of the popes and the Inquisition.

The Talmud from the 12th to the 18th century became the focus of Jewish education, usually to the neglect of the Bible and Mishnah. The Mishnah (*Avot* 5:21) suggested, "At the age of five study the Bible, at ten the study of the Mishnah . . . at fifteen the Talmud." While this was not followed rigorously, the only subject thought fitting for Jewish scholars was the Talmud. The study of the Talmud gave a rigorous and disciplined education to Jews for centuries, particularly while secular learning was discouraged. It truly encouraged Jews throughout history to become a literate, educated, and intellectual people.

34

MOHAMMED

Influenced by Judaism, the prophet Mohammed developed the monotheistic religion of Islam in the 7th century c.e. Although he initially tried to use Judaism as his basis, he was later rejected by Jews and turned against them, wiping out or sending into exile Jewish tribes in Mecca and Medina. Islam spread rapidly and by the 8th century, most of the Jewish population of the world lived under this new proselytizing religion.

As a young man, Mohammed (c. 572–632 c.e.) often sat alone in the barren, rocky hills outside the city of Mecca and meditated. Around 610 c.e., he began to have visions (Sura 53:1–18), in which he was told by God to recite verses. His wife's cousin, who was a Christian, said that Mohammed was reciting material similar to that of Moses. Mohammed built around himself a small group to study his revelations and teachings, as recorded in the Koran. He preached monotheism and a final judgment. The Arabs were polytheistic, although monotheistic concepts had infiltrated the area through exposure to Zoroastrianism, Judaism, and Christianity. Initially Mohammed tried to absorb local gods into his system by making them angels, but later rejected this approach.

While Mohammed made little headway in Mecca, in nearby Medina a group agreed to accept him as prophet and follow him. Since he was encountering opposition from tribes in Mecca, he also made these new converts pledge to fight on his behalf. The Muslim calendar begins with Mohammed's flight to Medina on July 16, 622, called the *hegira*. Mohammed assumed a position as religious leader and arbitrator in all disputes. Many of the tribes that settled in Medina and Mecca were Jewish. At first Mohammed tried to win over the Jews as his followers. Like the Jewish practice, he faced Jerusalem to pray. He observed the fast of the Day of Atonement, he established weekly communal worship, and he looked to Abraham as the ancestor of his religion. Although some Jews came to follow him as a prophet, in general he was opposed by the Jewish tribes. Soon he gave up trying to win Jewish adherents and began the steps to create a new separate religion. He abandoned the practice of facing toward Jerusalem and had his followers turn instead toward the Kaaba shrine in Mecca, which contained a black stone, the site of previous pagan worship.

Abandoning the one yearly fast, he directed his followers to fast during the day for the whole month of Ramadan. Abraham was heralded as the true founder of Islam, but Mohammed asserted that Abraham's teachings were perverted by Jews and Christians. The Arabs were seen as the descendants of Abraham through his handmaiden Hagar and their son, Ishmael. Mohammed argued that as Jews had wrongly rejected prophets in their past, so they rejected Mohammed as a prophet. Mohammed took the *Shema*, "Hear, O Israel, YHVH is our God, YHVH alone," and substituted the cry "There is no divinity but God, and Mohammed is his prophet."

In 624 Mohammed defeated the tribes of Mecca at the battle of Badr. He then turned on the Qaynuqa, a Jewish tribe in Medina who specialized in trading and goldsmithing. He besieged them in their fortresses, and after fifteen days they surrendered. Mohammed allowed them to leave without their possessions, and they migrated to Syria. The following year, Mohammed attacked the Jewish tribe of Banu Nadir. He swiftly defeated them and allowed them to go into exile. In 627 the Jewish clan of the Qurayza, the last major Jewish tribe in the area, was the victim of Mohammed's wrath. They agreed to surrender on the same terms as the Nadir. Mohammed, however, demanded an unconditional surrender, which they accepted. He then proceeded to have all the men of the tribe executed and the women and children sold into slavery.

By 630 Mohammed had collected a force of about 10,000 men with which he attacked and conquered Mecca. The Kaaba was cleansed of idols and became the central shrine of Islam. Shortly thereafter, a force of 20,000 Bedouins attacked Mohammed at the battle of Hudaybah, but they were defeated. Tribes from all over Arabia flocked to his banner and converted to Islam, and Mohammed quickly gained control of the whole country. He died in 632 C.E. in Medina.

Islam took on the character of a religion and state, driven by a great proselytizing zeal. Under Mohammed's successors Islam spread out from Arabia to the world. By 644 C.E. most of the Middle East, including Persia, Babylonia, and Egypt, was conquered. By 750 North Africa, Spain, the Indus River valley, and Afghanistan were converted, and in 762 Baghdad became the capital of the Islamic world for the next 500 years.

By the 8th century most of the Jewish world was under domination by Islam. While in the 1st century C.E. 80 to 90 percent of the Jewish population lived under the Roman Empire, with the Arab conquests the figure was reversed, with 90 percent of Jews living in lands ruled by Islam. The remaining Jewish population lived under Christianity.

Although both Christianity and Islam sprang from Judaism, both exhibited animosity toward the Jews. Christians were hostile because the Jews had refused to accept Jesus as the messiah. They claimed that God's New Covenant was with them, and that God had rejected his original Covenant with the Jews.

In turn, Jews viewed the worship of Christ and Mary as idolatry. Moreover, Christians rejected the concept of Jewish law and looked only to the spirit of the law for salvation, while the Jews continued their adherence to the law. Muslims were also hostile to the Jews, although not as intensely as the Christians. The Jews rejected Mohammed as a prophet of God and the Koran as a sacred text. However, the Muslims, like the Jews, shunned idols and had a similar view of the nature of God. Jews fared better under the Muslims, although they, along with Christians, were considered second-class citizens. For the most part they found tolerance and economic prosperity under Islam, although there were periods of persecution, but not nearly as frequently as in Christian countries.

Throughout history Jews had been influenced by the cultures in which they lived. The flowering of Islamic culture resulted in the absorption of Greek thought and science. Once these disciplines found their way into Arab culture, they became increasingly influential on Jewish thought and culture. From the 10th century onward we can see these growing influences brought to bear on the works of many Jewish thinkers, such as Saadiah Gaon, Ibn Gabirol, Judah HaLevi, and Maimonides (see nutshells #35, #39, and #40).

35

THE KARAITES

*The Karaites are a Jewish denomination that began in the 8th century
c.e. They believe that the Torah is supreme but that each person is able
to interpret it. Although the Talmud and Oral Law are rejected and not
considered binding, both influence Karaite philosophy. Branded as heretics in various periods, in general Karaites are considered Jews, and
existed on the same legal footing as other Jews until secular authorities,
particularly in Russia in the late 18th and early 19th century, tended to
set them apart. They are recognized as Jews in Israel and are free to
migrate there under the Law of Return.*

On the eve of the outbreak of World War II in early 1939, while Jews were
fleeing from Nazi Germany, the German Ministry of the Interior declared that
the Karaites were not Jews and that their "racial psychology" was not Jewish.
When Nazi soldiers invaded Eastern Europe, they were ordered to spare the
Karaites. At one point during the war, however, certain Germans wanted to
expand the Holocaust to include the Karaites, and a new investigation of them
was launched. Three distinguished Jewish scholars, Zelig Kalmonovitch, Itzhak
Schiper, and Meir Balaban, were extensively interrogated on the origin of the
Karaites. Knowing that if they identified the Karaites as Jews they would be
signing a death warrant, these scholars lied to the Germans and insisted that
the Karaites had non-Jewish origins. Kalmonovitch and Schiper perished in
the concentration camps, and Balaban died in the Warsaw ghetto, but they
helped save the Karaites, most of whom survived the Holocaust.

In Jewish history there have always been competing denominations and sects.
In the First Temple period we find struggles between various groups, such as
those who would permit elements of foreign worship in the Temple versus strict
monotheists. In the Second Temple period the Sadducees dominated the Temple
worship, but a large number of Jews were Pharisees. Many smaller sects existed,
such as the Essenes. Historically within these denominations, divisions
occurred. With the destruction of the Second Temple in 70 c.e. rabbinic Judaism, which grew out of Pharisaic Judaism, with its emphasis on Oral Law as a
means of interpreting the Torah or written law, became mainstream Judaism.

Other sects still existed, including the Sadducees, but were small and inconsequential, until the emergence of Karaism in the 8th century C.E.

Karaism was founded by Anan ben David. Its chief principle was a denial of the Talmud and Oral Law. The Karaites saw themselves as the continuation of the Sadducees. According to their doctrine, the true law had been preserved by the Sadducees. Part of the Truth had been discovered by the First Temple priest Zadok, but the whole Truth was found by Anan ben David. Karaism thus can be seen as a reemergence of a kind of Sadducean sect.

Many factors contributed to Karaism, including the religious upheavals caused in Babylon by the emergence of Islam, the socioeconomic conditions of Babylonian Jews, and the demographics of the Babylonian Jewish population, whereby Jewish settlement was increasingly on the frontiers of the country, further from a central authority. At the time, various other Jewish sects had sprung up, such as the Isawites and Yudghanites. This may suggest that the climate was ripe for the emergence of a new sect. According to the rabbinic Jews, now called Rabbanites, Anan ben David began the movement out of pique, because his younger brother Hananiah was elected exilarch of the Babylonian community over him. Another story, probably apocryphal, recounts that Anan ben David was not elected exilarch because of his religious views, and thus set himself up as counter-exilarch. When the secular authorities learned of this, they imprisoned him. While in prison he met Abu Hanifa, who founded the Hanifite Muslim legal system. Abu Hanifa urged Anan to appeal to the caliph on the grounds that he represented a religious community separate from the Rabbanites. This he did and was freed.

The new Karaite movement quickly absorbed other sects, including the remnants of older sects, such as the Sadducees and Boethusians, as well as many minor sects. Anan ben David's main thesis was that the Talmud was not binding and that each person could rely on his own interpretation, as stated in the principle "Search thoroughly in the Torah and do not rely on my opinion." While this doctrine brought some freedom from the authority of the Talmud, it contributed to a religious free-for-all. On the death of Anan ben David many new Karaite sects quickly arose, such as the Ukbarite sect in the 9th century.

Later in the 9th century consolidation of these divergent Karaite sects came about under the leadership of Benjamin ben Moses Nahawendi. Benjamin based his philosophy on a reading of the Bible. He recommended that if the Bible did not give a clear interpretation, then the Karaites should rely on the interpretation of the Rabbanites. In order to remove anthropomorphism from the Bible, he followed the neo-Platonism of Philo and interpreted all anthropomorphic references to be not of God, but of angels serving the will of God.

By the 10th century Karaism began to proselytize among the Rabbanites. This led to attacks from Rabbanites, the foremost being Saadiah Gaon, who declared Karaites heretics. Karaism reached its zenith in the early 12th century, when it had spread throughout Babylon, Palestine, and Egypt.

With the expulsion of the Jews from Spain, and the migration of many of them to Turkey, where the Karaite population was extensive, in the 15th and 16th centuries a rapprochement began between the Rabbanites and Karaites. By the 17th and 18th centuries, the Karaites had spread to the Crimea and Lithuania.

Karaites, wherever they settled until the late 18th century, were considered Jews both by the Rabbanites and by secular authorities. But in the late 18th century, when Russia gained control of Lithuania and the Crimea, Empress Catherine II treated the Karaites as a separate group and in 1795 removed the "Jew tax" from them.

By the eve of World War II, there were perhaps 12,000 Karaites remaining, 2,000 outside Russia and 10,000 inside. After the war most migrated to Israel, where their numbers remain about the same as in 1939.

While Karaites tend not to intermarry with Rabbanites, they follow Jewish practices, but with a lack of systematization of its laws. Minor differences in practices exist, such as observance of the Sabbath, structure of the religious calendar, and rejection of Hanukkah as a festival. Dietary laws are more restrictive, such as allowing the eating only of animals mentioned in the Bible. The range of prohibited marriages is greater among Karaites. The Karaite liturgy is rather different, consisting mainly of passages from the Bible. The *Shema* is included, but the *Amidah* is not.

If we were to compare, for example, Reform versus Orthodox Judaism of the 20th century, and Karaite versus rabbinic Judaism, we would find a much greater difference in theology and practice between Reform and Orthodox than between Karaite and Rabbanite. Karaite Judaism began as a reform movement in the 8th century C.E. Like many reform movements, its roots were in earlier movements, in this case the Sadducean. Like Pharisaic Judaism, which began as a reaction to the rigidity of Sadducean doctrine, Karaism began as a movement that challenged the authority of the existing religious hierarchy and attempted to restore decisions and interpretation to the populace. The modern Reform movement also began in much the same way. While Pharisaic Judaism prevailed and became rabbinic normative Judaism, Karaism prospered for four centuries but could not overcome its rival, although its tenacity has kept it alive to the present.

36

THE JEWS IN THE MUSLIM WORLD BEFORE 1400

From the 8th to the 13th century most of the Jewish population lived under Muslim rule. Although second-class citizens, they enjoyed great prosperity and freedom. Muslim policy tended to encourage them to move from agriculture and the countryside to the cities, where they flourished, in all walks of life, especially as merchants and traders. Arab culture thoroughly influenced Jews, and they adopted Arabic as their first language. Beginning in the 13th century, Jews tended to migrate to Christian lands, and by the 17th century half of all Jews still lived under Muslim rulers.

In 1159 C.E. a Jew named Benjamin left his native Tudela in Spain and began a journey from one end of the Muslim world to the other. His travels lasted until 1172. He began his odyssey in Muslim Spain, passed through France, Italy, Greece, and Byzantium, continued through Palestine, Baghdad, and Basra, around the Arabian peninsula to Egypt, and from there home. Although the main purpose of his journey is unknown (he may have been a gem merchant), he wrote a remarkable account of his trip called *Sefer haMassa'ot* (*Book of Travels*). He gives a detailed account of the Jewish life in all the places he visited, as well as much economic and social information not only about Jews, but about the general community. This book is perhaps the most important primary source for Jewish life in the 12th century.

Benjamin of Tudela gives Jewish population figures for each place he visited. If we add up the numbers from his book, we come to a total of 512,532 Jews. Although Benjamin did not visit all Jewish settlements, he did visit most of the larger ones. Thus, we can estimate that the Jewish population in the 12th century worldwide was perhaps 1.5 million to 2 million. Of these, perhaps 80 to 90 percent lived in Muslim lands.

Muslims, as set out in the *Covenant of Omar*, treated Jews and Christians similarly, as "the people of protection." This gave them the right, as "People of the Book," to live in Muslim countries, to have religious freedom, and in return to pay taxes. Since agricultural taxes for Jews were particularly heavy,

Jews tended to move out of agriculture and into the cities, where they came to pursue a variety of occupations.

Living under Muslim rule, Jews were heavily influenced by Islamic culture and civilization. The Jewish masses began to use Arabic as their primary language. The great philosopher Maimonides (see nutshell #40), for example, wrote many of his works in Arabic. Hebrew remained the language of prayer, and Aramaic of the study of the Talmud, but Arabic became the dominant language of Jewish philosophy. A dialect of Arabic developed, written in Hebrew characters, called Judeo-Arabic, largely Arabic with mixtures of Hebrew and Aramaic, much as later Yiddish developed from German, Polish, and Hebrew.

During this period Greek philosophy made heavy inroads into Arab and Jewish thought, particularly the works of Plato and Aristotle. Although Platonic influences had entered Judaism during the Hellenistic period, particularly through the works of the Jewish philosopher Philo, who lived in Alexandria in the 1st century C.E., this was a new route of influence.

Arab culture came to dominate Jewish life. Arabic poetic and literary forms were adopted. Jews donned Arab garb, and Islam came to influence the religious philosophy and practices of Jews, with emphasis on ritual repetition of prayers.

A product of his times and the Arab Jewish culture was Saadiah Gaon (882–942), who wrote the first real philosophical Jewish treatise since Philo. Saadiah was born in Fayum in Egypt, where he lived until he went to Israel to study as a young man, and from there to Babylon. In 921 we find him embroiled in a massive struggle over details of the calendar with Aaron Ben Meier, head of the Jerusalem academy. By this time Saadiah apparently had gone to Baghdad. Aaron Ben Meier attempted to assert the authority of the Jerusalem academy over that of the Babylonian on matters of the calendar. Ben Meir proclaimed that Rosh Hashanah, the Jewish new year, would fall on a Thursday, while Passover would fall on a Sunday. Despite efforts by Saadiah, acting for the Babylonian community, Ben Meir would not budge. One source records that in 922 the Jews in Israel celebrated Rosh Hashannah on a different day from the Jews of Babylon. In an effort to defeat Ben Meir and avoid a schism between the two communities, Saadiah wrote a treatise on the calendar, by which the Babylonian school achieved victory. Saadiah was appointed head of the *yeshivah* of Pumbedita in Babylonia in 922 and in 928 was named the Gaon of the academy at Sura. A difficult and competitive personality, Saadiah had an uneven career, was often embroiled in vicious struggles, and was even removed at one time from his post. Nonetheless, he was perhaps one of the greatest philosophers in the history of Judaism.

Under the influence of Aristotle and Plato, he saw the intellect as the basis of faith, the instrument through which divine will was made known. Law came from three sources: the Torah, intellect, and tradition (Oral Law). Only through intellect can the Torah and Oral Law be comprehended. Saadiah set out these beliefs in *Kitab al-Amanat wa-al-I'tiqadat* (*The Book of Beliefs and Opinions*). He intended this work to give spiritual guidance to Jews who were caught up in the confusions of various sects and religious disputes. Saadiah further believed that truth was obtainable by speculation, that is, through sense perception, assumptions, inference, and reliable tradition.

In addition to his philosophical works, Saadiah wrote three extremely important texts on the Hebrew language: a dictionary, one of the earliest works on Hebrew grammar, and a work on words that occur only once in the Bible. He also wrote an important Arabic translation and commentary on the Bible with the purpose of making the work accessible to the average reader.

Saadiah was perhaps one of the most important figures in Jewish philosophy and literature. He laid the basis for much philosophical work that was to follow, of scholars such as Maimonides. Saadiah was a product of two cultures, Arab and Jewish, and represents perhaps the best example of their synthesis.

Jews lived from one end of the Muslim world, in Spain, to the other at the borders of India. Although second-class citizens, they prospered in every sphere, especially economics, religion, and philosophy, and shared in the golden age of Islam, which in the 12th and 13th centuries was the height of world civilization.

By the 13th century Muslim power began to fade, particularly in Spain, and with the Christian reconquest of the northern part of Spain more Jews came under Christian rule. In the subsequent centuries Jews began migrating to countries dominated by Christians, particularly Poland and Lithuania. By the 17th century the population of world Jewry was about a million, with 50 percent living under Muslim rule and 50 percent under Christian, mostly in Poland and Lithuania.

37

THE JEWS OF ITALY

Jews first settled in Rome in the 2nd century B.C.E. They comprised a significant portion of the population of the Roman Empire, about 10 percent. When the Roman Empire became Christianized in the 4th century C.E., Jews were tolerated but discriminated against. Despite this, they continued to live in Italy, which was perhaps the third largest Jewish community in Christian Europe. With the Renaissance, they participated in the prosperity of Italy and the cultural and intellectual advancements of that era.

Yael Orvieto, a Jewish student at the Hebrew University in Jerusalem and through her mother a member of the de Rossi family, traces her Italian ancestry back 1,900 years. The family had been brought to Rome by Emperor Titus after the destruction of the Temple in 70 C.E. (see nutshell #25). Whether or not this account of the origin of the de Rossi family is true, the family can be traced in Italy as far back as the 13th century. Among its members were Azariah Rossi, the greatest scholar of Hebrew letters during the Renaissance, and Salamone de Rossi, the leading Jewish composer of the late Italian Renaissance. They represent but a small part of the rich Jewish life in Italy.

Jews have lived continuously in Italy from the 2nd century B.C.E. to the present day. By the 1st century C.E. there were nearly 50,000 Jews in the city of Rome, and twelve synagogues have been uncovered there from the Roman Empire period. In the 1st century Jews comprised about 10 percent of the population of the empire, or 7 million people. By the early 13th century the world Jewish population had dropped from about 8 million to 2 million, with only 250,000 living in Christian lands. Many factors devastated the Jewish population. The Jewish revolt of 70 C.E. and the Bar Kokhba revolt had proved disastrous to the Jewish population. Although early Christianity looked to Jews for converts, Paul had moved the direction of conversion to the gentiles. Nonetheless, many Jews converted. After the Roman Empire first tolerated Christianity, then adopted Christianity as its official religion in the 4th century, the numbers of converts grew. With the conquest of the Roman Empire by the Germanic tribes, the level of civilization for the entire society was retarded. There was a partial breakdown in many areas, including water delivery, sewage, and education, with the concomitant result that life expectancy, which had risen in the Roman Empire to over forty years of age, fell and infant mortality apparently rose. These general trends may have affected the size of the Jewish population.

Once the Roman Empire had become Christian in the 4th century C.E., Jews were tolerated because of religious doctrine, that is, they must be preserved so that they could turn to Christ. Consequently, forced conversion of Jews was discouraged and at times legally forbidden. But as deniers of Christ, their political, legal, and economic rights were restricted. They were forbidden to own Christian slaves, and at times to hire Christian servants. These restrictions by necessity forced Jews off the land and to the cities, since without slave or hired Christian labor it was almost impossible to compete in agriculture. Marriages were forbidden between Jewish men and Christian women, with the death penalty for violators. Often leaders of the early church would incite the populace against the Jews, such as in 388 C.E., when Philaster, bishop of Brescia, incited the people of Rome to burn a synagogue. Theodosius II banned the building of new synagogues and the enlargement of old ones. The legal code of Justinian (reigned 529–534), which was to become the basis of Roman law throughout most of Europe during the Middle Ages, laid out the position of Jews as second-class citizens, banned from public offices. All Jews who were not slaves had become Roman citizens in 212 C.E. under the Edict of Caracalla. But this was before the empire became Christian.

At the end of the 6th century the medieval papacy under Gregory I (590–604) began to establish its religious and political power over Italy. Gregory I firmly believed that Jews had to be converted by persuasion and not by violence. Thus he began a policy of protecting Jews in Rome, Naples, Palermo, and Ravenna from the local clergy who pressed for forcible conversion. Southern Italy and parts of Sicily were under the control of the eastern Roman Empire in Constantinople. In the 9th and 10th centuries Byzantine rulers were fanatical in trying to convert the Jews, which they did in many Italian cities in the south, such as in Oria, Brindisi, and Otranto. Relief came in Sicily and some cities in the south through the Saracen conquests (827–1061). Under Saracen rule Jews were free to practice their religion.

Very little is known of Jewish life in this period, though we find evidence from tombstones. After the 5th century C.E., we find tombstones inscribed in Hebrew instead of Greek or Latin. Some Jewish artisans and merchants plied their trade, especially in the south, as well as dyers and silk weavers. By the 10th century talmudic academies had sprung up in Rome and Lucca, as well as in Otranto. Under the influence of the academies in Babylon, Jewish learning prospered in the 9th and 10th centuries. Aaron of Baghdad is reputed to have taught the Kabbalah at Bari. One of Aaron's pupils, Shephatiah, son of Amittai

from Oria, became adroit at performing exorcisms. One story has him performing an exorcism on the daughter of Emperor Basil I (reigned 867–886). Turning down jewels for his reward, he asked that the edicts restricting Jewish
worship be repealed. The emperor refused this request, but did allow freedom
of worship at Oria, Shephatiah's native city.

Another prominent Italian Jew of this period was Sabbatai, son of Abraham
Donnolo (913–982), who was a physician and astronomer. Among his works
were a medical treatise and a commentary on the Book of Genesis.

The great Italian scholar of this period was Nathan, son of Jehiel of Rome.
Nathan's father had been head of the talmudic school at Rome and in 1070 on
his father's death, Nathan succeeded. He spent the next thirty-one years on a
monumental work, still used by talmudists today, called the *Arukh*. A dictionary, it gives the etymology of the words of the Talmud with not only the
Hebrew and Aramaic, but also the Latin, Greek, Arabic, and Persian roots.
Nathan's work is of particular importance, not only for its linguistic brilliance,
but because he quotes much from works that have been lost. He used all the
major talmudic literature of the time, including the commentaries of Hananel
ben Hushiel of Kairouan, the Mainz commentaries, and those from the Babylonian schools. Nathan and his brothers also were responsible for the building
of a new synagogue in Rome.

Between 1100 and 1300 the Jewish population of Italy continued to grow
and prosper. By 1300 their numbers had reached 50,000, making them the third
largest Jewish community in Christian Europe. They were scattered throughout Italy, with the greatest concentration in Rome. The attitude of sufferance
but not acceptance continued. Although religious freedom, protection from
attack on their persons and property, and protection from forced conversion
were codified by the bull of Pope Calixtus II (1119–1124), Jewish rights were
later curtailed. The Lateran Council of 1215 attempted to reduce Jews to the
level of serfs and required them to wear a badge identifying themselves as Jews.
By the middle of the 13th century the persecution of the Inquisition began,
particularly in southern Italy, which was under Spanish influence.

The zenith of Jewish life in Italy was the 14th and 15th centuries. In these
years many Jews grew wealthy as loan bankers. Banking activity was widespread and this created an entire class of wealthy Jews. As the Renaissance
began to flourish in the 14th century, Jews were caught up in the renewed climate of culture and learning. Religious studies, along with poetry, both secular and religious, were produced. One Italian Jewish scholar, Moses ben Isaac
Rietai, wrote *Mikdash Me'at*, a Hebrew work that used Dante's *Divine Com-
edy* as a model. The Jewish philosophers Elijah Delmedigo and Johanan
Alemmano were part of the Renaissance humanistic circle of Pico della
Mirandola. But perhaps the greatest stimulus to learning at this period was the

development of movable type. Within a few years of its invention in 1455, Jews in Italy began to lead the way in the printing of Hebrew books.

By the end of the 15th century the Jewish population of Italy had grown to about 120,000. This large increase could be explained partially by an increased birthrate and mirrored the growing population of Europe in general, but it also represented the migration of Jews to Italy from Spain and other areas of persecution and economic hardship. The end of the 15th century and the beginning of the 16th century saw two crises for the Italian Jews: the expulsion of Jews from Spain (see nutshell #45), which included the Spanish possession of Sicily, and the emergence of the Counter-Reformation in Italy.

The Jews of Italy from their first settlement lived a relatively stable and prosperous life, although after the Christianization of Rome, they became second-class citizens. This stability is evidenced by the De Pomi clan, an Italian Jewish family that in the 15th century could trace their roots back to the 1st century C.E. Jews participated in the Renaissance and benefited from the advancement of humanistic values. But those values would not translate into total equality for Jews until the 19th century.

38

THE JEWS OF SPAIN

Jews were part of Spain from at least the 3rd century C.E. until their expulsion in 1492. They lived under Christian rule in various places and times and under Muslim rule in others. The Spanish Christians treated the Jews with deceit, cruelty, and barbarity until they expelled them from the country, while for the most part under the Muslims Jews found tolerance. Particularly under Muslim rule the Jewish population prospered. Intellectually and culturally this period was one of the greatest in Jewish history, comparable to the height of Jewish civilization in Babylon and Poland.

"Ever since the day when we abandoned our homeland to go into exile, the persecution has never ceased; from our youth it has reared us as a father, and from our mother's womb has guided us," wrote Moses Maimonides in the *Epistle on Persecution.*

While the expulsion of Jews from Spain in 1492 represents the nadir of Jewish life in Spain, the career of Samuel ha-Nagid, philosopher-poet, general, and politician, illustrates the best. In 1056 Samuel ha-Nagid lay dying on campaign against the enemies of Granada. He had come far in the sixty-three years since his birth in Córdoba. Born into a prominent family, he was superbly educated in Hebrew, Talmud, mathematics, and philosophy. He was fluent in Arabic and six other languages. When he was twenty fate gave his life a strange twist. The Berbers conquered Córdoba, and he fled to Malaga, where he opened a spice shop. A maidservant came to his shop and asked him because of his fine handwriting to write a letter on her behalf to the vizier of Granada. When the vizier read the exquisite calligraphic handwriting, he advised King Habbus of Granada to appoint Samuel to his staff. Samuel began as a tax collector, then assistant to the vizier. He proved himself not only in penmanship, but also in affairs of state, and upon the death of the vizier, he was appointed to replace him. When King Habbus died, his sons vied for the throne. Samuel supported the elder son, Badis, who triumphed and brought Samuel to power with him. Badis was tyrannical and drank heavily. However, Samuel's influence was so great that he assumed much of the administration of the kingdom. Under his hand, Granada prospered economically and became the leading state in Spain. An able general, Samuel often took the field at the head of his troops. Except for two years of peace, he spent much of his career from 1038 to 1056 leading Granada's army, mostly at war against Arab Seville.

Samuel became a patron to the Jewish community, and in return received the title *nagid*, or prince. He supported scholars in Spain, Africa, Sicily, Jerusalem, and Baghdad. A bibliophile, he amassed a large collection of books, including numerous volumes from Babylon. At the same time he had copies of the Mishnah and Talmud made, which he gave to needy scholars. Annually he sent olive oil to synagogues in Jerusalem. He developed relationships with the leaders of the Jewish world, from Babylon, Jerusalem, and Kairawan in North Africa, and married his son to the daughter of Jacob ben Nessim of Kairawan.

Samuel founded a talmudic center and wrote several works on the Talmud, including *Sefer Hilkheta Gavrata*. A Hebrew dictionary called *The Book of Riches*, which he wrote, is consulted by scholars to this day. He composed poetry in Hebrew, although not on the level of his contemporary Ibn Gabirol. His major work was the *Diwan*, in which he tells of his many military campaigns. He also wrote treatises on the Koran. Samuel was a remarkable man, a polymath who was a statesman, warrior, religious thinker, poet, and aesthete. He was said to have worn four crowns: the crown of the Torah, the crown of political power, the crown of the Levites, and the crown of good deeds.

Despite the Inquisition (see nutshell #45) and persecution of Jews by Christians, Spain was a major center of Jewish life for 500 years. The major philosophers and poets of medieval Jewry came from there. They include the philosophers and religious scholars Moses Maimonides (see nutshell #40) and Ibn Ezra and the poets Judah HaLevi (see nutshell #39) and Ibn Gabirol. With such towering personalities, Spain succeeded Babylon as the major intellectual and religious center of Jewish life in the late Middle Ages.

The history of the Jews of Spain can be divided into three periods—the early Christian period, the Muslim period, and the Reconquest period. Anti-Jewish legislation began almost immediately after Spain became Christian. In 305 c.e. the Council of Elvira forbade Christians from eating with Jews or living with them in the same house. Spain, like the Roman Empire, fell to the Germanic tribes in the 5th century, and a Visigothic kingdom ruled from the 6th to the 8th century. The Visigothic rulers were converted to Christianity. Unlike the rulers in Rome, the Spanish Christian kings often forcibly converted Jews. King Sisebut in 613 ordered all Jews to be baptized or to leave Spain. This decree was softened after his death, but King Chintila (reigned 636–639) at the Sixth Council of Toledo (638) proclaimed that only Catholics could live in Spain. Despite these decrees, some Jews still remained in Spain. Many chose to be baptized and signed a document stating that they would follow Christian practices. In an attempt to force Jews to become Christians or to go into exile, and not practice their rites in secret, King Recceswinth (reigned 649–672) prohibited circumcision and observance of the Sabbath. Throughout the 7th century there were constant persecution, forced baptism, and conversion, but a small Jewish population persevered. Finally, in the 8th century relief came with the Muslim conquest of Spain.

In 711 Tarik ibn Ziyad crossed into Spain from North Africa and defeated the Visigoths. Although the country had nominally rid itself of Jews, many Jews had continued their religion in secret. Whenever the Muslims conquered a place, they sought out the local Jews, to whom they turned over the garrisoning of the town. The tables had turned and the Jews instead of being the oppressed, were now ruling. It was not that the Muslims were particularly well disposed to the Jews, but rather that the politics and military strategy dictated this situation. The Muslims did not have enough troops both for garrison detail and fighting, and so they turned to the Jews out of necessity. At the same time, many of the Visigothic landowners fled, leaving control of their lands to the Jews. Many of the Jews who had gone into exile in France and North Africa now returned.

In 755 the Umayyad dynasty was founded by Abd al-Rahman. He made Córdoba his capital. Under the Umayyads Spain prospered, as did its Jews. Arab geographers came to call Granada, Lucena, and Tarragona Jewish cities. The center of both Jewish and Muslim culture was in Córdoba, the political capital. Jews became influential in the fields of medicine, trade, commerce, and to some extent agriculture. In the 10th century a Jew, Hasdai ibn Shaprut, became the chief of customs and trade and was very influential with the caliphate. Under his patronage a *yeshivah* developed in Córdoba, and Hebrew learning in theology, religion, and philology flourished. The development of Córdoba as a religious center, which occurred at a time when the great academies in Babylon were in decline, meant that the Jewish community not only developed religious independence from Babylon, but also began to be the center of Jewish life and theology.

By the 11th century the Umayyad dynasty was in decline, and Muslim Spain was fragmented into smaller kingdoms. Partly as a consequence, the centers of Jewish life spread from Córdoba to other centers, including Seville. Jews increasingly became part of the ruling class. Many entered the profession of tax farming; that is, the Muslim ruler would decide the amount the state should collect in taxes and sell the tax farmer the rights to collect that amount. The tax farmer in turn would have the legal right to collect the levies. If he collected less than the contract, he lost money. If he collected more, he could keep the excess. The Jewish intelligentsia pursued the study of the Talmud and philosophy, as well as poetry, both religious and secular. Medicine was another profession pursued by the Jews. Physicians ministered not only to the body, but also to the soul. Many who took up this career were also religious philosophers and scholars of the Talmud. The epitome of philosopher-physician was Moses Maimonides.

In the 11th century the Christians from the north begin to reconquer Spain from the Muslims. The reconquest took 400 years, until 1492, when the last of the Muslims were driven from Spain. When the Christians first retook parts of Spain, the Jews were tolerated, mostly for economic and political reasons. They formed an important middle class and paid a good share of the taxes. The Jews became in name the serfs of the king and lived under an autonomous organization within the towns, called *aljama*. They collected their own taxes and paid them to the crown. Jews remained in their leadership positions in society. Many, particularly in Castile, held positions as administrators and financial officers in the government. However, often high taxes were levied on the Jews. During the 11th and 12th centuries Jews prospered in both Christian and Muslim Spain. However, by the 13th century a strong anti-Jewish reaction arose, which led to the persecution and ultimately the expulsion of the Jews from Spain, a land where they had experienced a cultural golden age.

39

A 12TH-CENTURY ZIONIST: JUDAH HALEVI

The literary output of Judah HaLevi (c. 1085–1141) represents the high point of Spanish-Jewish cultural creativity. A physician, poet, and philosopher, HaLevi was an early theorist of Zionism and Jewish nationalism.

Of how many poets can it be said that their words became the lyrics of popular music more than eight centuries later? While it may be hard to answer that question precisely, cognoscenti of Jewish history can name at least one: Judah HaLevi.

Judah HaLevi lived some 750 years before the word *Zionist* came into use. The political conditions of his time, however, led him to the conclusion that many future Zionist theorists would ultimately reach: that life in the Diaspora, even at its most comfortable, was not only insecure but also destructive of Jewish spiritual creativity.

During HaLevi's lifetime, the Iberian peninsula became a battleground as Christians sought to regain land from Muslims. In response, the Almoravids, whom we would now call Muslim fundamentalists, invaded from North Africa, establishing an intolerant regime in southern Spain. The Jews suffered at the hands of both Christians and Muslims. As he witnessed what was going on around him, HaLevi underwent a transformation.

Although as a young man he had been content to live under the illusion of security in Spain, he now foresaw that the days of the Jewish community of Spain were numbered. Like many other able Jews, anxious to have a trade that would be useful to whomever the Jews' ruler might be, HaLevi trained as a physician. But poetry was his true vocation, and he developed his theories of Zionism and Judaism in his literary works.

HaLevi is probably best known for his *Poems of Zion*. In them, he transformed a motif of medieval spiritual works—the sense of alienation from this world—into a proto-Zionist theme. Instead of longing for an other-worldly existence, HaLevi's poems see Israel as the only place where a Jew can feel rooted. While the poems lament the barrenness of the country, they praise its spiritual splendor. Life in Spain, by contrast, may seem more luxurious, but in fact it is a life of bondage to empty temptations. The poems argue that there is no physical security for Jews in other lands they call home. Furthermore, only in Israel can the Jewish people realize their spiritual potential.

The most famous of Judah HaLevi's *Poems of Zion* is chanted each year in congregations around the world as part of the service for the 9th of *Av*, the day of mourning commemorating the destruction of the First and Second Temples. In it, the poet laments the destruction of Jerusalem but looks forward to its restoration in the future. HaLevi compares his wails of sorrow to the howls of jackals, his words of hope to the plucking of a harp. More than 800 years later a popular song written to celebrate the reunification of Jerusalem in the 1967 Six-Day War (see nutshell #96) used some of HaLevi's words as its refrain: "I am a harp for your songs."

While much of HaLevi's original philosophy of Zionism and Jewish nationalism can be inferred from reading his poems, it is fully developed in his prose work *The Book of the Khazars*, usually called the *Kuzari*, from the Hebrew word for Khazars. The Khazars were a Turkish people living on the western bank of the Caspian Sea whose king converted to Judaism around the middle of the 8th century. HaLevi presents his philosophy in the form of a dramatic dialogue between the Khazar king and representatives of Greek philosophy, Christianity, Islam, and Judaism, each of whom has the opportunity to make the case for his beliefs to the king. Using this format, HaLevi makes his argument for the superiority of Judaism, despite its underdog status in the politics of his time. In fact, the full title of the *Kuzari* indicates that it is a "book of argument and demonstration in aid of the despised faith."

In the work HaLevi makes rather short shrift of Christianity and Islam as threats to Judaism; their representatives concede to the Khazar king that their religions are merely offshoots of Judaism. Because HaLevi believed that the rationalism of Greek philosophy was the greatest threat to Jewish belief, he devotes more attention to its tenets. Through reason one can conclude that there would be no universe without a divine intelligence. Such a divinity, however, has no interest in human beings. By contrast, Judaism is based on more than reason: it is grounded in God's revelation to 600,000 Israelites at Mount Sinai. The God of Judaism cares about individuals, whose happiness depends on their spiritual connection to God. While HaLevi does not dismiss the value of reason—as a physician, after all, he was a man of science—he stresses its limitations. The ritual law of Judaism and the spiritual effects brought about by their observance transcend human reason.

According to HaLevi, the Jewish people are God's instrument for the religious enlightenment of humanity. Jews alone have the gift of prophecy, which enables them to come into personal contact with God. This gift, however, can flourish only in Israel, among those who observe God's laws and speak the Hebrew language. The current powerlessness of the Jews is not a sign of their rejection by God. The meaning of their suffering will be understood only at the time of redemption, which will come when people accept God's sovereignty and observe His commandments. In the meantime, the Jews are like a seed that may appear to be decaying in the ground but is in fact taking root in preparation for growth and life.

At the end of the *Kuzari*, the Khazar king accepts the Jewish religion for himself and his subjects. Having fulfilled his mission, the scholar who presented Judaism's case to the king resolves to leave Khazaria for Israel. The king tries to dissuade him on the grounds that the Holy Land is in the possession of the Crusaders, enemies of the Jews. Further, argues the king, one can find God anywhere, assuming one approaches God with a pure heart. The Jewish scholar will not be deterred, however, rebutting that only in Israel, a land singled out by God, can the Jewish heart and soul attain purity.

In 1141, despite the objections of some colleagues, friends, and family, Judah HaLevi himself set out for Israel. Although he appears to have died in Egypt later that year, and thus never to have fulfilled his life's dream, a popular legend gave him a more poetically satisfying death. Upon finally making his way to Jerusalem, Judah HaLevi knelt to kiss its stones, reciting the most famous of his *Poems of Zion*. Just then, an Arab horseman passed by and trampled him to death.

Whatever the circumstances of Judah HaLevi's death, his arguments questioning the security of life in the Diaspora and promoting the return to Israel as a practicable solution resonated through centuries of Jewish history.

40

THE LEGACY OF MAIMONIDES

The greatest Jewish philosopher of all time, Maimonides also compiled an influential code of Jewish law. Known for his insistence that Judaism is a rational religion, Maimonides is a model for those who would combine secular with religious scholarship. He also exemplifies those Jews whose achievements earn them recognition in the gentile world but who nonetheless assume responsibility for leadership in the Jewish community.

If asked to name the greatest Jewish intellectual giant of all time, many scholars would choose Moses Maimonides (1135–1204), usually referred to in Hebrew as the Rambam, an acronym for *Rabbi Moses ben* (or son of) *Maimon*. (The suffix *ides* simply means "descendant of.") Either of Maimonides' two major religious writings—his code of Jewish law called the *Mishneh Torah* (*The Repetition of the Law*) and his philosophical masterpiece *The Guide for the Perplexed*—could have been a lifetime's work. In addition to these and other religious writings, he wrote influential treatises in his professional field of medicine and numerous letters both in a personal capacity and as a Jewish communal leader.

Just as striking as the scope of his learning is the fact that Maimonides amassed much of his knowledge under adverse conditions. When he was thirteen, his hometown of Córdoba, Spain, was taken over by fundamentalist Muslims called the Almohades, who vigorously persecuted minorities. For many years the Maimon family were wanderers, unable to live openly as Jews. Ultimately, they settled in Cairo, where by 1185 Maimonides had become a court physician to Egypt's Muslim ruler.

Although the broad scope of Maimonides' knowledge might suggest that he had to compartmentalize his various areas of expertise, in fact a common thread ran through all of his writings: the conviction that reason and religion reveal the same truths.

To help other Jews practice their religion under difficult conditions, Maimonides undertook the task of summarizing all Jewish law on a scale never attempted before or since. The fourteen volumes of the resulting *Mishneh Torah* (completed c. 1178) represent Maimonides' systematic location and processing of all the material on Jewish law, its classification according to subject matter, and his designation of a single ruling, without referring to differing views or assigning sources. One of the best-known passages of *Mishneh Torah*—the "Eight Levels of Charity"—reveals Maimonides' method. The discussion of charity in the Talmud is anything but methodical, consisting of a statement here, an anecdote there. By organizing all of the sporadic references to charity, Maimonides inferred that charitable behavior can be organized into eight hierarchical steps, depending not only on the donor's generosity and reasons for giving but also on the ability to give without embarrassing the recipient.

While Maimonides wrote the *Mishneh Torah* in Hebrew to be accessible to all educated Jews everywhere, his Arabic-language philosophical masterpiece *Guide for the Perplexed* (1185–1190) was intended for a much more limited audience: those who were troubled by what seemed to be contradictions between what they knew from their secular studies and what the Torah seemed to be saying. Maimonides believed firmly in the incorporeality of God—that God had no body. One of Maimonides' achievements in the *Guide* is his thorough analysis of the anthropomorphisms of the Bible, which ascribe human qualities to God. In forty-seven chapters in the first part of the *Guide* Maimonides gives rational explanations for the Bible's use of anthropomorphic language. The third section of the *Guide* includes an analysis of the reasons for the commandments. Maimonides denied the assertion that some commandments, such as the dietary laws, were arbitrarily given by God to test human beings' obedience. It was he who advanced the still-controversial idea that the dietary laws were given to enhance human health.

A third important religious writing by Maimonides is his commentary on the Mishnah (completed c. 1168). In it, Maimonides presented his famous "Thirteen Principles," or articles of faith. A restatement of these principles in poetic form can be found in the popular hymn "Yigdal" (c. 1300). Victims of the Nazi slaughter are known to have walked to their death in the gas chamber singing the words of the twelfth article, "I believe in perfect faith in the coming of the Messiah."

If Maimonides' religious writings reveal his powerful intellect, his letters reveal his compassion and tolerance. An anguished convert to Judaism from Islam wrote Maimonides, wondering if he was permitted to say prayers referring to a Jewish past in which he did not share. In a famous response, Maimonides assured the convert that by formally adopting Judaism the convert acquired all the rights and responsibilities of a born Jew. In a famous letter to the troubled Jews of Yemen, Maimonides argued that the community should not exclude those who in the face of persecution pretended to convert to Islam but who nonetheless continued privately to practice the Jewish commandments.

Maimonides' intellectual influence was not limited to Jewish circles. His attempt in the *Guide* to demonstrate that Judaism was compatible with Greek philosophy as formulated by Aristotle (384–322 B.C.E.) influenced Christian Aristotelian theologians, including St. Thomas Aquinas.

Among Jews, Maimonides was a controversial figure in his lifetime and in the centuries following. Many suspected, for example, that he intended to supplant the Talmud with his own *Mishneh Torah*, and others thought his emphasis on reason sold religion short. Today Jews of all denominations celebrate Maimonides' achievements, whether or not they agree with his every legal ruling or philosophical argument. Many try to implement in their own lives Maimonides' teaching that the task of human beings in this world is to develop their intellectual powers fully.

41

NAHMANIDES AND
THE 1263 DISPUTATION

Nahmanides, a physician like Maimonides, was one of the greatest biblical commentators and talmudic scholars in Jewish history. As the religious leader of the Jewish community of Spain, he was the Jewish representative in a debate with the Catholic church at Barcelona in 1263. Although standing alone, he successfully won the debate against an array of church leaders. However, this victory only led to Nahmanides' exile, the intensification of efforts to convert Jews, and the burning of the Talmud and other Jewish books.

The Inquisition came to Aragon in 1233. Raymond de Peñaforte, a member of the Dominican order of priests, was appointed as its head by Pope Gregory IX. The first efforts of the Inquisition were to convert the Jews through persuasion and education. The Dominicans built seminaries to teach Hebrew so they could argue from the Hebrew texts to refute Jewish religious claims. One of the disciples of Raymond de Peñaforte was Pablo Christiani, a baptized Jew. The attempt to proselytize the Jews was a failure, and Pablo came up with the idea of having a debate between the Jews and the Church. Reasoning that church scholars would win an easy victory, which would help the campaign to convert Jews, he persuaded King James I to order Nahmanides, the leading Jewish thinker and the foremost authority on the Talmud at the time, to debate at Barcelona in 1263.

By the 13th century the Jewish population had grown to about 150,000, 3 percent of the total population of Spain. Although antisemitism existed, it tended to be diffuse and without a specific agenda. But in the early 13th century the monastic orders became the center of antisemitism, and a process began that ended in expulsion. While the rulers of the various kingdoms of Spain historically had continued to employ Jews as advisers and bankers and Jews had contributed to much of the prosperity of the countries, the clergy in their religious zeal were particularly hostile, encouraging forced baptism and persecution. The religious orders gained increasing influence over the rulers of Spain, who became very antisemitic.

Moses ben Nahman (1194–1270), also known as Nahmanides or Ramban, was from Gerona in Catalonia. Like Maimonides, Nahmanides was a physician. He presided over a *yeshivah* in Gerona. A major leader in Jewish life in Catalonia, and in Spanish Jewish religious thought and the study of the Talmud, he wrote numerous works, of which over fifty have survived. They fall into three groups: biblical commentary, halakhic (legal) opinions, and kabbalistic works. In his biblical commentary he wrote extensively on the narrative as well as the legal sections of the Bible. The commentary contains Nahmanides' views of God as the source of all knowledge. He views the past as foreshadowing the history of the Jews. He makes moral comments on the behavior of the patriarchs and even criticizes Abraham. Nahmanides' commentary is upbeat and inspiring, and consequently was widely used. Parts of it have been incorporated into later commentaries, including those of the 20th century. Nahmanides' work on the Talmud and *halakhah,* or Jewish law, are equally influential. Although he wrote little on the kabbalah directly, many kabbalistic ideas are found in his writings, particularly his commentary on the Pentateuch. In the generations that followed, he was considered one of the most influential kabbalists, despite this paucity of writing on the subject.

This was the scholar called upon to defend Judaism in the Disputation at Barcelona in 1263, over four days, July 20, 27, 30, and 31. Nahmanides was at the time sixty-nine years old and at the height of his fame and influence in the Jewish world. The Catholic church sanctioned this debate with the idea that a public hearing of the issues would show the superiority of Christianity and thus induce Jews to convert. On the side of the Church were arrayed King James I of Aragon, who was presiding and who took some part in the debate; the Dominicans Raymond de Peñaforte, Raymond Martini, Arnold de Segarra; Pablo Christiani; and the head of the Franciscans, Peter de Janua. Nahmanides stood alone on the Jewish side. King James I was an honorable and fair man, and assured Nahmanides that he would have complete freedom of speech, something that often was not permitted to Jews in other debates. The debate began with a warning by Raymond de Peñaforte to Nahmanides not to criticize the Church. Nahmanides replied that he understood civilized behavior.

Pablo Christiani maintained that the messiah had appeared, and used haggadic material to prove his point. Moreover, he argued, the messiah was at the same time human and divine, and had died to atone for humanity's sins. Nahmanides replied that *aggadah* represented homilies from the *Midrash,* which were not binding on Jews. Examining the passages of the Talmud that were cited, Nahmanides argued that the literal interpretation of these passages simply did not state that the messiah had come, but the passages could be bent to mean that only through interpretative rather than literal meaning. Nahmanides continued that the controversies between Judaism and Christianity were not built around whether Jesus was the messiah. He angered his Christian opponents when he argued that Rome was a mighty empire before it adopted Christianity, and that it had declined and fallen once it did become Christian. In contrast, Islam had established a greater empire than that of the Christians. Nahmanides' implication was that Christianity had contributed to the deterioration of Rome, a sentiment echoed later in the 18th century by the great historian of antiquity Edward Gibbon, in his *Decline and Fall of the Roman Empire*. Another point of attack by Nahmanides was that "from the time of Jesus until the present the world has been filled with violence and injustice, and the Christians have shed more blood than all other peoples."

Because Nahmanides seemed to be gaining the upper hand over the church officials, the debate was adjourned. Church sources say it ended because Nahmanides fled the city. However, the Jewish sources have Nahmanides staying in the city for another week. On the Sabbath he attended a sermon delivered in the synagogue by King James I himself, which had as its purpose the conversion of the Jews. Nahmanides was allowed to reply, and the next day received a monetary gift of 300 maravedis from the king.

While the disputation may have been a personal triumph for Nahmanides, it had negative results for the Jews. Given the tenor of the Church toward the Jews, these results probably would have occurred anyway. Raymond Martini, in an attempt to strengthen the christological interpretations in the *aggadah*, wrote a book, *Pugio Fidei*, in 1280, which came to be the basis of Christian arguments against Judaism. Pablo Christiani was given permission to increase the debates with Jews in Aragon, with the Jews to pay the expenses. Pablo again could make little progress in converting the Jews, and consequently persuaded Pope Clement IV (1265–1268) to censor Jewish books; books in which offending passages were not censored were to be burned. Even the *Mishneh Torah* of Maimonides was consigned to the fire because he mentioned Jesus.

Nahmanides was persecuted because he defeated the Church in the debate. The bishop of Gerona, Nahmanides' native city, had asked for an account of the debate. When Nahmanides wrote this account, it was used as a basis for a charge before the Inquisition that Nahmanides had blasphemed Jesus. King James I wanted a light penalty, the burning of Nahmanides' account, and two years' exile. Fearful that this would not satisfy the Inquisition, King James I adjourned the trial. The fate of this great scholar foreshadowed what would happen eventually to all of Spain's Jews, death or exile. Nahmanides realized the time had come to leave his native land. He fled to Israel, where he arrived in 1267 and spent the last three years of his life.

42

THE BIBLE OF THE JEWISH MYSTICS: THE ZOHAR

The Zohar, which appeared in Spain during the last two decades of the 13th century, is the basic text of Jewish mysticism, known as kabbalah. The Zohar and the kabbalah are both attempts to understand the inner life of God.

The *Zohar* is the classical text of kabbalah, the esoteric and mystical teachings of Judaism. The root meaning of *kabbalah* is "that which is handed down through tradition." In fact, the *Zohar* was not presented as a new work written by a contemporary author. Instead, Moses de Leon (1250–1305), a Spanish Jew who in about 1280 began to circulate and sell passages from it, claimed that the material came from an old manuscript. The fact that the work was written in Aramaic, the language of the talmudic rabbis, strengthened Moses de Leon's claim that his role was merely that of scribe. The manuscript, he said, came from the times of the great Rabbi Simeon ben Yohai, who had lived in Israel more than a thousand years earlier.

According to traditional belief, Rabbi Simeon ben Yohai and his son, while living in a cave for thirteen years to avoid Roman persecution, were visited twice daily by the prophet Elijah. During those visits, Elijah instructed them in the Torah's mysteries. Moses de Leon asserted that the *Zohar* contained those mysteries, which in the succeeding generations had been handed down in secret from teacher to student. Now that the work had finally arrived in Spain, he had taken it upon himself to spread its mystical interpretation of the Torah.

After Moses de Leon's death, his wife told a different story: that her husband had admitted to her that the *Zohar* was his own work, but that he knew he would be better paid for a manuscript by an ancient revered sage than for his own words. Despite her claims, most readers of the *Zohar* accepted the book's antiquity. These readers were aware that the manuscript was riddled with such anachronisms as the names of rabbis living hundreds of years after Simeon ben Yohai. Such seeming discrepancies merely deepened their reverence for the sage, however, whose grasp of the mysteries of the Torah obliterated all distinction between the present and the future.

When the *Zohar* was first printed in 1556, a legend arose that the 2,000-page printed book represented only a fraction of the ancient work. While its acceptance as a holy and ancient book grew, so did the number of those who challenged its antiquity and cast aspersions on it by calling it a forgery. Only in the late 1930s did the scholar Gershom Scholem assert with confidence that Moses de Leon was the author. Scholem reached his conclusion in part by comparing de Leon's Hebrew works with the *Zohar*. Rather than calling the work a forgery, however, Scholem argued that the Jewish tradition of contemporary writers attributing their works to ancient authors goes back to immediate postbiblical times. Moses de Leon's wish to cloak his words in an aura of antiquity was neither new nor disreputable.

Scholem's scholarship has not shaken the belief of many hasidic Jews and many of Yemenite descent, for whom the *Zohar* still represents the words of Rabbi Simeon ben Yohai. (In a similar way, biblical scholarship over the past century has not shaken the belief of many traditional Jews that the Torah was transmitted in its entirety by God to Moses at Mount Sinai.)

While the question of the *Zohar*'s authorship may never be resolved to the satisfaction of all, no one challenges the assertion that it is the classical text, though by far not the earliest of the kabbalah. The aim of the *Zohar* was to satisfy the yearning of many Jews for a way to feel closer to God and, at the same time, to make Jews feel that they had a significant role to play in the world. The *Zohar* makes use of the concept of God developed in earlier kabbalistic works. Human beings can never grasp the ultimate reality of God. This unavailable world is, however, connected to the world of God's ultimate reality. Human beings can get to know God through the world of the *sefirot*, in which God is a responsive being, affected by humanity. In the realm of the *sefirot*, God not only had a body, which is the model of the human body, but also a combination of male and female principles, so that there is a romantic and sexual aspect to God. According to the *Zohar*, God can actually be comprehended in terms of the human image, which is merely a reflection of God's.

The *Zohar* teaches that one way for human beings to experience as intimate a personal relationship with God as that between bride and groom is to perform the commandments. The commandments also play another role in the *Zohar*. Performing commandments—or stirring up holiness on earth—arouses God, causing divine mercy to flow down upon the entire people.

The *Zohar* also describes the "other side"—the realm of cosmic evil, the antithesis of God's mercy. It implies that evil originated from the remains of earlier worlds that God destroyed. The text compares evil to a husk or shell that covered lower levels of existence as the emanations of divine light spread out. But even the realm of the "other side" contains a spark of holiness, and the task of humanity is to separate the holy from the evil.

By describing God, the commandments, and evil in mythic terms, the *Zohar* made Judaism more inviting for many who felt that philosophic interpretations sapped Jewish life of all vitality.

43

THE JEWS OF ENGLAND:
MASSACRE AND EXPULSION

Jews came to England with the Norman Conquest in the 11th century. They settled in most major cities in England, especially York and London. Like their brethren in Christian Europe, many turned to money-lending, banking, and other financial activities. They became prosperous and contributed to the economic life of England. With the coronation of Richard the Lionheart in 1189, conditions for Jews began to deteriorate. Throughout the 13th century there was a systematic confiscation of Jewish property. When there was little left to confiscate, they were expelled from the country in 1290.

In March 1190 the people of York massacred their Jews. First, an uncontrollable mob set fire to the houses of the Jews. The mob was a mixed lot—townspeople, Crusaders about to join King Richard I in his wars, nobles who owed money to the Jews. Antisemitic priests urged on the mob and aroused them to destroy the Jews.

Joseph ben Asher of Chartres, an eyewitness, whose father and relatives may have perished there, wrote several elegies on those killed in the massacre.

They were gathered together to the fortress, and Asher was with us, indeed the prince oppressed us and the adversary stood at his right hand; we said: "Plunder our property!" but they replied, "No, we have come for [Rabbi] Yom Tov. . . . The holy congregation was altogether worthy, they stood dumb like a lamb before the shearers; a heavenly voice moaned from Horeb like a dove: "Woe is me! Woe is me! My servant Moses [of York] is dead." (*Elegy for the Martyrs of York*)

Place in a bottle the tears of oppression of those who cleave to You with their soul and might. Utterly crushed, constantly driven from the port of their desire, where they had dwelt, taken from their land on which they had lived. I will go in the lead, and lighten your burden. My enemies crushed the breasts of my sister. Spilt blood—It did not please me. Dove of my captivity, live in spite of your blood. O sister, may you grow into thousand and myriads. (*Love*)

The local sheriff was powerless to stop the mob, but he did allow 150 Jews led by Josce, a local Jewish financier, into the keep of the royal castle. The mob, right on their heels, besieged them in the castle. Instead of protecting the Jews, the authorities soon joined the mob. A local noble, Richard Malebys, took command of the siege. Every day a monk said Mass in front of the besieged castle and stirred up the crowd. One morning a Jew threw a stone from the battlements. It struck the monk and killed him. Now the mob was ready for a massacre. Food was almost gone. Surrender meant death, or forced baptism at the very least. At the urging of Rabbi Yom Tov of Joigny, their religious leader, the Jews decided the only escape was suicide. First they burned their goods, lest the townspeople be enriched. Then Josce slit the throat of his wife. Next he took his knife to his two children. In turn, he was slain by Rabbi Yom Tov. Most of the Jews followed this example. When the mob broke into the citadel in the morning, they murdered the few Jews left alive. They next went to the cathedral and burned the records of the debts they owed the Jews. The royal chancellor, Longchamp, decided to punish the mob, not for killing the Jews but rather for destroying the records, which deprived the state of revenue. The Crusaders had dispersed, and the barons who had led the mob fled to Scotland. This left only the sheriff of York, who had tried to aid the Jews. He was removed from office.

Jews had come with William the Conqueror from France shortly after 1066. They became a well-to-do merchant class in England, particularly active in finance and banking. In the first part of the 12th century Jews were encouraged by Henry I to settle in England. But the civil unrest there in the 12th century led to a need for money by the warring sides, and the royal house. Since Jews were virtually the only banking source, they became a target for nobles and the Crown to extort needed cash. Often the king would cancel debts owed to Jews, and when a Jew died, insist that the estate revert to the Crown. The king claimed that the debts owed to the deceased Jew now were to be owed to the state.

The lot of Jews took a downward turn with the coronation of King Richard I, the Lionheart. A delegation of Jews had come to the coronation at Westminster Abbey with rich gifts from around the country, but they were denied admittance. A riot broke out on the steps of the abbey and soon spread through the city. Many in the delegation were murdered, and the houses of Jews throughout London were sacked. Richard, who financially depended on the Jews, in retaliation hanged the leaders of the mob and made a proclamation that in all his dominions in France and England, the Jews were to live in peace. Once Richard left for the Crusades, the anti-Jewish riots spread throughout the whole country, partially because of Christian hatred of Jews, and partially inflamed by a desire to default on debts owed to them.

Seeing his revenue at risk, King Richard established a system of duplicate records where all debts to Jews were to be recorded. This network of records throughout the country came to be called the "Exchequer of the Jews."

Succeeding Richard, King John too saw the Jews as a source of revenue for the Crown. When John's nobles forced him to sign the Magna Carta in 1215, they included a clause that restricted claims of Jews against debtors who died owing them money. As in Italy five years earlier, in 1222 the Council of Oxford declared that Jews had to wear badges to identify themselves as Jews. The 13th century saw a progressively heavy economic burden placed on Jews. In 1230 the king took a third of all Jewish property. Between the years 1255 and 1273 the Crown confiscated 400,000 pounds, an enormous sum at that time, by seizing the property of Jews upon their death.

In 1255 the Jews of Lincoln were accused of the ritual murder of a Christian boy, Hugh of Lincoln. A confession was extracted by torture from a Jew, and this led to the arrest of ninety-one Jews, who were sent to prison. Eighteen Jews demanded a trial before a jury, to which they were entitled by law. Instead of a trial, they were taken out and hanged. Eventually, the remainder of the Jews who survived the harsh conditions of imprisonment were freed.

The accusation of ritual murder of Hugh of Lincoln found its way into mainstream English literature in the pages of Geoffrey Chaucer's *Canterbury Tales*. In "The Prioress's Tale," in addition to mentioning Hugh, Chaucer relates the story of a young boy who has his throat cut by Jews as he walked through "Jewes Street" singing a hymn to the Virgin Mary. After they cut his throat, the Jews threw his body into a pit. Miraculously, even with its throat cut, the corpse continued singing, and thus the body was discovered. Though Chaucer wrote over a century after the death of Hugh of Lincoln and the expulsion of the Jews from England, he reflects English prejudices and hatred of Jews.

By the end of the 13th century Jews had been impoverished by years of heavy taxation. Then Edward I in 1275 prohibited usury, which took away the only real source of Jewish income. The next fifteen years saw increasing persecution of Jews. In 1279 the death penalty was imposed on Jews who blasphemed against Christianity. In 1280 they were forced to listen to sermons by the Dominicans to convert them to Christianity. By the Synod of Exeter in 1281 they were deprived of such rights as holding public office, hiring Christians, eating with Christians, and building synagogues. Finally, on July 18, 1290, Jews were ordered to leave England, taking with them only the property they could carry. Their houses and land were confiscated by the Crown. The entire Jewish population of England left their place of birth and sailed into exile in France and Flanders. Jews were forbidden to settle in England for almost 400 years until they were readmitted under Oliver Cromwell in 1655.

44

RASHI

Rashi (1040–1105) was one of Judaism's greatest teachers and scholars. His works on the Talmud and the Torah have become standard commentaries to this day. Rashi is responsible more than any other single scholar for making the Talmud accessible to nonspecialists. His commentary on the Torah in 1475 became the first book printed in Hebrew. It proved to be of such great influence that in the past 900 years over 100 commentaries have been written on his commentary. A brilliant grammarian, Rashi interpreted many passages of the Torah, which modern development in Semitic linguistics and the decipherment of other Semitic languages have confirmed.

A legend tells that one day the father of Rashi was attacked by Christians, who were after an expensive gem he had in his possession. He cast the gem into the ocean, rather than let the Christians get it. A voice came from the heavens and foretold that he would have a son who would bring wisdom to the world. Today, almost a thousand years later, virtually everyone who seriously studies the Talmud or the Torah reads the brilliant commentaries of Rashi. Even modern Hebrew writers have been influenced by his exquisite literary style. When the Israeli writer Shmuel Agnon accepted the Nobel Prize in literature in 1966, he especially acknowledged Rashi. The greatest modern Israeli poet, Hayyim Bialik, also singled out Rashi as a source of inspiration.

Rabbi Shlomo ben Isaac, called Rashi from an acronym of the first letters of his name, was born and lived most of his life in Troyes, a city in France that Charlemagne had made his capital 250 years before. For a short period he studied with the famous Rabbi Gershom at a *yeshivah* in Mainz, and at the age of twenty-five returned to his native city. Although he presided over a school that he founded in 1070, he needed an occupation to provide a livelihood for himself and his three daughters. He knew much about banking and trade, but his main occupation was growing grapes and producing wine. In one letter he apologizes for the briefness of his response, since he and his family had been busy harvesting the grapes.

Unlike other scholars of the time, Rashi insisted that his three daughters become literate and study the Talmud. He may have developed this view because he had no sons. One of his daughters became so gifted that she became his assistant, and often when he was ill would read requests for talmudic decisions and help frame the answers. The daughters all married distinguished students of Rashi and produced children who became great scholars. The most distinguished of his sons-in-law were Meir ben Samuel and Judah ben Nathan, who carried on their father-in-law's work. They began the "Supplements" (*Tosafot*) to Rashi's *Commentary on the Talmud*. His grandchildren included the famous Samuel, known as Rashbam, and Jacob, called Rabbeinu Tam, who became the leader of the French Jewish community.

Rashi's life, though spent in relative tranquility, was overshadowed by the massacre of the Jews in France and Germany during the First Crusade, including many of his relatives and friends. On November 27, 1095, Pope Urban II at Clermont in southern France summoned all Christians to join in a Crusade against the Saracens to recapture the Holy Sepulchre. Godfrey of Bouillon vowed that he would not set out on the Crusades until he had avenged the death of Christ by spilling the blood of Jews. The Jews of France faced forced baptism or death. Jewish communities were attacked in Rouen and Lorraine. However, the Crusaders soon left France for the Rhine valley and the route toward Jerusalem. The Crusaders massacred the Jews in Speyer and in Worms, where 800 Jews chose death or suicide over forced conversion. Worms had been the center of Jewish scholarship in Germany, and Rashi had spent several years there studying. One can still visit his home in Worms, now a Jewish museum. The massacres spread to Mainz, where a thousand Jews were killed, and to Cologne. There is a tradition that Rashi foretold that Godfrey of Bouillon would return to his native city with only three horsemen, having lost entirely the rest of his army. The persecutions continued until 1103, when King Henry IV guaranteed peace for the Jews.

Rashi's genius in his commentaries is his ability to explain even the most difficult material clearly. His *Commentary on the Bible* took a middle course between traditional talmudic interpretation and the use of aggadic, or homiletic, stories. Later scholars, such as Ibn Ezra, criticized Rashi for this method. However, the combination of legal arguments with *midrash* gives a humanizing tone to the legal interpretation and makes the material more easily comprehensible and enjoyable to read. Rashi said, "As for me, I am only concerned with the literal meaning of the Scriptures and with such stories as explain the biblical passages in a fitting manner" (*Commentary on Genesis* 3.8).

Rashi probably was one of the finest grammarians in the history of Hebrew. His theory of language derived from the rabbinic literature and the Spanish grammarians. His lack of Arabic, however, meant that he never read the important theoretical works of Jewish grammarians that elucidated the basic structure of Hebrew. But one example of his fine grasp of Hebrew is his interpretation of the first sentence of Genesis. The traditional translation from the Septuagint until the 20th century is "In the beginning God created Heaven and Earth." Following Rashi, most modern Hebrew scholars translate, "When God began to create the heaven and the earth." Rashi's interpretation has been confirmed by work in Semitic linguistics of Hebrew and Babylonian and with the parallel of the Babylonian creation epic *Enuma Elish*, not discovered until the 19th century.

Rashi also comments about the first verse of Genesis that the Torah begins with the creation of the world to illustrate that God owns the whole world, and that if anyone says to the people of Israel, "You are robbers in conquering the territory of the seven Canaanite tribes," that since all the earth belongs to God, He can give it to whomever He wants. Thus we see in Rashi's comments on the opening of Genesis a profound grammatical understanding and an intellectual and biblical justification for the Jews' claim on Israel.

Despite his vast learning, Rashi was humble. He often wrote, "I do not know what this is" or "At all events I made a mistake in that comment . . . I have now gone through it and have corrected it."

Rashi's writings on the Bible and the Talmud have taught Jews for the past 900 years. Any modern scholar who works on the language of the Bible still must consult Rashi. Next to Maimonides, Rashi is perhaps the foremost scholar in the history of Judaism.

45

THE INQUISITION
AND EXPULSION FROM SPAIN

The religious fervor of the Catholic church in Spain from the 13th century onward led to systematic persecutions to rid the country of all non-Catholics. While under this pressure, many Jews adopted Christianity in name only, although they secretly remained Jews. These Jews, called Marranos, were also soon persecuted, tortured, and killed. In a final effort to ensure that the country was Catholic, all non-Catholics, especially Jews and Muslims, were expelled in 1492.

Until the beginning of the 18th century the Spanish royalty was in the habit of burning heretics at the stake for public spectacles, to celebrate weddings and special events. The worst case occurred in June 1680 in Madrid. In honor of the marriage of Charles II to Marie Louise d'Orléans, in a celebration that lasted fourteen hours, fifty-one people were burned at the stake. Charles II himself was given the honor of lighting the fire.

The Inquisition began in the early 13th century. It was at first directed against Christian heretics, such as the Albigensians in France, but it soon spread over the Catholic world. If under torture a person became repentant, he was handed over to the civil authorities for life imprisonment. If he failed to repent, he was burned at the stake. This public burning was called auto-da-fé. While the Inquisition at first left Jews alone, by the mid-13th century authorities found excuses to attack Jews. For example, in June 1242 the Inquisition in Paris condemned and publicly burned the Talmud on the grounds that it blasphemed Jesus. In 1288 the Inquisition began to burn Jews instead of Jewish books. Spain, however, became the center of the most aggressive and bloodthirsty reign of the Inquisition. Even after Jews were expelled from Spain, the Inquisition continued, especially in Spanish territories, and Jews were burned until the late 18th century, with isolated incidents in the early 19th century. The Inquisition was not abolished until July 15, 1834.

Jewish life in Spain took a sharp downward turn at the end of the 14th century. In 1391 the archdeacon of Ecija, Ferrant Martinez, who had been preaching against Jews for years, finally got his opportunity when the archbishop died. He began to urge the populace to rise against the Jews, kill them, and destroy their synagogues. On June 4, 1391, the first riots began in Seville. The Jewish quarter was burned, with many Jewish men slaughtered and women and children sold into slavery. The riots spread to Toledo, Madrid, and Córdoba. The secular authorities did nothing to quell the disturbances. Under the threat of death, many Jews chose to convert to Christianity. Others like Asher, son of Jehiel, imitated the martyrs of Masada and cut the throats of his mother-in-law, wife, and children, then committed suicide. Virtually no area in Spain escaped these riots, including the Balearic Islands, where the Jewish community was wiped out. At the end of three months of rioting, perhaps as many as 50,000, or approximately 20 percent of Spain's Jewish population, were massacred, with possibly as many as 100,000 Jews adopting Christianity.

Curtailment of rights and oppressive legislation followed. In 1415 King Ferdinand I forbade Jews from studying the Talmud, increasing the size of existing synagogues, marrying Christians, or disinheriting any of their children who might become baptized. They were henceforth barred from public office. All Jews over the age of twelve were required three times a year to listen to a Christian sermon delivered in their synagogue.

With the marriage of Isabella of Castile and Ferdinand of Aragon, and the uniting of their two kingdoms, the stage was set for the expulsion of Jews from Spain. Isabella and Ferdinand removed from Jews the right to jurisdiction in their own communities and invited the Inquisition to expand their activities in Aragon. The Marranos (see nutshell #46), as well as the Jewish community, became targets. In 1483 the Jews of Andalusia were moved to new locations. They were forced to wear badges and were segregated in Jewish sections.

The persecution of Marranos and Jews was not uniform throughout Spain. Consequently, when persecutions began, they would move from one region to another. This ended in 1483, when Tomás de Torquemada, the queen's confessor, was made inquisitor general. He brought the Inquisition to every corner of the kingdom. Between his accession and the expulsion, Torquemada condemned over 13,000 Marranos to death.

Finally, on January 2, 1492, the last Muslim territory, Granada, fell. Having driven Muslims from Spain, now the only non-Christians that remained were the Jews, along with crypto-Muslims, called Moriscos. Ferdinand and Isabella, with advice from Torquemada, now issued a decree on March 31, 1492, expelling all Jews. Some 250,000 Jews of Spain went into exile. Approximately 100,000 went to Portugal, but were expelled from there in 1496. The rest went to North Africa or Turkey. Thousands of other Jews, including the chief rabbi Abraham Seneor and many members of rich families, chose baptism over exile. Many of them continued to practice Judaism in secret.

At the time of the expulsion Jews had lived in Spain over a thousand years, had produced a great culture, and lived in prosperity, contributing much to the economic, intellectual, and cultural life of the region. The expulsion of 1492 was a disaster for Spain, contributing to its decline by eliminating much of its middle class and educated elite.

The antisemitism of Spain has persisted to the present day. Only in 1990 were Jews in Spain, most of whom had migrated there since World War II, given the same legal rights as Catholics. Spain was one of the last Western countries to recognize Israel in 1986.

46

THE MARRANOS

Marranos were Jews who converted to Christianity in Spain and Portugal in the 14th and 15th centuries. Many Marranos continued to practice their Judaism in secret, and those who did became targets for the Spanish Inquisition, which burned them as heretics. Tens of thousands of Marranos gradually escaped from Spanish lands and settled in Muslim countries that gave them religious freedom.

In 1648 Fernando Cardoso, a poet and physician at the royal court of Madrid who was prominent in society and the intellectual life of Spain, suddenly left for Venice with his brother, Miguel. To the people of Venice, the brothers appeared to be like any other pair of well-to-do Spanish travelers. The two went through the city until they stood outside the ghetto, where the Jews were forced to live. They then walked through the gates and into the arms of their brethren. Venice had become a haven for Jews, although their rights were restricted. Once inside the ghetto, Fernando and Miguel revealed themselves as Jews, and that their real names were Isaac and Abraham. They would not have been able to conceal their Jewish identity from the Inquisition in Spain if they had been circumcised. To fulfill the commandment to admit Jewish males into the Covenant of Abraham by circumcision on the eighth day after birth, only a drop of blood was taken, rather than full circumcision. Now they underwent a proper circumcision, a painful process as an adult. For five years they studied Hebrew, Jewish law, and customs in Venice, and in 1652 they settled in Verona. Isaac Cardoso now had the freedom to speak and write, and authored his famous defense of Jews and Judaism, *Las Excelencias de los Hebreos*.

Isaac and Abraham Cardoso were Marranos, crypto-Jews, who had concealed their Jewish practices since the conversion of their ancestors in the 15th century. When the Spaniards, and shortly after the Portuguese, drove all non-Christians from the Spanish peninsula at the end of the 15th century, Jews were faced with three choices: to leave Spain for exile; to convert to Christianity and remain in Spain; or to convert outwardly, but to practice Judaism in secret. Those who converted to Christianity were called New Christians, *conversos* (converts), or abusively, Marranos, from the Spanish word for "pig." Some were converted by force, others voluntarily.

Many Marranos practiced Judaism in secret. According to church law, those who did were heretics, and therefore under the authority of the Inquisition. All Marranos became particular targets of the Inquisition because so many of them in fact were heretics, that is, secret Jews.

Marranos regularly left Spain and Portugal and then came out as Jews in their new lands all through the 16th and 17th centuries. To stem the tide, the Spanish and Portuguese authorities prohibited Marranos from emigrating. Many left in secret. Some even received permission to make pilgrimages to Rome. Once in Italy, where paradoxically the Inquisition was not very strong, they made their escape and joined the Jewish community.

Marranos most often fled to Muslim countries, which were the implacable enemies of Christianity and Spain. The most frequent choices were Morocco and Turkey, where there were already large Jewish communities that had been formed by the refugees from the expulsion from Spain in 1492. By the 16th century so many Marranos had settled in Salonika in Greece, that they outnumbered the rest of the population of the city.

The new Protestant countries became another refuge for Marranos, particularly Hamburg and other cities in Germany, and England. Jews had been banned from England since the expulsion in 1290. Consequently, the Marranos who settled there could not officially practice their religion, but the Protestant authorities turned a blind eye, until Jews were officially allowed to settle in the country by Oliver Cromwell in 1655. Holland, a country with a long history of toleration, opened its doors to the Marranos at the end of the 16th century. Marranos openly practiced Judaism there, and when combined with the existing Jewish community, made Amsterdam one of the leading Jewish centers in the 17th century.

Life for Marranos was precarious in other Catholic countries besides Spain and Portugal. Although tolerated in the early 16th century in the Papal States in Italy, the mid-century Counter-Reformation led to the denunciation of many Marranos as heretics. They were subsequently burned at the stake. Venice and Tuscany were relatively tolerant of the Marranos, though they were forced to live in ghettos.

Perhaps the most distinguished figure illustrating the fierce loyalty to Judaism and the precarious existence of Marranos is Beatriz de Luna, known also as Gracia Mendes Nasi, or in the Jewish world of the 16th century, La Señora, or the Lady. Beatriz de Luna was born in 1510 and at the age of eighteen married Francisco Mendes, who was a Marrano and a member of a wealthy banking and trading family in Lisbon. Beatriz de Luna found herself a young widow at the age of twenty-six, but heir to her husband's fortune. The Inquisition was gaining strength in Portugal, and Beatriz took her infant daughter, Reyna, and her unmarried sister, Brianda, and fled to Antwerp, where her husband's brother, Diogo Mendes, had established part of the family trading and banking business. Antwerp had become the center of the spice trade for northern Europe, and under the political sway of Portugal, was a primary market for Portuguese traders. Marranos found this city an attractive place to settle, since they were free to travel there and since it was a way station where they could move their assets before escaping to Arab lands that allowed them religious freedom.

The house of Mendes, particularly Beatriz de Luna, was the conduit for many of these escaping Marranos, a secret network through Europe by which Marranos, with their funds intact, could move through the Alps, into Italy, then on to Muslim lands. Fugitives were provided with bills of exchange, honored by the Mendes banking empire, which allowed them to move their assets without fear of seizure. Diogo Mendes was several times charged with heresy by the Inquisition. These charges stemmed from two sources: one was that in fact he was a heretic since he was a crypto-Jew; the other was the desire of the authorities to confiscate his vast wealth, since the property of heretics was forfeited on conviction. Although thanks to a series of economic and political ploys, including bribery, Diogo Mendes was never convicted of heresy, the pressure was mounting. Diogo had decided to leave Antwerp, but died before he could. Beatriz de Luna was left half of the Mendes fortune and made administrator of the rest of the estate on behalf of her sister, who was Diogo's widow, and Diogo's infant daughter.

In 1544, with the threat of exposure growing daily, Beatriz de Luna and her family slipped out of Antwerp along the route they had previously sent so many other Marranos. She left her nephew, João Miguez (see nutshell #50), in charge of the affairs in Antwerp and made her way to Venice, but not to the ghetto. Beatriz continued to live outwardly as a Christian. But her sister, Brianda, tired of having her inheritance controlled by Beatriz, denounced her to the Inquisition. The city of Venice quickly took an interest, in an effort to seize the great Mendes fortune. However, Beatriz, who had long desired to settle in Constantinople, was given help by Suleiman the Magnificent. Suleiman wanted to lure the Mendes trading and banking industry to Constantinople. Since Venetian officials depended on Constantinople for trade and were fearful of the military threat of Suleiman, when he ordered them to leave Beatriz alone, they complied. Beatriz now moved to the Italian city-state of Ferrara. There for the first time, at the age of forty, Beatriz declared that she was a Jew.

The Counter-Reformation was building in Italy, and the lot of Marranos and Jews was becoming more precarious, even in Ferrara. Finally, in August 1552 Beatriz de Luna left Ferrara and Italy for Constantinople. She was welcomed in Turkey like a visiting monarch. The Jews of the city swarmed around her. She was already known in the Jewish world as one of the wealthiest women in Europe, as well as a savior of Marranos and a patron of Jewish learning and institutions. She lived the rest of her life in Constantinople, until her death in 1569, continuing to help her brethren. Her philanthropy toward the Jewish community was felt all over the Mediterranean, as well as at home, where daily she fed eighty Jewish poor at her table. She used her wealth to help Jews escape Europe and to prosper in their business enterprises. She was probably the most powerful and influential Jewish woman since biblical times.

Economics and an unwillingness to face exile induced Jews to become Marranos. This meant Marranos as a group were middle class; consequently, wherever they migrated, they brought their skills with them and quickly came to dominate in banking, trade, and finance. They had a large role in the Dutch East Indies and West Indies companies, and through them in the development of the New World. Trade in coral, sugar, tobacco, and gems was virtually monopolized by the Marranos. Because of the network of Marranos that developed throughout Europe, they were well situated to dominate international finance. Others became diplomats, writers, scientists, physicians, and leading actors and musicians, as well as explorers, such as Diego Texeira de Sampaio, who circumnavigated the globe.

Marranos paid a high price for the secret practice of their religion. In the three centuries of the Inquisition about 30,000 Marranos were killed and another 17,000 were burned in effigy. Possibly as many as 300,000 Marranos, under indictment from the Inquisition, chose to renounce Judaism. Marranos in their devotional book added a special prayer for their brethren burned at the stake.

With the 18th century and the Enlightenment, Marranos could practice Judaism openly, and with the end of the Inquisition in the early 19th century, Marranos were thought to have all returned to Judaism or died out. However, in 1917 Samuel Schwarz, a Polish-Jewish mining engineer who had settled in Lisbon, traveled to Belmonte, a remote area near the Spanish border. There he found a community that practiced Jewish rituals; further investigation revealed that they were Marranos. Once discovered, and partially with the help of Schwarz, they began to espouse Judaism again. More recently such communities have come to light in the southwestern United States.

47

THE JEWS OF MEDIEVAL GERMANY

The first major Jewish settlements in Germany took place in the 10th century. Jews prospered in the city of Worms and other trading locales along the Rhine. They were merchants, and ran the money-lending and commerce of the country. Local rulers protected them as a major economic tax base, despite the antisemitic leanings of the population. With the rise of guilds, who opposed the nobility, the Jews came under increasing pressure. The fifty years from 1298 to 1348 saw the worst persecutions, in which hundreds of thousands of Jews were massacred. Despite the persecutions, the Jews of Germany survived and prospered, although in the 15th and 16th centuries many began to migrate to Poland and Lithuania, where there was greater toleration, as well as economic opportunities.

In 1965 the Roman Catholic church declared that the child Simon, who had been canonized in 1582, was no longer beatified. In turn, rabbis lifted the ban on Jewish settlement in Trent. The story of Simon began in 1475 in Trent, now in northern Italy, but which was then settled by Germans. In that year the fanatical Franciscan Bernardino da Feltre, in his Lenten sermons, preached against the Jews. When he got little response from the citizens, he shouted that come Easter Sunday they would find the truth in his words. A week before Easter, Simon, a two-year-old, was playing along the Adige River and fell in. When his parents realized that he had disappeared, they searched the neighborhood. Bernardino da Feltre immediately charged that the Jews had killed the child for his blood. Two days later Simon's body was discovered by the riverbank near the home of the leader of the Jewish community. The body was taken to the church, and the bishop immediately charged that the Jews had killed the boy. A Jewish apostate announced that the Jews were using Christian blood for their rites. Seventeen Jews were seized; after being tortured for fifteen straight days, they confessed. The Jew near whose house the body had been found repudiated his confession after the torture stopped, but to no avail. Thirteen of the Jews were burned at the stake, and the remaining four accepted baptism. A papal inquiry in 1476 investigated and validated the legality of the trial. Simon, however, had to wait a hundred years before he was canonized.

The story of Simon is indicative of the precarious existence the Jews of Germany have always led. When in this century Hitler systematically attempted genocide against the Jews of Germany and Europe, he followed a German tradition that went back 650 years.

While some Jews came with the Romans, the earliest continuous settlements along the Rhine began in the 10th century when Jews came as traders to such cities as Cologne, Mainz, and Worms. Jews were prosperous as merchants and moneylenders. The first widespread destruction of German Jews occurred during the First Crusade (1096) in the Rhine valley. By the 13th century Jews were mostly engaged in banking and money-lending. They were doubly outsiders in Germany, first because of the tribal and state concepts of many German regions, who would not accept outsiders, then because the condemnation and disapproval of the Church increased the hostile attitudes of the populace toward them. Yet they were tolerated because of their economic importance. In 1236 Emperor Frederick II declared that all the Jews of Germany were *Servi camerae nostrae* ("Servants of our Treasury").

By the end of the 13th century the Jewish population of Germany had grown in number and prosperity. But in 1298 disaster struck. The Jews of Roetingen were accused of taking the host, a consecrated wafer, and pounding it with mortar and pestle until blood flowed from it. A leading nobleman of Roetingen, named Rindfleisch, gathered a mob and rounded up the entire Jewish community, then burned them at the stake. With the taste of Jewish blood in his mouth, Rindfleisch led his mob from town to town throughout southern Germany and Austria, burning Jews wherever he could find them. In July the Jewish community of Würzburg was massacred. On August 1 the Jews of Nuremberg, who had held out in the castle there, were captured and executed. All of the Jewish communities of Bavaria were destroyed and massacred except those in Ratisbon and Augsburg. When the rampage was done, 140 Jewish communities had been annihilated and perhaps as many as 100,000 Jews murdered.

By the 14th century, despite the destruction of a large percentage of the Jewish population, Jews began again to rebuild. While persecutions in Germany were widespread, Jews managed to survive and prosper for two reasons. First, Germany at this period consisted of many quasi-independent towns and cities. Hence, when Jews were persecuted in one area, they simply moved to another nearby one. Second, much of the banking and finance of the economy depended on the Jews. As long as they were an integral part of the economics of the towns, and a large share of the tax base, they were needed and tolerated.

In 1348 the Black Death swept across Europe. Bodies lay unburied in the streets. Husbands deserted wives, parents their children. People fled in vain, and the bubonic plague followed. There was no place to hide. When the angel of death had finished his journey over Europe, 30 to 50 percent of the population lay dead. Since public baths had been closed around 1000 C.E., during the

late Middle Ages, Christians did not bathe at all. However, Jews regularly ritu-
ally washed and bathed, and their abodes were slightly cleaner than their Christian neighbors'. Consequently, when the rat and the flea brought the Black
Death, Jews, with better hygiene, suffered less severely than their neighbors.
When the townspeople saw this, their antisemitism raged, and they began to
accuse the Jews of poisoning the wells to spread the plague. Moreover, in many
of the towns of Germany, guilds had developed, and with them an increase of
power of the towns against the nobility. The nobility were strengthened by their
financial dealings with the Jews. Hence, the guilds were especially hostile to
the Jews, and often became the leaders in persecution. While the massacres of
the Crusades and other periods were sporadic and unorganized, the massacres
of 1348 and 1349 were organized and led by the town councils. The massacre
began in northern Spain in the summer of 1348. It spread to Switzerland, Bavaria, and in January 1349 along the Rhine, then to Magdeburg and Berlin,
and finally to Nuremberg.

Flagellants, called this because they whipped or flagellated themselves, incited the populace to kill the Jews. These people, convinced that by piety and
self-inflicted whipping they could purify themselves and avert the plague, went
from town to town, calling on people to repent and join them in self-flagellation.
Often the Flagellants, as they applied the whips to their own bodies, cried out
that the populace should kill the Jews. Sixty large communities and 150 small
ones were destroyed. The destruction of Jews only abated when the rulers saw
that their revenues and tax base were being destroyed, since Jews in many places
often contributed as much as 10 percent of the tax revenue.

Despite the persecutions in the 14th century, the Jews of Germany survived,
although with diminished numbers. Scholarship continued, although reduced
in scale. Religious poetry and works on Jewish law were written, and the study
of the Torah continued.

By the 15th century the conditions of Jews began to improve. They adopted
other professions than money-lending, becoming wine merchants and small
traders, for example. Jews also became middlemen between large agricultural
producers, such as monasteries, and the cities. They also became wholesalers,
buying up large quantities of goods and selling them to small merchants and
manufacturers.

With the upheaval in Germany, many Jews began to settle in Poland and
Lithuania, where political conditions were better. They brought with them the
German dialect they spoke, Yiddish, a mixture of German and Hebrew. In the
17th century the center of European Jewry shifted to this area, where Jews could
find freedom, toleration, and prosperity.

48

HEBREW PRINTING

Hebrew printing paralleled the development of printing in Europe. It caused the same explosion in learning in the religious sphere and ensured the preservation of Hebrew religious works. Hebrew printing grew faster than secular printing because of the great demand for Hebrew books by Jews. They wanted books and could afford to pay for them. The center of the Hebrew printing presses was Italy in the 16th century, particularly the Soncino Press; in the 17th century it moved to Amsterdam under the Marrano Manasseh ben Israel.

Johannes Gutenberg had a dream: to re-create by mechanical means the medieval liturgical manuscripts and to reproduce the Bible. He started life as a goldsmith and because of the high cost of books, saw the potential of printing as a means of spreading the word of God and of making some money. In 1455 he printed 150 copies of the Bible and began a new world for gentile and Jew alike. Were he alive today, he would be astounded by the billions of books printed by his method, which was used until the 20th century. The best-seller of all time is the Bible.

Jews were driven by the same motives as Gutenberg: to spread the word of God and to make money at the same time. Because reading was so important for Jews—to practice their religion, all Jewish men were required to read from the Torah—literacy among Jews was considerably higher than among non-Jews. Furthermore, Jews as a whole were richer than the general population because many of them were engaged in banking, trade, and commerce and therefore had the money to spend on books. Jewish printers saw the new books as a golden opportunity to enrich themselves and aid their brethren. At the same time, gentile printers realized that Jews made the best customers for books, and many of them started printing books in Hebrew.

Most Jews hailed this new invention as "the crown of all science" and a "divine or sacred craft." Now the prophecy of Isaiah—"Earth shall be full of the knowledge of the Lord"—would be fulfilled. But Hebrew copyists regarded this new invention as the "work of the devil" since they feared for their livelihood. The copyists were not driven out of business, however, since the ritual scrolls of the Torah for use in the synagogue continued to be done by hand, as they are to this day.

Printing revolutionized Jewish cultural and religious life. Dictionaries and grammars became easily available, as did commentaries on the Bible and Talmud. Now the Talmud was more accessible and the tools were available for study by individuals. Prayerbooks were now widely printed and tended to standardize local custom. While in the Christian world the development of printing encouraged the development of Protestantism, in the Jewish world it reinforced existing trends and spread Jewish literacy.

The two most famous of Hebrew printers were the Soncinos in the 16th century and Manasseh ben Israel in the 17th. Hebrew printing began in Italy, not in Germany, since in Germany Jews were not permitted to join the guilds that controlled the new invention. Only when German printers settled in Italy did Jews begin to learn the secret of this new invention. The first Hebrew book was published in 1469, and over the next thirty years at least twenty-two Hebrew presses sprang up in Italy and Spain. The greatest of these Italian presses was Soncino. Samuel and Simon Soncino left Germany for Italy and settled in the town of Soncino near Cremona, from which they took their name. Samuel's son, Israel Nathan, like so many other Jews, became a physician. But Israel became interested in this new invention of printing, and with his son Joshua, Solomon set up a Hebrew printing press that produced its first book, the talmudic tractate *Berakhot*. In 1488 Soncino issued the first printed edition of the Hebrew Bible. More than forty works were printed by Joshua.

Joshua had no sons to succeed him in the family business, so the control of the press fell to his nephew, Gershom ben Moses, probably the finest Hebrew printer of all time. Gershom had a difficult career. Gershom printed books not only in Hebrew but also in Greek, Latin, and Italian. He thus came into competition with Italian printers. We find his books printed in many Italian towns, including Brescia, Barco, Rimini, and Ancona. Gershom was the first to use woodcuts and the first to print secular Hebrew literature. Following the example of the Venetian publisher Aldus, Gershom printed small pocket-sized books, convenient for travel and transportation—equivalent to the first paperbacks. Whether because of economic reasons or harassment by the authorities, Gershom left Italy first for Salonika, then Istanbul (1530), where he continued publishing.

Manasseh ben Israel (1604–1657) was baptized in the Catholic church as Manoel Dias Soeiro. But when Manasseh was still a young boy, the Inquisition discovered that his family were Marranos. His father, Gaspar Nuñez, was condemned to be burned at the stake, but at the last moment, claimed he would be a true Christian. At the first opportunity, Gaspar took his family and fled to Amsterdam, where they revealed themselves as Jews. Manasseh was a child prodigy and excelled in religious studies. He wrote his first book on Hebrew grammar when he was only seventeen, and at eighteen became the preacher at the Neveh Shalom congregation. When he was twenty-two, he founded the first Hebrew press in Amsterdam. He continued to write books in Hebrew, Spanish, Portuguese, and Latin for the rest of his life.

Manasseh wrote on theology and codes of Jewish law for Marranos returning to Judaism. He was influential in the non-Jewish community, and even befriended Rembrandt, who lived across the street from him. Rembrandt painted his portrait and did an etching of him; in turn, Manasseh advised Rembrandt on Jewish and Hebrew matters in his paintings. One of Manasseh's works, *Piedra Gloriosa*, contained engravings by Rembrandt.

Although he became the leading Hebrew publisher of his day, and his press surpassed the presses of Italy and became the standard for European Hebrew publishing, Manasseh did not make much money from this business. As a result, he contemplated settling in Brazil in 1650, but was distracted by a new cause: he became the spokesman for Jews who were seeking readmittance to England. After prolonged negotiations, in 1655 he met with Oliver Cromwell. Although his petition to readmit Jews was not formally accepted, shortly afterwards Jews were allowed to build a synagogue and establish a cemetery. Manasseh died in 1657, having had a successful career as publisher, writer, theologian, Jewish statesman, and defender of Judaism to the gentiles.

49

MARTIN LUTHER AND THE JEWS

Martin Luther (1483–1546), one of the founders of Protestantism, began his career as a friend of the Jews, and ended it demanding their persecution and expulsion. Luther, an Augustinian monk, revolted from the Catholic church and founded Lutheranism, which became the dominant religion in Germany. The emergence of Protestantism was a positive development for the Jews, since the religious diversity created by it gradually led to toleration for Judaism in Europe.

Martin Luther nailed his Ninety-five Theses against indulgences to the door of the castle church at Wittenberg, thus declaring theological war against the pope and Catholicism. He tried to enlist the Jews in his new Protestant movement, but to no avail. When Julius Streicher, the head of Nazi propaganda, stood trial for war crimes at Nuremberg at the end of World War II, he maintained that he had done and said nothing worse regarding the Jews than had Martin Luther. When the Nazis rampaged through Germany on *Kristallnacht* on November 9–10, 1938 (see nutshell #84), pillaging and burning Jewish synagogues and stores, they proclaimed that this deed was a birthday present for Martin Luther, born on November 10.

Like Mohammed in the 7th century, Martin Luther saw that he was starting a new movement, and he too saw the Jews as potential converts to his cause. When the Jews refused to follow Mohammed, he turned against them. The same happened with Martin Luther.

In 1523 Luther published *Jesus Christ Was a Jew by Birth*. In this work Luther defended himself against charges of Judaizing tendencies, but more important, presented arguments to persuade Jews to convert, and at the same time called for kindly treatment of Jews:

> For our fools—the popes, the bishops, the sophists and the monks—these coarse donkey-heads, have hitherto treated the Jews in such a way that any man who is a good Christian could well turn into a Jew. And if I were a Jew and saw such stupid rascals as these leading the Christian faith and giving instruction in it, I would sooner be turned into a swine than a Christian. For they have treated the

Jews as though they were curs. . . . They continue to abuse them and take away their money even after they have baptized them.

When Jews refused to convert and follow Luther, the fury that he had expressed against the Catholic church was then turned against the Jews. He wrote in *About the Jews and Their Lies* in 1543:

> What should we Christians do with the rejected and accursed people the Jews . . . first that we burn their synagogues with fire; and what cannot be burnt shall be buried in dirt so that no one may ever be able to see a stone or cinder of it . . . secondly . . . uproot and destroy their houses . . . thirdly it is necessary that all their prayerbooks and their books of the Talmud shall be taken from them . . . fourthly that their Rabbis shall be forbidden on pain of . . . death to teach . . . fifth that the Jews shall be absolutely forbidden to move on the roads . . . sixth that they shall be forbidden their usurious transactions and all their ready money and . . . belongings shall be taken from them. Seventh that the young and healthy Jews and Jewesses shall be given mallets, hoes . . . and shall be required to earn their bread by the sweat of their noses. . . . Let us therefore use the simple wisdom of other peoples like those of France, Spain and Bohemia . . . and expel them from the land forever.

Luther put his antisemitic views into practice. He played a major role in the Jewish expulsion from Saxony in 1537, and in the 1540s influenced many German towns to drive out their Jews.

Although he became an antisemite, Luther loved the Hebrew Bible and encouraged the study of the Hebrew language and texts. He did this for theological reasons, since he wanted to bring the Bible into the hands of everyone. He began with a translation of the New Testament from Greek into German. This translation had a great impact on the development of Protestantism. Printing began in Germany in 1455 with Gutenberg's publication of the Bible in Latin (see nutshell #48). By 1522, when Luther's New Testament appeared, books had become widespread. Although his was not the first translation (there were fourteen other published versions), his became the most popular. Theologians of the Church, such as Erasmus, and the hierarchy opposed a literate laity who could read the sacred texts without restriction. They feared that such unrestricted access would lead to questioning of the authority of the Church, as indeed it did. Luther used the vehicle of a translation of the Bible to spread his Protestant message. A dozen years after his New Testament appeared, his translation of the Old Testament from the Hebrew was published. His interest in Hebrew encouraged many Protestant scholars to study the language, despite their antisemitism.

While Luther himself became rabidly antisemitic, many of his circle did not. Despite his teachings, the mass hatred of Jews, and the religious wars in Ger-

many, there were few anti-Jewish riots during that period. Luther and his followers were more concerned with defending themselves against the Roman
Catholic church and establishing their own independence and survival.

In the mid-16th century the Catholic church tried to stem the tide of Protestantism with the Counter-Reformation, which set out to suppress all heretics.
Jews were harshly treated, along with Protestants. Hebrew books were burned,
and in many places in Italy Jews were expelled from communities where they
had lived since Roman times.

Luther and Lutheranism set a basis for much of the antisemitism that followed. But the development of Protestantism was a positive event for Jews.
After the excesses of the Counter-Reformation Jews became more tolerated in
both Protestant and Catholic countries, as Catholics and Protestants turned their
energies to battling one another instead of Jews.

50

THE JEWS OF AMSTERDAM

Jews first settled in Amsterdam and the Netherlands in the early 16th century. The earliest immigrants were Marranos, who sought freedom from the Inquisition and economic opportunities. Most prominent among these 16th-century Marranos was the house of Nasi. When the Netherlands gained its independence from Spain in 1579, the immigration of Jews increased. Amsterdam was to become a center of Jewish commercial and intellectual life in Europe, particularly in the 17th century. It included Manasseh ben Israel, the most prominent of Hebrew printers, as well as the philosopher Baruch Spinoza.

Four centuries before Anne Frank and her family fled to Amsterdam as a refuge from Nazi Germany, the city had welcomed other Jewish refugees. The first influx of Jews into Amsterdam were the Marranos, who were granted the right to settle in the Netherlands in 1536. Although the Netherlands was under the rule of Spain, Marranos from Spain and Portugal found that the hand of the Inquisition was less strong there. Amsterdam was becoming a center of trade and commerce, and the economic opportunities were another inducement for Jews to immigrate. The Marrano community found that little attention was paid to their religious beliefs. Charles V, king of Spain, however, introduced the Inquisition into the Netherlands, which forced all Jews who openly professed their religion to leave the region. But the Marranos continued with their secret practices. Once the northern provinces declared their independence from Spain in 1579, a new influx of Marranos came into Amsterdam.

The most important Marrano family in the Netherlands in the 16th century was the Mendes clan, the house of Nasi, who settled in Antwerp. They exerted an enormous influence on Jewish life not only in the Netherlands, but in Europe and the Ottoman Empire. The family was headed by two brothers, Diogo Mendes and Francisco. Beginning with businesses in spices and gems, the brothers soon prospered. On the death of Francisco, Diogo was joined in Antwerp by his sister-in-law, Beatriz de Luna (see nutshell #46). Beatriz was accompanied by her nephew, João Miguez, who came to be known as Joseph Nasi.

The incredible career of Joseph Nasi exemplifies the Marrano role in the Netherlands. He became a student at the University of Louvain, then joined the banking firm of Diogo Mendes. A friend of royalty, he was the jousting partner of the crown prince Maximilian, the nephew of Charles V, the king of Spain and the Netherlands. When Beatriz left the Netherlands for Italy in 1544, Miguez stayed behind to settle the vast financial affairs of the family. As so many rulers had in the past, Charles V saw Beatriz's flight and her subsequent declaration in Italy that she was a Jew as an opportunity to seize the fortune of the Mendes family. Although a large percentage of the assets had been disbursed in anticipation of Beatriz's return to Judaism and possible confiscation, a large fortune still remained. Despite Joseph Nasi's fine negotiating skills and machinations, he was unable to prevent the king from confiscating what was left. He fled in 1547 and settled in France, where he managed to enter the circle of King Francis I. Next he went to Italy, where he tried to persuade the Venetian government to give one of its islands as a refuge for the Marranos. Finally, in 1554 Miguez joined his aunt in Constantinople. Like her, he declared himself a Jew and took on a Jewish name, Joseph Nasi. Like many Marranos, he had not been circumcised. But he eagerly submitted himself to this painful operation to declare his Judaism. He then married his cousin, Reyna, Beatriz's daughter. His ties with Marranos in the Netherlands allowed him to continue and expand commerce between the East and the Netherlands, particularly with the spice trade.

Joseph Nasi quickly rose to prominence in Constantinople, which was to have a profound effect on the Netherlands. Suleiman the Magnificent, the sultan of the Ottoman Empire, warmly welcomed Beatriz de Luna and her family. Soon after Joseph arrived in Constantinople, he found he was often at court and quickly became a trusted adviser. His influence increased even more after the death of Suleiman the Magnificent in 1566. In the ensuing struggle between the sons of Suleiman, Joseph supported and helped Selim, who emerged as sultan. Selim appointed him *muterferik* ("gentleman of the imperial retinue") and made him the duke of Naxos. Joseph's political and economic ties with Europe led to his development of a network of agents, both economic and political, whom he could call upon, as well as friends at royal courts in Spain, France, and Italy. This made him an ideal adviser on foreign affairs for the Ottoman Empire. His influence increased daily. In 1562 he was responsible for negotiating a peace treaty between Poland and Turkey.

In 1569 Joseph Nasi played a decisive influence in the affairs of the Jews of the Netherlands and the country where he had spent his youth. He encouraged the Netherlands to revolt from Spain, and even promised the support of the Ottoman Empire in such an endeavor in a letter, which was read in a Calvinist meeting in Amsterdam. When the Netherlands successfully revolted from Spain, the encouragement and support of Joseph Nasi was remembered. For the next decade, until his death in 1579, Joseph wielded his power for the benefit of Jews in Europe and in the Ottoman Empire. He even became involved in the rebuilding of Tiberias in Israel, of which he became lord until his death. Throughout the Netherlands Jews prospered because of the commercial and trading ties that had been the basis of the Mendes family empire, and were only enhanced when Joseph settled in Constantinople.

With the independence of the Netherlands from Spain, toleration increased. The first public Jewish service in Amsterdam was held in 1596. On Yom Kippur of that year sixteen people gathered together in a private house to worship. When the local Protestants heard people praying, they thought it was Catholics and attacked them. But the leader of the Jews, Jacob Tirado, was able to communicate in Latin, and told the city fathers that they were Jews who were fleeing from the Inquisition. He persuaded them that they could contribute much to the city since they were well-to-do traders and merchants. His eloquence was persuasive, and the Jews were allowed to settle and build a small synagogue, which was called Beth Jacob (House of Jacob) in honor of Jacob Tirado.

Once Marranos and other Jews learned of the toleration in Amsterdam, they came in increasing numbers. A dozen years later, in 1608, another synagogue, Neveh Shalom, was founded by wealthy Marranos who were now practicing Judaism openly. By 1675 they built the magnificent Portuguese Synagogue, where Jews still worship to this day. The Jews of Spain and Portugal, called Sephardic Jews, were joined in Amsterdam by Jews from Germany, northern France, and the Slavonic countries, known as Ashkenazic Jews. In 1635 the first Ashkenazic synagogue was formed.

In the 17th century Amsterdam became an intellectual center of Jewish learning. Hebrew writers and poets flourished here. The center of Jewish publishing, both by Ashkenazic and Sephardic Jews, was located here. Manasseh ben Israel (see nutshell #48), Joseph Athias, and others published their books, which were sold throughout the Spanish-speaking Diaspora, in Eastern Europe, and even in Asia. The great philosopher Baruch Spinoza (see nutshell #55) was a product of this rich intellectual Jewish center.

The 17th century saw Jews engaged in modern capitalist activities. They invested in foreign trade in Spain, England, Italy, Africa, India, and the East and West Indies. The tobacco industry, as well as diamonds and printing, was almost entirely Jewish. The East India Company had 25 percent of its stock owned by Jews, and Jews became very active on the stock exchange. They played an important role in the prosperity of Amsterdam and contributed to its prominence in the world of commerce as long as they lived there. Amsterdam and the Netherlands opened its doors to Jewish refugees. The refugees found freedom and toleration, and in turn made major contributions to the economic and intellectual life of their adopted home.

51

ISAAC ABRABANEL

When the Jews were expelled from Spain in 1492, many of them settled in Italy, where they found refuge with the Jewish community that had existed there since Roman times. Most prominent among these refugees was Isaac Abrabanel (1437–1508), a statesman, entrepreneur, banker, biblical scholar, and philosopher. Since Italy was fragmented into many states, no uniform policy of persecution existed, and when one state persecuted its Jews, they simply moved to another region. Abrabanel and his family followed this pattern, settling first in Naples, then Ferrara and Venice. Abrabanel died in Venice in 1508 and left his mark on Jewish thought and on the lives of his fellow Jews.

Once King Ferdinand and Queen Isabella defeated the kingdom of Granada, the last Muslim state in Spain, they expelled all Muslims and Jews. Ironically, the man who financed their war against Granada, and who loaned them 1.5 million gold ducats, was a Jew, Isaac ben Judah Abrabanel. When the edict of expulsion was signed on March 31, 1492, Abrabanel went to the monarchs and tried to persuade them to revoke the order. One story, probably apocryphal, relates that when Abrabanel offered vast sums of money to the king and queen to revoke the decree, Torquemada, the head of the Inquisition (see nutshell #45), threw his cross on the floor in front of them and cried out, "Will you betray our Lord Jesus for thirty thousand dinars, as Judas did for thirty pieces of silver?" The monarchs tried to persuade Abrabanel to accept Christianity and to remain in Spain, but he refused. However, they did permit Abrabanel to take a thousand gold ducats with him when he went into exile.

Spain's loss of its productive, educated, and commercially sophisticated Jewish population was the gain of the countries to which they migrated, particularly Italy and Constantinople. Abrabanel chose Italy.

Abrabanel had known exile before. Born in Portugal, he was the son of Judah Abrabanel, who was engaged in commerce and state finance. On his father's death, he succeeded him as treasurer of King Alfonso V of Portugal. He and his family were immensely wealthy. When in 1480 King Alfonso needed funds, 12 million reals were raised from both Jews and Christians. Abrabanel personally contributed over a million reals. Abrabanel prospered until the death of Alfonso, who was replaced by João II. When a group of nobles rebelled against the new king, Abrabanel was suspected of complicity. He fled to Spain and joined the service of King Ferdinand and Queen Isabella in 1484. Meanwhile, the king of Portugal sentenced him to death in absentia.

Exiled in 1492, like so many of his fellow Jews, he made his way to Italy. Although the pope resided in Italy, which was the center of Catholicism, the country was politically fragmented into many independent states. This fragmentation prevented the Inquisition from gaining a strong foothold. Once in Italy, Abrabanel was warmly welcomed by Ferrante I, king of Naples, who made him an adviser and financier. Two years later the French sacked Naples, and Abrabanel fled with the royal family to Messina, where the king died in 1495. Abrabanel next fled to Corfu in Greece, and in 1496 was able to return to Naples. In 1503 his son Joseph persuaded him to settle in Venice, where he died in 1508.

If the career of Abrabanel were only of Jewish statesman, merchant, banker, and entrepreneur, it would have been more than enough accomplishments for two lifetimes. But like so many of Spain's Jews, he was schooled in the Talmud, the Bible, and philosophy. He was among the most important philosophers and biblical exegetes of his time, and his works are consulted to this day. Because of the heavy influence of Christianity among the Jewish community of Spain, Abrabanel chose to study Christian theology as well as Jewish. A man of wide interests, he began to read the works of non-Jewish Renaissance thinkers, and was influenced by the new Renaissance ideas of humanism. He was the first Jewish philosopher to introduce these ideas into Judaism.

His works, which consumed his time and energy throughout his life, can be divided into two main categories: biblical exegesis and philosophy. He wrote commentaries on many of the prophets, as well as a major commentary on the Pentateuch. He also wrote a series of three books designed to convince the Jews of Spain that the messiah was coming in their days. These books were combined under one title, *Tower of Salvation* (*Migdal Yeshuot*). In his commentaries he compared the social structure of biblical society with the present society. He also concerned himself with Christian exegeses, and even borrowed from them, if he thought the interpretations were correct. Since some of his commentaries accepted Christian exegeses, they were welcomed by Christians. Some of his works were translated into Latin and thereby influenced Christian biblical study.

As a philosopher, Abrabanel emphasized prophecy, history, politics, and eschatology. Influenced by Aristotle and Maimonides (see nutshell #40), he viewed the Bible as the basis for the history of the universe and man. He maintained that God did not give control of the universe to nature, but that nature acts as an intermediary between man and God. He also saw the state as necessary after the expulsion of Adam and Eve from the Garden of Eden. According to Abrabanel, the ideal state serves both the spiritual and the political needs of the people and should have two legal systems, the civil and the religious. He saw monarchy as a curse, but a limited necessity outside Eden. Abrabanel argued against the Christian interpretation of scriptures that Jesus was the messiah, and speculated that the messiah would come in the present time. His writings and influence led to a strong messianic movement among Jews in the 16th and 17th centuries.

The family of Abrabanel, now settled in Italy, played a prominent part in the life of 16th-century Italy. When Isaac settled in Naples, his two brothers, Jacob and Joseph, accompanied him. Isaac's children were almost as successful as their father. His son Judah, known as Leone Ebreo, became a distinguished philosopher. Joseph, another son, was a famous physician, practicing in Ferrara and later Venice. The third son, Samuel, was a major financier and leader of the Naples community. Naples expelled all its Jews in 1540, and many went to Ferrara, which benefited from the presence of the Abrabanels. Another member of the family became the private banker of Cosimo de' Medici.

The family of the Abrabanels, along with many other Spanish Jews, gave a tremendous stimulus to the Italian Jewish community, which had lived in Italy continuously since Roman times. They also brought wealth, commerce, banking, and medical skills to Italy, which profited tremendously from their presence. The Spanish exiled some of their most productive citizens, who brought that productivity to wherever they settled.

52

THE JEWS OF VENICE
AND THE FIRST GHETTO

Jews settled in Venice in the 11th century, and despite some brief expulsions in the 16th century, have lived there continuously to the present day. The expulsion of Jews from Spain and Portugal brought a great influx of new settlers and increased population and prosperity. The Renaissance brought the advent of printing, and Venice became a center for Latin, Greek, Italian, and Hebrew publishing. The Renaissance also brought with it new ideas in philosophy and religion, including Protestantism. The reaction to Protestantism was the Counter-Reformation, in which all non-Catholics were attacked. Jews were confined to ghettos throughout Italy. Despite these restrictions, Jewish life in Venice was prosperous and intellectually stimulating. By the 17th century the Jewish population there had grown to 3 percent of the population.

Venice was a center of Jewish economic and cultural life in the 16th and 17th centuries. Philosophers, musicians, Hebrew printers, Talmud scholars, merchants, and even female poets flourished there. Deborah Ascarelli in the late 16th century translated poems and hymns from Hebrew into Italian. Sarah Copia Sullam in the 17th century composed Italian poetry. But perhaps the most colorful of all of the Jewish inhabitants of Venice was Leone Modena (Judah), a gambler, rabbi, actor, alchemist, philosopher, and writer.

Leone was born in Venice in 1570, but was brought up in Ferrara. He was a child prodigy, at least according to his autobiography. At the age of two and a half he was publicly reading the Torah in synagogue, and at the age of three translating the Pentateuch into Italian. When he was twelve he translated the famous poem of Ariosto, *Orlando Furioso*, into Hebrew verse. One of his most clever works, written when he was thirteen, was a poem, whose words made sense as both Italian and Hebrew. He was equally outstanding in Jewish law and the Talmud, and at the age of twenty-two was appointed preacher and teacher in Venice. His sermons were so entertaining and insightful that Jews and non-Jews alike came to hear him preach. His skill at versification led him into a second profession, as a writer of epitaphs. Most of the tombstones of the Jewish cemetery at Venice of the late 16th century were written by him.

But like many great figures, Leone had a tragic flaw. His was a love of gambling. Not only was he a compulsive gambler, but he was also a bad one. He did nothing but lose. Because of his gambling, he associated himself with the most disreputable elements of Venice, and he dragged his sons into the same bad company. Because he was always in debt, he worked like a fiend to support his addiction.

Fortunately for us, Leone wrote an autobiography, the first of its kind to portray the real life of the writer. In it, he recounts that he pursued twenty-six occupations to pay his debts. These included brokering marriages, translating, writing amulets, ghost writing sermons, and acting. He was also head of the Jewish music academy in Venice and wrote at least one play in Italian. Perhaps his least successful occupation was his attempt at alchemy. His experiments were a total failure, and the only concrete result was that he accidentally killed one of his sons by lead poisoning. A liberal interpreter of Jewish law, he defended the playing of ball games on the Sabbath, probably because he was an active participant. He was a major force in introducing music into the synagogue services, particularly the compositions of his friend, the great composer of Jewish and gentile liturgical music Salomone de Rossi. Naturally, he was ambivalent when it came to gambling. At times he wrote that it should be permissible, and at other times attacked it. Perhaps his greatest legacy was his contribution to Hebrew letters, his sermons, polemics, and works on the Talmud and the *Zohar*. While Leone regarded his life as a failure because he could never conquer his compulsive gambling, his literary achievements have given him a place in the history of Hebrew literature.

What sort of place was the Venice where Leone Modena lived? Jews had lived continuously in Italy since the 2nd century B.C.E., and in Venice at least since the 11th century. Venice was an important commercial center and had strong trading ties with Constantinople and the Byzantine Empire. When Constantinople was sacked in 1453 by the Turks, Venice and all of Italy benefited from the influx of scholars. By the beginning of the 16th century, the Turkish domains, called the Ottoman Empire, were conducting extensive trade with Venice and Italy. Influential in this trade were the Jews. When Spain expelled its Jews in 1492, and Portugal in 1497, Jews and Marranos in great numbers came to Venice, and to the Ottoman Empire. Many Jews, such as Beatriz de Luna and Joseph Nasi (see nutshells #46 and #50), who lived for a time in Venice and later rose to prominence in the Ottoman Empire, became the conduits for trading between the Ottoman Empire and Venice and Italy. Jews from Germany and the Levant also settled there. We find in the 16th century six great synagogues that reflect the origins of their members—the Spanish Synagogue, the Luzzatto Synagogue, the Synagogue of the Levant, the Italian Synagogue, the Canton Synagogue, and the Great German Synagogue. Today, the remaining community of Jews in Venice weekly alternate their Sabbath observances among these synagogues, in order that their sites not become just relics.

Despite the economic benefits Jews brought to Venice, the most restrictive of all anti-Jewish institutions, the ghetto, originated there and spread to all of Europe. In March 1516 the rulers of Venice declared that all Jews must live in a separate section of the city, known as the *ghetto* ("foundry") from the activities conducted there. The word *ghetto* came to be applied to any area that was restricted to Jews. This region of the city was particularly unhealthy and far from the center.

In 1555 Pope Paul IV, in the face of the spread of Protestantism, instituted harsh measures against all enemies of the Catholic church. In his papal bull *Cum nimis absurdum* he wrote that it was absurd for Christians to tolerate Jews, whom God had shunned and condemned for their sins. Using Venice as a model, he ordered that throughout the Papal States, Jews were to be restricted to the ghetto. Each ghetto was to be enclosed, and its gates were to be shut at night and on all Christian holy days. Jews could venture out of the ghetto during the day, but they had to wear a yellow hat to identify themselves. Ghettos rapidly spread beyond the Papal States to all Italy, and hence to many cities of Europe. In Italy the Vatican had jurisdiction over the ghettos until 1870, when papal control of Italy ceased. Not until then did the institution of the ghetto end in Italy.

53

KABBALISTS AT SAFED

The 16th-century community of kabbalists—Jewish mystics—in the northern Galilee town of Safed introduced a version of kabbalah that would prove historically significant. They also introduced a number of customs that have been accepted by nonmystic Jewish circles. A concept these kabbalists developed is helping shape American politics of the late 20th century.

In 1993, the small circle of readers of the American Jewish periodical *Tikkun* suddenly found the name of the publication and of its editor, Michael Lerner, getting wide coverage in the mass media. Bill and Hillary Rodham Clinton, it appeared, were committed to the periodical's "politics of meaning." While most of *Tikkun*'s readers were aware that the periodical's title was the Hebrew word for "repair" or "improvement," fewer knew of the historical context in which the term was elaborated. The concept of *tikkun* was popularized among a community of 16th-century Jewish mystics—kabbalists—based in Galilee.

Many of the exiles from Spain, including Marranos, made their way to the Middle East. A large number of them were attracted to the northern Galilee hill town of Safed, to which neither Islam nor Christianity laid claim as a holy site. Perhaps more important, because of its proximity to Syria's commercial centers, Safed was a good business location. The talmudic and kabbalistic scholars who chose Safed as their home nearly all engaged in trade, whether in textiles, clothing, spices, or grain. For the mystics, Safed had the additional attraction of being close to Meron, site of the tomb of Simeon ben Yohai, whom kabbalists venerated as the author of the *Zohar* (see nutshell #42). By 1522, Safed easily rivaled Jerusalem as a center for Jewish life.

The difficulties of adjusting to a new home at first absorbed the energies of the refugee community. But as time passed, they began to ask the central question posed by the expulsion: why, if the Jews were God's special people, was intense suffering seemingly their lot in life? The answer that was formulated in Safed would not only help make sense of Jewish suffering for the generation following the expulsion but would also affect Jewish life and thought down to our own times.

The formulator of the kabbalistic system that provided the answer was Isaac Luria (1534–1572). His interpretation of kabbalah would have an enormous impact on Jewish history. Luria is often called Ha'ARI, a name that is both an acronym and a pun: the acronym makes use of the initial letters of the Hebrew words *HaElohi Rabbi Itzhak*—the divine Rabbi Isaac; the pun is that *ari* is the Hebrew word for "lion." Like a lion's roar penetrating the silence of the jungle, Luria's interpretation of the links between cosmic and Jewish history reverberated far and wide.

Lurianic kabbalah, as his system is known, addresses three basic questions: (1) what accounts for the existence of evil? (2) does the exile of the Jews serve a purpose, or is it merely a punishment for their sins? and (3) are Jews only victims, or do they have a more positive role to play in the world? To answer these questions, Luria focused on what he saw as the overlap between Jewish history and the history of the universe.

Luria's starting point was the moment of creation itself. According to the *Zohar*, creation began when God sent forth a ray of light that became the *sefirot*, the emanations of divine light. For Luria, this view of creation was flawed: given that God was by definition infinite, there was no place that was not God. From what source, then, came the space that the universe occupies?

In order to solve this problem, Luria developed an older idea about creation that had been mostly overlooked until then. In order to create the universe, God first had to draw Himself back. Withdrawal was the first act of creation. Only after God's withdrawal was there room to radiate the divine light that formed the *sefirot*.

For Luria, each one of the *sefirot* is actually a vessel for light, intended to hold the divine rays. Only the first three *sefirot* proved worthy vessels, however; too much divine light struck the remaining *sefirot* all at once, shattering them.

The existence of evil in the world is the direct consequence of the shattering of the vessels. As the vessels shattered, sparks of divine light became trapped by the shards. As a result, since the very moment of creation, nothing in the universe has been where it belongs. Everything is in exile. Even part of God is in exile, since sparks of divine light are not in their intended place. To restore everything to its intended place in God's original plan, everything must be repaired.

According to Luria, that repair—or *tikkun*—is the purpose of human existence. Only part of the divine light that overran the vessels made its way back to its source. It is for human beings to complete the task of repair: to liberate the divine sparks that remain trapped in the shards, and by doing so not only to eliminate evil from the world but also to put God back together properly.

According to Lurianic kabbalah, Jews have a central role to play in the process of *tikkun*. By performing God's commandments, Jews speed up the redemption of the world. In fact, each Jew has a specific task to fulfill, a task that cannot be filled by anyone else. By performing that personal assignment, each Jew contributes to the perfection of the world. For Luria, the messiah will come only when the Jews have completed the process of *tikkun*. In other words, the messiah's coming will not redeem the Jews and the world but will simply confirm that the world is finally in accord with God's original intent.

It is not difficult to see why the generations immediately following the expulsion found the message of Lurianic kabbalah so heartening. Exile no longer seemed like a curse restricted to the Jews; the universe and even God Himself shared the state of exile with the Jewish people. In addition, Jewish exile had a constructive purpose: by performing God's commandments in all the lands of their dispersion, and thereby liberating divine sparks entrapped in the remotest corners, each Jew had a unique role to play in advancing the world's development.

In the years following Luria's death his version of kabbalah made its way throughout the Diaspora. Its effect on Jewish history in the short term is evident in the Shabbetai Zevi affair (see nutshell #58). But its effect on Jewish thought continues down to our own time. Twentieth-century Jewish thinkers like Martin Buber (1878–1965), Abraham Isaac Kook (1865–1935), and Abraham Joshua Heschel (1907–1972) all make use of imagery and concepts developed by Luria.

In addition, some of the customs of the mystics at Safed are practiced even in the least mystically inclined and most rationalistic communities to this day. For example, such typical Friday night customs as singing the hymn "*Lekhah Dodi*" and reciting Proverbs 31 ("A woman of valor who can find?") come from the mystics of Safed and were originally intended as references to the mystical marriage between God and the *Shekhinah*, God's Presence.

That 16th-century kabbalistic thought should be affecting 20th-century American politics may seem unlikely but appears to be a fact. Bill and Hillary Rodham Clinton, like other readers of *Tikkun* magazine, are hopeful that their political activity can help repair the world as we know it, to make it more like the world as God originally intended it.

54

JOSEPH CARO AND THE *SHULHAN ARUKH*

The Shulhan Arukh—*the guide to traditional observance for Jews around the world—was written in the 16th century by Spanish-born Rabbi Joseph Caro. The additions of Rabbi Moses Isserles of Poland made it acceptable to Jews everywhere.*

Among the truly strange facts of Jewish history is that the author of the most influential Jewish legal code believed that the words of a heavenly mentor (a *maggid*) came forth from his mouth. But Joseph ben Ephraim Caro (1488–1575), the author of the *Shulhan Arukh*, was—like others of his time—not only a talmudic scholar but also a mystic.

Born in Spain, Caro and his family fled to Portugal in 1492; five years later, when the Jews of Portugal faced the choice of conversion, death, or exile, the Caro family left for the Balkans. But that was not to be Caro's ultimate destination, however, for among the words of professional and personal advice the *maggid* imparted to Caro was the suggestion that he migrate to Israel. He heeded this voice and in 1535 moved to Safed.

Like other Jewish legal scholars before him, Caro worried that people might not know which opinions were authoritative because there were so many legal codes and treatises, often contradicting one another. To end the confusion, he undertook a major work, called *House of Joseph*, to probe every relevant Jewish law, starting with its talmudic source, examining all stages of its development, including all opposing views, and stating finally the conclusive decision.

Initially, Caro thought he would present his work as a commentary on Maimonides' *Mishneh Torah*, since all would agree that its author (see nutshell #40) was the best-known Jewish legal scholar of all time. Ultimately, however, Caro fashioned his work as a commentary on a later code. Caro's stated reason for rejecting his initial plan was that the author of the later code presented opposing views, which Maimonides did not. Caro possibly had two other reasons. First, Maimonides paid little attention to the views of Ashkenazic scholars—those not rooted in Spanish-Portuguese culture—while the author of the later code took account of Ashkenazic views. Second, while Maimonides considered every law, even those no longer applicable to Jewish life, such as the laws of kings, the author of the later code limited himself only to those laws currently relevant to Jewish life.

Although Caro believed that it was important for him to state openly what the authoritative law was, he was a modest man. (His *maggid*, after all, recommended modesty as a worthy trait even in the most distinguished scholar.) Rather than make decisive rulings on his own authority, he relied on the opinions not only of Maimonides and the author of the later code but also of a third, earlier, renowned legal scholar. In general, Caro accepted the ruling agreed to by two of three of his chosen predecessors. If he did otherwise, he modestly stated that if his ruling deviated from a community's established practice, its members should feel free to ignore his decision.

While *House of Joseph* is an extraordinary achievement, Caro realized that its strength was also its limitation: its encyclopedic nature meant that it was too long to use as a handy guide to Jewish law. As a result, Caro decided to write a condensed version to enable students, scholars, and judges alike to look up legal rulings with relative ease. The result was the *Shulhan Arukh* ("Prepared Table"), which appeared first in 1564. This book became the most authoritative summary of Jewish law down to the present day.

Earlier codes had circulated through the Jewish world relatively slowly, in the form of hand-copied manuscripts, with errors often creeping in as a result of numerous transcriptions. But Gutenberg had developed the movable press in the 15th century (see nutshell #48), and by the 16th century printing had spread throughout Europe. This new technology enabled important books, such as the *Shulhan Arukh*, to reach a wide audience immediately after their publication.

In general, Caro followed the legal principles and customs of the Sephardic, or Spanish-Portuguese, community. Although he had taken into account the laws and customs of the Ashkenazic world down to the 14th century, he had ignored all such developments over the succeeding two centuries. As a result, the *Shulhan Arukh* was not immediately embraced by the Ashkenazic community.

The Ashkenazic community's initial difficulty in accepting the *Shulhan Arukh*, however, was soon overcome by the work of a distinguished Polish rabbi, Moses Isserles (c. 1520–1572). Isserles had independently prepared his own commentary on the same 14th-century code as Caro, but following the law and customs of Ashkenazic Jewry. After he became acquainted with the *Shulhan Arukh*, Isserles prepared a summary of the differences between his rulings and those of Caro. He published this summary, along with a number of clarifications of the *Shulhan Arukh*, under the clever title *Mappah* ("Tablecloth").

Isserles' work, by spreading a cloth of Ashkenazic design over the table prepared according to the Sephardic arrangement, helped lead to the acceptance of the *Shulhan Arukh* as the guide par excellence to Jewish life from the end of the 16th century to this day.

55

THE EXCOMMUNICATION
OF SPINOZA

Baruch Spinoza (1632–1677), one of the major figures of Western intellectual history, was excommunicated for his views in 1656 by the Jewish community of Amsterdam.

Many people associate excommunication with the Roman Catholic church only. They are unaware of the fact that the threat of *herem*, or involuntary banishment from the community, was used as a penalty by Jewish leaders from the time of Ezra (see nutshell #15) on. The most famous case of excommunication in Jewish history, though hardly the only such case, was the *herem* pronounced on Baruch Spinoza on July 27, 1656.

To understand why the Jewish authorities in Amsterdam felt compelled to excommunicate the young Spinoza, who would become one of the great philosophers of modern times, it is necessary to examine his Marrano background and the nature of the Amsterdam Jewish community. Spinoza was the son of a former Marrano who settled in Amsterdam, where he returned to Judaism and became a successful merchant. Many Marranos, who continued to experience discrimination and oppression in Spain and Portugal (see nutshell #46), viewed the Netherlands as a particularly attractive destination. Toward the end of the 16th century, the Netherlands proclaimed itself independent of Spain. Although the Jews of the Netherlands were not citizens, they were permitted to worship as they chose and experienced a greater degree of political security and social acceptance than Jews elsewhere. This tolerance in a former Spanish ally was a spur to the Marranos to settle there. A Marrano community began to develop in Amsterdam, which was fast becoming the capital of European finance and trade. The new immigrants sought not only to play a role in the growing capitalist economy but also to establish themselves as Jews once again. By the end of the 17th century the Amsterdam Jewish community was the largest in western Europe.

That so many former Marranos were able to make the transition back to Judaism is a testimony to their commitment to the religion of their forebears.

That others could not make the transition, is also understandable. As Marranos, they had grown used to criticizing the Church's leaders, laws, and legends; they imagined that Judaism, unlike Catholicism, was accepting of freedom of thought. The Jewish community leadership they encountered in Amsterdam, however, was far from tolerant.

This intolerance, too, is understandable. After suffering greatly in order to retain Jewish identity, the leaders of the Jewish community may have felt horror at what they perceived as Jewish betrayal of the faith. Also, challenges to the underpinnings of Jewish religious tradition were also often challenges to Christian faith; Jewish leaders were afraid that Jews who expressed such views would discredit the entire Jewish community in the eyes of the Christian leadership and endanger the Jews' tolerated status.

In addition, the cultures in which they lived did not welcome challenges to religion. In Italy in 1630 Galileo was condemned by the Roman Catholic church for espousing the Copernican sun-centered view of the universe over the earth-centered Aristotelian view. (Only in 1992 did the pope officially reverse the condemnation.) And although the Dutch church had broken with Catholicism, its Calvinist orientation involved close scrutiny of congregants' habits and thoughts. No wonder that opinions and behavior that the Jewish leaders perceived as threatening were punished, with punishments ranging in severity from fines to excommunication.

Spinoza, excommunicated at the age of twenty-four, had been a star pupil in the Sephardic community school. Familiar with the works of such earlier Jewish rationalists as Maimonides (see nutshell #40), Spinoza developed aspects of their thought to extremes unacceptable to the community leadership. Although Spinoza had not yet published any works at the time of his excommunication, it was known that he questioned the holiness of the Torah. After Spinoza refused to keep his opinions to himself, he was excommunicated in the standard way: in the presence of the Torah, to the sound of the shofar, with the symbolic extinguishing of candles to symbolize his spiritual death and the pronouncement of several biblical curses.

While Spinoza's excommunication effectively banished him from the Jewish community, he went on to become a seminal figure in philosophy. Supporting himself as a polisher and grinder of lenses, he settled in The Hague, where he lived modestly, dying of tuberculosis at an early age.

During his lifetime he published one book, anonymously; several other works of his were published following his death. In them Spinoza expressed his views on the Bible, God, the role of religion, and the relationship of church and state.

His approach to the Bible makes him a precursor of modern biblical criticism. Denying that it was a God-given document, Spinoza insisted that the Bible be analyzed as one would any other ancient document, on its own terms. Close evaluation of the various biblical documents led him to the conclusion that Moses was only one of several biblical authors and that Ezra probably collected the earlier documents. Denying that biblical law was of value to anyone other than the ancient Israelites, Spinoza asserted that, in the aftermath of the defeat of the ancient Jewish state, the laws had no binding power. As for biblical stories, they were written for the uneducated, in order to inspire them to devotion. The miracles they describe could not have happened, because nothing can happen to negate the laws that govern the universe.

Spinoza's views on God are considered an extreme form of pantheism— the doctrine that God is not a personality, but that all aspects of the universe are manifestations of God. Although Spinoza denied accusations that he was an atheist, it is understandable why people thought him one. By denying that God is involved in human history or in dispensing divine reward and punishment, Spinoza effectively challenged traditional views of God. He also denied the possibility of free will; according to Spinoza, God predetermines everything.

As for religion, it serves one purpose only, according to Spinoza: its moralistic tales, supposed prophecies, promises of rewards, and threats of punishment can make the uneducated masses follow laws. But enlightened individuals have no need for organized religion as such; for them, the religion of reason is all that is necessary.

The last point leads Spinoza to his concept of the proper relation between church and state: as long as citizens obey the law, the state should not interfere with their beliefs or with their right to declare those beliefs.

That much of Spinoza's thought may not seem radical to us today should not obscure just how groundbreaking it was in its day. Spinoza was a pathbreaker on the road to modernity. Not only were later Jewish thinkers, notably Moses Mendelssohn (see nutshell #60), deeply influenced by Spinoza but also modern thought in general.

56

JEWS ARRIVE IN THE NEW WORLD

The first Jewish community in North America was formed in New Amsterdam, now New York, with the arrival in 1654 of a small number of refugees fleeing the Inquisition in Brazil.

American Jewish schoolchildren and their parents tend to know more about the arrival of the Pilgrims at Plymouth Rock in 1620 than about the arrival some thirty-four years later of the first Jews to what would become the United States. Who were those first Jews, and under what circumstances did they come here?

Although the long arm of the Inquisition reached across the ocean, and Jews were forbidden by law to live in Spanish and Portuguese territories, nonetheless, in the first half of the 16th century both Marranos and Jewish traders are known to have done business in parts of the New World claimed in the name of Ferdinand and Isabella. A Jew—Antonio de Montezinos, better known as Aaron Levi to his Jewish brethren in the community of Amsterdam—was the first to describe the Native Americans as members of one of the Lost Tribes of Israel (the ten tribes of Israel carried off into Assyrian captivity in 721 B.C.E.). Whether because the Inquisition was perceived to be less active there or for economic reasons, Marranos and Jews found the New World an appealing place to settle.

The Netherlands, as the world's foremost economic power, sought its own footholds in the New World, and in 1621 the Dutch West India Company was chartered for that purpose. In 1630 the Netherlands wrested control of the northern Brazilian province of Pernambuco from Brazil. Unlike Catholic Spain and Portugal, the Dutch West India Company practiced a policy of religious toleration. Consequently, many Marranos already living in Recife, Pernambuco's principal city, and in other minor centers, returned to open Jewish life. Some Jewish soldiers involved in the successful Dutch invasion of Brazil joined them in establishing a Jewish community, as did some Jewish traders from the Netherlands. In 1642 the Amsterdam Jewish community sent abroad one of its own to serve as the Western Hemisphere's first rabbi.

Despite its auspicious beginnings, the Dutch Jewish community in Brazil did not thrive. Thwarting the Dutch West India Company's policy of toleration, Calvinists and Catholics alike discriminated against the Jews, some of whom left for Amsterdam and others for homes elsewhere in the New World. By 1654, when the Portuguese retook Recife, the Jewish population of Dutch Brazil had declined from about 1,000 to 600. The flight of these Jews from the encroaching Inquisition led to the founding of Jewish communities elsewhere in the New World.

A small group of these refugees—four men, six women, and thirteen children—made their way in September 1654, aboard the French warship *Sainte Catherine*, to New Amsterdam, where at least two other Jews had preceded them. Shortly after their arrival, Governor Peter Stuyvesant wrote to his Dutch West India Company employers asking for permission to turn the newcomers away. Stuyvesant had no love for Jews, whom he considered "hateful enemies and blasphemers of the name of Christ." He felt that the Jews of Curaçao, where he had previously served as governor, had betrayed him by turning to trade despite their initial claims that they sought to be farmers. Stuyvesant argued at the same time that the present poverty of the twenty-three refugees from Recife would make them into a public burden and that their undoubted certain future success would undercut the profits of local merchants. His arguments were seconded not only by New Amsterdam's merchants but also by a local official of the Dutch Reformed church.

Among the influential shareholders of the Dutch West India Company, however, were a number of Jews. Together with others in the Amsterdam Jewish community, they lobbied the Dutch West India Company to ignore the pleas of Stuyvesant and his supporters in New Amsterdam. Their arguments not only included the fact that the Jews and Dutch had a common enemy in Spain and Portugal but also contained veiled economic threats. The Jewish lobby prevailed, and the company ruled that the refugees were to be granted permission to live, trade, and travel throughout the Dutch New World. Perhaps as a concession to Stuyvesant and the Dutch Reformed church, the Jews were granted the right only to a burial ground, not to a synagogue.

Confrontations between Stuyvesant and the New Amsterdam Jews over the granting of rights continued over the next decade. Using two tactics, the Jews succeeded in overcoming Stuyvesant's challenges: a series of petitions to the Dutch West India Company secured for them "burgher rights" to conduct retail and wholesale trade, as well as the rights to engage in the fur trade and to hold property; and a court action won them the right to serve in the militia to defend the settlement rather than paying a special tax.

These and other victories for religious tolerance aside, however, New Amsterdam never became a thriving Jewish center. It remained very much an outpost, a place where transients conducted business and then left. Competition from Britain, whose settlements lay to the north and south of New Amsterdam, began to seem insurmountable, and the Dutch West India Company's interest in its investment waned. The Jewish community there never exceeded fifty people. Although the Amsterdam Jewish community had initially nurtured hopes for a Jewish presence in the Dutch New World, lending a Torah scroll to their coreligionists in New Amsterdam, in 1663 the scroll made the return voyage home, back to Amsterdam. This symbolic end of Jewish New Amsterdam foreshadowed the demise of the Dutch colony itself. In 1664 New Amsterdam surrendered to the British.

Only one of the Recife refugees remained, in what was now New York, to take the oath of allegiance to Britain. Under British rule, Asher Levy (d. 1681) continued to stand up for the rights of Jews as he had successfully done under the Dutch. His prominence not only won him the privilege of serving on a jury but also enabled him to intercede with the court on behalf of a poor coreligionist.

Today the original Jewish cemetery can be found in Manhattan, on 11th Street between 5th and 6th Avenues, and New York City is home to about 2 million Jews.

57

THE CHMIELNICKI MASSACRES

In the Chmielnicki massacres of 1648–1649 tens of thousands of eastern European Jews were slaughtered. This catastrophe, one of the most devastating in all Jewish history, intensified Jewish hopes for a messianic deliverance in the 17th century.

Until the atrocities of the Holocaust eclipsed all previous disasters in Jewish history, the name *Chmielnicki* evoked for many Jews what the name *Hitler* evokes today.

The causes of the Chmielnicki massacres of 1648–1649, sometimes called the Cossack massacres, extend back some three centuries and were rooted in the social and economic structure of the region. Starting in about 1340, Lithuania and Poland gradually took control of the rich farming region of the Ukraine, with the Ukrainian peasants bound to the land as serfs. Attracted by the economic opportunities that the Ukraine's fertile lands presented, the Polish nobility carved out large estates worked by the local peasants.

Most Polish nobles, however, had neither the interest actually to administer the estates nor the capital and commercial expertise necessary to develop them. Many turned to Jews to run the estates on their behalf. In a typical arrangement, a Jew loaned a Polish landlord a sum of money, in exchange for which the Jew not only leased but also managed the property, paying a certain percentage of the profits to the nobleman. Leases had to be renegotiated from time to time, and each renewal generally meant a rise in the percentage the Jewish lessee had to turn over to the Polish landlord. In turn, the Jewish estate managers put increased pressure on the peasants to make the estate more productive.

Although this economic system prevailed throughout much of Poland, it was particularly resented in the Ukraine. Tensions were fueled not only by ethnic differences but also by religious ones. The Ukrainian peasants were Greek Orthodox, while their Polish landlords were Roman Catholics and the estate managers Jewish. As a result, in the 15th century many disgruntled peasants joined bands of independent soldiers known as Cossacks, from the Turkish word meaning "adventurer" or "guerrilla." The Polish government organized these Cossacks as a defensive force against the Tartars, which gave them some group cohesion and military power.

Jewish leaders were not unaware of the potentially explosive economic situation. For example, rabbis and other leaders at a meeting held in 1602 in Volhynia in the northwest Ukraine strongly urged Jewish lessees to lessen tensions by giving the peasants a day off each Jewish Sabbath and festival.

Contributing to the smoldering situation in 1638, the Polish legislative body replaced the traditional head of the Cossacks, elected by his fellows, with a commission of Polish noblemen. Finally, in the spring of 1648, under the leadership of Bogdan Chmielnicki (1595–1657), the Cossacks revolted in the Ukraine against Polish rule. The son of a minor aristocratic landowner, Chmielnicki became embroiled in a controversy with the Polish governor of his province, and was jailed. Released from prison, Chmielnicki resolved to drive the Poles and the Jews out of the Ukraine. Contrary to Polish law, he was elected hetman, or chief, by the Cossacks in 1648, and the revolution began.

Poland's very strategy of militarizing the Cossacks proved its undoing. The Cossacks, now a potent military force, attacked their rulers. Both in an effort to keep the Tartars from attacking the Cossacks while they were in the midst of a revolt, and to increase his military strength, Chmielnicki turned the tables on the old military alignment. Instead of fighting the Tartars, he induced them to join the Cossacks and unite against the Polish gentry, who were economic oppressors, political tyrants, and heretics, with Jews as their allies. For his efforts, Chmielnicki has gone down in Ukrainian history as a patriotic hero.

In May 1648 Chmielnicki defeated the main Polish army. Throughout the Ukraine the serfs rose against the Polish nobility and their Jewish stewards, even though their leader was no peasant himself and had as his agenda the replacement of the peasants' Polish and Jewish masters with Cossacks. The Cossacks of the Ukraine and their allies went from town to town, bringing death and destruction in their wake. Although the exact number of Jews massacred is unknown, with estimates ranging from 40,000 to 100,000, eyewitness accounts relate the horrific slaughter. Cossacks looted synagogues, defaced Torah scrolls and other holy books, used the leather bindings for sandals, then forced Jews to lie on the shreds and submit to torture. They ripped babies from the bellies of pregnant women and replaced them with hungry cats, making sure first to cut off the women's limbs so that they could not remove the creatures. Other Jews, in areas controlled by Tartars, met a more benign fate, being merely sold into slavery in the slave markets of Istanbul.

Later that year Chmielnicki marched into Poland itself, where he destroyed many Jewish communities. In August 1649 he was recognized by the Polish king as a semiautonomous prince, and Jews were forbidden to reside in the Ukraine. But after renewed hostilities and a defeat in 1651, Chmielnicki transferred his allegiance in 1654 to the Russian czar. A Russian army invaded eastern Poland, and the Jews of that region were exterminated or expelled.

Whatever the total number of dead may have been, there is no disputing the catastrophic psychological effects of the Chmielnicki massacres on the Jews of eastern Europe. Since according to traditional Judaism, suffering was the result of sin, many Jews blamed themselves for the massacres and were overcome by feelings of sinfulness. Others lived in hope of messianic deliverance, certain that such desperate suffering could only signal the time of turbulence that, according to tradition, will precede the coming of the messiah. As refugees fled from the Ukraine to Germany, the Netherlands, and other countries of western Europe, they brought with them a renewed sense of the fragility of life in the Diaspora.

58

THE SHABBETAI ZEVI AFFAIR

The messianic movement that gathered around the figure of Shabbetai Zevi in 1665–1666 was the most widespread such movement in Jewish history. Its consequences lasted for generations after the conversion and death of Shabbetai Zevi himself.

According to Jewish tradition, the coming of the messiah will be preceded by a period of troubles, called "the birth pangs of the messiah." Since troubles were never lacking in the lives of Jews, messianic expectations were never completely absent. The expulsion from Spain in 1492 and the Chmielnicki massacres of 1648–1649 in the Ukraine and Poland kept alive hopes that the messiah's coming could not be too far off.

Two other factors made the mid-17th century a ripe time for messianic fervor even in places where the Jewish population led lives of relative security. Thanks to the spread of printing, the entire Jewish world had been exposed to the ideas of Lurianic kabbalah (see nutshell #53). An important aspect of Luria's system taught that the messiah would come once each Jew had fulfilled the particular role assigned to him in redeeming the sparks of holiness that had been trapped in evil husks at the time of creation. In addition, much of the European Christian world looked to the years 1665–1666 as a gateway to the millennium, the period of a thousand years during which, they believed, Christ will reign on earth.

The figure on whom Jewish messianic hopes centered, Shabbetai Zevi (1626–1676), in fact had proclaimed himself the messiah as early as 1648, some seventeen years before anyone took him seriously. Born in Turkey, this scholarly son of a merchant had a good background in both rabbinics and kabbalah, but a mental affliction stood in his way. A manic-depressive, Shabbetai Zevi could be charming and impressive in some states of mind, but in others he displayed bizarre behavior. He took a Torah scroll for his wife in a ceremony under a marriage canopy; using his erudition to make a play on words, he rewrote the benediction blessing God for freeing captives (*matir asurim*) into one blessing God for permitting the forbidden (*matir issurin*), and proceeded to perform various forbidden acts, most notably pronouncing God's explicit name—the tetragrammaton—in public.

Finally, the rabbis in his community expelled Shabbetai Zevi. He spent many years wandering through various areas of the Ottoman Empire, impressing many people while in his normal state of mind, and from time to time looking for help in freeing himself from his mood swings.

The turning point in Shabbetai Zevi's life came when he heard that a young kabbalist, Nathan of Gaza, was able to help each individual understand precisely what his role was in the Lurianic process that would correct the cosmic errors introduced at the time of creation.

Rather than helping Shabbetai Zevi overcome his manic-depression, however, Nathan of Gaza (c. 1643–1680) confirmed his messianic claims. In 1665 Nathan sent out letters to various locations in the Diaspora announcing that shortly Shabbetai Zevi would peacefully wrest the sultan's crown and usher in the redemption. Nathan called for Jewish communities everywhere to repent to hasten the arrival of the great moment. The response to the proclamation was astounding. Jews everywhere prayed, fasted, and flagellated themselves. Many made their way to Israel. Books appeared marked with the date "the first year of the renewal of the prophecy and the kingdom."

In February 1666 Shabbetai Zevi arrived in Turkey, and was promptly arrested. In September, given the choice of conversion to Islam or death, the pretender, first denying that he had ever made messianic claims, chose conversion. According to Nathan, however, Shabbetai Zevi's conversion was merely part of the messianic process. Like a spy within enemy territory, the messiah had to pretend to embrace Islam in order to free the holy sparks trapped there. Only by descending into the realm of evil, by flouting the laws of the Torah itself, could the messiah complete the process leading up to the redemption.

Shabbetai Zevi died in exile in Albania in 1676, and Nathan's death followed four years later. But Nathan's theory explaining Shabbetai Zevi's conversion enabled the so-called Shabbatean movement to survive in different forms for over a hundred years. One Shabbatean sect, the Donmeh (Turkish for "apostates"), practiced Islam in public but in private continued to believe not only that Shabbetai Zevi was the messiah but also that each Donmeh leader was his reincarnation. A second Shabbatean sect, the Frankists, flourished in Poland into the late 18th century. Its leader, Jacob Frank (1726–1771), claimed that he was a reincarnation of Shabbetai Zevi. In turn he converted to Islam, Catholicism, and Eastern Orthodoxy, and proclaimed his own variation of the Trinity. Both the Donmeh and the Frankists adopted sexual practices forbidden by Jewish law. Although neither the Donmeh nor the Frankists ever had large numbers of adherents, the very existence of such sects was a terrible blow to traditional Jewish values.

The response of many Jewish community leaders to the outcome of the Shabbetai Zevi affair was to pretend that it had never happened. There was a concerted effort to destroy documents recording the overwhelming response to Shabbetai Zevi's claims. Among the Jewish masses, many felt a tremendous disillusionment. For many years after the death of the false messiah, Jewish communities around the world continued to feel the aftershocks of his extraordinary rise and fall.

59

THE DEVELOPMENT OF HASIDISM

Hasidism, the Jewish pietistic movement emphasizing joyous worship of God, originated among Polish Jews of the 18th century. It continues to play a significant role in Jewish life and politics to this day.

In major cities around the world, Jewish men dressed in black wool clothing, with long earlocks dangling beneath broad-brimmed black hats, are a familiar sight. Although most people know that these are the Hasidim, many are unaware of the historical factors that led to the development of this distinctive, tightly knit, and influential group of Jews, or of the differences that distinguish them from other Jews.

Hasidism, as the way of life of the Hasidim is called, originated in the Polish Ukraine in the mid-1700s. Not having yet recovered from the effects of the Chmielnicki massacres of the previous century (see nutshell #57), the Jews of the Ukraine were once again being subjected to persecution by the Cossacks. Many still felt a void following the disturbing outcome of the Shabbetai Zevi affair (see nutshell #58). To purge themselves of feelings of guilt, many Jews adopted ascetic practices. Many felt abandoned by a leadership that seemed obsessed with scholarship but uninterested in the spiritual needs of the masses.

The founder of the new movement that was to appeal to many Jews, including some scholars, was the highly charismatic, if not intellectual, Israel ben Eliezer, better known as the Baal Shem Tov (1700–1760), or by the acronym of that name, the Besht. *Baal shem* ("master of the Name") was the title given to any itinerant faith healer who used God's name in amulets to cure people of diseases or rid them of demons. The addition of the word *tov* ("good") to Israel ben Eliezer's title distinguished him from the run-of-the-mill wonder-worker.

It is difficult to separate fact from legend in evaluating the circumstances of the Besht's life, but the main principles of his movement can be summarized with confidence. His adaptation of certain aspects of the Lurianic kabbalah (see nutshell #53) transformed Judaism into a joyous religion as accessible to the masses as to the intellectual elite. The holy sparks that were scattered everywhere meant that God was in everything. One could achieve the goal of total cleaving to God primarily through prayer but also through every other activity, no matter how mundane. Thus not only the most learned scholars but also the common people could draw close to God, by eating, drinking, transacting business, and so on, as long as they undertook these activities with the intent of cleaving mentally and joyously to God. Joyous involvement in all of life's activities, rather than ascetic withdrawal from life, was the proper way to approach God.

The Besht also developed a new concept of community leadership. In each generation there were a certain number of spiritually gifted individuals who were endowed with a special ability to cleave to God. These were the completely righteous ones, or *zaddikim*. But each *zaddik* had as his special task the responsibility of raising the souls of his followers—his *hasidim*, or pious ones—closer to God. By pleading to God for his *hasidim*, by advising them on spiritual and worldly matters alike, the *zaddik* as community leader was personally involved in the lives of his followers. The responsibility of the *hasidim*, in turn, was to cleave to the *zaddik* as a step toward cleaving to God. Never before in Judaism had veneration of the religious leader been of such great importance.

When the Besht died in 1760 he had many followers, but there was as yet no hasidic movement. His disciple Dov Baer (d. 1772) undertook to spread his master's teachings, and to that end he sent emissaries out through much of eastern Europe. As the movement grew, however, opposition to it also grew. The central figure in the opposition camp was the great intellectual Elijah ben Solomon Zalman, known as the Gaon (or rabbinic "genius") of Vilna (1720–1797). Among the objections of the Gaon of Vilna to Hasidism were that its reverence for the *zaddik* was a type of idol worship and that its stress on prayer rather than study would lead adherents of the new movement to transgress the law. The opponents of Hasidism saw nothing wrong with denouncing the movement's leaders to the secular authorities, and more than one hasidic leader was imprisoned. Eventually, however, the antagonism abated. Realizing that a greater threat to traditional Jewish values came from the growing trend toward secular studies, the Jewish establishment begrudgingly accepted Hasidism into the fold.

Large numbers of Hasidim perished in the Nazi slaughter, but the movement still flourishes. The Hasidim, as ultra-Orthodox religious fundamentalists, continue to live segregated lives in their own communities, with an almost fanatical devotion to the minutiae of Jewish law. Not only have hasidic communities attracted many new adherents in recent years, but Hasidim also play a significant role in the politics of cities like New York as well as in the state of Israel.

60

MOSES MENDELSSOHN AND THE JEWISH ENLIGHTENMENT

Moses Mendelssohn (1729–1786) was the father of the Jewish Enlightenment, which contended that Jews would no longer be persecuted if they learned the language and the culture of their gentile neighbors. Not all the premises upon which the Jewish Enlightenment was based have proven true, but it succeeded in bringing Jews into the modern world.

For better or for worse, most American Jews these days live lives not very different from those of their gentile neighbors. For the most part, neither their dress nor their speech nor their occupations can distinguish them from other Americans. Whether they know it or not, they are products of the so-called Jewish Enlightenment, which began in 18th-century Germany.

The Jewish Enlightenment, which ushered Jews into the modern world, is called the *Haskalah*, from the Hebrew word for "intelligence." Those active in the *Haskalah* were influenced by the leaders of the European Enlightenment of the 17th and 18th centuries. Philosophers like Descartes, Rousseau, Voltaire, and John Locke taught that all people are born with the capacity to reason. They also taught that all human beings, regardless of their origin, have the same natural rights. Enlightenment philosophers optimistically believed that human progress was guaranteed if all people would be properly educated, allowing their rational human will to develop and ridding them of ignorance and superstition.

The individual most often associated with the *Haskalah* is Moses Mendelssohn, whose life in many ways seems to exemplify the beliefs of the European Enlightenment. The son of a pious scribe in the German town of Dessau, from his boyhood Mendelssohn was possessed by the desire to increase his store of knowledge. Most of the Jews of Europe at the time were unaware not only of the ideas of the Enlightenment but also of other changes that were moving Europe into modernity. Most spoke only Yiddish or other mixtures of Hebrew and the local dialect. The standard Jewish education, in fact, not only did not include study of the local languages but also ignored the nontalmudic Hebrew heritage along with secular subjects. Rebelling against this system, young Mendelssohn taught himself biblical Hebrew. He also managed to find some of Maimonides' works, and was very impressed by the great medieval philosopher's emphasis on reason (see nutshell #40).

At the age of fourteen Mendelssohn followed his hometown rabbi and teacher to Berlin, the cosmopolitan city only thirty miles from Dessau. Though some of the wealthy Jews of Berlin spoke German and were permitted to own property and conduct business on an equal footing with gentiles, even they were often humiliated because of their religion. Under the tutelage of some young Jewish professionals in Berlin, Mendelssohn was introduced to modern and ancient languages, to Enlightenment philosophy, and to Christian theology. Eventually, he was hired as tutor to the children of a wealthy Jewish silk manufacturer. Mendelssohn impressed his employer so much that he eventually became his business manager, and after his employer's death, Mendelssohn took over the business.

Mendelssohn might have lived and died an obscure if well-to-do and well-educated Jewish businessman if a friend had not introduced him to the German playwright and critic Gotthold Ephraim Lessing, born in the same year as Mendelssohn. Although friendships between Jews and gentiles were extremely rare in mid-18th-century Germany, Lessing and Mendelssohn forged a friendship that would launch Mendelssohn on a literary career and help spread his fame throughout Europe. The two colleagues began a literary magazine, and Lessing saw to the publication of Mendelssohn's first book, a study of the English philosopher Shaftesbury. In the succeeding years, Mendelssohn's fame as a philosopher in his own right grew, and he became a much sought after figure in the literary salons of Berlin.

Far from letting his fame distance him from his roots, Mendelssohn used his position both to dispel the anti-Jewish prejudice of the German public and to assist Jewish communities in distress. In addition, aware of the doors that had been opened for him as a result of his education, he determined to help other German Jews enter the modern world. In order to achieve this end, he directed his efforts toward improving their skills in German, awakening their interest in Hebrew, and rethinking the goals of Jewish education. These three goals would shape the common aims of the *Haskalah* over the next century as it spread from Prussia through the Austrian Empire and into Russia.

Convinced that only after Jews could speak, read, and write German fluently would they be equipped to enter the modern world, Mendelssohn undertook a unique translation of the Five Books of Moses into elegant German—but written with Hebrew letters to ease the task of reading. Although male Jews of his day could read Hebrew, most considered it a sacred language fit only for prayer and religious scholarship. Mendelssohn, however, believed that the Yiddish his coreligionists used as a daily language held back their progress in the modern world. To make them aware of the contemporary expressive potential of their ancient tongue, Mendelssohn accompanied his Torah translation with a Hebrew commentary. He also began a Hebrew periodical with the twofold purpose of teaching Jews about a variety of secular topics of contemporary importance and of broadening their skills in Hebrew. Finally, the changes Mendelssohn and his younger colleagues and their followers elsewhere in Europe introduced in the Jewish educational system involved replacing Yiddish as the classroom language and expanding the curriculum to include Hebrew, other languages, and a wide variety of subjects ranging from bookkeeping to geography. An intense Talmud-centered education, they argued, should be limited to those intending to become rabbis, but other students should be prepared to take up a trade in the world.

To today's reader, the changes Mendelssohn and his followers sought to make do not seem particularly revolutionary, but many Jews at the time viewed them with horror. The value of studying religious works for their own sake, reinforced over the centuries, was being challenged. Many feared that if Jews learned the language and culture of the gentiles, they would abandon Judaism altogether. When Jewish communities did not embrace the changes put forth by the leaders of the *Haskalah*, some of the latter joined forces with those rulers who saw that such modifications might serve their own purposes. After all, one way to rid their countries of unseemly, ill-mannered, boorish Jews was to educate them to be like their Christian neighbors. Needless to say, such collaboration on the part of some *Haskalah* leaders did not endear them to the traditional Jewish communities.

In 1782 traditionalists' concerns about Mendelssohn's attitude to Judaism were confirmed when his book *Jerusalem* appeared. Beginning with the tenet that no religious institution has the right to use force to control people's beliefs, Mendelssohn offered an idiosyncratic explanation of what Judaism and the Torah are. According to Mendelssohn, God gave all people, not just Jews, the power of reasoning to determine how to behave. Judaism is special for the specific laws listed in the Torah, which only Jews are required to observe. He went on to argue that under the ancient Israelite nation, an offense against the Torah's laws was also an offense against the nation's laws. Since it is a legitimate right of civil governments to compel citizens to obey even those laws with which they disagree, violations of the Torah were punishable offenses at that time. But when the Jewish state came to an end with the destruction of the Temple, Judaism lost its power of force. Although Mendelssohn argued that the end of the Jewish state destroyed the binding effect of some of the Torah's laws, such as those relating to the Temple, he asserted that observance of the Torah was still necessary to keep the Jewish people united and to preserve the pure belief in God. If the time ever came when the Torah was no longer needed, God would provide an unmistakable sign to that effect.

Despite his controversial philosophy of Judaism, throughout his life Mendelssohn himself remained committed to observance of Jewish law. But the effects of the *Haskalah* that he initiated included one that Mendelssohn would have deplored. Many of his followers in the movement and, in fact, several of his own children abandoned Judaism completely. (His son Abraham, for example, had all his children baptized, including the great composer Felix Mendelssohn, and subsequently converted to Christianity himself.) In addition, he would have regretted learning that some of the basic premises both of the European Enlightenment and of the *Haskalah* were flawed. For example, a little more than a century after Mendelssohn's death, Sigmund Freud's theories undermined the idea that people's behavior is determined by rational will. And by the end of the 19th century it was apparent that antisemitism would not go away simply because Jews were educated according to European norms.

On the other hand, the *Haskalah* did make some lasting positive contributions to Jewish history, among which are the revival of the Hebrew language and the restructuring of the goals of a Jewish education. The forces of the Enlightenment that swept Europe could not leave the Jews untouched. Many Enlightenment figures, such as Voltaire, turned their backs on organized religion. Mendelssohn, as the father of the *Haskalah*, provided an intellectual framework for Judaism in the modern world, the influence of which persists to this day.

61

EMANCIPATION

Emancipation, the lifting of restrictions against Jews and the granting of equal rights of citizenship to them, took place in the United States and western and central Europe in the century following the American Revolution.

As anyone who has learned about the Emancipation Proclamation in American history knows, the concept of emancipation is not limited to Jewish history. The word has its root in Latin, for in ancient Rome a young man achieved emancipation when he was freed from his father's control and became an independent legal entity. In world history, one speaks of the emancipation of feudal serfs, of United States slaves, of English Catholics, and of women in many countries. But in Jewish history, the term refers to the abolition of restrictions specifically affecting Jews and to their being granted all the rights and responsibilities of citizenship. Although the Jews of the United States and western and central Europe achieved emancipation in different ways and with different degrees of long-term success, the process was complete by the end of the 19th century.

The United States was the first country to emancipate its Jews. During the colonial period Jews enjoyed full civil rights and experienced no restrictions in the practice of their religion. Such political discrimination as there was against them resulted not from the fact that they were Jews in particular but rather because they were not Protestant; holders of public office were required to take a Protestant form of oath. After the American Revolution, the federal Constitution specifically stipulated that religion could not be a factor in qualifying for federal office, and the Bill of Rights disestablished all religions. Although most of the individual states ratified similar constitutions from the outset, Maryland, North Carolina, and New Hampshire maintained a Christian oath requirement for some time after.

In France, home of many of the philosophers of the European Enlightenment, ideas of the equality of all men led to discussions of Jewish rights in the decades before the French Revolution of 1789. The Declaration of the Rights of Man of that year, which states that no one should be harmed for his opinions, including religious ones, implies the equality of Jews. Two years later Jews were specifically emancipated, although with the understanding that as their part of the bargain Jews would become true Frenchmen: they were not to form "a nation within a nation." In other words, in exchange for equal rights, Jews would have to relinquish their autonomous communities and sense of national identity as Jews. Despite a temporary setback under Napoleon, Jewish legal equality was not challenged in France, and Jews played an increasingly active role in French life. The fact that in 1870 it was the French Jewish statesman Adolphe Crémieux who issued the law granting French citizenship to the Jews of Algeria is testimony to this fact.

Despite the fact that Moses Mendelssohn was exposed to European Enlightenment philosophy in Germany (see nutshell #60), and despite the fact that he exemplified for Germans how "acceptable" a Jew could be, Jewish emancipation did not run a smooth course in Germany. Having witnessed first the bloody aftermath of the French Revolution and then Napoleon's aggressive foreign policy, Germans, along with Italians and Austrians, rejected all the philosophical claims and political reforms associated with France. In addition, many educated Germans began to view all the egalitarian beliefs of the French and English Enlightenment philosophers as the product of an "alien spirit." For pure Germanic inspiration, they looked back to an idealized past of the medieval "Christian state." For many, the question of Jewish emancipation meant not granting rights to Jews but rather emancipating Christians from Jewry.

Ironically, what made Jewish emancipation a fact by 1871 in Germany, Italy, and the Austrian Empire was the rise of nationalism. Although there was not necessarily a true change of heart toward Jews, the wish to unify formerly unassociated territories led to more inclusive definitions of who could be considered a citizen. In their search for widespread support, nationalist groups often could not turn their backs on liberals. For pragmatic reasons, they found themselves having to accept such liberal positions as Jewish emancipation.

The road to emancipation in England was different. Although France had been England's enemy for years, the British did not reject liberal ideas associated with the French Revolution. The Enlightenment, after all, was as much an English product as a French one. Instead, such restrictions as there were against Jews began to be lifted from the mid-1830s on. Although in theory Jews were full citizens, the problem lay in the oath of loyalty that was required of all candidates for public office and university degrees, and in some places even of those wishing to register to vote. Originally the oath included the words "according to the usages of the Anglican church." In 1828, in order to emancipate English Catholics, a new formula—"on the true faith of a Christian"—was substituted with the intent of discriminating against Jews only. The offending portion of the oath was deleted by law in 1866, following several decades in which other restrictions against Jews were abolished.

By the early 1870s, then, the Jews of the United States and of western and central Europe were fully enfranchised citizens. For the largest Jewish community in the world, however, that of the millions of Jews in eastern Europe, emancipation was still far off. And although in the mid-1800s the Ottoman Empire granted civic equality to Jews, along with Christians, there was never a Western-style reform movement toward emancipation of the Jews of the Islamic world.

Upon emancipation of French Jewry, some traditional Jews worried how the new rights and responsibilities would affect their religious life. Most Jews, however, welcomed emancipation wholeheartedly. Clearly, however, the lifting of restrictions and the granting of rights and duties did affect Jewish religious life, not only in France but also in all the other countries where Jews achieved emancipation. The new freedom had its price. Along with the many benefits that emancipation brought, for the first time remaining Jewish was a matter of private choice, not of involuntary legal status. Many began to question whether Jewish forms of worship should be modernized to bring them more into line with those of their Christian countrymen, and whether some traditional Jewish beliefs—such as in the messianic redemption from exile—still had meaning. The broadened possibilities available to Jews not only forced a reassessment of Jewish identity but also encouraged intermarriage and assimilation, major problems with which Jews are still grappling today.

62

RELIGIOUS RESPONSES
TO MODERN CHALLENGES

During a single generation of German Jewry, the roots were sown for the three main movements of modern Judaism—Reform, Modern Orthodox, and Conservative. Each movement coalesced around a single rabbi with a specific vision of what it meant to be a Jew in the modern world. Abraham Geiger (1810–1874) was the founder of the Reform movement, Samson Raphael Hirsch (1808–1888) of the modern Orthodox movement, and Zacharias Frankel (1801–1875) of what was to become the Conservative movement.

In most large communities today, Jews have different options about what kind of synagogue they want to belong to and what kind of Jewish education they want to provide for their children. When they decide to affiliate as Reform Jews or as Conservative Jews, they know they are opting for a more liberal "brand" of Judaism than they would find in most Orthodox congregations. The idea that such options should be available to Jews first emerged in 19th-century Germany.

As Jews began to take a greater part in the secular world, they began to confront and to address new concerns related to their Jewish identity. Some Jews wondered why they should bother to remain true to the ancestral faith, which in so many ways seemed to lack the aesthetic appeal and the decorum of the Christian denominations. In response, groups of laypeople in different German cities set about to reform Jewish worship. To make the service more agreeable, they shortened it, began to use some German in the prayers, included a weekly topical sermon in German, and introduced choral singing to an organ accompaniment. The rabbis they chose to lead them looked like modern men, who often wore no beards and were dressed in the same black robes that the Lutheran clergy favored.

Young, secularly educated Jews also began to apply for the first time the same impartial, critical approach to classical Jewish texts as they used in universities to study other ancient documents. Several reasons led them to favor this new approach to Jewish study. On a scholarly level, they were disturbed about the contrast between the objective, scientific approach to history being taught in the universities and the old-fashioned approach to the Talmud and other classical texts of the Jewish tradition. On a social level, they were certain that scientific study of the Jewish past would reveal its glories to non-Jews, who would then learn to respect the Jews' contributions to modernity. On a religious level, most were concerned that their reforms not be arbitrary but be grounded in Jewish tradition. Only by uncovering the Jewish past could they legitimize the reforms they made, such as the use of the vernacular in prayer and in weekly sermons.

Although these reforms in worship and scholarship were begun not by rabbis but rather by laypeople, by the mid-19th century three clearly defined approaches to the challenges of modernity were associated with three different rabbis. The spiritual fathers of the modern Reform, Orthodox, and Conservative movements shared much in common. They all had rigorous Jewish educations as well as secular educations. They all believed that modern synagogue worship should be more decorous than the traditional services of the past. But the three differed both in their views about what was the essential aspect of Judaism and in their understanding of such issues as revelation, Jewish peoplehood, Jewish aspirations for the distant future, and the appropriate methods for studying Judaism.

The Reform movement did not originate with Abraham Geiger, but as the major developer of its ideology, he is considered its founding father. For Geiger, the essence of Judaism was the creative spirit that produced each age's religious principles and moral ideals. Geiger believed passionately in the scientific study of Judaism and did much groundbreaking work himself. His scholarship convinced him that all the "sacred" texts of Judaism, including the Bible, were the products of the specific periods in which they were written. Therefore, there were outdated elements in all of them, and none of them alone could provide all the guidelines for modern Jewish practice and belief. This realization, however, was not a reason to reject the texts, because all were sources of traditions that could still be meaningful to today's Jews.

Geiger's research led him to compare Judaism to a living organism, constantly growing and developing. Just as Judaism of biblical times, with its priesthood and animal sacrifice, differed from Judaism of rabbinic times, with its emphasis on prayer and good deeds, Judaism took on new forms in each historical period. Just as the early rabbis kept Judaism from dying after the destruction of the Second Temple, the rabbis of each age were responsible for keeping Judaism alive by helping it to accommodate to new circumstances. But Geiger emphasized that the changes of each period had to develop out of the past, not represent a rupture with it.

Geiger found in what he called "prophetic Judaism" the timeless component of the Jewish creative spirit. The prophets' emphasis on social justice, their disdain for ritual acts that did not go hand in hand with social morality, and their vision of a peaceful future for all humanity were—or should be—the underpinnings of the Judaism of each and every age. Through a process of "progressive revelation," it is incumbent on the Jews of each generation to turn the prophets' demands into reality in ways appropriate to each historical period.

For Geiger, as a result of the evolution of Judaism, Jews, who had once constituted a nation, were now a religious community only. He considered himself a patriotic German "of the Mosaic persuasion," and as such rejected prayers looking forward to a return to Zion and to the restoration of the Temple cult. He also rejected the idea that a personal messiah would come to restore nationhood to the Jews, and looked forward instead to a better future for all humanity.

While Geiger was a student at the University of Bonn, among his friends was Samson Raphael Hirsch, who was to become the father of modern Orthodoxy. Hirsch was unlike traditional Orthodox rabbis in many ways. Rather than viewing emancipation as a threat to Jewish values, he worked to promote political rights for Jews. He wore modern clothes and introduced a choir and a biweekly German sermon into the services he led. He believed in the importance of secular education, and considered the ideal Jew one who was proficient in both traditional Jewish subjects and modern secular ones. He emphasized the educational value of the Bible and prayerbook, as well as the Talmud.

Essentially, Hirsch was extremely traditional. For him, the essence of Judaism was Jewish law. He was committed to the traditional belief that at the revelation at Mount Sinai (see nutshell #3) God had transmitted to Moses not only the Written Law, or the Torah, but also the Oral Law, consisting of all the rabbinic interpretations. Because God was the source of the law, Jews were not permitted to decide which laws it was permissible to discard. Ritual laws and moral laws were equally binding. Instead of trying to adapt Judaism to fit the times, Jews should work to adapt the times to Judaism: "Only then, when the times will conform with God, will Judaism also conform with the times," Hirsch maintained. Hirsch's belief that God's revelation is unchangeable through time led him to reject the new scholarly approaches to Jewish studies that considered all the texts as human products of a particular age.

Hirsch's focus was not on the Jewish people but rather on the individual Jew. Like Geiger, he believed that Judaism was a religion, not a nationality. Unlike Geiger, however, he believed in a messiah who would come at some time in the distant future foreordained by God.

If prophetic Judaism and the creative Jewish spirit were the essence of Judaism for Abraham Geiger, while immutable God-given law was its essence for Samson Raphael Hirsch, for the father of Conservative Judaism the essence of Judaism was faith anchored in a people and its history. Zacharias Frankel is associated with an approach to modern Judaism that falls between the ideological positions staked out by the other two men. Although Frankel was a productive scholar of the new modern science of Judaism, he believed that historical inquiry could go only so far: at the core of Judaism lay the revelation at Sinai. For Frankel, however, unlike Hirsch, the Pentateuch alone was transmitted through direct divine revelation. The Oral Law may have been divinely inspired, but it was the product of human beings.

Like Geiger, Frankel believed that Jewish law had to be responsive to the changing needs of every age. But in his estimation, traditions—though of human origin—were not to be easily overturned. In fact, Frankel linked tradition to revelation in a novel way: the traditional heritage of the Jewish community is an indirect form of divine revelation as worthy of recognition as the revelation at Sinai, which it supplements and transmits. As long as the majority of a community felt emotionally committed to certain traditions, reformers should consider those traditions sacrosanct.

Frankel's attitude toward Jewish peoplehood and hopes for the distant future also distinguished him from Geiger on one hand and Hirsch on the other. While he agreed that the Jews of his day were but one religious community among many, he believed that hopes for future political independence were a source of self-respect. Even though German Jews were devoted to the German fatherland, hopes for a messianic delivery had a more immediate resonance in lands where Jews suffered persecution.

For many Jews, first in Germany and later in America, Frankel's position was appealing because it suggested that Jews could face the challenges of modernity without undergoing radical change. Over the next century, the Conservative movement developed on the basis of the framework Frankel provided.

63

THE PALE OF SETTLEMENT

The Pale of Settlement, the giant ghetto where Jews in Russia were forced to live from 1791 to 1917, exemplified the restrictions on Jews in czarist Russia. These included residential and occupational restrictions, onerous military obligations, and education designed to promote assimilation.

The word *pale* in the term "Pale of Settlement" has nothing to do with color. Like the same word in the phrase "beyond the pale," it comes from the Latin word for a stake or picket used in a fence. A pale is an enclosed area. Czarist Russia's Pale of Settlement consisted of the provinces and districts where Jews were allowed to reside.

During the 15th century, Jews were expelled from Russia. But in the late 18th century, as a result of the partitions of Poland among Russia, Austria, and Prussia (1772, 1793, 1795), Russia found itself home to too large a Jewish population to eliminate so conveniently. Although the policies toward the Jews of the individual czars who ruled Russia until 1917 differed in their specifics, their general attitude was that the "Jewish problem" could be solved through two main routes: assimilating the Jews or driving them out.

In order to achieve this solution, the czars undertook an experiment in social engineering, with the Jews as objects to be manipulated for the "improvement" of society. The first step, in 1791, was to confine the Jews to the Pale of Settlement, an area of about a million square kilometers—more or less the size of the American Southwest—stretching from the Baltic to the Black Sea.

Without special legal dispensation, Jews were forbidden not only to live but also to travel outside the Pale. Even within the Pale they were restricted to certain areas, comprising only about 1/2,000 of the territory. In addition, formerly permitted zones might become illegal overnight. Tevye's family in the popular musical *Fiddler on the Roof*, for example, finds itself driven from its *shtetl*— or small, preponderantly Jewish town—when by czarist decree the town is suddenly put off limits to Jews. Similarly, in 1835 Jews found themselves banned from the formerly permitted city of Kiev.

Restrictions applied not only to where Jews might reside in the Pale of Settlement but also to what occupations they might pursue there. The czars' initial intent was to eliminate "evil" Jewish influence on the peasantry by forbidding Jews to live or work in villages. In particular, Jews were forbidden from selling alcoholic beverages to peasants. Since about a third of the Jewish population had previously run village estates as leaseholders of absentee noblemen or had managed village inns, these new rules wreaked havoc on the lives of many. In theory, the czars wanted the Jews to pursue agricultural careers, but since little land was available, the towns and *shtetls* of the Pale became crowded with Jewish merchants and shopkeepers, tailors and shoemakers. The combination of intense competition and a high birthrate led to conditions of poverty and overcrowding.

Perhaps the most devastating czarist orders against Jewish residents of the Pale were Nicholas I's "Cantonist Decrees" (1827–1856), requiring Jewish males to serve for twenty-five years in the Russian military. In drafting boys as young as twelve, the government hoped to turn them into assimilated and Christianized Russians who would become role models for future generations of Jews. While the government's hopes did not materialize, the Cantonist Decrees caused unspeakable horrors for thirty years. Dissension was sown within the Jewish community, with resentment growing toward those communal leaders who seemed all too ready to turn over the children of the poor to meet the draft quota, while sparing the children of the rich and powerful. *Chappers*, or the kidnappers who stalked the *shtetls* looking for draft-age boys, were more terrifying than any imaginary bogeyman. Many of the boys who were drafted died from the rigors of the forced march into the Russian interior. Large numbers committed suicide by drowning rather than allow themselves to be baptized.

Not unreasonably, Nicholas I also looked to education as a means of reshaping the identity of the Jews of the Pale. He sought to replace independent Jewish schools with state-run schools for Jews, and imported a German-born proponent of the Jewish Enlightenment (see nutshell #60) to run them. At first Dr. Max Lilienthal was too naive to believe the fears of the Russian Jews that the government saw its schools as roads to conversion. After four years, however, he came to the same conclusion, and in 1845 Lilienthal fled Russia for the United States. All the same, the government did establish schools for Jews, with Jewish teachers for Hebrew subjects only. Although at first Jews bribed officials to fabricate lists of Jewish pupils supposedly enrolled at these schools, the state schools eventually attracted a large number of Jewish pupils. The draft deferments granted to those enrolled there convinced parents that worse fates might await their children than a secular education.

Over the period that the Pale of Settlement endured, varying categories of Jews were permitted to travel and even live outside its bounds. These included former soldiers, medical workers, university graduates, and those engaged in commerce or crafts who were considered especially "useful." But even these privileged Jews smarted under restrictions. They were required to carry special papers, obtainable only with difficulty and always revocable by bureaucratic whim. A privileged Jew outside the Pale who ran afoul of the law was subject to a fine for the first offense, and to expulsion for the second. The situation was a bonanza for corruptible officials. Instigating Christians to accuse Jews of disrupting the peace, the officials would then extort money from wealthy Jews to allow them to remain outside the Pale. Without hesitation, they would send poor Jews back to join the many other paupers already living within the Pale.

The Pale of Settlement was abolished in 1917, at the end of the czarist period. Despite the many oppressive policies directed toward the Jews unwillingly restricted within its boundaries, recent scholarship has begun to focus on some of the unintended positive effects of their confinement. Despite economic and political hardship, Jewish culture thrived within the cities and towns of the Pale. Many of the classics of Yiddish and Hebrew literature were written by Russian Jews. The culture of the *shtetl* has left its imprint on the outside world as well, as in the paintings of Marc Chagall and the popularization of Sholem Aleichem's Tevye and other characters in *Fiddler on the Roof.*

64

THE HOUSE OF ROTHSCHILD

The House of Rothschild became the foremost privately owned interna-
tional banking enterprise in 19th-century Europe. In their heyday, with
five major banks in Frankfurt, London, Paris, Naples, and Vienna, the
Rothschilds were bankers to Europe's governments, financed some of
Europe's first railroads, and influenced the economic and political his-
tory of the continent. Unlike other 19th-century banking families of Jew-
ish origin, the Rothschilds maintained their Jewish identity, often put-
ting Jewish interests ahead of purely financial ones.

What Jewish family has not only provided models for characters in 19th-century
British literature but has also been the subject of a 20th-century American
musical named for them? In modern Jewish history, only one family name has
such universally recognized cachet and almost mythological grandeur, and that
name is Rothschild. One looks in vain for a comparable family in American
history, although there are some parallels between the Kennedys in 20th-century
America and the Rothschilds in Europe. Like Joseph P. Kennedy, the patriarch of the Irish-Catholic American family, Mayer Amschel Rothschild
(1744–1812) was passionately devoted to furthering the fortunes of his sons
through business and political connections. Like the Kennedy name, the
Rothschild name has symbolic overtones, positive or negative, depending on
one's orientation. For over two centuries, the Rothschild name has for some
connoted not only Jewish wealth and influence but also philanthropy; for others,
the name has conjured up demonic images of an international Jewish conspiracy.

Many people know that the family name comes from the German words for
"red shield." In the Jewish quarter of Frankfurt, where the family originated in
the 16th century, in the days before numbered street addresses, each house had
a distinctive marker. For several generations the family did in fact live in the
house there marked by a red shield. Fewer people know, however, that by the
time the patriarch of the House of Rothschild was born, a decline in family
fortunes necessitated a move from the relatively opulent house with the red
shield to a lesser dwelling marked by a saucepan. Later, when Mayer Amschel
began to turn things around for himself and his family, they moved to a better

house, marked by a green shield, where Mayer Amschel's wife lived well into her nineties. Even though Rothschild became something of a misnomer, the name stuck.

Born into a family of indifferent merchants, Mayer Amschel himself had been designated for another career entirely. Recognizing him as the cleverest of their children, his parents had hoped he would become a rabbi. Shortly after he began his rabbinical studies, however, both parents died, and he returned to the family home in Frankfurt, where his brothers ran a used-goods store. Mayer Amschel's interest in old coins brought him into contact with the first of many chiefs of state with whom Rothschilds would form mutually beneficial ties. Mayer's initial connection with William of Hesse-Kassel set a precedent for future Rothschild generations: first, to do business with ruling houses, and second, to produce sons to facilitate the carrying out of that business.

Mayer knew, for example, that William had acquired much of his wealth by supplying Hessians (mercenary soldiers) to fight for Britain against the colonists in its revolutionary war, and the patriarch soon saw how useful it would be to have a Rothschild in England. To protect his financial resources from the ravages of battles fought on the continent, William eventually turned to Mayer's London-based son, Nathan. While investing William's fortune in British securities, Nathan managed to enrich himself as well. Some time later, it became clear that a Rothschild presence in France would facilitate Nathan's transfer of products and funds from England to the rest of Europe despite Napoleon's ban on British trade. Mayer thus sent the youngest of his five sons, James, to Paris.

Although the Rothschilds made their initial fortunes in wartime conditions, spanning the French Revolution and the ensuing Napoleonic Wars, the family later recognized that their investments were only as stable as the countries where those investments lay. Passionate advocates of peace that they became, however, they continued to make use in peacetime of one of the keys to their wartime success: an efficient system of communication among Rothschild bases in different countries. Thanks to their reliable couriers, Rothschilds often knew of key financial and political developments well before others did. Aware that transmitted information was not always secure, they often communicated with one another in code. To bamboozle Napoleon, patriarch Mayer referred to himself as "Arnoldi," to William of Hesse-Kassel as "Herr Goldstein," and to English investments as "stockfish" (fish cured without salt by being hung in the open air). Years later, in a telegram from an agent informing him of a likely truce in a South American war, Nathan's son Lionel read that "Mr. Sholem [Yiddish for peace] is expected soon." The Rothschild courier system was so well regarded for its speed and inviolability that Queen Victoria sometimes preferred to entrust her private mail to it rather than to the diplomatic pouches.

Which is not to say that the Rothschild communications network could not be used to spread disinformation as well. When James first arrived in Paris in

1811, with the intent of helping brother Nathan make money at Napoleon's expense, he let a false rumor spread: that Great Britain was anxious not to let money leave British shores. In fact, just the opposite was true, since the Duke of Wellington's troops behind the Pyrenees were in need of funds. But the false leak did the trick, and Napoleon did nothing to stop the flow of gold through France to the beleaguered British forces.

An early success of the private communications network enabled the Rothschilds to develop a questionable financial tactic that would serve them well time and again. Nathan was among the first to know of Wellington's victory over Bonaparte at Waterloo. He took advantage of his early knowledge in a somewhat unscrupulous way. As if anticipating a British defeat, he dumped huge quantities of Britain's funded securities on the market. Naturally, the price dropped. Rothschild agents then bought even greater quantities of securities at the newly lowered price. When the news of Napoleon's defeat finally broke, the securities' price soared. Nathan had made a killing.

Perhaps the most dramatic example of how the Rothschild family fortune affected European history came during the time of Nathan's son Lionel. One Sunday evening in 1875, Lionel was at home in his London mansion, hosting his weekly dinner with the prime minister, Benjamin Disraeli (himself proud of his Jewish roots, though he had been baptized as a boy, and author of one of the novels that lionizes a fictionalized Rothschild family). A telegram arrived from a Paris-based Rothschild informant: the khedive of Egypt was in such financial straits that he had offered his 177,000 shares in the Suez Canal to the French government; having now grown impatient with France's terms, the khedive was prepared to sell to the country that would come up with the 4 million pound sterling ante most quickly. The next morning, Disraeli met with his cabinet. All agreed that England, which had long yearned for the canal, one of the world's prime assets, had to grab the opportunity before other countries learned of it. But there was a constitutional problem.

Because Parliament was in recess, it could not appropriate the necessary 4 million pounds. Similarly, the Bank of England could not loan money to England unless the House of Commons was in session. Enter Lionel Rothschild to the rescue. The London branch of the House of Rothschild immediately loaned the money to the nation. England benefited from the canal militarily and financially until Nasser's Egypt took it over in 1956 (see nutshell #94).

Making money, investing it, and lending it were not the Rothschild family's only concerns. The Rothschilds often put Jewish interests ahead of business considerations. In 1820, while the fortune was still in the making, Nathan publicly refused to deal with German cities that denied the rights of Jews. In 1840 his younger brother James took time out from a battle for control of France's fledgling railway system to protest an outbreak of antisemitism in Syria. In 1850 another brother, Carl, founder of the short-lived Rothschild bank in Naples (1821–1861), on the verge of concluding a loan to the pope, took the occasion to lecture the bishop of Rome on the need to do away with that city's ghetto. Later in the century, the head of the Rothschild bank in London made a habit of refusing to grant loans to the czar because of Russia's mistreatment of the Jews.

The activities of two Rothschilds on behalf of Jews were particularly significant. Lionel (1808–1879), head of the London branch, fought for eleven years to make it possible for Jews to serve as members of Parliament. Between 1847 and 1858, Lionel was elected as a Liberal representing the City of London. While the House of Commons immediately passed a bill permitting a Jew to take a seat in Parliament, the House of Lords refused. Eventually, the House of Lords agreed to a bill that permitted each House to amend the oath of admission required of those who serve in Parliament. Instead of having to forswear allegiance to the Stuart dynasty "upon the true faith of a Christian," Lionel was the first MP to be sworn into office on the Hebrew Bible, with covered head. Lionel's French cousin Edmond (1845–1934) became a mainstay of early Jewish colonization projects in Palestine. Although he never became a Zionist per se, he not only provided the necessary financial support for early pioneer activities but also gave the Zionists a desperately needed infusion of cash in 1931.

Although the Rothschild family's prominence and wealth began to decline after World War I, it has survived even the French government's nationalization of the Paris bank in 1981. The House of Rothschild today operates not only a London bank but also an American investment company. While the family may no longer have the financial or political clout it once had, the name retains its allure. Several generations of family members were among those who proved that hard work together with native ability can exceed the capabilities of title and ancestry alone.

65

SIR MOSES MONTEFIORE AND 19TH-CENTURY JEWISH HISTORY

Sir Moses Montefiore (1784–1885) was the best-known Jew of the 19th century. He exemplified the highest hopes of Jewish emancipation by using the great distinction bestowed upon him by the English government to champion Jewish causes throughout the world. His involvement with Jewish life in the land of Israel helped shape that country in pre-Zionist days. While his intervention on behalf of Jews in Christian and Muslim lands did not always succeed in ameliorating their living conditions, it did show that Jews could be taken seriously by heads of state as spokesmen for humanitarian causes.

The name Montefiore today has lost some of the instant recognition it once had. Even New Yorkers may be ignorant of that city's Montefiore Hospital, and visitors to Jerusalem may be only dimly aware that the incongruous windmill that figures so prominently on that city's landscape was a gift of someone by that name. In today's world Rothschild is a better known name than Montefiore. Yet when marriage linked the two families in 1812, it was the former family that was the Johnny-come-lately on the British scene. When Moses Montefiore married the sister of Nathan Rothschild's wife, the Rothschilds had been in England for only a little more than a decade. The first Montefiores, by contrast, had arrived in England in the early 18th century and had already established themselves as one of Anglo-Jewry's premier families.

Partly as a result of the connection with the Rothschilds, Montefiore became a wealthy man. While the lure of financial wizardry kept a hold over Montefiore's brother-in-law Rothschild long after the latter became rich, Montefiore himself retired from business in 1824. From then on he devoted himself to serving the cause of Jews around the world. Because Montefiore lived for over a century, his involvement in Jewish affairs provides a window into what was going on in the Jewish world of his time.

By 1840, when Montefiore made his first and probably greatest success in international diplomacy on behalf of the Jews, he had already been knighted by Queen Victoria (1837) and was serving as president of the Board of Deputies of British Jews. Tall, strikingly handsome, and well-spoken, and with the diplomatic backing of Great Britain, Montefiore made an ideal emissary on behalf of a Jewish community in distress.

In February 1840, a Capuchin friar who had long lived in Damascus disappeared without a trace together with his Muslim servant. The Capuchins immediately spread a blood libel implicating the Jews of Damascus in the deaths: the Jews, argued the friars, sought blood for use in their Passover rituals. The French consul in Syria, who was responsible for the protection of all Catholics there, was less interested in conducting a responsible investigation than in supporting the reckless charge against the Jews. He did nothing to protest the rounding up of Jewish "suspects," the extortion of "confessions" under torture, the conversion of one of the suspects to avoid torture, or the seizure of sixty-three Jewish children as a means of forcing their mothers to reveal the hiding place of the friar's blood. Together with the French Jewish statesman Adolphe Crémieux, Montefiore traveled to Damascus. They succeeded not only in winning the release of the imprisoned Jews but also in convincing the Turkish sultan to issue a decree condemning blood accusations. Montefiore's success in this so-called Damascus affair proved that European Jewry was prepared to help beleaguered Jews in other locales.

Over the next several decades, Montefiore undertook other diplomatic ventures on behalf of far-flung Jewish communities. In 1846 Czar Nicholas I issued an order expelling the large Jewish population of the frontier area bordering Germany and Austria. With the backing not only of the Jewish communities of "enlightened" Europe but also of the British government, Montefiore and his wife traveled to Russia. His reception by the minister in charge of Jewish affairs and by the Czar himself made clear how seriously the Russian authorities viewed his visit. The withdrawal of the order of expulsion seemed to indicate that Montefiore's mission was successful, but Russian persecution of the Jews continued, with varying degrees of severity, for the duration of Montefiore's life and beyond. In 1872, when Montefiore was well into his eighties, he made a second trip to Russia, this time to represent the Board of Deputies of British Jews on the occasion of the bicentennial of the birth of Peter the Great. Once again, his reception by the Russian authorities was impeccable, and Montefiore expressed his conviction that the situation of Jews in Russia had improved. Within the decade, however, his conviction was proven wrong when a wave of the most vicious pogroms to date swept over the country (see nutshell #68).

Shortly after Montefiore's return to England from his first trip to Russia, Queen Victoria raised him to the rank of baronet with the explicit intention of aiding his efforts on behalf of Jews elsewhere in the world. He did not have to travel as far as Russia in order to attempt to do so. In 1858 he went to Rome to see what he could do in the so-called Mortara case. In June of that year the six-year-old son of the Jewish Mortara family of Bologna was taken by the papal police to a Roman institution for converts to Catholicism. It turned out that during an illness the child had suffered some five years earlier, his Catholic nurse had performed an irregular baptism in order to save the child's soul. Montefiore's visit, however, had no effect. The child, trained by the church, grew up to be not only a professor of theology but also an antisemitic missionary who preached his conversionary message in six languages.

Montefiore's other efforts on behalf of distressed Jewish communities took him on missions to Morocco in 1863, where he pleaded before the Muslim ruler for more humanitarian treatment not only of the Jewish population but of the Christian population as well, and to Rumania in 1867, where Montefiore's own life was threatened by an antisemitic riot. In 1865 he was on the verge of a visit to Persia to see what he could do to mitigate the persecution of the Jewish community there, when the British Foreign Office dissuaded him on the grounds that he might be risking his life in undertaking it. But he took the occasion of the shah of Persia's visit to London in 1873 to make a plea—unsuccessful, as it turned out—for better treatment of Persia's Jews.

For nearly half a century, Montefiore not only made occasional visits to different hot spots in the Jewish Diaspora but also seven trips to the Jewish settlement in the land of Israel. World Jewry considered Montefiore its delegate to the Holy Land as well as to the rest of the world: when American Jewish philanthropist Judah Touro died, his will stipulated that it was to be Montefiore—whom Touro had never met—who would allocate the money Touro had left for the development of Jewish life in the ancient homeland. Montefiore's contributions to living conditions there were numerous, and were a factor in more than doubling the number of Jewish inhabitants over the period. His building projects in Jerusalem include the central area of what is now the Israeli capital. He made efforts to improve the purity of the city's water supply, to educate the inhabitants of the country, and to improve conditions at the Western Wall. His windmill is one example of his attempt to industrialize the country.

One aspect of Montefiore's lifelong involvement in Jewish causes is perhaps less well known. Although as a young man he was not strictly Orthodox, he became so by the 1830s, and as such he became an inveterate foe of the burgeoning Reform movement in England, though his younger brother was one of its founders. Montefiore drew up a ban against the Reformers, and for years it was difficult for Reform Jews to be married or buried as Jews. Ironically enough, a grandnephew, Claude Goldsmid Montefiore (1858–1938), was to become the founder of what became Liberal Judaism in England.

It cannot be argued that Montefiore succeeded in all his undertakings on behalf of the Jews of his own country or around the world. Without question, however, he succeeded in providing a model from which Diaspora Jews today can still learn a lesson: Jews fortunate enough to live lives of financial ease and political security have a responsibility to their less fortunate brethren scattered around the globe.

66

EARLY ZIONIST VOICES

In the mid-19th century two Orthodox rabbis, Yehudah Alkalai (1798–1878) and Zevi Hirsch Kalischer (1795–1874), along with a secular Jew, Moses Hess (1812–1875), published writings that foreshadowed many themes of the later Zionist movement. The rabbis presented arguments challenging traditional beliefs that only God could bring about the return to Zion. Hess overcame an estrangement from Judaism to become the first spokesman for Zionist socialism.

Not until 1891 was the word *Zionism* first used to describe the movement promoting the return of the Jews to the land of Israel. But beginning over fifty years earlier, Jewish writers from two strikingly different backgrounds began to publish writings that touch on many later Zionist themes. Two Orthodox rabbis steeped in Jewish mysticism and a secular Jew steeped in socialist ideology found common ground in the belief that the future of the Jewish people was linked to their return to the land of Israel.

Not only did the *themes* of these early Zionist voices presage later Zionist messages. The different psychological *obstacles* these early spokesmen had to overcome also parallel those faced by two schools of later Zionist thought, the religious and the secular. According to traditional Orthodox belief, it was heretical to suggest that a return to Zion should be brought about by human intervention. The "ingathering of the exiles" would come about only when God sent the messiah. The rabbis had to overcome this objection. The secular Jew, an early socialist theoretician, had to find his way back to an involvement with his people before he could link the new ideology to their future.

As early as 1834, Rabbi Yehudah Alkalai was writing arguments suggesting that far from waiting passively for God to send the messiah to redeem the Jews from exile, Jews had to initiate the divine act by their own efforts. He used his training in Jewish mysticism to find and interpret texts to justify such human intervention. His background as a mystic also influenced his interpretation of current events. In mystical circles, where calculating the date for the Redemption was a time-honored activity, many believed that 1840 would be the long-awaited year. In that year the Jews of Damascus, charged with a blood libel, suffered terrible persecutions but were ultimately saved by the intervention of Moses Montefiore and Adolphe Crémieux, the leaders of English and French Jewry (see nutshell #65). Alkalai, rather than losing faith when the Redemption itself failed to occur, drew a different conclusion: the salvation of the Jews of Damascus was but one step toward, and the model for, the process of Redemption. Just as that community had been saved by the actions of notable Jews, similar actions by other outstanding Jews would little by little bring about the Redemption for all Jewry.

As rabbi of Serbia, Alkalai was also aware that the Serbs were beginning to demand independence from the Turkish Empire and that the nearby Greeks had already shaken off Turkish rule. Using the Bible as his guide, Alkalai believed that the Jews could buy the land of Israel from the Turks, just as the patriarch Abraham had bought a burial cave from Ephron the Hittite. Alkalai went so far as to suggest this scheme directly to Montefiore.

Nothing came of Alkalai's plans at the time, but later Zionists independently carried out some of Alkalai's suggestions. The Zionist Congresses that were held beginning in 1897 (see nutshell #71) recall Alkalai's plan for a "Great Assembly." The fifth of these congresses set up the Jewish National Fund, to perform a function likewise suggested by Alkalai: to acquire and develop land in Israel on behalf of the entire Jewish people.

Like Alkalai, Zevi Hirsch Kalischer viewed modern political events through a Jewish mystical lens. The fact that whole communities of Jews were securing rights through the process of emancipation (see nutshell #61), and that some Jews, like Rothschild (see nutshell #64) and Montefiore, were achieving unprecedented distinction were, for Kalischer, signs that the process of Redemption had begun. Just as human actions had secured these miraculous achievements, the next stages of the Redemption would be brought about by human intervention as well. The basic text of Jewish mysticism, the *Zohar*, teaches that by their actions "below" Jews on earth have the opportunity to influence the "upper world" directly (see nutshell #42), and Kalischer believed that Jewish actions would further the redemptive process. In the late 1830s, therefore, he suggested first to the head of the Rothschild family and then to Moses Montefiore that he buy from the Turks all of the land of Israel—or, at the very least, the Temple site in Jerusalem. Kalischer also argued that if other peoples were liberating themselves from foreign overlords in the name of their glorious national ancestry, "how much more should we exert ourselves, for our duty is to labor not only for the glory of our ancestors but for the glory of God who chose Zion!"

While Kalischer's entreaties encouraging well-placed Jews to buy up the Holy Land had no more effect than Alkalai's, his activities did yield some results. Under his influence, in 1866 a group purchased land for settlement on the outskirts of Jaffa, and four years later an agricultural school was set up there by the Alliance Israélite Universelle, the ten-year-old French organization formed to defend Jewish rights around the world.

But Kalischer's modest successes led to no bandwagon effect. On the contrary, traditional Jews in Israel resented and denounced his actions. They feared that the founding of agricultural settlements, to be worked by Jewish labor, would take Jews away from their true calling: the study of Torah.

Unlike Alkalai and Kalischer, Moses Hess presented a call for a return to Zion not from a mystical-rabbinical perspective but from a thoroughly secular one. Although as a young boy he had had some Jewish training from his grandfather, he became a secular intellectual. From an interest in philosophy, he moved into early socialist circles, even collaborating on two books with Marx and Engels before their groundbreaking *Communist Manifesto*. By the time the *Manifesto* appeared in 1848, Hess had broken with his former collaborators, who now felt nothing but contempt for Hess's "unscientific" ethical socialism. In fact, because of Hess's commitment to ethical socialism, which he equates with "Mosaic principles," he has been called "father of Zionist socialism."

Hess began his *Rome and Jerusalem* (1862) with an announcement that after a twenty-year "estrangement," he once more felt a part of his people. Impressed by the efforts of the Italian states to band together as the Italian nation, and aware of their hopes that the center of a new world of nations be in Rome, Hess proposed that that center be in Jerusalem instead. Laying out the foundations of Zionist socialism, Hess envisioned a return of the Jewish people to the ancestral homeland on these terms: the nation as a whole would acquire the land; legal conditions would be set up to govern work on the land; and a Jewish state based on social justice and other Jewish values would be established.

In an era when most Western Jews felt confident that Jews would eventually be fully accepted in the Diaspora, Hess expressed some doubts. He sensed that his own country, Germany, would never overcome its hostility to Jews, and that Jews must accept the fact that their true nationality is Jewish. His belief in a Jewish nationality also led him to reject much of the work of the religious Reformers. According to Hess, as long as the Jewish nation is denied a homeland, its national spirit finds embodiment in religious institutions alone. The Reform movement, by threatening those institutions and by denying Jewish nationality, also threatens to destroy the Jewish national spirit. Only by reconstructing national life in the land of Israel can that spirit be revived. Once the Jewish nation is restored to its homeland, then and only then can Jewish law begin to address the question of how religious institutions should be modified to reflect new circumstances.

For the most part, the early Zionist voices of Alkalai, Kalischer, and Hess fell on deaf ears. As long as the Jews of Europe remained convinced that their struggle for political rights would prove successful, they felt threatened by claims that the Jews were a nation. They did not want to arouse suspicion that

Jews were anything but true patriots, devoted to the national interests of the countries where they resided. As long as Jews were optimistic about their future in the Diaspora, as long as they felt that it was just a matter of time until they were fully accepted, they saw no need for a "homeland" elsewhere. Although Alkalai, Kalischer, and Hess touched on many themes of later Zionist theory in their works, none of them focused on what would become a major theme by the end of the 19th century: that Jews needed a homeland to ensure their very physical survival.

67

MODERN ANTISEMITISM

In the last decades of the 19th century, the term antisemitism was coined to describe and legitimize a new kind of hatred of Jews. No longer were Jews hated simply because of their religion. The new antisemitism, now a pseudo-scientific theory based on supposed racial contrasts, blamed Jews for all the dislocations of modern life. Like earlier hatred of the Jews, modern antisemitism was based on what was perceived as the alien nature of Jewish civilization. This perception caused ideological-religous and then racial antisemitism to arise. The new antisemitism was expressed in both economic and social ways.

According to 20th-century American Jewish novelist Joseph Heller, "Nothing succeeds as planned." Certainly, 19th-century European Jews did not expect that the successes Jews were experiencing in economic, social, and political life would lead to anything but their full acceptance into European society. Instead, by the last decades of the century, partly as a result of these very successes, Europe was in the grip of a new kind of anti-Jewish hatred. Jews were discovering that though they might dress, speak, and worship very much like their gentile neighbors, they were still considered an alien presence. Nor was this modern version of hostility toward Jews restricted to the uneducated sector of society. Indeed, the new science of Jew hatred became very fashionable among the intelligentsia as well.

Dramatic change had swept across Europe during the course of the century, and the Jews provided a convenient scapegoat for many of those whose existence was destabilized as old established social roles were overturned. The political revolutions that furthered democracy across Europe meant a loss of status and power for the old nobility and clergy. In the estimation of some of the losers, the Jews seemed the most obvious gainers, and anti-Jewish resentment built. Similarly, the Industrial Revolution and the rise of capitalism meant new challenges to agricultural laborers and more intense competition for shopkeepers. To them, too, the Jews seemed the group who most benefited from the painful changes.

The financial success of many Jews led critics on the left to smear Jewish capitalists. As early as 1808, French left-wing anti-Jewish sentiment identified commerce as the root of all evil and labeled Jews the embodiment of commerce. By the middle of the century, Karl Marx, the major theoretician of modern socialism and himself the grandson of a rabbi, had launched a major attack against the Jews along these lines. Not only were Jews the slaves of Mammon, but they had also corrupted their Christian neighbors into believing that all that matters is money. Marx even redefined emancipation to accommodate his contemptuous characterization of the Jews: true emancipation meant freeing society from the Jewish emphasis on money and unscrupulous financial practices. The striking successes of the Rothschild family, with its base in five European countries (see nutshell #64), also fostered suspicions of an "international Jewish conspiracy" (see nutshell #80).

Of course, not all Jews were wealthy capitalists. Large numbers were struggling workers, and in Russia and elsewhere many became involved in radical politics seeking to overthrow repressive governments. Supporters of those governments were quick to suggest that Jews everywhere were involved in a conspiracy to topple rightful regimes.

Jews were depicted on one hand, then, as the evil incarnation of exploitative capitalism, and on the other as the promoters of political and social unrest. For some, the goal of the Jew was to dominate the established social order; for others, to annihilate it. It sometimes seemed that conservatives and radicals could agree on only one thing: the Jew was to blame for all the problems of society. A respected professor of history at the University of Berlin summed up the matter with a phrase that the Nazis would adopt: "The Jews are our misfortune."

Hatred of the Jews, of course, was nothing new. But in the past it had been based on religious difference. The Jew was viewed as a rejecter and the killer of Christ, but by accepting the divinity of Jesus, a Jew could overcome these disabilities. But the new anti-Jewish sentiment no longer had a purely religious basis. It was broadened to reject Jews on the basis of specious racial differences. Linguists had distinguished between the Indo-European Aryan languages, based on Sanskrit, and the Semitic languages, based on Hebrew and other languages of the ancient Near East. Now social "scientists" broadened the distinction between languages into a contrast of racial traits: the Aryan races of northern Europe were physically strong and culturally creative, while the Semitic races lacked these positive traits and excelled only in selfish, materialistic cunning. With their noxious Semitic traits, Jews, unrooted in a single land and thus aliens in all the European countries, threatened the cultural life of those countries. The new term *antisemitism* was coined in 1879 to describe this racist theory.

In the older form of anti-Jewish hatred, conversion wiped the slate clean and enabled a Jew to enter society. But in modern antisemitism this was no longer the case. Semitic racial traits, it was argued, endured from generation to generation, and mere conversion would not eliminate them. Assimilation and even conversion were no longer tickets enabling Jews to gain entry into European society. To the contrary: by their attempt to blend into the Aryan societies where they lived, assimilated Jews and converts to Christianity threatened the biological purity of the Aryan race.

This pernicious racial theory led to some unexpected and terrifying but completely logical conclusions. If Jewish racial traits persisted over the generations, then not only Judaism but also Christianity was a threat to Aryan culture. Not only was the Christian God a Jew, but St. Paul, the originator of Christianity, was a Jew. In addition, Christianity sympathized with the underdog rather than glorifying physical strength, as true Aryan culture did. Thus in certain German antisemitic circles, one offshoot of the new racial theory was the rejection of Christianity and a call for the return to the pagan roots of Germanic culture.

A second consequence of the new antisemitism was, with benefit of hindsight, much more unsettling. If Jewish racial traits were not only a cultural but also a biological threat to Aryan cultures, the argument went, then every effort must be made to eradicate those traits. Just as medical science takes no pity on life-threatening viruses and bacteria but seeks to exterminate them, so must Aryan culture seek to exterminate the Jewish threat. By the end of the 19th century, the seeds had been sown for the vicious Nazi campaign against the Jews that would begin only decades later.

68

THE POGROMS OF 1881

The word pogrom—*Russian for "riot"—became associated during the last decades of czarist rule with attacks against the Jews. While pogroms varied in intensity, they often included looting, rape, and murder. Russian Jews had been victims of pogroms earlier in the 19th century, but the series of pogroms beginning in 1881 mark a watershed in Russian Jewish history. When neither the government, the press, nor the intelligentsia rallied to the victims' cause, Russian Jews in ever larger numbers turned to revolutionary movements seeking to overthrow the czar, to mass migration, and to Jewish nationalism.*

Many Jewish historians today lament the emphasis often found in popular surveys on the woes that have beset the Jews over the ages. They reject the so-called "lachrymose theory" of Jewish history and seek to redress it by stressing the many positive contributions of Jews to civilization. Nonetheless, historians recognize that certain tragic events in Jewish history mark significant turning points. No one questions, for example, that the years 586 B.C.E. and 70 C.E., in which the First and Second Temples, respectively, were destroyed, or 1492, when the Jews were expelled from Spain, mark crucial watersheds in Jewish history. Although the significance of the year 1881 is not as universally recognized, Jewish historians consider it a major turning point in Jewish history as well. Russian Jewish reactions to the pogroms of that year decisively shaped not only the future history of their own country but of world Jewry as well.

The pogroms of 1881 were sparked by an important event in general Russian history. In March, members of a revolutionary group assassinated the czar, Alexander II. Ironically, Alexander II was a relatively liberal despot; he had liberated the Russian serfs, did not initiate any significant new anti-Jewish restrictions, and opened up certain professions to Jews.

Among the minor participants in the plot was a young Jewish woman, and the press, with the government's blessing, aroused popular sentiment against the Jews. About a month later a pogrom broke out in a town in Ukraine, where a tradition of anti-Jewish sentiment ran deep. A wave of pogroms ensued, and before the year's end over a hundred cities and villages in southern regions of the czarist domain witnessed attacks of varying degrees of severity against the Jewish population.

The extent to which the government itself was implicated in initiating the pogroms is not clear, but in many cases the local authorities did little to curb the violence or to assist the victims. Both victims and perpetrators had the sense that the attacks were carried out with the government's blessing.

In fact, the new czar, Alexander III, blamed the Jews themselves for causing the pogroms. The government went through the motions of uncovering the root causes of the attacks by appointing local investigative commissions. The highly biased data-seekers came to the conclusion that Jewish control of commerce, industry, and real estate, coupled with Jewish exploitation of the "general population," were at the root of the problem. From the government's point of view, the only way to prevent the outbreak of such attacks in the future was to protect "the general inhabitants" from Jewish economic exploitation.

These self-styled protective measures included new severe restrictions on the Jews. In May 1882, a series of laws was passed placing new limits on where Jews could live (they were forbidden to settle outside towns and townlets), what real estate they could hold (all deeds of sale or lease of real estate to Jews outside the towns and townlets were canceled), and when they could work (they were prohibited from doing trade on the Christian Sabbath or holidays). Although these laws were called "temporary," in fact they were not repealed until 1917, when the czarist regime was finally toppled. During that period, the laws were alleviated in some locations, but the general effect of the May Laws on Jewish livelihood was devastating.

In addition to the May Laws, other restrictions on Jews followed the pogroms of 1881. In the past, the czarist government had sought to impose secular education on the Jewish population as a way of encouraging assimilation. Now, in an about-face, the government concluded that educating the Jews gave them a competitive edge. Thus, in 1884, the government shut down the first Jewish craft school in Russia, which had been in operation for over twenty years, since the "general population" did not have such schools. The government also instituted the infamous *numerus clausus*—or fixed proportion—that limited the number of Jews admitted to Russian high schools, universities, and various professions. For example, between 1882 and 1887, institutions training military physicians limited the number of Jews to 5 percent of the entire student body, and secondary schools and universities set aside for Jewish applicants a maximum of 3 percent to 10 percent of openings, depending on location.

In the years following the pogroms of 1881 the government continued to exert different types of administrative pressure on the Jews. Although the Ministry of the Interior announced none too subtly at the beginning of 1882 that "the western border is open to the Jews"—in other words, that the government encouraged the Jewish population to leave—heavy fines were imposed on Jewish families whose sons failed to show up for military duty because they had emigrated. In 1891, 20,000 Jewish artisans living legally in Moscow were expelled—bound in chains, with a police escort—in order to "purify the sacred historic capital." With each new repressive decree, it became clearer that, far from seeking to protect its Jewish populace, the government had seized on the pogroms of 1881 to declare an ongoing open season on the Jews.

The physical cost to Russian Jews of the pogroms of 1881 seems modest compared to other massacres in Jewish history; the numbers of maimed and homeless could be counted in the hundreds. But the psychological impact was staggering. Until 1881, many Russian Jews, like their counterparts in western Europe, lived in hope that the czarist regime would ultimately become a democratic constitutional monarchy that would foster the well-being of all its subjects. The government's response to the pogroms, however, disabused even the most optimistic Jews of this expectation. Russian Jews were disappointed not only in the government, but also in their compatriots. Participants in pogroms included educated people; noted intellectuals like Tolstoy and Turgenev did not rally to the Jews' cause, and even the most respected newspapers supported the anti-Jewish frenzy.

Loss of faith in the state led Russian Jews in different directions. Even before the pogroms of 1881, many Jews had become involved in revolutionary groups seeking to overthrow the czars. Those numbers now escalated. By the end of the century, a group of eastern European Jewish socialists and workers formed the Jewish socialist party called the Bund. The Bund believed in the solidarity of the Jewish working class with the working classes of other peoples, and considered the Jewish bourgeoisie its enemy as much as any other capitalist group. For the Bund, Yiddish rather than Hebrew was the appropriate language for the Jewish working class, and Zionism (see nutshell #66) represented a form of bourgeois nationalism. Significant numbers of Bundists eventually migrated from Russia to the United States, where they played an important role in the American labor movement.

Emigration itself was another Jewish response to the pogroms of 1881. As large numbers of eastern European Jews poured into the United States and other countries, the center of gravity of Jewish life began to shift. The composition of American Jewry changed dramatically, and the American Jewish community would ultimately seize the mantle of Jewish leadership from its western European counterpart.

The most significant intellectual response to the pogroms of 1881 was the publication of a pamphlet that would help transform Zionism into a force in Jewish and world affairs. *Auto-Emancipation*, the anonymously published pamphlet by a secularly trained Russian Jewish physician, Leo Pinsker, became a basic document in Zionist literature. In it, Pinsker despairs of finding a solution to antisemitism among so-called enlightened humanity. He argues that Jewish emigration to other nations is not a solution because antisemitism will eventually arise there. The only hope for the Jews is to assert themselves as a nation and find a home—if possible, in the ancient land of Israel—where they can no longer be considered aliens, as they are everywhere else they live.

The pogroms of 1881, then, galvanized Russian Jews in ways that would powerfully affect world history over the course of the next century and beyond.

69

THE BEGINNINGS OF ALIYAH

Immigration to Israel is called aliyah, *from the Hebrew word "to go up."*
Organized aliyah *began even before the word* Zionism *entered the lexi-*
con. Following the pogroms of 1881, groups calling themselves "Lovers
of Zion" encouraged settlement in the land of Israel. The immigrants who
left Europe for Israel in the two decades beginning in 1882 constitute
the First Aliyah.

The Russian pogroms of 1881 (see nutshell #68) convinced nearly all the Jews
of Russia that the solution to their problem lay in emigration. Not all Russian
Jews, however, agreed on which country would be the most sensible place to
immigrate to. There was a large group who favored America, but a tiny group
actively promoted immigration to the land of Israel as offering better long-term
prospects for Jewish national revitalization. This group, which consisted of
numerous local organizations, called themselves "Lovers of Zion," and their
overall movement "Love of Zion." Beginning in 1882, members of these groups
began to emigrate to the land of Israel.

The Love of Zion movement sprang up in response to the same wave of
pogroms that led Dr. Leo Pinsker to publish *Auto-Emancipation* in 1882.
Pinsker's pamphlet first appeared anonymously, but when it became known
that he was its author, he agreed reluctantly to assume leadership of the entire
Love of Zion movement. Pinsker, despite his intellectual acuity, however, was
neither a very effective nor a very willing leader, and the Lovers of Zion never
cohered into a tightly knit organization.

Pinsker and other spokesmen of the Love of Zion movement basically believed that a real solution to the "Jewish problem" required a political basis:
governments must be made to acknowledge the plight of the Jews and to support the founding of a Jewish homeland. But for two reasons the Love of Zion
movement avoided what would soon become known as "political Zionism" and
focused instead on what became known as "practical Zionism"—namely, encouragement of small-scale settlement in the land of Israel. First, for nearly a
decade the Russian government forbade the movement to operate officially,
forcing the Lovers of Zion to avoid the political arena and focus not on deal-

ing with heads of state but on helping individuals settle in the land of Israel. Second, Russian Lovers of Zion hoped to encourage western European Jews to join the movement, and most Western Jews shunned any undertaking that might cast suspicion on the depth of their patriotic commitment. As a result, Pinsker's opening address at the first Lovers of Zion conference in 1884 avoided all mention of national revival and stressed instead the need for Jews to return to working the land.

Although Pinsker's decision to tone down his aspirations is understandable, many young Jews wrote off the Love of Zion movement for its timidity. Where Pinsker's pamphlet had inspired young Jews to make invidious comparisons between emancipation—a mere gift of gentile hosts—and "auto-emancipation," or self-liberation, the Love of Zion movement seemed to satisfy itself with much more modest goals. The lack of enthusiasm of young Lovers of Zion was only one reason for the failure of the movement ever to become a coherent whole. Hampered by a small income, which made major undertakings impossible, the Love of Zion movement was also plagued by Pinsker's ill health and growing pessimism, by poor organization, and by internal feuds.

All these shortcomings of the Love of Zion movement notwithstanding, it was the prime force behind the First *Aliyah*, the first organized wave of settlement in the land of Israel. From 1882 for the next two decades, approximately 30,000 Jews left Europe for their ancient homeland. Upon arriving, they discovered a preexisting Jewish community that could hardly have been more different from the newcomers demographically, culturally, and religiously.

The "old settlement," as it was called, consisted of about 25,000 Jews, living primarily in Jerusalem but also in the three other "holy" cities—Safed, Tiberias, and Hebron—as well as in the two newer cities of Jaffa and Haifa. Nearly all the old-timers, whether of Sephardic or Ashkenazic descent, and whether hasidic in lifestyle or not, were extremely religious. Many were opposed to anything that smacked of modernity or even of change. Most were supported by donations from Jewish communities abroad but were suspicious of philanthropy intended to promote careers in agriculture or handicrafts.

Not surprisingly, members of the old settlement did not greet the newcomers with enthusiasm, and for over a decade the two groups were engaged in divisive clashes. The new settlers included many who were not religious, and some rabbinical leaders of the old settlement, horrified by what they perceived as the immigrants' loose morals, went so far as to notify the Turkish authorities that leaders of the newcomers were inciting the Jews to rebel against the established government. By the late 1890s, however, the religious old-timers and the secular newcomers had worked out a modus vivendi, allowing for peaceful, if often tense, coexistence between the two groups.

The clash between the old settlement and the new was neither the only nor the worst problem that the participants of the First *Aliyah* faced. In addition to

the malaria they contracted by working in swampy land, they faced the opposition of the Turkish government, which perceived almost immediately that the
new *aliyah* was different from the smaller-scale migrations of the past. Fearing that the new immigrants might indeed represent a political threat to their
rule, the Turks banned immigration completely in May 1882. In order to gain
entry into Israel, the settlers had to infiltrate the country secretly, often relying
on bribery. In addition, the Turks not only did their best to make it difficult for
Jews to purchase land but also required a special permit from Constantinople
for every building project.

Another serious problem arose almost from the outset. Although the participants in the First *Aliyah* quickly set up some agricultural settlements, they
soon discovered that they lacked both the professional expertise and the financial wherewithal to make them succeed on a long-term basis. They were forced,
therefore, to seek outside help. Pinsker and other Love of Zion leaders turned
to the head of the French branch of the Rothschild bank (see nutshell #64), the
Baron Edmond de Rothschild (1845–1934).

From 1883 to 1899, many of the settlements were in effect run by experts
from abroad handpicked by the baron. While the baron's assistance kept the
early settlement project from collapsing, it was not without serious drawbacks.
While the baron's people were trained professionals, they were not Jewish nationalists themselves nor did they comprehend the nationalist aspirations of
the settlers. Instead, many had contempt for the settlers, whom they dismissed
as charity cases. As the baron's managers took over the long-range planning
and day-to-day operations, the settlers began to view themselves as hired hands
and consequently became less personally committed to the success of their
endeavors. As interest among the Jewish settlers waned, the baron's people
began to rely more and more on Arab labor, further alienating the settlers from
the undertaking. Only in 1899 did Baron Rothschild address these problems
by transferring management of "his" settlements to the Jewish Colonization
Association, which helped train the settlers to become independent.

One of the first to focus on the shortcomings of the Love of Zion as a movement in general and on its implementation of the First *Aliyah* specifically was
Ahad HaAm (1856–1927), himself a member of the movement and one of the
important Zionist thinkers. Ahad HaAm—the pen name of Asher Ginzberg,
whose modesty led him to sign his work as "one of the people"—argued that
the Lovers of Zion had hastened to set up settlements without adequately preparing the immigrants. The would-be settlers were often given incomplete or
misleading information about the conditions they would find upon arrival in
the land of Israel. Small wonder that numbers of them chose not to remain to
work the land.

Ahad HaAm also insisted that the Lovers of Zion were wrong to look to a
well-meaning but absent philanthropist to prop up numbers of shaky settle-

ments. Far preferable would be to have a single model settlement, entirely run by truly committed settlers themselves. He also criticized the settlers for treating the Arab inhabitants of the land with disrespect, and forecast that such behavior could only result in arousing resentment toward the Jews in a region where it had hitherto been largely absent, namely, the land of Israel.

In general, Ahad HaAm felt that the focus of the Love of Zion movement was misguided. The Jewish national homeland should not be seen as a panacea for all the economic and spiritual problems of the Jewish people as a whole. Instead, the movement should seek to establish a "national spiritual center" in the ancient homeland: a committed group of Jews based there would bring about a cultural revival of the Jewish people that would ultimately energize Jews everywhere.

Ahad HaAm recognized that he himself lacked practical leadership qualities, and although his writings were very influential, he never sought leadership positions. Nonetheless, his views helped shape the thinking of future Zionist leaders.

The Love of Zion movement and the First *Aliyah* carried out under its auspices achieved only limited success. The approximately 1,000 Jews a year who left Europe for the land of Israel during the period of the First *Aliyah* succeeded in establishing about twenty agricultural settlements. But as the settlers relied increasingly on Arab labor, many lost interest in developing a distinctively Hebrew culture, and—even among those who retained their early enthusiasm—many were unable to transmit their ideals to their children. The main achievement of the First *Aliyah* was in preparing the groundwork for the Second *Aliyah*, whose participants were mostly young Russians fleeing the pogroms of 1903. The idealism and commitment to national cultural rebirth of these later immigrants truly transformed the nature of Jewish settlement in the land of Israel. In the meantime, the Love of Zion movement was largely absorbed by the World Zionist Organization, founded after Theodor Herzl's arrival on the scene (see nutshell #71).

70

THE DREYFUS AFFAIR

The Dreyfus affair, beginning with the 1894 arrest for treason, convic-
tion, exile, and imprisonment of a Jewish officer in the French army, tore
apart French society for the rest of the century. Despite the officer's
eventual exoneration, the affair's repercussions had long-term effects on
world history, as well as on Jewish and French history.

Many Americans have become so cynical about government that late-breaking
news of another scandal and cover-up sometimes elicits only a ho-hum response.
Where Watergate engaged the passions of many people, fewer people follow
in great detail the unfolding of the later instances of government skulduggery
known colloquially as Irangate and Iraqgate. But the first modern government
scandal to convulse an entire nation took place not in this country in this century but rather in France in the late 19th century. The focal figure in the affair
was Alfred Dreyfus, the sole Jew (albeit an assimilated one) on the General
Staff of the French army. If the Dreyfus affair were to occur today in America,
it would probably be dubbed Dreyfusgate. Just as the American head of state
tried to calm down the citizenry during the unfolding of Watergate by assuring
them that their president was "not a crook," so French officials tried to defuse
the situation at the time by announcing that "there is no Dreyfus affair."

Although the detailed chronology of the events in the Dreyfus affair is anything but uncomplicated, one can paint a picture in broad strokes. It began very
much like a spy thriller, with a memorandum pulled out of a garbage pail by a
supposed cleaning woman at the German embassy in Paris. The cleaning woman
was actually an agent for the division of the French military concerned with
counterespionage. The memorandum, though unsigned, was clearly from a
French officer offering to sell military secrets to the German military attaché.
Once the memorandum was turned over to the War Office, suspicion settled
on Captain Alfred Dreyfus, who was not only a probationer on the army's
General Staff but also the only Jew. Although handwriting experts did not
unanimously confirm that Dreyfus wrote the memorandum, in short order he
was accused of high treason and arrested, court-martialed, sentenced to deportation, and exiled to Devil's Island in French Guiana.

Neither Dreyfus's family nor a growing number of French intellectuals who were convinced of the convicted man's innocence were willing to let the matter die, however. Over the next few years, evidence was uncovered and leaked to the press proving not only that another officer was guilty but also that the military had forged documents to implicate Dreyfus. Reluctantly, the army agreed to set aside the first conviction and brought Dreyfus back from prison for a second trial. Though the second court-martial found Dreyfus "guilty with extenuating circumstances," he was soon pardoned. Not content with a pardon that left the presumption of guilt, Dreyfus's supporters—known as Dreyfusards—continued their struggle. Finally, in July 1906, nearly twelve years after his implication in a crime he did not commit, Dreyfus's conviction was annulled. He was not only reinstated in the French army as a captain but was also decorated with a military award in the courtyard of the Ecole Militaire—the site where, over a decade earlier, he had been degraded and stripped of his military paraphernalia.

Although Jewish scapegoats were not a new phenomenon, several noteworthy aspects of the Dreyfus affair combined to make it a major event in modern history, and not just for French citizens and Jews. Nowadays, we are familiar with full-page ads in major newspapers signed by university professors, clergy, and other professionals, who lend the prestige of their names and affiliations in support of various causes. Until the time of the Dreyfus affair, intellectuals acting only as individuals sometimes publicly supported or opposed political events, but for the first time the intelligentsia emerged as an organized political force. The first "petition of intellectuals" appeared, with Dreyfusard members of the intelligentsia collecting signatures of like-minded colleagues willing to identify themselves publicly. It should be noted, however, that not all intellectuals aligned themselves with the Dreyfusards. The question of what role an intellectual should play in society formulated itself in terms that guaranteed a division in the ranks: should an intellectual identify with such universal values as "justice" even if doing so threatened the stability of the nation? Or should an intellectual put the nation's security and well-being above all, even at the expense of an individual's rights?

Another way in which the Dreyfus affair marked a turning point in modern history was in the use both sides made of the press and of two fledgling art forms, photography and cinema. The already active French antisemitic press first leaked the story of an officer's arrest for espionage and identified him as Dreyfus the Jew. This early press involvement forced the army into a hasty conviction with no real evidence. Three years later, after the real author of the memorandum was acquitted by a court-martial, novelist Emile Zola's famous letter "J'accuse!" ("I accuse!") was printed in a Dreyfusard newspaper. Zola charged the army with knowingly convicting an innocent man and exculpating a guilty one. In many ways, the uproar that followed—including antisemitic riots that spread throughout France and its colonial possessions—transformed the Dreyfus case into "the affair." The release in France of photographs of the resulting attacks on Jews in

Algiers helped keep passions inflamed. The following year, Dreyfus's second court-martial led to the filming of the first docudrama. Because the film actually caused fistfights in movie theaters, it also led to the first instance of government film censorship; in France, until 1950 it was forbidden to show films on the Dreyfus affair, and until 1974 to produce a film on the subject. Interestingly enough—and indicative of the curiosity the affair stimulated beyond French borders—films have kept the English-speaking public aware of the Dreyfus affair throughout the 20th century. The Academy Award winner *Life of Emile Zola* (1937) was followed by *I Accuse* (1958). A 1992 American made-for-television movie starred Richard Dreyfuss (no relation) as the French military officer who first became convinced of Dreyfus's innocence.

Other consequences of the affair include a decisive turning point in the history of political Zionism on the one hand and the institutionalization of French antisemitism on the other. Theodor Herzl, father of political Zionism (see nutshell #71), was present in Paris at the time of Dreyfus's degradation. As correspondent for a prestigious Viennese newspaper, he was among the few journalists allowed to witness the humiliation of the Jewish officer. Herzl, although long aware of antisemitism in Vienna, had cherished the thought that France, home of "liberty, equality, and fraternity" and the first European country to emancipate its Jews, was free of such prejudice. The sight of his coreligionist's disgrace led Herzl to doubt the efficacy of emancipation and assimilation in lessening the plight of the world's Jews. Shortly thereafter Herzl was to write *The Jewish State*, a book that would change the course of Jewish history.

Although the Dreyfus affair concluded with the exoneration of Dreyfus and the seeming victory of pro-Jewish forces over antisemitism, it actually reshaped and hardened divisions in French society. The Dreyfusards may have won the immediate battle, but the anti-Dreyfusards merely went underground and regrouped for the next skirmish. When the Nazis emerged on the scene, there were many French who announced that Hitler was preferable to Leon Blum, the left-wing Jewish prime minister who had been among the young Dreyfusards. The Vichy government that collaborated with Hitler has been called "the revenge of the anti-Dreyfusards."

Remarkably, the Dreyfus affair is still able to arouse passions in France. In 1982 a French sculptor was commissioned by the minister of culture to create a piece commemorating Captain Dreyfus. After the work's completion, however, the minister of defense refused to have it installed, as originally planned, at the Ecole Militaire, the site of both Dreyfus's degradation and rehabilitation. And in February 1994, nearly a century after the arrest of Dreyfus, the lingering divisions between Dreyfusards and anti-Dreyfusards surfaced once again. France's defense minister dismissed the head of the army's history section for issuing a report that stopped short of confirming that Dreyfus had been framed. According to the report, "Dreyfus's innocence is the thesis now generally accepted by historians."

71

THEODOR HERZL, THE JEWISH STATE, AND THE FIRST ZIONIST CONGRESS

Theodor Herzl (1860–1904) is considered the founding father of the modern state of Israel even though he died nearly half a century before the state's establishment. As author of The Jewish State, *Herzl was first to address the Zionist message not to a small coterie of like-minded Jews alone but to the heads of state and citizens of gentile Europe. As convener of the First Zionist Congress, he organized the first representative body of the Jewish people in modern times.*

For decades, assessments of the life and work of Theodor Herzl—the man who transformed a fractious bunch of Zionist dreamers into a powerful popular movement—bore more than a passing resemblance to hagiography. In recent years, however, biographers have directed attention to the hero's clay feet, focusing on his immature attachment to his mother, his vengeful attitude toward his estranged wife, his propensity toward impractical and self-aggrandizing schemes, and his unwillingness to recognize serious obstacles (including the presence of a large Arab population in the historic homeland). Yet even his most unforgiving critics acknowledge the amazing force of Herzl's personality and the relentless drive that enabled him to bring parochial Jewish interests into the international arena.

Born in Budapest and raised there and in Vienna by well-to-do assimilated parents, Herzl struggled for many years with his Jewish identity. Tormented by a generous measure of Jewish self-hatred, he would confide to his diary that antisemitism had some beneficial aspects: it would, for example, help curb the rapacious instincts of Jewish businessmen. Nonetheless, he was obsessed with the problem of how the Jew could overcome society's hatred. He toyed with the idea of challenging the leading Austrian antisemites to a duel: if he were to die, a letter he would leave behind would open people's eyes to his insights on the subject; if he succeeded in killing one of his opponents, he would turn his trial into an indictment of antisemitism, culminating in his acquittal. For a while,

Herzl tried to convince himself that antisemitism could be overcome by complete assimilation. To help achieve that goal, he dreamed of leading a procession of all the Jews of Vienna to St. Stephan Cathedral to undergo mass baptism. But his awareness of the hatred directed centuries earlier to the Marranos (see nutshell #46) even after their conversion worried Herzl. On some level he knew that assimilation and even conversion would not keep antisemites from hating Jews or former Jews.

Herzl later claimed that what turned him into a Zionist was his connection to the Dreyfus affair (see nutshell #70): as Paris correspondent of Vienna's leading liberal newspaper, he watched Captain Alfred Dreyfus be stripped of military rank in the courtyard of the Ecole Militaire on January 5, 1895, while the mobs outside chanted antisemitic slogans. For a variety of reasons, historians reject Herzl's claim as an oversimplification. He had already written for his paper about the resurgence of antisemitism in France, home of "liberty, equality, and fraternity," and was aware of recent political gains by antisemites in Vienna, one of Europe's most culturally advanced cities. But regardless of what marked the decisive moment in Herzl's life, it is clear that by the spring of 1895, Herzl had come to believe—completely independently, without the slightest inkling that other Jews, both secular and religious, had reached the same conclusion—that the only answer to the "Jewish problem" was the establishment of a Jewish homeland.

Hoping to gain the support of wealthy and influential Jews, he first wrote to Baron Maurice de Hirsch (1831–1896), a financier and philanthropist who was already engaged in settling Russian Jews in Argentina. In asking for an appointment with Hirsch to discuss the "Jewish problem," Herzl implied that his proposal would finally give the baron a chance to do something really worthwhile with his money. The meeting—Herzl's first action on behalf of the Zionist cause—took place in early June 1895, but ended in failure. Baron de Hirsch dismissed Herzl without giving him a chance to spell out the details of his scheme. Undaunted, Herzl followed up with a letter, his first written statement of his Zionist views. When de Hirsch ignored the letter, Herzl decided to turn to the Rothschilds (see nutshell #64). Over the next week or so, he worked out in his diary an "Address to the Rothschilds." He hoped to convince the wealthy family that the best way to protect its fortune from being undermined by jealous gentiles was to support a program of migration to and settlement in a Jewish state. Herzl was dissuaded from presenting his plan to the family, however, when a physician friend in whom he confided told Herzl he must be suffering from a nervous breakdown.

But Herzl did not give up. Resolved to put his plan before the public, he revised his notes. The result, his Zionist pamphlet *The Jewish State*, appeared first in the *London Jewish Chronicle* in January 1896, and was published in Vienna the following month. The most famous sentence from the pamphlet reads, "We are a people—one people." Herzl, who once accepted antisemitic stereotypes of eastern European Jews, now concluded that Eastern and Western Jews are in the same boat: all are the victims of antisemitism. But his belief in the inevitability of antisemitism as long as Jews lived in gentile lands led him to a novel theory: in order to rid themselves of the "Jewish problem," governments of all countries would actually help set up the Jewish state. Herzl distinguished between the "teakettle phenomena" of current Zionist projects and the steamroller "political Zionism" he had in mind: instead of settlers illegally sneaking into Israel and establishing small settlements, a Jewish state should be established through diplomatic means—by meetings between heads of state and representatives of the newly acknowledged Jewish nation. Herzl was not adamant about the location of the Jewish state, and considered Argentina a possibility along with the historic land of Israel.

Unlike earlier Zionist tracts, *The Jewish State* was aimed not solely at Jews but at a general audience. Herzl hoped to demonstrate that antisemitism was not merely a scourge that Jews had to bear but also an international political issue to be resolved on the level of international diplomacy. If the idea of a Jewish nation had until now been discussed only in small groups with no influence, Herzl was now attempting to make it an issue worthy of the attention of heads of state.

Although *The Jewish State* would be published in eighty separate editions in eighteen languages, it did not win over the hearts and minds of Western Jews. The head of the English branch of the Rothschilds publicly announced his refusal to meet with Herzl. In Paris, Herzl succeeded in meeting with Baron Edmond de Rothschild in July 1896, but the philanthropist raised objections to "political Zionism": it would call into question the patriotism of Diaspora Jews and would endanger the settlements already under way in Israel.

Even as he was being snubbed by the Jewish establishment, however, Herzl discovered that eastern European Jews were more than eager to respond to his call. Lord Rothschild might refuse to meet with him in Piccadilly, but eastern European immigrants in London's East End welcomed him and his message with thunderous applause. Russian Jewish students studying at Western universities rallied around him. And in eastern Europe itself, where censorship prevented Jews from reading *The Jewish State*, word spread of the remarkable, handsome, well-educated assimilated Jew who had returned to his people, to lead them, like Moses or the messiah, to the Holy Land. In June 1896, while en route to what he hoped would be a meeting with the Turkish sultan in Constantinople, Herzl's train stopped in Sofia, Bulgaria; hundreds of Jews met the train at the station, eager to greet their new leader.

Aware now of the potential power of the Zionist movement, Herzl began to issue invitations to a conference for all who shared similar views. The result was the First Zionist Congress, which met in Basel, Switzerland, during the final days of August 1897. The very opposition of the Jewish establishment to the proposed meeting helped publicize it, and about 200 delegates from nearly twenty countries attended. Herzl's own newspaper, owned by assimilated Jews who rejected Zion-

ism, boycotted the event, choosing instead to cover an Oxford conference of
Jewish tailors to discuss fashions for women cyclists. But twenty-six newspapers
did send correspondents to cover the proceedings of the First Zionist Congress.

Herzl, whose journalistic career was punctuated by unsuccessful attempts to
make a big name as a dramatist, gave free rein to his theatrical skills in staging the
Congress. He insisted that all delegates wear black tie, thus conferring an aura of
dignity on the proceedings. Lacking a curtain and scenery, he transformed Basel's
Municipal Casino into a parliamentary hall with the prototype of the flag of the
state of Israel: a large white-and-blue banner with a blue Star of David in the center.

The First Zionist Congress adopted what came to be known as "the Basel
Program." Every word was examined for possible connotations that might upset
governments or factions. The Zionist goal was defined as the establishment of
"a home for the Jewish people in Palestine secured under public law"; the word
state was rejected, so as not to antagonize Turkey. The Congress established
the World Zionist Organization—the political organization of the "Jewish
people en route"—and elected Herzl its president. It also set up institutions,
along the lines projected by Herzl in *The Jewish State*, that were to serve the
Zionist movement for the next fifty years.

In his diary Herzl assessed what he had achieved at the Congress: "In Basel
I founded the Jewish State." Although the idea might provoke laughter at the
moment, he said, it would surely be realized within fifty years. In fact, just
over fifty years later, on May 14, 1948, the state of Israel was founded (see
nutshell #89). Herzl died decades before that goal was attained, without, in
fact, achieving any significant diplomatic success. Yet, although his meetings with heads of state yielded little by way of actual results, each meeting
in itself was a triumph; each was an acknowledgment that there was a Jewish
nation, with Herzl its leader. In fact, a recent—and critical—biographer concludes that Herzl was the *only* Jewish leader in modern times, dismissing all
other contenders for the title as mere "politicians."

Ironically, only two decades after Herzl's dream was fulfilled with the founding of the state of Israel, the Palestinian national movement began to adopt some
of the tactics that had served Herzl so well. In the 1970s, Yasir Arafat, chairman of the Palestine Liberation Organization, began to focus his attention on
securing international diplomatic recognition for his movement. In November
1974, Arafat addressed a plenary session of the United Nations General Assembly, the first representative of a nongovernmental organization to do so.
To establish his legitimacy as head of a nation waiting to be born, Arafat began
to pay official visits to Eastern-bloc countries and arrange meetings with Western leaders. Within six months after proclaiming the "state of Palestine" on
November 15, 1988, the Palestine National Council elected Arafat president
of the Palestinian state, just as some ninety years earlier Herzl had been elected
president of the World Zionist Organization by the First Zionist Congress.

72

THE EMERGENCE
OF AMERICAN
CONSERVATIVE JUDAISM

Conservative Judaism emerged as a separate American religious move-
ment in the late 1880s when the Reform movement proved itself too radi-
cal to encompass more traditional modernist Jews. After a slow and
unpromising start, the Conservative movement was reinvigorated by in-
fluential Reform Jews, who hoped it would help Americanize Jewish
immigrants from eastern Europe. The Conservative movement was con-
solidated by the appointment of Solomon Schechter to the presidency of
the Jewish Theological Seminary in 1901.

That a caterer's gaffe was the immediate, if not the underlying, cause for the
emergence of American Conservative Judaism is among the odd facts of Jewish history.

Before Conservative Judaism with a capital *C* emerged as an independent
movement on the American religious scene, it constituted the most traditional
segment of the Reform movement. The pioneer of Reform Judaism in America,
Rabbi Isaac Mayer Wise (1819–1900), hoped to be able to unify all of liberal
Judaism in the United States. Wise's dream led to the establishment of the Union
of American Hebrew Congregations (UAHC) in Cincinnati in 1873 and of the
Hebrew Union College (HUC) in 1875. As president of this first rabbinical
school in the United States, Wise developed a curriculum that focused on traditional texts, not on radical doctrine. This curriculum, he hoped, would not
only train rabbis acceptable throughout the country but also do away with the
need for competing rabbinical schools.

Wise's dream was short-lived. In 1883 HUC threw a big party to celebrate
the ordination of its first four students. Jewish law dictates that many religious
acts be accompanied by a festive meal, and ordination is no exception. The
problem in this case, however, was what was served. No one had bothered to
instruct the caterer in the laws of *kashrut*, and to the dismay of the more tradi-

tional—or conservative—guests, the first course consisted of a variety of shell-fish. Since shellfish are not *kosher*, the celebratory meal has gone down in history as the *Terefah* (Hebrew for "unfit," or not *kosher*) Banquet. Not sur-prisingly, a group of guests left the banquet in a huff. When Wise made no attempt to apologize for what had happened, his fragile union began to fall apart.

The gap separating the more radical liberal Jews from the more traditional ones became unbridgeable following the meeting of a group of rabbis in Pitts-burgh in 1885 to define the Reform movement's principles. The so-called Pitts-burgh Platform claimed, among other things, that only Judaism's moral laws are binding in modern times; that biblical or rabbinical laws regulating diet are not only outmoded but also destructive of true spirituality; that since the Jews are no longer a nation but only a religious community, a return to the land of Israel is neither to be longed for nor expected. These positions (which have been superseded by the more centrist positions given in the 1937 Columbus Platform and the 1976 Centenary Perspective) led a group of conservative lib-erals to conclude that a more traditional rabbinical school must be set up to produce rabbis less radical than those who would be trained at HUC.

By the end of 1885, those who had broken away from the UAHC were being called "Conservatives." The Conservatives believed that the positions laid out by the Pittsburgh Platform threatened the link connecting American Jews to Jews around the world, as well as the historical continuity of Judaism. The Conservative position was rooted in the positive-historical school of Judaism, which emphasized Judaism's ability to adapt over the ages without breaking with tradition. Since the positive-historical school had been centered in Eu-rope at the Jewish Theological Seminary at Breslau, the American Conserva-tives decided to name their new rabbinical school the Jewish Theological Semi-nary of America.

The new Jewish Theological Seminary (JTS), which opened in 1887, was to become the central institution of Conservative Judaism. Its early years, how-ever, were inauspicious. By the turn of the century—its *bar mitzvah* year—JTS had ordained only seventeen rabbis; six of its affiliated congregations had defected to the Reform camp, and its funding was in perilous condition.

Ironically, it was a group of wealthy and influential Reform Jews who saved the seminary. Their motives were somewhat self-serving: they feared that the influx of eastern European immigrants into the United States would lead to a rise in antisemitism unless the newcomers were quickly assimilated into Ameri-can life. They correctly understood that the immigrants were likely to reject Reform Judaism as too abrupt a break with tradition. But if a reinvigorated seminary could produce rabbis who combined traditional Jewish knowledge with American know-how, the newcomers could turn to them as models.

One of the seminary's founders, who was also its first president, had under-stood from the outset that what JTS lacked was the right leader. As early as

1890 he began trying to woo the great scholar Solomon Schechter (1847–1915) to come to the United States from England. At the very end of 1901, Schechter agreed to assume the presidency of JTS. In the intermediate years, Schechter had enhanced his scholarly reputation by his work in recovering the contents of the Cairo *Genizah*, or storeroom of ancient Jewish documents.

Schechter's arrival transformed the seminary into a center of Jewish intellectual activity. He handpicked a distinguished faculty who would train generations of Conservative rabbis. He clarified the middle-ground position that would come to define Conservative Judaism: a willingness to confront both modernity and tradition without being overwhelmed by either. He emphasized the responsibility of each generation to examine its own spiritual needs in order to define its relation to Judaism. In addition, despite the opposition of the non-Zionist (and sometimes anti-Zionist) stance of many of the Reform backers of the seminary, Schechter early on identified the Conservative movement with Zionist aspirations.

Schechter is often associated with the concept of "Catholic Israel," which makes the community of prime importance in determining the course of Jewish life. (In this context, the word *Catholic* means "all-inclusive" and has nothing to do with Roman Catholicism.) Schechter, like Zacharias Frankel (see nutshell #62), believed that the Jewish legal system, like all others, involves not only legislation but also custom. On the one hand, a law ceases to be authoritative if large numbers of people ignore it, and on the other, a custom takes on the authority of law if it becomes firmly established in people's practice. Schechter's concept helped shape Conservative Judaism's approach to Jewish law: in evaluating how Jewish law should be amended, the practices of today's community have to be taken into account as much as the law codes and rabbinic decisions of the past.

In Schechter's day and for some decades thereafter, most Conservative Jews observed Jewish law, and therefore the concept of "Catholic Israel" was sensible. By the middle of the century, however, it became clear that fewer and fewer Conservative Jews were observant. Since it made no sense to determine the content of Jewish law based on the behavior of those who ignore it, the Conservative movement decided to limit the concept of "Catholic Israel" to those Jews who do try to observe Jewish law. Many Conservative rabbis today feel that the movement's priority should be to encourage a much broader base of Jewish observance. Only in this way can Schechter's original concept of "Catholic Israel"—and his understanding of the role of Conservative Judaism— become truly meaningful again.

73

THE KISHINEV POGROMS

Kishinev, the capital of Moldova, was the site of a major pogrom in 1903 and of a second pogrom in 1905. Throughout the world, the name of the city became synonymous with anti-Jewish incidents instigated by the czarist regime. The Kishinev pogroms had wide-ranging effects, including a steep increase in Jewish emigration from Russia, a meeting between Zionist leader Theodor Herzl and Russian officials, the organization of movements for Jewish self-defense in Russia and in Israel, and the formation of an effective American Jewish political action committee.

Just as Pearl Harbor is indelibly associated in American minds with the bombing of December 7, 1941, so in spring 1903, Kishinev, Moldova, achieved worldwide infamy. When a vicious anti-Jewish riot in April of that year was followed by a second in the autumn of 1905, the association of the city's name with the word *pogrom* was ensured.

By the end of the 19th century Kishinev had a large Jewish presence, with Jews comprising nearly half the total population. Jews also played an important role in the economy of the city, with, for example, Jewish ownership of nearly all the factories. But in the aftermath of the two pogroms, large numbers of Jews left Kishinev, and its economic development ground to a halt.

The Kishinev pogroms of 1903 and 1905 were much more violent than the pogroms of 1881, with murder, torture, and rape the order of the day. In the pogrom of April 6–7, 1903, about fifty Jews were killed and approximately ten times that number injured; rioters mutilated many of the injured and dead. Thousands of Jews were left homeless and without work as houses, businesses, and shops were looted and destroyed. Both local and czarist government forces were behind the pogrom. *The Times of London* published an order sent by the Russian minister of the interior ordering the provincial governor not to open fire on the pogromists. While the order's authenticity was never proven, in any case the 5,000 soldiers stationed in the city were ordered not to intervene. Russians from other towns were brought in to participate in the mayhem.

The Kishinev pogrom of October 19–20, 1905, was one in a series of upheavals that swept through Russia that autumn. In its wake, over fifty Jews were left dead, and material damage was extensive.

The underlying cause of both Kishinev pogroms was the growth of the Russian revolutionary movement. Nicholas II, who was to be the last czar, ascended the throne in 1894. His failure to introduce liberal reforms led to growing dissatisfaction, particularly among the intelligentsia. Many intellectuals, who until then had turned a blind eye toward official repressive policies toward the Jews, began to realize that the regime was using antisemitism as a political tool, to curry favor with the uneducated masses. As a result, intellectuals, including writers like Maxim Gorky, began to speak out on behalf of the Jews. But the czarist regime manipulated this new support for Jews to serve its own purposes: it claimed that the revolutionary movement was a Jewish plot. The government began to coordinate antisemitic activity, financing antisemitic newspapers and organizations. When Russia experienced defeats in the Russo-Japanese War (1904–1905), the press began to blame the Jews for sympathizing with the enemy and fomenting revolution to weaken the Russian position.

Among the antisemitic newspapers receiving support from the government was a paper widely read in Kishinev. The local police chief was a coauthor of a series of vicious anti-Jewish diatribes. When the body of a Christian boy was found near Kishinev in February 1903, the newspaper, assisted by the Russian Orthodox church, circulated a blood libel: that the Jews had killed the child in order to use his blood for Passover *matzot*. When a young Christian woman patient committed suicide in the Jewish hospital, the crowd went mad. No matter that in truth the child was a victim of his relatives and the young woman's suicide was unconnected to the Jews. The pogroms were orchestrated to coincide with Easter.

The immediate cause of the second Kishinev pogrom, as of other even more violent pogroms that took place in Russia at about the same time, was a manifesto issued by the czar in October 1905. In the hope that some liberal concessions would quell revolutionary ferment, the czar agreed to establish a Russian parliament and to guarantee the basic freedoms of Russians. Liberal and radical opponents of the czarist regime responded in spontaneous celebrations. In response, government-supported "patriotic" organizations mounted counter-demonstrations, with thugs displaying the portrait of the czar. These counter-demonstrations, as intended, dissolved into pogroms. Once again, the central regime circulated orders to local authorities not to interfere with the pogromists.

The results of the Kishinev pogroms were numerous and far-ranging. Not surprisingly, the number of Jews leaving Russia shot up. Of the 672,000 Jews who entered the United States between 1904 and 1908, most came from the Russian Empire. Thousands also left for the Land of Israel. More committed to the ideal of national renaissance than many of their predecessors, they transformed the nature of the Jewish settlement in the homeland.

An immediate result of the 1903 Kishinev pogrom was a crackdown on the Zionist movement in Russia. In June, the minister of the interior, who had been implicated in fomenting the riot, announced that Zionists were to be dealt with harshly. The secret police had learned, he said, that the Zionists were responsible for encouraging Jewish youth in the struggle against the regime. In order to ease the situation, Theodor Herzl, the leader of the Zionist movement (see nutshell #71), arranged a meeting in Russia with the minister of the interior and other high Russian officials. The idea of negotiating directly with the man responsible for the pogrom did not sit well with everyone in Zionist circles, but Herzl went through with his plan. He had hoped that the czarist regime would be so anxious to rid itself of its Jews that it would agree to speak to the Turkish sultan on behalf of political Zionism and of a Jewish state on Turkish-held soil. He also hoped to convince the Russian authorities to legalize Zionist activity. But Herzl's hopes were only partly fulfilled. Although the minister of the interior promised to speak to the sultan on behalf of Zionism and not to interfere with Zionist attempts to encourage Jewish emigration from Russia, he insisted that all Zionist political activity within Russia would continue to be severely disciplined.

A striking effect of the 1903 Kishinev pogrom was the formation of Jewish self-defense organizations. Although some Jews in Kishinev did strike back at the perpetrators of the violence, many Jews throughout Russia reacted to the event with disgust at the defenselessness of the victims. H. N. Bialik's poem "The City of Slaughter" captured this mood, casting shame in strong verse on those who submitted themselves like "calves for the slaughter." Two weeks after the pogrom, the Hebrew Writers League called for the establishment of a defense organization. Interestingly, not all Jews supported such an organization. Some Jewish revolutionaries argued that pogroms were a legitimate expression of anger on behalf of the awakening proletariat, and that the people's voice should be heard. But many Jews joined self-defense groups, which were active during the 1905 pogroms.

The idea of Jewish self-defense made its way to Israel along with the Russian Jewish immigrants. A group of these men were distressed to learn that Jewish settlements were being guarded not by Jews but by paid Bedouin, Circassian, and other non-Jewish guards. Before 1910, an association of Jewish watchmen was in place, and Jews in Israel were in charge of defending Jewish lives and property. The association of Jewish watchmen is considered a forerunner of the Israeli army, and in that sense the Kishinev pogroms ultimately inspired the ideology of the armed forces of the Jewish state.

The Kishinev pogroms also led to the formation of what today would be called an American Jewish political action committee. On the surface, the response of the U.S. government to the 1903 pogrom was gratifying, with President Theodor Roosevelt decrying the "dreadful outrage upon the Jews" in Kishinev and "the appalling calamity that has occurred." But the American Jewish establishment was not long in noticing that the government was not willing to put its money where its mouth was. Then, as now, it is easy enough for governments to pay lip service to a commitment to human rights, but other strategic goals often take precedence. The U.S. government did not issue a condemnation. When the czar refused to accept a petition sent by the B'nai B'rith via the American diplomat in St. Petersburg, Secretary of State John Hay announced that the petition had been placed in the State Department's archives, where it would be considered one of the department's treasures. It was clear that sympathy was all the U.S. government was willing to offer the Jews. Russia, after all, might be useful to the United States in stanching Japanese expansion in the Far East and in providing a market for American goods.

In the face of this lack of real government action on behalf of the Jews of Russia, the established leaders of American Jewry correctly assessed the limits on their abilities. They were proficient at raising the public consciousness about the plight of Jews abroad, but they were inept at translating that awareness into direct governmental response. In order to change that situation, they set up the American Jewish Committee (AJC) in 1906. Its aim was to intercede discreetly with government officials on behalf of Jewish interests at home and abroad. The AJC thought of itself not as an ethnic group acting on behalf of interests different from those of other Americans but as a product of the American democratic system, working within and on behalf of it.

The Kishinev pogroms, then, galvanized Jews into action on many fronts and in several lands. Determined not to be passive pawns in the face of assaults, Jews reacted by shaping their destiny in different ways.

74

THE UGANDA CONTROVERSY

In August 1903, at the Sixth Zionist Congress, Theodor Herzl reported the British government's offer to explore setting up an autonomous Jewish settlement in East Africa. The crisis that ensued almost destroyed the Zionist Organization. The resolution, which occurred only after Herzl's death, committed the movement to a state in the Land of Israel only.

Theodor Herzl's original hope for political Zionism was that the Turkish sultan, who controlled the Land of Israel, would be convinced to give the Jews a legal charter for settlement there. Over seven years had now passed since Herzl had originally published the plan in 1896. During that time his diplomatic encounters with world leaders had gained recognition for the Zionist movement as a whole, as well as personal recognition for him as leader of a nation waiting to be born (see nutshell #71). But he had nothing truly substantive to show for all his activity. Herzl had begun to despair of achieving his end through the sultan and began to look for other powerful sponsors. In the long term, the most productive political connection he made was with Great Britain. Ironically, the British plan he presented to the Sixth Zionist Congress, held in Basel, Switzerland, in August 1903, nearly destroyed the Zionist movement.

Earlier that month, the British government proposed that if the Zionist Organization sent a commission to British East Africa, and if that commission found a suitable area for Jewish settlement, Great Britain would sponsor a self-governing Jewish colony there. Since the name *Uganda* was used then for the part of East Africa where the British had attempted to maintain a presence since the 1870s, the government's proposal to the Zionist Organization was known as "the Uganda scheme." (Actually, the area in question is in today's Kenya.) Joseph Chamberlain, the colonial secretary, had alluded to the plan in April, but Herzl had shown no interest. But in the intervening months the news of the Kishinev pogroms (see nutshell #73) had spread, and during his subsequent visit to Russia, Herzl had seen for himself the misery of the Jewish masses there. He decided to consider the Uganda scheme more seriously.

Britain, of course, did not propose the Uganda scheme for purely humanitarian reasons. Opening up East Africa to Russian Jewish immigration would not only spare Britain itself an additional influx of ghetto types. It would also, it was to be hoped, enable the area—thus far unsuccessfully colonized—to be developed by a combination of Jewish capital and labor.

Herzl had three main reasons for reconsidering the plan: (1) to strengthen the Zionist Organization's political connection with Great Britain, a country that could do much to help achieve Zionist goals; (2) to put pressure on Turkey, which might make some concessions upon realizing that Jewish money would now go to British East Africa instead of Turkish Palestine; (3) to channel Russian Jewish immigration to a single area that might serve as an outpost to the main Zionist state in the land of Israel.

When Herzl announced the British proposal to the delegates at the Sixth Zionist Congress, he was quite clear in stating that the Uganda scheme in no way supplanted the basic Zionist goal, to achieve a homeland in the land of Israel. But the political realities of the moment suggested that a temporary asylum was needed, which might be found in East Africa.

Although before the Congress, Herzl's closest confidant in the Zionist movement, the author Max Nordau, had expressed reservations about the scheme, Herzl was unprepared for the impassioned opposition to the plan expressed mainly by the Russian Zionists, the very people whom the plan was intended to benefit most directly. Nordau argued that if the Jews of eastern Europe were unable either to stay where they were or to go to the land of Israel, they would leave for England, the United States, or Australia. He feared that transplanted to the African tropics, they would end up, like other colonialists, exploiting native labor. Such an outcome would hardly foster the spiritual revival of the Jewish people. Nordau, however, agreed not to speak out against the plan at the Congress, and in fact he was the main spokesman for it.

The Russian Zionist delegates, however, were very outspoken about their objections. To many of them, a proposal to establish a Jewish national settlement anywhere other than the land of Israel was as unacceptable as would be a proposal that they change religion. Herzl's audacity in entertaining such a scheme enraged them. In fact, many of those who opposed Herzl were already active in a Zionist opposition group formed in 1901. Its members saw Herzl as an autocratic leader who relegated most of the movement's adherents to passive roles. Only Herzl and a few select Zionists were involved in diplomatic encounters to secure the still-elusive charter for settlement. In the meantime, Herzl insisted that Zionists refrain from becoming politically involved in the internal politics of the countries where they lived, lest they antagonize governments toward Zionism. Many movement members chafed under this restriction. In addition, his opponents felt that Herzl ignored the importance of Jewish cultural development. Now, with the new incitement of the Uganda scheme, all these latent resentments came to a head.

When Herzl called for a vote on his proposal to elect a commission to help advise on the Uganda scheme, 295 delegates voted for, 178 against, with 132 abstaining. The announcement of the tally was followed by the walkout of the opponents, now calling themselves "Zionists of Zion." The large group gathered in another room, where many actually broke into tears over what they perceived as the abandonment of Zion.

Much of the rest of the Sixth Zionist Congress was taken up with Herzl's attempts to pull the movement back together. He met privately with the disaffected to convince them of his devotion toward securing a national settlement in the land of Israel. He convinced them to attend the final session of the Congress, where he publicly quoted from Psalm 137, "If I forget thee, O Jerusalem, may my right hand wither." On the surface, the rupture was mended.

But the resentment toward Herzl and the Uganda scheme continue to seethe just below the surface. In November 1903 the Russian Zionists held a conference in which they decided to issue Herzl with an ultimatum: he must agree in writing to withdraw the Uganda scheme, not to propose in future any such scheme, and to resume immediately small-scale settlement in the land of Israel. If he rejected the ultimatum, the group agreed to various measures, including presenting the case to a British court for withholding Zionist funds from supporters of the Uganda scheme. In the meantime, the group decided not to forward to the general Zionist treasury any funds raised by Zionists in Russia.

A group of the "Zionists of Zion" traveled to Vienna in April 1904 to present Herzl with the ultimatum, but he refused to receive them officially. Instead, he met with each one individually, managing to appease them by repeating his commitment to the idea of a national home in the land of Israel. Herzl thus managed to save the Zionist movement. But the accumulated strain of the crisis, added to the stress of his exhausting travel schedule, worsened his heart condition. Months later, on July 3, 1904, Herzl died.

The crisis itself had not yet been fully resolved, however. Although Britain had already withdrawn the offer, as a result of internal opposition, the Seventh Zionist Congress (summer 1905) officially rejected it. The Congress also rejected the notion of Jewish settlement anywhere except the land of Israel and its immediate environs. The Zionist movement thus officially devoted itself to pursuing a Jewish homeland in Zion, and there only.

A sizable number of delegates, however, had been enthusiastic about finding an asylum for Jews elsewhere. A number of them, led by the British author Israel Zangwill, now broke off from the Zionist Organization. Known as the Territorialists, this group hoped to establish an autonomous Jewish settlement in some sufficiently large territory, including but not limited to the land of Israel. The departure of this group from the Zionist Organization had little impact, and the movement survived both the Uganda crisis and Herzl's death.

Interestingly enough, we find some fallout from the Uganda controversy in, of all places, Galveston, Texas. Though the Territorialists did not play a significant part in Jewish history and rejoined the Zionist movement in the mid-1920s, their single practical success was in the United States and involved abandoning the group's official aim. Instead of achieving a Jewish national settlement, the Jewish Territorial Organization participated in a project to encourage the settlement of eastern European Jewish immigrants in the American West. The Galveston Plan, from 1907 to 1915, sent more than 10,000 Jewish immigrants through Galveston to Fort Worth, Oklahoma City, Omaha, Minneapolis, Los Angeles, and other interior cities, thus alleviating to some extent the overcrowding in eastern port city immigrant neighborhoods.

75

THE BEILIS BLOOD-LIBEL CASE

The 1913 trial of Russian Jew Mendel Beilis for the ritual murder of a twelve-year-old Christian boy aroused worldwide interest. Although the authorities knew the child had been murdered by a criminal gang, they pursued the rumor of ritual murder in an attempt to discredit liberalism. Opponents of czarist despotism viewed Beilis's acquittal as a telling blow to the regime.

Although few people today are familiar with the Beilis blood-libel case, in its time it aroused passions as deeply as did the Dreyfus affair (see nutshell #70) some years earlier. Just as the Dreyfus affair underscored the political and social divisions in France, the Beilis case pitted most of the Russian people against the forces of extreme reaction. While antisemitism certainly played a major role in the Beilis case, as it had in the Dreyfus affair, in both cases the struggle was as much for the soul of an entire nation as for the exoneration of the single Jew at the center.

Mendel Beilis did not figure in the case for several months, and was hardly a central player at all. In March 1911 the body of a Christian boy was found in a cave eight days after his disappearance from his home in a Kiev neighborhood. Nearly fifty puncture wounds had been made in the body, which had lost most of its blood. At the time of the funeral, members of the local antisemitic nationalist group distributed leaflets making a blood accusation: Jews had committed the murder to get blood for Passover *matzot*. The leaflets also called for revenge against the Jews.

No pogroms occurred, however. The czarist regime had let the various local police departments know that international response to the last wave of pogroms, from 1903 to 1906, had been detrimental to Russia's stature in the world community. As a result, more discreet ways of repressing Jews should be pursued. When local officials' suspicions almost immediately identified a Kiev criminal gang as the likely murderers, it seemed that nothing would come of the blood accusation.

But as it turned out, the regime was looking for some way to discredit liberal and revolutionary forces in the country. Nicholas II had been certain for some years now that the Russian people on their own would never challenge the czar's divine rule. He saw a Jewish plot underlying all the revolutionary impulses in the country. Most recently, just a month before the murder, he had been outraged when 166 members of the Duma, or Parliament, had pushed for a bill to abolish the Pale of Settlement. Although the bill had never reached the floor, the very fact that it had been suggested was a bad sign. Since it was a given that there was a poisonous link between liberalism and attempts for Jewish emancipation, some way must be found to undermine both. Perhaps the Kiev murder would prove the very thing.

By July, a trumped-up case was made against Mendel Beilis, an uneducated and nonobservant Jew who worked in the brickworks halfway between the boy's home and the cave where the body had been found. Although officials knew that there was no case against him, and that the originally suspected criminal gang had almost certainly committed the murder, the decision was made to pursue the blood accusation.

The fraudulent nature of the case was apparent from the outset to a large segment of the Russian population. When the government published the "medical evidence" it had collected in support of the charge of ritual murder, a Russian medical society issued a statement condemning the use of pseudoscience to support racist claims. In assembling a legal staff for the prosecution, only lawyers willing to put career goals above a commitment to justice were willing to become involved. Nor could any Russian church official or scholar of any repute be found to testify on behalf of the blood accusation. The government had to content itself with a Catholic priest from remote Tashkent, who some years before had written a pamphlet to prove that Judaism sanctioned ritual murder. Fearful that a randomly selected jury would reject the blood libel and acquit Beilis, the government handpicked a group of mostly illiterate peasants who, it was hoped, would be convinced by their prejudices to endorse the blood accusation.

The government found itself faced with a more serious problem when a newspaper began a series of articles identifying the criminal gang as the murderers. Fearful that the defense had conclusive evidence that Beilis was not involved, the government came up with additional "proof" linking the Jew to the crime, and drew up a new indictment against Beilis.

The indictment spent more time exonerating the leader of the gang than accusing Beilis. It also acknowledged expert opinion denying the blood accusation. In disgust at the document, two members of the judicial board resigned rather than sign the document as required. Following the reading of the indictment in court on the second day of the trial in September 1913, a greater shock awaited the regime. A devastating assessment of the indictment was published in an editorial—but not, as might have been expected, in a liberal newspaper. Rather, the editorial was signed by a well-known antisemite, editor of the Kiev semiofficial monarchist and reactionary newspaper. He wrote that one did not need legal training to see that there was no case against Beilis, and that the government's mock trial could only bring shame on Russia before the world. He warned that the time might soon come when those in charge today would be tried by others. In fact, the end of the czarist regime came within three years.

Beilis had been in jail for several months before it dawned on the Jewish community of Kiev that the regime's objective was twofold: not only the conviction of a single hapless Jew but also the conferral of judicial sanction on the blood libel. To frustrate both goals, the Kiev Jewish leadership assembled a defense team of impeccable credentials. Its one Jewish member was the leading Jewish criminal lawyer of his generation, who had already involved himself in cases involving Jewish causes. Its other members were non-Jews, including not only "the Clarence Darrow of Russia" but also the brother of the reactionary minister of the interior, who was deeply involved in the regime's perversion of justice in this case. The members of the defense team sought both to exonerate the persecuted Jew and to salvage their country's reputation.

Jews from around the world also organized a Beilis Defense Committee. Nor was it Jews alone, in Kiev or elsewhere, who organized on Beilis's behalf. In Russia, professionals, workers, and peasants throughout the country protested the government's contempt for justice. Trolley-car workers in Kiev collected money for Beilis's wife and five children. A bishop of a dissident group within the Orthodox church denounced the blood libel, and a high-ranking Catholic official censured the priest from Tashkent whom the government had found to make the case for ritual murder. Notable figures in the arts, sciences, and politics, not only in Russia but also in Germany, England, France, and the United States, signed manifestoes condemning the Beilis case. In fact, more international outrage was expressed against the czarist regime's falsified case than against Nazi antisemitism in the late 1930s and early 1940s. The foreign press recognized that the Beilis case was more than an antisemitic incident; it was proof of a desperate regime's utter lack of principle and its willingness to sell its soul to forestall revolution. (There were, however, antisemitic voices raised abroad as well. Strong support for the regime came from the anti-Dreyfusards in France, and a scholarly British review claimed that while most Jews certainly do not practice ritual murder, it might be that some Jewish sects did.)

The Beilis trial itself was a travesty of justice. When faced with trained lawyers of the highest caliber, many of the witnesses for the prosecution recanted their original testimony. The state prosecutor claimed that all such retractions were due to Jewish bribes or threats. When no witness could be found to say anything negative about Beilis, the prosecutor claimed that the better a Jew's reputation, the more likely he would commit ritual murder. He also asserted that the difficulties encountered in finding evidence against Beilis were likewise attributable to Jewish money and power. As the trial progressed, it became clear that less and less of the testimony had to do with Beilis at all. Not only did the newspapers begin to question "Where is Beilis?" but when a member of the defense team raised the same question, the judge called a ten-minute recess as nearly everyone in the packed courtroom—the state prosecutor included—began laughing.

The prosecution's attempt to prove the blood libel also ran into trouble. Only one "expert" could be found to interpret the wounds on the body as being likely proof of ritual murder; it later came out that the "expert" had accepted a bribe of 4,000 rubles. The testimony of the priest from Tashkent was also undermined when the defense exposed his pretensions to scholarly knowledge of the Talmud and other Jewish texts by revealing his ignorance of some basic terms. In addition, the defense called not only on the chief rabbi of Moscow but also on four Christian scholars who testified that Jewish ethical principles contradicted the concept of blood libel.

In the end, on October 28, 1913, the jury found Beilis not guilty, although its findings on the blood libel question were unclear. Perhaps their statement that the murder victim had "lost five glasses of blood" could be interpreted as implying that the lost blood was intended for drinking. In any case, both sides claimed victory. As if in response to news of a great military victory, a wave of joy spread throughout Russia in response to what was seen as a defeat for the administration. Strangers kissed each other on the street. Telephone operators in the major cities announced "acquitted" before asking callers for the numbers they sought. But the following day the reactionary press let leak that on the question of Beilis's guilt, the jury had been split 6 to 6, technically an acquittal, but hardly a trouncing of antisemitism. The French antisemitic press joined the czarist regime in claiming that the blood libel had been proved, and a celebratory banquet was held for the prosecuting team. But the foreign press in general felt that the regime's bluff had been decisively called, and that Beilis's acquittal was the most devastating blow to the czar since the Russo-Japanese war.

The miscalculations of the regime in the Beilis case symbolized the general failure of the czar to understand the mood of the country at large. While the end of the czarist regime would surely have come whether or not the Beilis trial had occurred, the case certainly played a role in hastening the inevitable. As the correspondent for *The Times of London* at the trial stated, "This is not the Beilis case. It is possibly a final fight for existence on the part of the innermost powers of reaction against all modern forces in Russia."

76

ELIEZER BEN-YEHUDA AND THE EMERGENCE OF MODERN HEBREW

Eliezer Ben-Yehuda (1858–1922), born Eliezer Perelman, is considered the father of modern Hebrew. He and his successors adapted Hebrew to modern use along the lines they believed it would have followed on its own if its use as a spoken language had been continuous. Ben-Yehuda is best known for his multivolume dictionary of modern Hebrew, published largely after his death (1910–1959).

Nowadays, when Hebrew is not only the language of the state of Israel but is also routinely taught to Jewish children in the Diaspora, it is hard to remember how different the situation was only a century ago. At that time, Jews around the world studied Hebrew, but primarily to enable them to read the prayers and the Torah. More scholarly Jews studied it as the language of the Mishnah and of other important texts. The inhabitants of the Land of Israel spoke different languages, depending on their religious or ethnic community, including Arabic, Armenian, French, Italian, Greek, and Russian. The spoken language most Jews had in common was not Hebrew but Yiddish. The change in the situation was due largely to the efforts of a single individual, Eliezer Ben-Yehuda.

At birth, the future "father of the modern Hebrew language" was given the name Eliezer Perelman. Born in Lithuania into a hasidic family, through a variety of circumstances he was able to acquire a secular education. Inspired by the nationalist movements in Europe, he came to believe that Jews too had a homeland and a national language. His initial use of the name Ben-Yehuda was in signing, at the age of twenty-one, the first published article calling for a modern Jewish nation, with its spiritual center in the land of Israel and with Hebrew as its language. He would later officially assume his pen name.

Ben-Yehuda was determined to move to the land of Israel but only after he had trained for a profession that would sustain him there. Having settled on medicine, he entered medical school in Paris. Although a bout with tuberculosis kept Ben-Yehuda from ever finishing his medical studies, he had several significant encounters in Paris that kept his attention focused on the Hebrew language as the key to the unity of the Jewish people. First, a Jewish journalist there told him that in traveling through Asia and Africa, he was able to converse in Hebrew with the Jews in those continents. Next, when tuberculosis forced him to leave medical school, Ben-Yehuda decided to train for a teaching career in the Jewish homeland. The Alliance Israélite Universelle, the world Jewish organization founded in Paris in 1860, had opened the first Jewish school in the land of Israel in 1870. Ben-Yehuda enrolled in the Alliance's teachers' seminary in Paris. Among his lecturers there was an Assyrologist who believed that Hebrew could be brought into modern times if new words were developed. Finally, when his health worsened, Ben-Yehuda entered the Rothschild Hospital. There he met a scholar from Jerusalem who not only spoke Hebrew in the Sephardic pronunciation with Ben-Yehuda but also told him that Sephardic Hebrew was the only language in which the different Jewish communities of Jerusalem could speak to one another.

Confirmed now in his belief that a common language was crucial for a united people, in 1881, as soon as his health permitted, Ben-Yehuda moved to the land of Israel. He and his wife made a self-conscious decision to speak only Hebrew not only with each other but also with whatever children they might have. Ben-Yehuda and his wife thus began through personal example to transform Hebrew into a living language. Two years later, Ben-Yehuda helped organize a secret society, "The Revival of Israel," whose members swore to speak only Hebrew to one another, even under circumstances where less committed individuals might be too embarrassed to do so.

To achieve his goal of making Hebrew the living language of a renewed people, Ben-Yehuda undertook many different but interrelated activities. Although he did not remain a classroom teacher for long, he continued to help shape Hebrew education in the land of Israel throughout his lifetime. He introduced what is now called the immersion method of teaching a language by speaking it from the outset. Concerned that only male students were being exposed to spoken Hebrew, he helped establish a girls' Hebrew school in Safed in 1891. His example led teachers around the land to teach not only Jewish subjects in Hebrew but also secular subjects. He also saw to it that professional journals for teachers and periodicals directed to children were published in Hebrew.

In fact, different facets of publishing became Ben-Yehuda's primary profession. When he arrived from Paris, he began writing for one of the already established Hebrew-language papers being published in the land of Israel. But three years later, when he left its staff to begin his own newspaper, Ben-Yehuda began to change the nature of the modern Hebrew press. The journalistic changes he brought about have led him to be considered the father of modern Hebrew journalism. Ben-Yehuda's paper was the first in the land of Israel to deviate from Orthodox religious tradition. As the paper secularized the field of journalistic coverage, its editor felt a need for a broader vocabulary. As a result, Ben-Yehuda began to coin new Hebrew words.

Neologism, the practice of creating new words or giving new meanings to established words, was not new to Hebrew. But Ben-Yehuda was the first to undertake the enrichment of the language in a systematic way, in order to make it flexible enough to respond to the changes of the modern world. In a charming article he pointed to a limitation in the work of Peretz Smolenskin (1842–1885), one of the great eastern European writers committed to the revival of the Hebrew language. Smolenskin's stories, said Ben-Yehuda, are skillfully written, but you will never read about any of his characters being tickled, simply because Smolenskin had no Hebrew word for tickling. In order to make up for such deficiencies, and for more serious ones, Ben-Yehuda undertook a thorough study of Hebrew in all its periods and of Hebrew's Semitic roots.

The job of revitalizing the Hebrew language was obviously too immense for a single individual to accomplish on his own. In 1890 Ben-Yehuda was one of the founding members of the Hebrew Language Committee, whose self-imposed tasks included establishing a Hebrew vocabulary for daily use; determining rules of spelling, punctuation, and grammar; and standardizing Hebrew pronunciation. The committee settled on Sephardic pronunciation because it most closely resembled Hebrew speech in ancient times.

Ben-Yehuda's most monumental task, with which his name is most closely associated, is his *Complete Dictionary of Ancient and Modern Hebrew* (1910–1959). It was the first Hebrew dictionary organized by word, like modern European language dictionaries, rather than by root words, as all previous Hebrew dictionaries had been. The seventeen-volume dictionary is noteworthy both for what it includes and for what it excludes. Ben-Yehuda tried to include all Hebrew words used in the different developmental stages of the language, but unlike other lexicographers he chose to omit not only all foreign words found in Hebrew texts over the ages but also all Aramaic words.

Ben-Yehuda was helped in his efforts to make Hebrew into a spoken language by the historical fact that it had been the original language of the people in their land. Whenever archaeologists uncovered ancient Hebrew inscriptions, the connection between the ancient people and language and their contemporary successors was underscored. But other factors stood in the way of universal recognition of Hebrew as the appropriate language for the Jews in the land of Israel. In fact, Ben-Yehuda and his colleagues were embroiled in various conflicts in their attempts to revive Hebrew.

First of all, many Orthodox Jews considered Hebrew a holy language only; the language of the Torah and of the prayers should not be defiled by being used to discuss sewage systems and agricultural technology. A group of Orthodox extremists were so enraged by Ben-Yehuda's activities that they alerted the Turkish authorities to a supposedly seditious statement in an article in his newspaper, resulting in his arrest and sentence to a year's imprisonment. Although world Jewish protest succeeded in securing his release, Turkish censors continued to keep a close eye on Ben-Yehuda's newspaper.

In addition, the Jewish philanthropic organizations based in different European countries sought to maintain their own influence in the country partly through language. Thus the officials of Baron de Rothschild promoted French, not Hebrew. In 1913 the efforts of the German-Jewish philanthropic organization that was sponsoring the new technical institute in Haifa (the Technion) to have classes taught in German led to a strike of students and teachers throughout the Jewish settlement. The formation of a national Hebrew school system in Israel is traced to this so-called language conflict.

A third source of opposition to Ben-Yehuda and his colleagues came from those who favored Yiddish as the Jewish common tongue. They feared that the emphasis on the rebirth of Hebrew would lead to the demise of Yiddish.

Nonetheless, by the time the British took over political control of Palestine, Hebrew was already firmly established in that country. In December 1917, when General Allenby issued a two-sided sheet repeating the announcement of martial law in Jerusalem in seven languages, Hebrew was the first of four languages on one side, and English the first of three on the reverse. In 1922, the year of Ben-Yehuda's death, Hebrew was recognized along with English and Arabic as an official language of the country under the British Mandate. And when Israel became a state in 1948 (see nutshell #89), Hebrew was not only its official language but also the sole language of communication for over half of its Jewish inhabitants. So successful had been the efforts of Eliezer Ben-Yehuda, who devoted his life to refashioning Hebrew as an instrument of national revival.

77

TEL AVIV AND DEGANYAH: A NEW CITY AND A NEW TYPE OF COMMUNITY

The second wave of immigration to the land of Israel—the Second Aliyah (1904–1914)—transformed the nature of the Jewish settlement and laid the groundwork for the future Jewish state. In 1909, to help accommodate the newcomers who chose an urban life, the first Jewish city in Palestine was founded. Tel Aviv was to become a national center of industry, commerce, and entertainment. In the same year, idealistic Russian immigrants also founded Deganyah, the forerunner of the kibbutz, or communal settlement, movement. The kibbutz movement was to play a crucial role in forming the state of Israel.

Beginning in 1904, a wave of Russian Jews, ultimately totaling more than 40,000, began to arrive in the land of Israel. These immigrants of what became known as the Second *Aliyah* had several things in common. Most were young. In the wake of the Kishinev pogroms (see nutshell #73) and of the czar's failure to liberalize his regime, they had lost hope for their future as Jews in Russia. In addition, they had all been affected to some extent by the socialist ideals circulating among liberal groups in their former country.

But the immigrants of the Second *Aliyah* did not share identical personal aspirations. Upon arriving in the land of Israel, some chose to live in one of the four cities traditionally considered holy in religious Jewish circles: Jerusalem, Safed, Hebron, and Tiberias. Others, middle-class and not necessarily religious, chose to live in other cities or towns. Still others, adherents of the Zionist belief in the importance of working the land, chose to live in rural settlements.

The "gate to Zion" for all these immigrants of the Second *Aliyah* was the port city of Jaffa, as it had been for the immigrants of the First *Aliyah* (see nutshell #69) before them. Many new immigrants simply chose to stay in Jaffa, instead of moving on elsewhere. The First *Aliyah* had brought some 5,000 new

Jewish settlers to Jaffa, quintupling the size of the Jewish presence there. To accommodate the newcomers, wealthy Jews established the first Jewish quarter in Jaffa in 1887 and a second in 1891. These quarters, like other Jaffa neighborhoods, were characterized by narrow dirt lanes, little room between houses, and an absence of sanitary facilities.

But when the Second *Aliyah* brought several thousand more Jewish settlers to Jaffa, demand for housing far exceeded supply. Rents became exorbitant. In summer 1906 a group of over 100 Jaffa Jews, old-timers and new immigrants, began plans not for another Jewish quarter in Jaffa but for a modern garden suburb on its outskirts. The group had to overcome various obstacles put in its path by the Turkish authorities, who suspected the motives underlying such a plan. The group also failed to win financial support from the Zionist Organization, whose first priority was to establish agricultural settlements. Nonetheless, the group's members succeeded in collecting enough money to buy a plot of land northeast of Jaffa. They also secured a loan from the Jewish National Fund for building the suburb's first 60 houses. On April 11, 1909— traditionally considered the day on which Tel Aviv was founded—the group held a lottery to distribute the housing plots.

In the course of the next year, not only were those sixty houses built, but a network of streets was also laid out, with each street named after a major figure in the Zionist movement (e.g., Herzl, Ahad HaAm) or in the annals of Jewish history (e.g., Yehudah HaLevi). The foundations were prepared for a new building for the Gymnasia Herzlia, the first Hebrew secondary school in Israel, established three years earlier in Jaffa by young teachers who had arrived as part of the Second *Aliyah*. On May 21, 1910, the suburb was officially named Tel Aviv. On the one hand, its name echoed the Bible: a Babylonian city, Tel-abib, is mentioned in Ezekiel 3:15. On the other, it referred to contemporary Zionist literature: the title of Theodor Herzl's (see nutshell #71) 1902 novel of a Zionist utopia, *Altneuland*, or "old-new land" in German, had been translated into Hebrew as Tel Aviv. Since a *tel* is a mound consisting of the remains of ancient settlements, and *aviv* is the Hebrew word for spring, the name of the new suburb suggested the connection between the new enterprise and the Jewish people's historic past in the homeland.

Among the outstanding immigrants of the Second *Aliyah* was the original thinker Aaron David Gordon (1856–1922). Gordon, who made *aliyah* at the age of forty-eight, had a profound influence on many of the younger immigrants, as much as a result of his personal example as of his theories. Although he had been a land official in Russia, he had never worked the soil with his own hands until he arrived in Israel. Gordon's philosophy has been called "the religion of labor," a term he never used himself but one that adequately summarizes his basic beliefs. Gordon believed that the renewal of the Jewish people could come about only through their physical labor on the land. In a general sense, he maintained that an individual can regain a sense of unity with the cosmos only by returning to nature, which is also the key to rediscovering religion. More specifically, he argued that cultivating the soil of the ancestral homeland would do much more than make the land flourish; it would also give the Jews a moral claim to that land and would result in their individual and national rebirth.

Gordon rejected ties with international socialism, because he believed that Jewish workers needed to work out their own path through a life of labor to a just society. He rejected Marxist socialism because, in his opinion, it put the horse before the cart: instead of seeking to transform the individual, it sought to change the political system. Gordon believed that a new social order could not succeed unless the human beings who initiated it had already undergone fundamental change. According to Gordon, the Jewish people had been the first to recognize that all humanity was created in God's image. It was now the Jewish task to create a Jewish nation in God's image.

Gordon's inspiration led to the development in 1905 of the Young Worker party. One of the party's priorities was the "conquest of labor"—basing Jewish agriculture on Jewish, not Arab, labor. In 1909 several members of the Young Worker party received permission from the head of the Palestine office of the Zionist Organization to farm a plot of land on their own collective responsibility. They named their communal settlement Deganyah. Gordon soon moved to Deganyah, where he spent the remaining years of his life, contributing to the ideology of the communal settlement movement, and helping Deganyah earn the sobriquet "mother of the communal settlements."

Communal settlements—in Hebrew, *kibbutzim* (singular: *kibbutz*)—are voluntary collective communities whose members traditionally neither earned wages nor owned private property but whose needs were provided for by the settlement. The *kibbutz* movement stressed the importance of personal labor and valued all kinds of work equally. (In recent decades, and particularly following the collapse of communism in eastern Europe, a small number of *kibbutzim* began to move toward free-market ways, paying members salaries based on the market value of their work, hiring outside laborers, encouraging members to work elsewhere, and designating boards of directors to run *kibbutz* factories.)

Despite the fact that since the creation of the *kibbutz* movement, only a small percentage of the total population of Israel chose to follow that way of life, the movement had an enormous impact on the country in its early years, in matters both practical and moral. Even before statehood, *kibbutz* members helped reclaim land considered untillable. They formed the nucleus of the army that fought the War of Independence. The communal settlements also helped in absorbing new immigrants, including children who came to Israel unaccompanied by family members. To this day a significant number of army officers come from a *kibbutz* background, as do members of the Israeli Knesset, or legislature.

With the founding of the first modern Jewish city in Israel and the first communal settlement, 1909 was a significant year for the Zionist movement. The role Tel Aviv continues to play in the commercial and cultural life of the State of Israel and the role *kibbutzim* like Deganyah played for many decades in Israeli economic, political, and military life show how thoroughgoing was the impact of the Second *Aliyah*.

78

THE BALFOUR DECLARATION

The Balfour Declaration, an official statement of the British government's "sympathy with Jewish Zionist aspirations," was conveyed in a letter dated November 2, 1917, from Foreign Secretary Arthur James Balfour to Lord Rothschild. The declaration, which endorses the "establishment in Palestine of a national home for the Jewish people," was recognized by international law when it became part of the British Mandate for Palestine in 1920. The Balfour Declaration was a turning point in modern Jewish history, enabling the dream of a Jewish state to become a political fact.

Two of the protagonists in the events that led to the Balfour Declaration had their first significant meeting eleven years earlier. In 1906, Chaim Weizmann (1874–1952), who was later to become the first president of the state of Israel, was a researcher in chemistry at Manchester University. Arthur James Balfour (1848–1930), who had been prime minister when the British government had proposed the Uganda plan to Herzl (see nutshell #74), was electioneering in Manchester. Curious to learn why the Zionists had not accepted the Uganda plan, he asked to speak with Weizmann, who was among its opponents. Although there are no contemporary records of what was actually said at the meeting, the following story appears in encyclopedias and history books alike, conferring on it a certain verisimilitude. When Balfour asked Weizmann why he had rejected Uganda, the young scientist replied with a question of his own: if Balfour were offered Paris, would he turn his back on London? Of course not, said Balfour, but London is my country's capital. To which Weizmann replied, Jerusalem was the capital of our country when London was still a marsh.

Whatever actual conversation occurred between the statesman and the scientist, Balfour is known to have left the meeting not only with a deeper understanding of Zionism but also with great admiration for Weizmann. The prime minister at the time of the Balfour Declaration, David Lloyd George (1863–1945), also was personally drawn to Zionism. A Welshman, Lloyd George believed that small nations were destined for great things. As things developed, Lloyd George became minister of munitions in 1915, during the

First World War (1914–18). A chemical process Weizmann was working on was crucial for the production of munitions, and Weizmann was brought to London as a chemical adviser to the ministry. Weizmann's important wartime contribution made him an especially forceful advocate for the Zionist cause, and his advocacy began to bear actual fruit when Lloyd George became head of the government in December 1916, with Balfour his foreign secretary.

But it was not sentiment alone that led the British government to issue the Balfour Declaration. For a number of reasons, mostly based on miscalculations of one sort or another, the British felt a statement of support for Zionist aims would strengthen the British war effort. For example, the British seemed to believe that Russian Zionists could somehow either keep postrevolutionary Russia in the war on the Allied side or at least prevent the Germans from commandeering Ukrainian produce. They also hoped that an expression of British sympathy with Zionist aims would influence American Jews to speak out against the voices of pacifism in that country and support the entry of the United States into the war. The British also seemed to fear that if they delayed in expressing sympathy with the Zionist cause, the Germans might beat them to it, which would encourage Jews around the world to support Germany, Britain's enemy, in the war.

The official expression of sympathy with Zionism was to take the form of a letter from Balfour to Lord Rothschild, whom the government recognized as leader of the English Jewish community. By arrangement, Lord Rothschild submitted a draft of such a letter to Balfour on July 18, 1917. Rothschild's draft, carefully edited by Weizmann and others, summarized the position the Zionists hoped the British would endorse: all of Palestine should be "reconstituted" as the Jewish national home (stressing the historic connection of the Jewish people to the land), and the British government would seek to achieve this end in concert with the Zionist Organization.

Opponents of Zionism strenuously objected to this wording, however. Four drafts and three and a half months later, the final version was much more ambiguously worded: "His Majesty's Government view with favour the establishment in Palestine of a national home for the Jewish people." The Jewish national home was no longer synonymous with all of Palestine but was merely to be located in it. In addition, the final letter contained two provisions missing from the original draft: "it being clearly understood that nothing shall be done which may prejudice the civil and religious rights of existing non-Jewish communities in Palestine, or the rights and political status enjoyed by Jews in any other country."

As the British cabinet discussed what was to be the final version of the letter, Weizmann sat in an anteroom, awaiting the results as anxiously as a prospective father outside a hospital delivery room. In fact, a cabinet member emerging from the meeting with the final document is reported to have said,

"Dr. Weizmann, it's a boy." Weizmann later wrote, "I did not like the boy at first. It was not the one I expected."

Nonetheless, Weizmann took to heart the Balfour Declaration's expression of concern for the Arab population of Palestine. As head of the British government's Zionist Commission sent to Palestine in 1918 to help advise on the future of the country, he met with the Emir Faisal, a leader of the Arab movement. In January 1919 the two men signed an agreement endorsing "the closest possible collaboration in the development of the Arab State and Palestine" and "the immigration of Jews into Palestine on a large scale." The agreement, however, was linked to the realization of Arab nationalist aims in Iraq and Syria. When those aims were dashed the following year, Faisal reneged on the agreement, which, in any case, more extreme Arab nationalists had never accepted as binding.

Nor was Arab rejection of the Balfour Declaration the sole problem the Zionists faced. Even though Lloyd George and Balfour truly sympathized with Zionist aims, the British administration in Palestine had at best mixed feelings. For two years, no attempt was made to publicize the Balfour Declaration in Palestine, and few British officers there were even aware of it. In the eyes of some antisemitic British officers, the Zionist settlers were merely a band of Bolsheviks. Even after the League of Nations gave Great Britain the mandate for Palestine, to put "into effect the declaration originally made on November 2, 1917," many members of the British administration in Palestine bent over backwards to protect Arab interests over Jewish ones.

The 1920 appointment of Herbert Samuel as the first British high commissioner in Palestine led many Jews to hope that Zionist aims would be realized in short order. Samuel, after all, was not only a Jew and a Zionist, but had also been a member of the cabinet that had issued the Balfour Declaration. It is certainly true that Samuel made some sincere efforts on behalf of the Jewish settlement. For example, he made Hebrew one of the official languages of the country. But precisely because he was Jewish, he was anxious not to seem to be favoring his coreligionists at the expense of the non-Jewish inhabitants of the country, in whose interests the Balfour Declaration also committed him to act. He informed the Zionist Organization that it would be responsible for funding development projects in Palestine, that aid from Great Britain would not be forthcoming. Perhaps Samuel's most destructive act was his appointment in 1921 of a radical as grand mufti, or chief legal authority for the Muslims, of Jerusalem. Anti-Jewish riots, fomented by the mufti, spread throughout the country.

By summer 1922, responding to Arab pressure, the British government publicly disclaimed that the intent of the Balfour Declaration had been to convert all of Palestine into a Jewish state. Nor should the declaration have given Jews hope that Palestine would become thoroughly Jewish. Indeed, "His

Majesty's Government regard any such expectation as impracticable and have no such aim in view."

The British government's belated attempts at backtracking, however, could not expunge what the Balfour Declaration had already succeeded in doing. No matter how vague and noncommittal the letter's wording, it had transformed Zionist aspirations from fantasies into political facts. Despite the British government's subsequent attempt to retreat from the implications of the Balfour Declaration, its appearance in 1917 made possible the emergence of the state of Israel some thirty years later.

79

THE BRITISH MANDATE
OVER PALESTINE:
"THE WHITE PAPER REGIME"

The term white paper *refers to an official government report or policy statement. The six White Papers on Palestine presented to Parliament between 1922 and 1939 reflect Great Britain's movement away from concern for the development of a Jewish national home and toward appeasement of Arab extremists. The Mandatory government has been called "the White Paper Regime."*

White Papers got their name from the fact that British governmental policy statements were once bound in the same white paper used for the pages. For Zionists, however, the pages and the covers of the official government reports on Palestine seemed to grow blacker and blacker. Although there were six White Papers in total, the three that are most important are those often called by the names of the colonial secretaries who issued them: the Churchill White Paper (1922), the Passfield White Paper (1930), and—most infamous of all—the Malcolm MacDonald White Paper (1939). Each of these official reports resulted from a similar sequence of events: a riot or other disturbance led to one or more investigative commissions, with the findings and recommendations summarized in a White Paper.

The Churchill White Paper. In May 1921 Palestine experienced the worst outbreak of Arab rioting to date, culminating in more or less equal numbers of Jewish and Arab deaths (47, 48) and twice as many wounded Jews as Arabs (146, 73). The commission of inquiry into the disturbances identified as their fundamental cause Arab concern over Zionist policy, particularly immigration. Because it represented the first official British statement on the subject since the Balfour Declaration, the subsequent Churchill White Paper was of particular interest. To the Zionists, it signified the erosion of British commitment to Jewish national aspirations. It flatly stated that the intent of Balfour's 1917 letter had never been to convert all of Palestine into a Jewish national home and reassured Palestinian Arabs that they would never be subordinated to Jewish culture. It also diminished the area originally covered by the Balfour Declaration, forbidding Jewish settlement in Transjordan. Most critically, it introduced qualifications into the concept of Jewish immigration: without specifying precisely what the restriction meant, the Churchill White Paper stipulated that the number of new immigrants could not exceed "the economic capacity of the country" to absorb them.

Nonetheless, some assertions of the Churchill White Paper enabled the Zionists to take heart. It envisioned a Jewish national home as a Jewish "center" in Palestine in which Jews around the world could pride themselves. It reaffirmed that the development of such a home was based on international guarantees, so that its inhabitants might know that they were in Palestine "as of right and not on sufferance."

With some reluctance, the Zionist Organization accepted the principles of the Churchill White Paper, while the Arabs rejected them outright.

The Passfield White Paper. After a period of relative calm, a new disturbance broke out in 1929. The issue was the right of Jews to worship at the Western Wall, the only remnant of the wall surrounding the ancient Temple. The grand mufti of Jerusalem claimed that the Jews intended to rebuild the Temple there, and thus posed a threat to the two mosques on the Temple Mount. The ensuing riots led to 133 Jewish deaths, with hundreds wounded and much property damage. For many Jews, the British administration's lackadaisical response to the riots conjured up memories of czarist tolerance of pogroms.

The commission of inquiry's conclusions did nothing to allay Zionist concerns. Although it clearly stated that the Arabs had attacked the Jews, in essence the commission blamed the victims: there would have been no riots if not for the Jewish presence, which the Arabs perceived as a threat to their political and economic future.

The subsequent Passfield White Paper dealt additional blows to the Zionist cause. It rejected the view that Britain's primary responsibility under the Mandate was to ensure the development of a Jewish national home. It unequivocally asserted that, as long as agricultural development in Palestine remained at its present standard, "there is no room for a single additional settler." It charged that the Zionist goal of employing only Jewish employees in Jewish enterprises had contributed to the Arab unrest. It imposed new restrictions on the transfer of land from Arabs to Jews. It also reinterpreted the linchpin of the Churchill White Paper's immigration policy: before Jewish newcomers could be admitted, the "economic absorptive capacity" of the entire populace must be considered, so that Arab unemployment constituted grounds for restricting immigration.

Reaction to the clearly anti-Zionist positions of the Passfield White Paper was immediate. Several British statesmen voiced their objections, including the former high commissioner of Palestine, Sir Herbert Samuel, known for his willingness to yield to Arab demands. By way of protest, Chaim Weizmann—a protagonist at the time of the Balfour Declaration and the acknowledged leader of the Zionist movement since—resigned as president of the Jewish Agency, the executive body of the Zionist Organization, formed to advise the Palestine administration with regard to the Jewish national home.

So intense was the negative response to the Passfield White Paper that Prime Minister Ramsay MacDonald felt constrained to soften the anti-Zionist blow it had dealt. In February 1931 he published a letter to Chaim Weizmann, in which he stressed Great Britain's commitment, through the Mandate, not only to the Jewish community in Palestine but also to world Jewry. He also reaffirmed the British responsibility to help implement Jewish immigration to and settlement in Palestine.

Although some Jews wondered why the government did not simply revoke the Passfield White Paper, the Zionist Organization accepted the prime minister's letter and agreed to cooperate once again with the Palestine administration.

The Malcolm MacDonald White Paper. In the eight and a half years between the Passfield White Paper and the infamous Malcolm MacDonald White Paper of May 1939, the clouds of war began to thicken over Europe. Following Hitler's rise to power in 1933, it became more necessary than ever for Jews to have a place of refuge. But British strategic interests stood in the way of unrestricted immigration to Palestine. The British government was loath to anger the Arabs, who controlled not only the route to India but also most oil resources, lest they side in case of war with Britain's enemies. The Arab extremists, on the other hand, saw in the rise of Nazism a new potential, and powerful, ally.

Aware of their increased leverage, the Palestinian Arabs announced a general strike in 1936. The grand mufti and his associates made three demands of the British: Jewish immigration must be halted; further sale of land from Arabs to Jews must be prohibited; and an Arab "democratic government" must be set up, one that could impose its will on the Jewish minority. Although these demands had not been met when the strike was ended after six months, it was disruptive enough: it was accompanied not by riots but by paramilitary operations, in which officer-led units blew up the oil pipeline from Iraq to Haifa, damaged railways, and mined roads.

The report of the ensuing investigative commission is noteworthy for the depth of its understanding of the roots of Zionism. The commission solicited opinions from a wide variety of Jews and Arabs. Weizmann's testimony was particularly poignant. He divided the world into two kinds of places—those where Jews "cannot live" and those where they "cannot enter"—and stressed that the doors to the Jewish national home must not be shut to Jewish refugees.

The commission's conclusion was balm to the Zionists: the primary responsibility of Great Britain under the Mandate was to "promote the establishment of the Jewish National Home." That home, said the commission, was thriving at present but severely threatened. To ensure its survival without reneging on the British mandatory commitment to the Arabs, the commission saw only one solution: "a surgical operation," or partition of the country into separate Jewish and Arab states. The establishment of a Jewish state was thus for the first time formally recommended by an official body of a world power.

After vigorous debate, the Zionist Organization accepted the concept of partition, but the Arabs rejected the proposal out of hand. While the British proceeded to publish a White Paper accepting the concept of partition (July 1937) and another appointing a commission to consider how to implement it (December 1937), a full-scale Arab revolt broke out, which was not suppressed until spring 1939. Not only Jews and British but also moderate Palestinian Arabs were among its victims.

This time the investigative commission withdrew the partition plan, and the subsequent White Paper (November 1938) announced that since no such plan could work, the government would strive to bring about an understanding between Arabs and Jews. The 1938 White Paper called for a conference of representatives of the Jewish Agency, on the one hand, and of representatives of the Arabs of Palestine and of the other Arab states, on the other. When nothing constructive emerged from the conference—really two separate conferences, because the Arabs refused to meet with the Jews—the government issued the Malcolm MacDonald White Paper of 1939.

With the statement that "His Majesty's Government now declares unequivocally that it is not part of their policy that Palestine should become a Jewish state," the Malcolm MacDonald White Paper completely withdrew from the pro-Zionist stance of the 1936 commission. The emergence of such a state, it added, would be "contrary to their obligations to the Arabs under the Mandate." The White Paper went on to propose the creation, within ten years, of "an independent Palestine state," which would safeguard the interests of both Arabs and Jews. During the transition period, based on their respective populations, Arabs and Jews would be placed in charge of government departments.

The White Paper went on to say that nothing in the Mandate supported the idea that Jewish immigration should be permitted to "continue indefinitely." Even if the economy were able to absorb an infinite number of newcomers, the Arabs' fear of Jewish immigration had to be taken into account. In view of the difficult situation in Europe, over the next five years a total of 75,000 Jews would be admitted. Following that five-year period, no new immigration would be allowed without Arab approval.

The implications of the policies of the White Paper were dire for both the Jews of Europe and the Jews of Palestine. The strict immigration quotas amounted to a death sentence to the millions of European Jews who needed a refuge. The proposed "independent Palestine state" would have a permanent Arab majority, exposing the Jewish minority to persecution, expulsion, or worse.

Not surprisingly, many saw the Malcolm MacDonald White Paper as a betrayal of Britain's obligations to the Jews under the Balfour Declaration; the League of Nations itself concluded that the White Paper violated the Mandate. Although the White Paper seemed to constitute a great victory for the Arabs, they too rejected its proposals. Many Arab extremists had by this time formally allied themselves with the Nazis, hoping that with this crucial assistance, they might finally wipe out the Jewish settlement in Palestine.

The outbreak of war led many to hope that the White Paper's provisions would at least be suspended for the duration of the conflict. But Britain immediately began to put its draconian policies into effect. In the eyes of the Jews of Palestine, the restrictions on immigration were illegal, not to mention immoral, and with clear conscience they began to organize the rescue of European Jews. Palestinian Jews thus found themselves fighting *with* the British and *against* them at the same time. In the words of the Zionist leader David Ben-Gurion (1886–1973), soon to become the first prime minister of Israel, "We must fight Hitler as if there were no White Paper, and we must fight the White Paper as if there were no Hitler."

At the Zionist Congress in December 1946, Chaim Weizmann said of the Malcolm MacDonald White Paper, "Few documents in history have worse consequences for which to answer." Two months later, still clinging despite rising opposition to the restrictive immigration policy of the White Paper, Great Britain opted out of the Mandate completely by turning the matter over to the United Nations. In November 1947 the United Nations Special Commission on Palestine recommended that the Mandate for Palestine be terminated as soon as possible and the country partitioned (see nutshell #88). The end of the "White Paper Regime" was at hand.

80

THE PROTOCOLS OF THE ELDERS OF ZION

The Protocols of the Elders of Zion has for nearly a century been a basic text for antisemites. It has been used to prove the existence of an "international Jewish conspiracy" to dominate the world and subvert Christianity and existing governments. Though revealed as a forgery in 1921, The Protocols continued for years thereafter to bolster antisemitic claims even in Western democracies, and they are still promoted by antisemites and anti-Zionists.

For centuries, *elder* was an honorific term in Jewish usage. The Bible describes several different kinds of elders, all of whom share social prominence and leadership roles. In rabbinic times, sages of whatever age were called elders, and until the mid-18th century scholars and community leaders alike were respectfully addressed by this title. As Jews entered the modern world, where respect for age as a repository of wisdom and leadership abilities was no longer a given, the term fell into disuse. But it took anonymous antisemites in the 20th century to turn the term on its head. Far from conferring honor, the term "elders of Zion" was intended to arouse fear and loathing. The image of a revered statesman was transformed into a caricature of a bogeyman, scheming with others of his ilk to destroy all civilized values.

Although the specific term "elders of Zion" came into use only at the turn of this century, in fact the conspiracy theory it denotes had been circulating in anti-Jewish circles from ancient times. Writers in Alexandria over 2,000 years ago reported a secret Jewish plot to bring evil upon the Greeks. During the Middle Ages, stories were rife of collaborations between Jewish sages and satanic forces to undermine Christians and their religion by poisoning wells (a theory used to explain the Black Death in the 14th century), performing ritual murder, and the like. In more modern times, Napoleon's convoking a "Great Sanhedrin" in 1807 gave new life to these conspiracy theories. The actual Sanhedrin, the supreme legal institution of the Jewish state during the Second Commonwealth, had not met since the early 5th century (c. 425 C.E.). Entirely for reasons of state, Napoleon assembled seventy-one rabbis and Jewish lay-men from France and Italy to translate secular political rulings into legal terms that would be religiously binding on the Jews. In the popular imagination this meeting of Jewish notables recalled old tales of secret meetings of Jews from different countries to choose the site for each year's ritual murder. The rise to success during the mid-19th century of the Jewish international banking fam-ily, the Rothschilds (see nutshell #64), helped convince believers in the theory of "the international Jew" that such a figure was more than a metaphor.

In 1868 the German novelist Hermann Goedsche reworked the conspiracy theory into a major plot element in his novel *Biarritz*. A German scholar and a baptized Jew secretly witness a nighttime meeting in the Prague Jewish cem-etery of a representative from each of the twelve tribes of Israel, a 13th dele-gate representing "the unfortunates and exiles," and a disembodied Devil. According to the novelist, each of the representatives has a specific assignment to help bring about Jewish domination of the world. The delegates arrange to meet again in a century, by which time their descendants will have success-fully completed the task.

It was not long before antisemitic forces in Russia presented a reworking of this horror fiction as actual fact. The resulting pamphlet, *The Rabbi's Speech*, changes the venue from a cemetery to a secret rabbinical conference, where the participants make plans to overthrow Christian society.

Popular as these modern versions of Jewish conspiracy theory were, they did not have the lasting impact of *The Protocols of the Learned Elders of Zion*. The text first appeared in Russia in late summer 1903, in the St. Petersburg newspaper edited by one of the instigators of the Kishinev pogroms (see nut-shell #73) some months earlier. Two years later, during the 1905 revolution in Russia, *The Protocols* was reprinted. Neither of these early appearances had much of an effect, however. But the text was given new life when a new edi-tion came out in 1917. This edition claimed the contents as a report of a series of meetings of "the Council of Elders" called by the "Prince of Exile"—Theodor Herzl—at the time of the First Zionist Congress (see nutshell #71). Since the Zionist Congress was actually a meeting of Jews from many different coun-tries to discuss the idea of a Jewish state, the scurrilous claim had just enough basis in fact to confer upon it an aura of verisimilitude.

This version became popular in Russia among the pro-czarist forces. Al-ready having condemned the revolutionary movement as a Jewish plot, with this new grist for their mill, they led systematic pogroms that left over 100,000 Jews dead and many more wounded and orphaned. These pogroms constituted the most devastating attack on Jews from the time of the Chmielnicki massa-cres (see nutshell #57) until the Holocaust. When the czarist regime was fi-nally overthrown, large numbers of Russian émigrés made their way to other countries, where they began to spread the conspiracy theory. Translated into different languages, *The Protocols* convinced many readers in western Europe that the Jews were bent on undermining society. The common knowledge that several Bolshevik leaders were of Jewish ancestry bolstered this fear.

That the text found an eager audience in Germany and France, both of which had active antisemitic movements, is not surprising. But the fraudulent document also had a powerful influence in the United States and England. In 1920 American automobile magnate Henry Ford published a series of articles on the "Jewish world-conspiracy" based on *The Protocols*, and an American edition appeared under the title *The International Jew: The World's Foremost Problem*. In England, the Russian correspondents of two major newspapers, *The Times* and *The Morning Post*, accepted its authenticity. Both papers noted that Jewish Bolsheviks appeared to be fulfilling the plan for subversion of society. In May 1920, *The Times*, in a long article evaluating a recent translation of *The Protocols* into English, asserted that the truth about the "document" must finally be unearthed: if it were authentic, the group responsible for its plans must be identified. But the newspaper also raised the possibility that the text was a forgery.

It took a little over a year for *The Times*'s Constantinople correspondent to prove that *The Protocols* was in fact a fraud. Just as Woodward and Bernstein were to have their "Deep Throat" more than a half-century later, Philip Graves had an anonymous tipster, too. The reporter was approached by a Russian monarchist who had begun research on *The Protocols* fully committed to its authenticity. But recently he had bought some old books from a former officer of the czarist secret police, the Okhrana. One of the books, in French, dated 1864, contained passages bearing a striking similarity to the text. The Russian's French volume lacked a title page, but with the book in tow, Philip Graves went off to the British Museum Library, where he identified it as a French journalist's satire against the regime of Napoleon III. Interestingly enough, the Jews do not figure at all in the French satire.

The fact that the Russian had purchased the book from a former czarist secret police officer suggested that the Okhrana was behind the plagiarism. Investigations soon confirmed that in the late 1890s, a Paris agent of the Okhrana was asked to prepare a document to convince Czar Nicholas II that Jewish radical conspiracies had to be more forcefully suppressed. The agent felt free to plagiarize from the 1864 satire, which had become a rare book, the whole edition having been confiscated by the French government. With the French book providing the basic framework for *The Protocols*, he fleshed out his forgery with material from *Biarritz* and other sources.

Interestingly enough, it turned out that the czar was not taken in by the claim that *The Protocols* was an authentic report. Although no great fan of the Jews, he scribbled in the margin of the copy given him, "A worthy cause is not defended by evil means." Lest the work of their Paris agent go for naught, however, the Okhrana let the text find its way into the Russian press, starting the forgery on its infamous career.

The London Times ran Philip Graves's revelations in August 1921. Although anti-Jewish sentiment in England soon died down, *The Protocols* continued to flourish nonetheless. In early 1921 in the United States, even before its fraudulent nature was confirmed, President Wilson and former president Taft had lent their prestige to a declaration signed by 119 leading Americans denouncing the idea of an international Jewish conspiracy. But it took a consumer boycott of Ford's cars and the intervention of the American Jewish Community to exact a formal apology in 1927 from Henry Ford.

The damage had already been done, however, and the bogeyman image of "the international Jew" continued to stoke the flames of American antisemitism over the next few decades. As the Nazis rose to power in Germany, *The Protocols* became one of their chief weapons. Editions of the text usually bore covers reminiscent of those on horror comics, often with the image of a snake—representing "international Jewry"—entwining itself around the world. Nor did the defeat of Nazism signal the demise of *The Protocols*. A new Spanish edition was published in 1963, evidently in the attempt to influence the Second Vatican Council not to revise the Church's traditional attitude toward the Jews. Arab propagandists also borrowed the idea of the "international Jewish conspiracy," perhaps as a way to explain the success of Israel's army against the combined Arab forces: the small state could not have been acting on its own, but must have been supported by "world Jewry." In 1956 the United Arab Republic published an Arabic edition, and two years later Nasser was reported in an Indian newspaper to have said that *The Protocols* proves the existence of a Zionist conspiracy that governs "the fate of the European continent." When the Ayatollah Khomeini came to power in Iran in 1979, a new readership was introduced to the text. *Imam*, the Ayatollah's publication, not only printed excerpts from the forgery but also claimed that, during the 1982 war in the Falklands, under the influence of the "Elders of Zion," British soldiers committed atrocities on their Argentine opponents. Even more recently, the leader of Pamyat, the antisemitic Russian nationalist movement, has promoted the text. Although in November 1993, a Russian court ruled that *The Protocols* was a forgery and that to publish it was an act of antisemitism, ultranationalists in Russia and elsewhere still talk with conviction of an "international Jewish conspiracy."

Belief in *The Protocols* not only rationalized antisemitism in the early 20th century, thus contributing to the Holocaust, but continues to contribute to anti-Jewish agitation to this day. It is a sad truth that the fraudulent document compares in the number of its translations and editions to the Bible itself.

81

THE OPEN DOOR CLOSES

Approximately 2.5 million Jews from eastern Europe entered the United States between 1881 and 1924. As a result of the restrictive immigration acts of 1921 and 1924, the great wave of Jewish immigration into the United States slowed to a trickle. Although the laws were not specifically antisemitic in intent, they had decisive long-term effects on the Jewish communities of Europe and America alike.

On a bronze plaque on the interior wall of the pedestal of the Statue of Liberty, a poem is inscribed. Composed in 1883 by the American Jewish poet Emma Lazarus (1849–1887), "The New Colossus" attributes the following welcoming words to the Statue:

> . . . "Give me your tired, your poor,
> Your huddled masses yearning to breathe free,
> The wretched refuse of your teeming shore.
> Send these, the homeless, tempest-tost to me.
> I lift my lamp beside the golden door!"

In 1903, when Lazarus's poem was affixed to the statue's pedestal, the doors to the United States were not only "golden" but also open. Jews, along with Germans, Italians, and Irish, represented one of the largest ethnic groups to take advantage of the Statue's invitation. In response to the Kishinev pogrom of that year (see nutshell #73), over 75,000 Russian Jews were able to migrate to America, followed by over 100,000 in 1904. But two decades later, laws restricting immigration effectively dimmed the welcoming beacon represented by the statue's lamp.

While the doors of the United States were open to immigration, about a third of east European Jewry made its way to the United States. That influx was responsible for a sixteen-fold increase in the American Jewish population, from about 250,000 in 1880 to over 4 million in 1925. The American Jewish community became the largest in the world, with the Jewish population of New York, its premier city, outranking that of Warsaw—the world's next largest

Jewish community—by more than 5 to 1. As a result of the great wave of Jewish immigration, the Jewish population of the United States increased at a pace five times that of the American population in general. Furthermore, once they had arrived in the United States, Jewish immigrants tended to stay in greater numbers than other immigrants. According to immigration data for the period 1908 to 1924, one out of every seven immigrants who came to and stayed in the United States was Jewish.

Many citizens of the United States supported the so-called open-door immigration policy, viewing the immigrants as potential builders of the country. But by the turn of the century voices were heard opposing unrestricted immigration. Some adherents of the Populist movement, which began among American farmers, associated Jews with oppressive financial practices and favored restricting their immigration. Organized labor saw the immigrant mass as undermining the growing strength of unions. And for a surprising number of intellectuals, nothing less than the American gene pool was endangered by unrestricted immigration. In the view of the Immigration Restriction League, founded by a Harvard professor in 1894, the "wrong kind" of immigrants threatened to "mongrelize" America. By 1891 a law was enacted to exclude would-be immigrants "likely to become a public charge," in addition to those with physical or mental handicaps or undesirable morals.

The racist bent of those favoring restriction became unmistakable in the results of a study conducted from 1907 to 1911 contrasting northwestern Europeans—English, Irish, German, Scandinavian—and southeastern ones—Mediterraneans, Slavs, and Jews. The forty-two–volume report prepared by the U.S. Immigration Commission characterized the former group as skilled workers who helped stabilize the economy, while the latter were not only unskilled as a group but also likely to concentrate in slums that posed a threat to the moral and physical health of the country. A policy was beginning to evolve in the United States that bore more than a passing resemblance to the racist laws that would characterize Nazi Germany.

Following World War I, public sentiment against the open-door policy strengthened. Although the war's outcome seemed to be a victory for democracy, the period that followed marked a rise in antisemitism and in "nativism." Not only Jews but also Catholics and blacks were the targets of "nativists" who promoted themselves as guardians of the "real America." By 1924 the Ku Klux Klan had a membership of over 4 million. Its revival helped fuel the movement to restrict immigration.

The Bolshevik victory in Russia led to a "Red Scare" in the United States, the main victims of which were Jews. Many people noted the prominence of Jews in the new Communist regime, which not only called for the overthrow of capitalist governments but also denounced religion as the "opium of the masses." No less a personage than the U.S. attorney general himself warned against "foreign-born subversives and agitators." Among the documents he circulated was one showing that the decision to overthrow the czar had actually been made by New York Jews in February 1916.

The economic devastation the war had caused in the Jewish communities of eastern Europe also led to rumors of a flood of foreigners poised to enter the United States. Unfortunately, the rumor was supported by a metaphor used by an American Jewish leader to describe the parlous situation of Jews in Poland: if there were a ship large enough to hold 3 million people, he wrote, all of Polish Jewry would board it in order to escape to America.

The rumor was among the factors leading to the passage of the "emergency immigration law" of 1921. This law established the principle of limiting immigration by quotas based on national origin. It provided that in any given year, the number of immigrants from any given country could not exceed 3 percent of the number of people from that country living in the United States in 1910. The law was thrown together so quickly that neither shipping companies providing passage to would-be immigrants nor American consuls issuing visas understood it clearly. As a result, ships sometimes arrived bearing passengers whose countries' quotas had already been filled. These immigrants were in fact sent back to Europe, often with no resources whatsoever.

A more restrictive law still, one that essentially held sway for four decades, was enacted in 1924. By reducing the quota to 2 percent and by rolling back the definitive year to 1890—which predated the arrival of large numbers of Jews and other "undesirable" immigrants—this law gave clear preference to immigrants from northwestern Europe.

Although the Jews were not the only target of the restrictive immigration laws of 1921 and 1924, the impact of those laws on the Jews of Europe and of America was decisive. Before World War I, about 100,000 Jews emigrated each year from Russia, Poland, Rumania, and the Baltic countries. Now the combined annual quota for those countries, including non-Jews as well as Jews, was fixed at under 9,500. Ironically, the influx of "Nordic" Europeans favored by the laws never came. While the quotas for the countries of northwestern Europe went unfilled, those for southeastern Europe were oversubscribed.

The American Jewish population from its earliest days had been continuously invigorated and renewed by the arrival of Jews from abroad. With the severe restrictions on immigration, Yiddish culture in the United States began to decline, as did religious observance. By 1940 a majority of American Jews were native-born. As Jews continued to acculturate, some began to wonder whether Judaism would survive in America.

Laws are an expression of national sentiment. American Jews correctly saw the restrictive immigration laws of 1921 and 1924 as indications that official America might pay lip service to the words of "The New Colossus," but the ideology of the poem no longer influenced American policy. The full effect of the laws of 1921 and 1924 on world Jewry could not have been foreseen at the time, but essentially they were to spell catastrophe for the Jews of Nazi Europe.

82

BIROBIDZHAN: THE SOVIET UNION'S "JEWISH AUTONOMOUS REGION"

In the late 1920s the Soviet government began to encourage Russian Jews to become agricultural settlers in a distant region of Siberia called Birobidzhan. By the time Birobidzhan was declared the "Jewish Autonomous Region" in 1934, it was already a failure. A brief renaissance of Jewish settlement there after World War II was followed by official government repression of Jewish life both in Birobidzhan and throughout the rest of the country. Nonetheless, throughout the late 1970s and 1980s, Soviet propaganda continued to hail Birobidzhan as a viable center of Jewish life.

The Birobidzhan project, which would turn out to be a prime example of Soviet cynicism vis-à-vis its Jewish populace, had at its core some humanitarian concern. World War I and the civil war that followed the 1917 Bolshevik revolution not only destroyed Russian industry but also undermined the economic basis of Jewish life in the *shtetls*, or townlets. Hoping to improve their lot, many Jews moved to larger towns and cities, where they simply added to the problem of unemployment. The introduction of communism also forced over a million Jews to close down their small businesses by 1925. Some Jews turned to the black market as a way to keep body and soul together. In order to combat the impoverishment of the Jewish masses and to turn the "little profiteers" into productive members of society, the Soviet leadership decided on a policy of Jewish agricultural settlement. In 1924 it set up a Committee for the Settlement of Jewish Workers on the Soil.

The involvement of Soviet Jews in agriculture won the wholehearted support of Mikhail Kalinin, who was president of the country from 1923 to 1946. Though he was little more than a figurehead, Jews were heartened by Kalinin's remarks in 1926, when he urged the self-transformation of several hundred thousand Jews into "a compact farming population" as "one of the most efficient means of preserving the independent existence of the Jews as a nation." Special areas in the Crimea and Ukraine were designated for Jewish agricultural settlement.

Central planning, however, had failed to take into account the reaction of Ukrainian and Crimean farmers. Complaints were voiced that the Jews were being given the best lands in the country, and a wave of antisemitism broke out.

For a number of reasons, not the least of which was its relatively sparse population, Soviet leadership turned next to Birobidzhan, a remote area in eastern Siberia, about the size of Massachusetts and Connecticut combined. Although Russia had annexed the region in 1858, czarist attempts to colonize it with Cossacks had not succeeded. By the mid-1920s, the population of about 30,000 included the descendants of those Cossacks, some Koreans and Kazakhs, and members of a primitive tribe.

By choosing Birobidzhan as a center for Jewish agricultural settlement the Soviet authorities hoped to achieve several political objectives at one time. Security concerns topped the list. Birobidzhan's geographical situation made it vulnerable to invasions from neighboring Manchuria, and when Japan occupied Manchuria in 1931 and 1932, it became more important than ever to strengthen the Soviet presence in the region.

Two other items on the Soviet leadership's agenda had less to do with the specific location of Birobidzhan than with the general idea of establishing a Jewish enclave within the Soviet Union. The first was the propaganda potential of such a region among Jewish communities abroad. Soviet leaders had perhaps an inflated view of the weight of Jewish political influence in the United States, which had not yet recognized the Soviet Union. They hoped that the Birobidzhan project would arouse the sympathies of American and European Jews, who would convince their governments to reverse their hostile policies toward the Communist country. They also anticipated—not incorrectly, as it turned out—that Jewish philanthropic organizations would foot a large part of the bill for developing Jewish settlement in the region.

The Soviet leadership also hoped that Birobidzhan would undermine the influence of Zionism both in the Soviet Union and abroad. According to Soviet propaganda, Zionism not only was a tool of British imperialism but also required superimposing Jewish rule on the local Arab population, whereas Jews would encounter no local opposition in the sparsely populated Soviet Far East (a claim not completely borne out by the facts, however). Soviet rhetoric extolled the virtues of the Jewish national experiment in Birobidzhan, where "for the first time in the history of the Jewish people, under socialism, they are developing sovereign, soviet, national upbuilding."

In sum, while the Soviet leaders had several reasons for undertaking the Birobidzhan project, Soviet interests, not Jewish ones, were uppermost in their minds.

One of the clearest signs of how cynical the Soviet attitude toward the project quickly became was its dubbing Birobidzhan a "Jewish autonomous region" in May 1934, by which time it was clear that the project had failed. Soviet Jewish enthusiasm for it had been less than overwhelming from the outset. Among the Jews who, to paraphrase a contemporary Jewish journalist, raised their feet and not merely their hands in support of Birobidzhan, more than half left not long after their arrival. As a result of poor planning on the part of the Soviet authorities, the first Jews to arrive found no roads, insufficient housing and sanitary conditions, land unsuitable to agriculture, and an infestation of insects, in addition to the harsh climate. At the same time, incentives for Jews to make the radical move to the Siberian wilderness began to decline. As the 1920s drew to a close, the economic hardship of the Soviet Jewish population was on the wane. As opportunities for young Jews opened up in the large cities, fewer were attracted to life on the land in the remote wilderness and more to professional, administrative, and managerial careers.

Furthermore, it became increasingly clear to Soviet Jews that there was no consistent government commitment to the idea of an internal Jewish state. To be sure, on the occasion of naming Birobidzhan a Jewish autonomous region, President Kalinin gave an optimistic view of the region's future: "In ten years' time, Birobidzhan will become the most important guardian of the Jewish-national culture. . . . We already consider Birobidzhan a Jewish national state." He announced that once the region had a Jewish settlement of 100,000, the Soviet government would consider forming a Soviet Jewish republic. On the other hand, in November 1936, Joseph Stalin, the general secretary of the USSR's Communist party (1922–1953) and its future premier (1941–1953), envisioned a rather different future for Birobidzhan. Without specifically mentioning either Jews or Birobidzhan, he outlined three conditions without which no autonomous region could become a republic. Birobidzhan met only one condition: it was a border region. But it failed to meet the other two: the nationality whose name the republic bore must constitute a majority there, and the region's population must exceed a million. To this day, the population of Birobidzhan as a whole is under a quarter of a million, and the Jewish presence there never accounted for more than about a fourth of the entire population.

Two signs of the government's lack of commitment to a Jewish state in Birobidzhan became clearer as World War II approached. Although in 1928, the government had banned settlement there to non-Jews, it began to welcome non-Jewish immigration as well, as defense of the Soviet Far East became more pressing. Also, the Soviet government did not open up the area to Jewish refugees from Nazi persecution.

The small number of Jews who went to and stayed in Birobidzhan witnessed a brief but intense flowering of Yiddish culture. Not only Russian but also Yiddish appeared on street signs and postmarks; a Jewish state theater was established; a library named for the Yiddish author Sholem Aleichem (1859–

1916) specialized in Judaica; and Jewish publications thrived. But Jewish cultural hopes in Birobidzhan were dashed with the onset of the purges of 1936–1938, which included as victims Jewish leaders throughout the Soviet Union. The particular charges brought against the Jewish leadership of Birobidzhan included their being spies and Japanese agents, their neglect of the settlers' needs, and their sabotage of the agricultural enterprise.

A superb example of the Soviet leadership's cynicism toward the Birobidzhan project can be found in the extravagant rhetoric used during the spring and summer of 1938, as the purges continued. Even as the Jewish leadership was being decimated, official celebrations were held in Birobidzhan and elsewhere to commemorate the passage of ten years since Jewish settlement had begun there and of four years since its designation as a Jewish autonomous region.

Following World War II, in the aftermath of the Nazi horrors, there was a brief revival of Jewish interest in Birobidzhan. Between 1946 and 1948, hundreds of Jews, including well-known writers, made the long trip to the region, longing for a Jewish rebirth there. But once again the cultural revival was decisively ended by a new set of purges. These purges of 1948–1949 were intended to undermine Jewish activity throughout the Soviet Union. In Birobidzhan, all Jewish institutions were closed. Accusations against the Jewish leadership included their being American agents, aimed at turning the Soviet Far East into an American anti-Soviet base. Despite the fact that many administrative offices in Birobidzhan were held by non-Jews, only Jews were accused.

As a result of the purges, Jewish life in Birobidzhan declined even further. But cynical Soviet claims about the region continued to be made in the 1970s and 1980s, when the Jewish population there accounted for less than 10 percent of the total. In spring 1984, as a means of countering criticism of Soviet mistreatment of Jews, the government mounted an impressive, if hollow, celebration of the 50th anniversary of Birobidzhan's designation as the Jewish autonomous region. The propaganda value of the Birobidzhan project to Soviet policy long outlived whatever actual function the project served in the lives of Soviet Jews.

83

MORDECAI KAPLAN AND RECONSTRUCTIONIST JUDAISM

Reconstructionist Judaism is the youngest and smallest of American Judaism's organized religious movements. Its ideology is tightly linked to the writings and teachings of its founding father, Mordecai M. Kaplan (1881–1983). Reconstructionism derives from Kaplan's definition of Judaism as an evolving religious civilization.

The ideas behind Reconstructionist Judaism first reached a wide audience in 1934, with the publication of Mordecai M. Kaplan's first and most influential work, *Judaism as a Civilization: Toward the Reconstruction of American-Jewish Life.* In fact, however, Kaplan had been implementing Reconstructionist ideas since 1922 as rabbi at New York City's newly created Society for the Advancement of Judaism. Although Kaplan had no intention of creating a new movement, his ideas not only gave birth to a new major American Jewish grouping but also profoundly influenced the American Reform and Conservative movements and, to a lesser degree, left its mark on modern Orthodoxy in America as well.

Kaplan, son of an Orthodox rabbi, came as a young boy from Lithuania via France to the United States. His wide reading, particularly in the newly emerging social sciences, led him to reject all the supernatural claims associated with Judaism. At the same time, his studies left him convinced that Judaism, like all other religions, is only part of a larger civilization. Kaplan felt that the three traditional pillars of Jewish life and thought—God, Torah, and Israel—needed to be reconstructed to be acceptable to modern, educated Jews. He stressed that, while the idea of reconstructing Judaism might seem threatening, in fact Judaism had been reconstructed at various times in the course of Jewish history.

To begin with, Kaplan insisted that the traditional placement of the three pillars needed rethinking. Not God but the Jewish people needed to be at the center of a reconstructed Judaism. But a reconstructed Judaism had no place in it for the supernatural concept of "the chosen people," not only because such a concept implies that God makes choices like a person but also because it smacks of ethnocentrism.

Since for Kaplan Judaism represented an entire civilization, the land of Israel played a significant role in his blueprint for reconstruction. But unlike the Zionists of his day, who denied the value of Jewish life anywhere besides the ancient homeland, Kaplan promoted "Diaspora Zionism," in which Zion is a spiritual center for Jews around the world. Zionism, however, should not be allowed to supplant the Jewish religion: Diaspora Jews and Jews in Palestine alike must practice Judaism. Without the support of Jewish ethical teachings, which help bring about a just social order, a Jewish government would run the risk of being nothing more than another country. Kaplan also believed that Jewish civilization closely links land and language, and he promoted Hebrew education for American Jewish children and adults alike. The American synagogue of his day seemed inadequate to address all the needs of Jewish civilization, and so Kaplan recommended a new type of institution: the Jewish Center, sometimes referred to as "a *shul* with a pool and a school." Kaplan was the first to conceive of this now-familiar institution.

Kaplan's reconstruction of the concept of Israel also called for a larger role for the American Jewish woman. The first *bat mitzvah* in the United States was celebrated in 1922, when Kaplan's daughter Judith entered religious majority by reading the blessings over the Torah and chanting the *Haftarah*, just as her male counterparts had been doing for centuries. The *bat mitzvah* was subsequently adopted by the American Conservative and Reform movements.

Kaplan also called for reconstructing the concept of Torah. He rejected the supernatural concept of divine revelation. In his view, God did not reveal the Torah to the Jewish people. Rather, the people reveal God through the Torah. According to one of Kaplan's theological definitions, God is a lasting power that not only encourages human beings to strive for righteousness but also guarantees that it can be realized on earth. By demanding righteous behavior in God's name, the Torah reveals God to the world.

Reconstructing Torah called for reconstructing the concept of *mitzvah* as well. Kaplan rejected the supernatural implications of the term's root meaning of "commandment," and insisted that Jews should not observe *mitzvot* out of fear of heavenly punishment or anticipation of heavenly reward. Instead, Kaplan urged Jews to observe Jewish rituals in order to strengthen their ties to the Jewish people. He also insisted that since Jewish people—not God—devised the laws of Judaism, Jews of every period of history have not only a right but also a responsibility to make sure that Jewish law responds to the needs of the moment.

Kaplan's reconstruction of God, not surprisingly, was the most controversial of his innovations. Various passages of his writings present different definitions of God, but all focus on individual self-fulfillment. For example, God is the natural forces that enable us to achieve our ideals, or the sum of everything that makes life worthwhile, or the force in the universe making for goodness, justice, mercy, and truth. Likewise, salvation for Kaplan does not imply a reward in another world but rather striving for self-fulfillment in this world. Because Kaplan felt strongly that modern Jews should not have to pray using words offensive to modern beliefs, he and some colleagues at the Society for the Advancement of Judaism made bold innovations in the traditional prayer book. Although an influential group of Orthodox rabbis responded by banning him and his works, his efforts led the way to the variety of Reform and Conservative prayer books available today.

Kaplan saw shortcomings in all of the movements of organized American Judaism of his day but he did not intend to create yet another movement. He hoped, instead, that within a reconstructed Judaism in America there would be a place for the Orthodox, Reform, Conservative, and Zionist movements. For many years he resisted the call of some of his students and colleagues to set up a separate Reconstructionist movement, but in 1968, when Kaplan was eighty-two, the Reconstructionist Rabbinical College opened. Although Reconstructionism thus became a separate Jewish movement, the number of Jews identifying themselves as Reconstructionists remains small.

Yet the influence of Kaplan and of Reconstructionism on American Judaism remains great. Many aspects of Judaism as routinely observed in the United States today reflect ideas that when introduced by Kaplan half a century ago were viewed as radical if not heretical. Today American Jews of all persuasions agree that Jewish religion and culture are part of a whole. Even in Orthodox day schools, students learn not only Torah and commentaries but also modern Jewish literature and Israeli history. The Jewish feminist movement that began in American Judaism in the 1970s (see nutshell #99) has its roots in Kaplan's egalitarian vision of reconstructed Israel. And while Kaplan's concept of God has left many unsatisfied, his Reconstructionism continues to enable many Jews to practice Judaism without feeling intellectually dishonest.

84

KRISTALLNACHT: THE NIGHT OF THE BROKEN GLASS

Kristallnacht—Crystal Night, or Night of the Broken Glass—is the German name for the pogrom sponsored by the Nazi government throughout the German Reich on the night of November 9–10, 1938. The pogrom shattered not only vast quantities of plate glass but also hopes for continued Jewish existence in Germany. After Kristallnacht, *German Jews lost their place in the German economy, saw their cultural organizations dissolved, and desperately sought out countries willing to take them in.*

Kristallnacht did not occur until after the Nazi party had been in power for five and a half years, but the party's antisemitic ideology was hardly a secret. The 1920 party program called for stripping Jews of their citizenship rights and for expelling all Jews who had entered Germany after 1914. The party's bible, Adolf Hitler's *Mein Kampf* (1925), blamed all the world's problems on the Jews, who, Hitler alleged, threatened everything of ethical and national value. Even before Hitler became chancellor of Germany in January 1933 the Nazis not only conducted a vigorous anti-Jewish propaganda campaign but also committed acts of violence against Jews.

Once Hitler was legitimately in control of the country, he began to systematize his attack on the Jews. In 1933 Jews were dismissed from government jobs. In 1935 the Nuremberg Laws reversed the 19th-century emancipation of the Jews (see nutshell #61). Now only second-class subjects and no longer citizens, Jews were forbidden to marry or have sexual relations with "Aryans." In 1937 the Nazis undertook widespread "Aryanization" of Jewish businesses, thus beginning to eliminate Jews from the nation's economy.

In the months prior to *Kristallnacht*, it became clear that in 1938 the pace of the assault on the Jews was picking up speed. Jews were required by law to register not only their businesses but also their other property. For the first time a German census was made on a racial basis. Jewish physicians were forbidden to treat non-Jews, and Jewish lawyers were denied the right to practice altogether. In addition to having to use a Jewish middle name—*Israel* for men and *Sara* for women—all Jews had the letter *J* stamped on their passports. In the summer of 1938 Hitler was further emboldened by the outcome of an international Conference on Refugee Affairs. Although sympathy was expressed for the plight of the victims of Nazi persecution, the participants showed little willingness to extend themselves on behalf of the Jews. The concentration camps already in operation on German soil—Buchenwald, Dachau, Sachsenhausen, and Mauthausen—were expanded.

The immediate pretext for the *Kristallnacht* pogrom was the assassination on November 7, 1938, of an official at the German embassy in Paris. Herschel Grynszpan, a seventeen-year-old Jewish student studying in Paris, shot Ernst vom Rath to avenge the suffering inflicted on the other members of the Grynszpan family. On October 27, Grynszpan's parents—along with some 18,000 other Jews originally from Poland though long resident in Germany—were transported against their will and under inhumane conditions to the Polish border. A postcard from his father having brought the matter to Herschel's attention, the young man took his anger out on vom Rath, the first German official whom he could get to see.

The Nazis attempted to depict the events of *Kristallnacht* as the spontaneous expression of the nation's impulse to avenge Grynszpan's outrage. But the pogrom was in fact well orchestrated by Nazi officials. On November 8, as soon as the news was broadcast that vom Rath's wounds were serious, local Nazi officials organized meetings to encourage mob action against the Jews. When news of vom Rath's death arrived the following evening, the head of the Gestapo, the Nazi secret police, sent orders to all state police units not to interfere with anti-Jewish actions, particularly those directed against synagogues; to arrest not the perpetrators but rather the victims; and to let arsonists have a free hand except where the fires they set posed a threat to nearby "Aryan" property.

In the ensuing night of terror that swept the German Reich (which as of March 1938 included Austria, and as of October 1938 the Czech Sudetenland as well) nearly 100 Jews were killed. Approximately 30,000 Jews—one in ten of the 300,000 still remaining in Germany—were arrested and sent off to concentration camps. Thousands of Jewish shops, warehouses, and homes were burned or otherwise destroyed. Fires were also set not only to hundreds of synagogues but also to the Torah scrolls and prayerbooks they housed. As day broke, throughout the country the embers of fires still smoldered, and heaps of shattered glass lined the streets. The broken window glass that spawned the name *Kristallnacht* yielded some remarkable statistics: the amount destroyed equaled half the annual production of plate glass in Belgium, its source, and the replacement cost came to 5 million marks.

The days following *Kristallnacht* dealt further blows to the Jews. Although the Nazis decided that insurance companies had to go through the motions of satisfying Jewish claims, the government would confiscate all compensation paid to Jews. The Jews would not only be held responsible for repairing all damage but would also be fined a billion marks. To make sure the fine was paid, the government would confiscate 20 percent of the property of every German Jew. In addition, whatever businesses or industries remained in Jewish hands would now be "Aryanized." Beyond the economic punishment meted out to the Jews, their social isolation was intensified. On November 15, Jewish children were denied further access to German schools. On November 28, Jews became subject to local curfews. Before the year was out, Jews were forbidden access to public places including theaters, beaches, and sleeping-car compartments. By banning all Jewish institutions, the Gestapo also limited the ability of Jews to socialize with one another.

The devastation *Kristallnacht* and its aftermath wreaked on the Jews of Germany was not only physical but psychological as well. Before *Kristallnacht* many hoped that there was still a future for them in Germany. *Kristallnacht* shattered all such hopes. The Jews of Germany sought desperately to emigrate, but immigration restrictions in the United States, Great Britain, and British Mandatory Palestine thwarted the hopes of many. Only tens of thousands of the hundreds of thousands seeking sanctuary abroad found it before the Nazis closed off the possibility of emigration in 1941. In the months following *Kristallnacht* many German Jews resorted to suicide.

Since 1938 memories of the night of November 9 have been searingly imprinted on Jewish minds. That the date was not so memorable in the minds of all Germans became startlingly clear fifty-one years later. On November 9, 1989, the Berlin Wall was opened, as the East German government eliminated all travel and emigration restrictions to the West. The mayor of Berlin joyfully announced that the day would now enter the annals of German history. Berlin's mayor obviously still had much to learn from Germany's thoughtful and distinguished president, Richard von Weizsacker, who has commented that "whoever closes his eyes to the past becomes blind to the present."

85

THE WANNSEE CONFERENCE:
GENOCIDE BECOMES STATE POLICY

At the Wannsee Conference of January 20, 1942, SS official Reinhard Heydrich met with representatives of fourteen different government and Nazi party agencies to coordinate the "Final Solution": the systematic murder of the Jews of Europe. The minutes of the conference reveal the acquiescence of the Nazi bureaucracy in the genocide that resulted in the death of 6 million Jews. Because the "Final Solution" was formally articulated and bureaucratically confirmed there, the Wannsee Conference is considered a milestone in Hitler's war against the Jews.

An elegant villa on a lakeshore road in an affluent suburb seems an unlikely site for a coldblooded bureaucratic discussion of the mechanics of genocide. But the January 1942 conference, where representatives of different Reich and Nazi party departments agreed to participate in the "Final Solution," took place in such a site. The villa's location in the Wannsee suburb of Berlin, then the nerve center of Hitler's regime, gave the conference its name. The villa had been built in 1914 for a wealthy businessman, whose anti-Nazi views some quarter of a century later resulted in the seizure of his home by the SS (the Nazi party's special police).

The meeting was called by Reinhard Heydrich (1904–1942), head of the Reich security main office, who had six months earlier received instructions from Hermann Göring, one of the highest-ranking Nazi officials, to undertake all necessary preparations for "the complete solution of the Jewish question." To coordinate the efforts of the various agencies that would have to be involved, Heydrich invited not only the Gestapo chief but also other high-ranking party and state officials. Although the representatives of the state agencies came from the second echelon, seven of the participants were SS officers and eight held doctorates from German universities. As fate would have it, the lowest-ranking participant, Adolf Eichmann (1906–1962), survived the war to achieve the greatest notoriety as a result of his capture in Argentina in 1960, trial in Jerusalem in 1961, and execution in 1962 (see nutshell #95). It was Eichmann who prepared Göring's instructions to Heydrich, sent out the invitations to the Wannsee Conference, drafted the statistics and other material Heydrich presented there, and wrote up a report of the proceedings, the so-called Wannsee Protocol. More damning, it was Eichmann who, following the Wannsee Conference, managed the deportations of Europe's Jews to the Nazi death camps.

Heydrich's presentation at the Wannsee Conference began with a review of the measures taken to date to deal with the "Jewish problem." The regime's removal of Jews from positions of influence had been followed by an attempt to expel them from German "living space." But this policy of "emigration" had not proven workable. Not only were other countries unwilling to take in the Jews, but as the Reich expanded across western and eastern Europe its Jewish population grew appreciably. For this reason, a different policy was being adopted: "evacuation of the Jews to the East." Heydrich spoke only in such euphemisms, but there is little doubt that his audience fully understood their host's veiled references to the systematic extermination of Europe's Jews in death camps.

Next, Heydrich introduced statistical information about the numbers of Jews involved in the "Jewish problem." The accuracy of the 11 million figure he presented has been challenged, but it included the Jewish population not only of neutral countries but also of unconquered England. Heydrich proceeded to outline the different situations in the various countries whose Jews had to be dealt with. Although he anticipated little difficulty in rounding up the Jews of France, for example, and foresaw no problems in finishing up an operation already well underway in Slovakia and Croatia, he suspected an adviser on Jewish questions would have to be placed in Hungary. Something would have to be done, too, about the irregular situation in Romania, where Jews were encouraged to enrich the government treasury by buying false identity papers.

Heydrich also outlined the general procedure to be undertaken to implement the "Final Solution." Segregated according to sex, all Jews able to work would be sent to the East. Although large numbers would doubtless "fall away" as a result of natural processes, the stronger ones who survived would have to be "dealt with appropriately," lest they perpetuate the Jewish species. In order to ensure thoroughness, the European continent would have to be "combed from West to East."

None of the participants opposed the drift of Heydrich's presentation in any way. They voiced no concerns beyond the narrow needs of their particular agencies. There was even some jockeying for position to see whose "Jewish problem" would be attended to first. Heydrich suggested that the Jews in the Reich area would "have to be placed ahead of the line" because of such problems as the shortage of apartments. But the administrator of what was formerly Poland expressed his hope that the Jews be removed from his area "as fast as possible": most of them were incapable of labor; because of their location, transport was not a major concern; their involvement in the black market was wreaking havoc with the local economy; and their living conditions made the spread of epidemics a live threat.

For the participants, the Wannsee Conference was just a morning's hard work, followed by drinks and lunch. At his trial nearly two decades later, Eichmann recalled sitting around over brandy with Heydrich at the meeting's end, "to rest after long hours of work."

The morning's events did not have a decisive effect on the victims of the "Final Solution." The Wannsee Conference was designed merely to ensure the efficiency of a state enterprise already in the works—not to set the murder machine in motion but rather to make certain that its gears meshed smoothly. Even as the conference was in session, the Nazis were busy gathering "practical experience," as Heydrich put it, that would affect the implementation of the "Final Solution." Mobile gas vans were busy murdering Jews at the death camp at Chelmno in Poland, and gas chambers were under construction at Belzec, another death camp. Within six months of the conference, mass deportations of Jews from occupied Europe to all six extermination centers (including Auschwitz, Treblinka, Sobibor, and Majdanek) had begun under Eichmann's orders.

The Wannsee Protocol prepared by Eichmann based on the notes a stenographer took the morning of the conference and carefully edited by Heydrich are a unique document. Hitler himself left no written orders with respect to the "Final Solution." Although the protocol notes in bloodless language only that "there was a discussion of the various types of solution possibilities," giving no details, at his trial years later Eichmann reported that they spoke "of methods of killing, about liquidation, about extermination."

A copy of the Wannsee Protocol is a central exhibit at the "House of the Wannsee Conference," Germany's first permanent memorial to the 6 million Jewish victims of the Holocaust, which was dedicated in the Wannsee villa on the occasion of the 50th anniversary of the conference, in January 1992. The fact that such a museum exists in Berlin is a sign to some that Germans are finally ready to confront the facts of its past. But a poll taken by a German magazine at the time of the 1992 anniversary of the Wannsee Conference yielded some disturbing statistics: 42 percent of those polled held that there were positive aspects to the Nazi regime, and 60 percent claimed that there would always be "a certain amount" of antisemitism in Germany.

86

THE WARSAW GHETTO UPRISING

The Warsaw ghetto uprising was the most sustained confrontation between armed Jewish resistance groups and the Nazis. Undertaken in April 1943 when the Nazi intent to liquidate the ghetto and destroy the site became known, the uprising was an unequal fight between a few hundred poorly armed Jewish youths and a much more numerous, better equipped, and better trained enemy. Although only a few Jewish participants in the Warsaw ghetto revolt survived, the uprising symbolized the affirmation of Jewish honor in the face of unprecedented evil.

The Warsaw ghetto uprising, acknowledged as the most dramatic instance of active Jewish resistance against the Nazis, had its roots in the more passive resistance demonstrated by the ghetto inmates in the early years of the war. When the Nazis entered Warsaw in September 1939, its 400,000 Jews comprised about 30 percent of the city's population, and constituted (next to New York City) the world's second-largest concentration of Jews. Shortly after entering Warsaw, the Nazis began to impose restrictions on the Jews. By October 1941, when it became an offense punishable by death for Jews to leave the ghetto, which was established in November 1940, its inhabitants had devised many strategies to circumvent Nazi directives.

Ghetto inmates defied the Nazis in numerous ways. To supplement the 184-calorie per day per person food allocation, they refined the art of smuggling. Although some schools and all public religious worship were forbidden, even forbidden courses were taught regularly and religious services held secretly. To prevent the Nazis from obliterating the memory of Polish Jewry, archives documenting ghetto life were hidden under the supervision of a trained historian. Illegal publications appeared to help the ghetto's inhabitants make some sense of the ordeal they were undergoing. To maintain their human dignity in the face of the indignities imposed on them, the ghetto inhabitants supported a network of charitable and cultural institutions.

By early 1942 an underground combat organization was set up, representing Zionist youth movements and young Communists. By late 1942 Bundist groups had joined as well, and the Jewish Fighting Organization—the ZOB—

was formed. Hampered by lack of arms and largely ignored by the Polish underground, the organization could only start active fighting in early 1943. By then, mass deportations to the Treblinka death camp during the previous summer had left only about 50,000 Jews alive in the ghetto, most between the ages of twenty and thirty-nine. Uninhibited now by family responsibilities and having learned that the destination of the cattle cars transporting Jews from the ghetto "to the East" was not labor camps but rather death camps, the young activists resolved at least not to die passively.

ZOB members began to negotiate with the Polish underground for weapons. They organized secret workshops to produce bombs and grenades and began to construct a network of bunkers to enable fighters to elude the Nazis and civilians to hide. In essence assuming leadership of the ghetto, they ordered all Jews to resist deportation.

The first opportunity for the ZOB to put its plan into effect came in January 1943, when the Nazis attempted to resume deportations. To the Nazis' surprise, members of a group selected for deportation opened fire and escaped their guards. Street fighting went on for several days, with losses on both sides. When the Nazis halted the deportations, the ZOB's popularity surged.

Everyone knew, of course, that it was only a matter of time until the Nazis decided to liquidate the ghetto entirely. That moment arrived on April 19, 1943, the eve not only of Passover but also of Hitler's birthday. The Germans had hoped to complete their task in three days, but the ghetto fighters held out against the Nazi onslaught for several weeks—longer, it has been noted, than some European countries. Several hundred Jewish fighters, armed mainly with grenades and explosives, with only a few hundred pistols, some rifles, and barely any automatic weapons, impeded the plans of an enemy about three times as numerous, equipped with machine guns, armor, and artillery. Failure to overcome the ZOB led one German commander to be replaced by another, who resorted methodically to burning down the ghetto and sending gas into the bunkers. On May 8, the bunker of the ZOB leadership fell to the Nazis. Most chose to commit suicide rather than fall into enemy hands. Although the German commander reported on May 16 that the ghetto had been completely destroyed, sporadic armed resistance lasted for at least four months more.

A number of ghetto fighters escaped through the sewers and continued to fight the Nazis as partisans in nearby woods. Among the survivors was a married couple who, after the war, made their way to Palestine, where they helped found a *kibbutz* honoring the memory of the ghetto fighters.

News of the Warsaw ghetto uprising made its way to the Treblinka death camp, where it inspired an underground group to revolt in early August 1943, enabling about 100 prisoners to escape and avoid recapture. There were also uprisings at Sobibor and Auschwitz.

Recent research has revealed that the first use of the word *Holocaust* to refer to the Nazi slaughter of the Jews may have come from an underground Christian Polish daily newspaper. On May 14, 1943, the Polish word for holocaust—*calopalenie*—appeared in an article describing the suppression of the Warsaw ghetto uprising.

In April 1993 the 50th anniversary of the Warsaw ghetto uprising was commemorated on the site. To honor the occasion, Yitzhak Rabin became the first Israeli prime minister to visit Poland. Dignitaries from the United States also attended the ceremonies, with Vice President Al Gore describing the ghetto uprising as "sacred text for our time."

87

THE *EXODUS* 1947
AND ILLEGAL *ALIYAH*

The Exodus *was a ship carrying 4,500 "illegal" immigrants—Jewish survivors of the Holocaust—to Palestine. When the British government not only refused to allow the refugees to enter Palestine but also forcibly returned them to an internment camp in Germany, the world was aghast. The affair of the* Exodus, *which took place between July and September 1947, reinforced Great Britain's resolve to terminate the Mandate.*

For a time, thanks to Leon Uris's 1958 novel *Exodus* and Otto Preminger's 1960 film of the same name, the most dramatic story of postwar "illegal" immigration into Palestine was common knowledge. The saga of the *Exodus* symbolized for readers and moviegoers Britain's incomprehensibly harsh refusal to open the gates of Palestine to refugees from Hitler's Europe.

In July 1947 more than 4,500 Jewish survivors of the war left the French port of Sète for Palestine. Apparently hoping for a liberation as complete as that of the Israelites from Egyptian slavery, the passengers changed the name of their vessel from the *President Warfield* to the *Exodus.* Their hopes were dashed, however, the following week, when British destroyers opened fire on the *Exodus* as it neared the coast of Palestine. Several passengers were killed, more wounded. The British brought the vessel to the port of Haifa, where the passengers were removed to three transports for the return voyage to France. The French government agreed to accept the passengers but refused to remove them from the transports against their will. Passively resisting attempts to make them disembark in France, the refugees went on a hunger strike. The British finally took them to Hamburg, where, on September 7, the use of tear gas forced them ashore. To the world's horror, the Holocaust survivors were then taken to a British internment camp in Germany.

The passengers aboard the *Exodus* were only a fraction of the tens of thousands of Holocaust survivors to whom a new life in Europe was out of the question. Jews attempting to return to their prewar homes often encountered violent antisemitism, notably in Kielce, Poland, where a pogrom in the summer of 1946 resulted in forty-one Jewish deaths. For other survivors, Europe was too drenched in Jewish blood and too readily called up nightmares of the Nazi ordeal. Having no place to call home, the refugees illegally crossed borders in very large numbers and congregated in camps for displaced persons in Germany, Austria, and Italy. By 1947 there were 250,000 Jewish Holocaust survivors in DP camps. For many in the camps, a Jewish home in Palestine was all that was worth living for.

A mass movement toward Palestine began, led by an organization called *Brichah* (flight). But Britain clung stubbornly to the provisions of the 1939 White Paper (see nutshell #79), which had strictly restricted immigration to Palestine. In fact, in an official statement in November 1945, Foreign Secretary Ernest Bevin indicated that Palestine was *not* the solution to the problems of the Jewish survivors, who should, instead, devote their strength and talents to rebuilding Europe. The British government heeded neither President Harry Truman's call for the immediate admission into Palestine of 100,000 DPs nor the similar recommendation of an Anglo-American Committee of Inquiry.

But the survivors and the Jewish inhabitants of Palestine were resolved to find a way for all who wanted a new life in the Jewish homeland to enter it. In their eyes, the would-be immigrants were not "illegal." Rather, Great Britain itself was illegally violating the terms of the Mandate by severely restricting Jewish immigration.

By late summer 1945, vessels carrying Holocaust survivors began to arrive in Palestine. Between then and May 1948, when the state of Israel was proclaimed, about 70,000 Jews made the trip aboard sixty-five ships, but British intervention prevented most of them from settling in the country until after independence.

As a rule, the boats carrying "illegal" immigrants set sail from small European ports under the supervision of the Mossad, the precursor of Israel's intelligence agency. The vessels, though not really fit for carrying human cargo, were tightly packed with passengers. The refugees were escorted by members of the Haganah, the precursor of the Israel Defense Forces, and by volunteers from the Diaspora. Under the best of circumstances, the boats arrived under cover of darkness at remote spots on the coast of Palestine. There they were met by Haganah members and other Palestinian Jews, who carried to shore those passengers unable to wade on their own. Once on shore, the refugees were transported to *kibbutzim*, where a change of clothes enabled them to escape detection by the British police.

More often than not, however, the plan was foiled by the intervention of the British. The Mandatory government exerted pressure on other countries to prevent refugee vessels from embarking. To detect vessels that had set sail, the British used aerial patrols and coastal radar installations. As soon as British patrol boats intercepted refugee vessels, they would attack if their orders were not obeyed, ramming the vessels, using tear gas, batons, even firearms. Refugees would sometimes respond with sticks, stones, or jam jars. Typically, however, they would resist passively, requiring the British to drag them off to deportation boats. Injuries and even some deaths often resulted.

In effect, Britain's policy vis-à-vis the Holocaust survivors caused war to break out between the Mandatory government and the Jewish population of Palestine. The Jews undertook a series of terrorist actions, although the most famous one—the July 1946 explosion at the King David Hotel, headquarters of the Mandatory government's civil and military administrations—aroused revulsion among mainstream Zionists for the deaths it caused. Two Israeli prime ministers would later emerge from among the anti-British terrorists.

The British response to the terrorism included the decision to expel intercepted "illegal" immigrants to internment camps in Cyprus. Each month some internees were admitted to Palestine, but the number admitted was deducted from the quota set by the White Paper. The British had not anticipated, however, that world opinion would rally to the cause of the Holocaust survivors. Among the witnesses to the violence perpetrated by the British on the *Exodus* refugees at Haifa, for example, were some members of the United Nations Special Committee on Palestine. Not surprisingly, the committee's first recommendation was that the Mandate be terminated.

Within two and a half years after Israeli independence, all those in the DP camps of Europe and the internment camps in Cyprus who wished to settle in Israel had been brought there.

88

THE UN PARTITION RESOLUTION

On November 29, 1947, the United Nations General Assembly voted to partition Palestine into two separate states—one Jewish, the other Arab—with Jerusalem under international control. By recognizing the idea of Jewish sovereignty, the resolution was a significant step leading to the birth of the state of Israel. The partition resolution also ushered in an unofficial war during the final months of the British Mandate that threatened the future of the embryonic Jewish state.

The historic vote in the United Nations General Assembly on November 29, 1947, unleashed passions that are still at work today. The resolution called for partitioning Palestine into an Arab state and a Jewish state, with Jerusalem to fall within neither but to be under UN trusteeship.

Of the fifty-six member states voting on the future of Palestine, more than the required two-thirds majority favored the partition of Palestine. Remarkably, among the thirty-three votes in favor were those not only of the United States but also of the Soviet Union. The thirteen votes against included all the Arab states, while the ten abstentions included Britain, at whose request the UN had undertaken the issue. The Arab states were narrowly defeated in their proposal to refer to the International Court of Justice the legitimacy of a partition resolution thwarting the wishes of a majority of the country's inhabitants. (In 1946 there were 1,269,000 Arabs compared to 678,000 Jews in Palestine.) The Arabs rejected the partition resolution not only because it challenged the Arab identity of Palestine but also because it set aside 55 percent of the territory for a Jewish state, a substantial minority of whose population would be Arab.

One historian of the event, the Israeli diplomat Abba Eban (who was at the time a member of the Jewish Agency delegation to the General Assembly, and who would become Israel's chief delegate to the UN), describes the partition resolution in these significant terms: "The international community took the line of lesser injustice." Eban explains that the presence of an Arab minority in a single Jewish country would not decisively undermine the idea of Arab nationalism, whereas a Jewish minority in an Arab Palestine would deliver a deathblow to the hopes for a Jewish nation.

291

The response to the resolution among the Jews of Palestine and Zionists around the world was jubilant. The idea of Jewish sovereignty was finally no longer a dream, and a Jewish state seemed near at hand. The general joy did not mean that Zionists applauded all aspects of the resolution. The exclusion of Jerusalem from the Jewish state's portion was a particular disappointment. In addition, the Revisionist faction of the Zionist movement—precursors of today's right-wing Likud coalition—remained committed to the idea of a Jewish state on both sides of the Jordan, and another faction favored the formation of a binational state. But despite the reservations, the Jews of Palestine resolved to work together to support the resolution and to ensure that it would lead to the formation of a Jewish state.

By contrast, the representative body of Palestinian Arabs immediately announced its intention to use force to prevent the resolution's implementation. Its spokesman accused the United States of using unscrupulous methods to force the vote of smaller UN members, called the resolution a declaration of war against the Arab countries, and threatened that it would lead to an anti-Jewish crusade. Hostilities began immediately, with the ambush of two buses in Jerusalem, resulting in six Jewish deaths.

Despite their different perspectives on the Palestine issue, all the Arab states opposed the partition resolution. Immediately following the vote, in Syria—which under Ottoman rule had itself controlled Palestine—angry mobs marched on the Soviet, American, and French legations in Damascus, removing and burning those countries' flags. Volunteers from the different Arab countries formed a "Liberation Army" to assist the Palestinian Arabs in their armed struggle.

The British response to the partition resolution might be dismissed simply as "immature," if its consequences had not been so serious. Claiming impartiality, the British resolved to do nothing to implement the resolution since it was not acceptable to both sides. They refused to cooperate with the UN Palestine Commission to supervise the transition period until the termination of the Mandate, set for May 15, 1948. Since the UN at that time lacked a military force to carry out the resolution, it fell to the Jewish settlement in Palestine to create the conditions that would enable the Jewish state to be born. The task would not be easy.

The unofficial but bloody war that broke out as soon as the partition resolution was passed was marked by Arab assaults on Jewish settlements and attacks on the convoys bringing food and replacements to them. When they provoked hostilities on the morrow of the UN vote, the Palestinian Arabs had no professional army, only an assortment of uncoordinated military and paramilitary organizations. But their manpower potential far exceeded that of the Jews, even without the additional support of Arab irregulars from nearby states. In addition, a variety of mercenaries eagerly joined forces with them, among them not only British deserters but also former fascist sympathizers. By contrast, the Jewish settlers' striking force, the Haganah (the forerunner of the Israel Defense Forces) numbered only a little over 2,000 men and women.

Under the terms of the Mandate, still officially in effect, the Jewish settlement could neither import nor produce weapons legally. As a result, the Jewish arsenal was also woefully inadequate. It consisted of some equipment purchased abroad and smuggled in and a variety of homemade items manufactured in illegal workshops.

In theory, the British were still responsible for maintaining law and order in the country. In practice, however, they tended to hound the Jews while for the most part benignly neglecting to restrict Arab attacks. While the British continued actively to track down Jewish illegal immigrants, who might enhance Jewish fighting strength, they allowed Arab "liberation troops" to enter the country to support the local Arabs in their opposition to the UN resolution.

Furthermore, the British stubbornly refused to oversee a smooth transferal of administrative authority. On the contrary, they prepared to leave the country in a state of what was then called "planned chaos." In order to avoid cooperating with the UN resolution, Britain allowed the Mandate's administrative infrastructure to cease operation on May 1, 1948, without arranging for successor facilities. As a result, Palestine's membership in the International Postal Union ended and there was no mail service; trains simply stopped running; and the British police and justice systems were disbanded, leaving a vacuum in their wake. Instead of helping in any way to set up a Jewish state—an act that would be provocative in Arab eyes—the British burned official files and shipped to England, put up for auction, or gave to the Arabs whatever assets remained from the Mandate.

To make matters worse, beginning in March 1948 it seemed that the Arabs would succeed in their aim not only of undermining the UN partition resolution but also of destroying the dream of Jewish statehood. In the face of the ongoing unofficial war, the United States decided that partition would not work and that attempts to implement it should be halted. Withdrawing support for the partition resolution, the United States called instead for the United Nations to explore a new plan for a trusteeship in Palestine.

This diplomatic reversal was a blow to the Jewish settlement, which determined to pursue the aims of the partition resolution nonetheless. But despite significant Haganah military gains in April 1948, prospects for the future of the Jews of Palestine on the eve of the British departure were disheartening. Although the Haganah had begun to import some arms from Czechoslovakia, the arsenal included only four field guns, one tank, one fighter plane, and a few private planes. Jewish leaders hoped for the best, however, and began setting up all the organs of governance that the new state would require. On the eve of independence, David Ben-Gurion—soon to be Israel's first prime minister—outlined a plan for success, including enlarging the Jewish fighting force by additional recruitment in Palestine and absorption of immigrants from abroad, and enhancing the arsenal by domestic manufacture and importation from abroad. Just how realistic Ben-Gurion's hopes were remained to be seen.

89

THE BIRTH OF THE STATE OF ISRAEL

At midnight on May 14, 1948, the British Mandate over Palestine ended. A few hours earlier, David Ben-Gurion read out the Declaration of Independence of the new state of Israel. Within minutes of the end of the Mandate, the new state was recognized by the United States. Within hours, it was invaded by Egypt, beginning the Arab attempt to destroy the fledgling state. As a result, May 14–15, 1948, has been described as the most eventful day in modern Jewish history.

In the hours before the termination of the British Mandate over Palestine and the birth of the state of Israel on May 14, 1948, the United Nations continued a debate initiated two months earlier by the State Department. In March, the State Department had proposed that the United Nations partition resolution of November 29, 1947, be altered. Since, the State Department argued, the hostilities in Palestine proved that partition was unworkable, the UN should establish a temporary trusteeship in Palestine.

When the Mandate formally ended, at 6 P.M. New York time (midnight in Palestine), no vote had been taken modifying the partition resolution, which had given international sanction to a Jewish state in Palestine. Without the knowledge of the United States UN delegation, President Truman announced the recognition of the newly proclaimed state of Israel. Ironically, State Department officials had been speaking out on the floor of the United Nations against the establishment of the Jewish state, even as local news agency office tickers were flashing President Truman's recognition of Israel.

A few days earlier, preparations had begun in Palestine for announcing the birth of the new nation. The thirteen-member National Administration—soon to become the provisional government of the Jewish state—began to draft a Declaration of Independence. The language and contents of the document were debated. A suggestion that the declaration specify the boundaries of the new state was rejected, for example. As David Ben-Gurion—soon to be Israel's first premier—pointed out, the United States Declaration of Independence did not define the country's frontiers. A suggestion that the document include articles condemning the British Mandate was also dismissed.

On the afternoon of Friday, May 14, the National Council—soon to become the provisional legislature of the new Jewish state—met in Tel Aviv Museum Hall. On hand for the historic proclamation of the state of Israel were 240 witnesses. Not all the members of the National Council were able to attend. Thirteen were unable to leave Jerusalem, which was under siege. But these thirteen were able to convene in the embattled city, where they approved a draft of the Declaration of Independence.

David Ben-Gurion, until then the chairman of the Jewish Agency Executive, presided over the Tel Aviv gathering. Dressed in a blue suit, with the Zionist banner—soon to be the Israeli flag—flying over his head, Ben-Gurion began to read the Declaration of Independence of Israel, its "Foundation Scroll," which had already been approved by the National Council.

The founding document begins by summarizing Jewish claims to the land of Israel, the birthplace of the people, where they first became a nation and formed "cultural values of national and universal significance." Although the Jews were subsequently exiled from the land, they had never ceased to pray for their national restoration in it.

The Declaration of Independence then reviews three milestones in Zionist history: the First Zionist Congress of 1897, which asserted the Jewish people's right to a national renaissance in its own land (see nutshell #71); the Balfour Declaration of 1917, which recognized that right (see nutshell #78); and the Mandate of the League of Nations, which gave international sanction to that right (see nutshell #79).

Referring next to the Holocaust, which demonstrated the necessity for a Jewish homeland open to any Jew in distress, the document refers to the UN partition resolution as irrevocably recognizing the right of Jews to a state of their own.

All of the preceding can be considered the preamble to the essence of the Declaration of Independence, the announcement of the establishment of the state of Israel "by virtue of our natural and historic right and on the strength of the resolution of the United Nations General Assembly." Going on to identify absorption of Jewish immigrants as a basic aim of the new state, the declaration guarantees equal social and political rights to all the country's inhabitants, regardless of religion, race, or sex; ensures "freedom of religion, conscience, language, education and culture"; and makes a commitment to protect the Holy Places of all religions.

The document concludes with appeals to four different groups: the United Nations, the Arabs of Israel, the Arabs of neighboring states, and the Jews of the Diaspora. While appealing to the UN to admit the Jewish state into its family of nations and to assist the Jewish people in building its new country, the document affirms Israel's readiness to cooperate with the UN in implementing the partition resolution. The declaration then entreats the Arabs within the

Jewish state to participate in developing the new country as full and equal citizens. Offering peace to the Arabs of neighboring states, the declaration urges them to join hands with Israel in furthering the development of the Middle East as a whole. Finally, the document asks Jews around the world to help bring about "the redemption of Israel."

When, seventeen minutes later, the recitation was concluded, the audience rose at Ben-Gurion's request to signify its unanimous acceptance of the Foundation Scroll. A rabbi led the assemblage in reciting the *Sheheheyanu* blessing, thanking God for enabling them to reach this long-awaited occasion.

Having announced the first act of the Council of Government—the nullification of the 1939 White Paper's restrictions on immigration and land transfer—Ben-Gurion proceeded to sign the Declaration of Independence. The names of the other thirty-six signatories were announced. Each of those present went up to the dais to sign, leaving space on the document for those who were unable to leave Jerusalem to sign later. With the words "the State of Israel has arisen," Ben-Gurion closed the session.

Sabbath began shortly after the session's adjournment, and there was no newspaper until Sunday morning, May 16. Headlines on the front page of that morning's *Palestine Post*—the precursor of today's *Jerusalem Post*—include PROCLAMATION BY HEAD OF GOVERNMENT of the new state, SPECIAL ASSEMBLY ADJOURNS without altering the 1947 UN partition resolution, and US RECOGNIZES JEWISH STATE. Another item, SIR ALAN SAILS FROM PALESTINE, describes the departure of the last British Mandatory High Commissioner. Several articles describe the status of the ongoing unofficial war and give details of the new Arab invasion. Fairly crackling with jubilation tempered by tension, these articles verify the newspaper's claim in yet another front-page story that the weekend just experienced encompassed "the most crowded hours in Palestine's history."

90

JERUSALEM AND ISRAEL'S WAR OF INDEPENDENCE

Israel's War of Independence not only ensured the viability of the state of Israel but also left more land in its territory than envisaged in the 1947 Palestine Partition Resolution. Since Transjordan occupied the remainder of the former Palestine, no Arab state was formed there. Highly valued by both sides was Jerusalem, the central city of Jewish life from biblical days. Although the Jewish Quarter of the Old City fell to the Arabs, the Israelis consolidated their control of the New City. In early 1950, despite UN disapproval, Jerusalem became the official capital of the Jewish state.

On May 15, 1948, shortly after David Ben-Gurion proclaimed the new Jewish state, five Arab countries invaded Israel: Egypt, Syria, Transjordan, Iraq, and Lebanon. Ben-Gurion shared a conviction in common with the ruler of one of the invading countries, King Abdullah of Transjordan. In the eyes of each man, Jerusalem was the major prize to be won in the war, which the Israelis would come to call their War of Independence.

For Ben-Gurion, possession of Jerusalem would mean renewing rule in the ancient capital of biblical kings, for whose restoration Jews had prayed during the millennia since the kingdom had fallen in 586 B.C.E. For Abdullah, not only was Jerusalem the third holiest of Muslim cities, but his reign there would also help compensate for his father's loss of the other two, Mecca and Medina. Ben-Gurion also believed that if Jerusalem were lost, the Arabs could easily swoop down from its surrounding hills into the Jewish areas in the coastal plain below, thus wiping out the entire Jewish settlement in Palestine. Abdullah believed that if he let the Jews take Jerusalem, his hope of occupying the Arab parts of Palestine would be impeded.

The battle for Jerusalem—indeed, the entire first phase of the War of Independence—began half a year before the official birth of the state of Israel. Immediately following the UN Palestine Partition Resolution of November 29, 1947, Arab attacks began on Jewish convoys bringing supplies to Jerusalem along the western road, leading to the Jewish coastal plain. When the British did little to intervene, Jerusalem found itself in effect in a virtual state of siege.

In the winter of 1948 attacks within Jerusalem intensified. Arabs—and possibly anti-Jewish terrorists in the British police—blew up several Jewish buildings in the city. In retaliation, two Jewish terrorist groups attacked an Arab village near the western outskirts of Jerusalem, resulting in the infamous Deir Yassin massacre of April 1948. The vengeful cycle—again, within British view but without British intervention—continued with an Arab massacre of medical and other personnel bound to the Hadassah Hospital on Mount Scopus. Eastern Jerusalem's Mount Scopus and the Jewish Quarter of the Old City became cut off from the rest of the Jewish settlement in western Jerusalem's New City.

Also in the spring of 1948, the Jewish forces undertook two operations to open the road to Jerusalem. Although each enabled some large convoys of vehicles bearing food and arms to reach Jerusalem, Arab forces retook the strong points protecting the road to the city. The siege of Jerusalem seemed unbreakable.

The Arab grip on Jerusalem tightened when Abdullah's army—the famous Arab Legion with its British officers—took control of the military situation, despite British assurances that the legion would withdraw along with the British. In late May, the 1,700 Jews in the Old City surrendered to the Arab Legion. For months they had been isolated from the Jews in the New City, receiving only small amounts of food every two weeks via British-escorted convoys. Among the 1,300 Jews evacuated to the New City were the wounded, the elderly, and children. The remaining Jews were taken prisoner.

Following the surrender, no Jews remained in the Old City. The Arabs began to demolish most of the Jewish Quarter, including its historic houses of study and worship. They also desecrated the ancient Jewish cemetery of the Mount of Olives. Transjordan proclaimed Jerusalem its "second capital." For Jews, the loss of the Temple Mount and its Western Wall was emotionally devastating.

In late June, during a monthlong truce imposed by the United Nations, the official UN mediator proposed that Jerusalem be given to Transjordan. When Israel rejected this proposal, he later proposed demilitarization of the city. Acceptance of this proposal would have left the city's Jewish population defenseless. Not surprisingly, Israel rejected this proposal too. In the ten days of all-out fighting that followed the expiration of the truce, the Israelis attempted to retake the Old City, but they were forced to withdraw shortly before a second truce went into effect. In September 1948 the UN mediator was assassinated by members of the Jewish terrorist groups that had perpetrated the Deir Yassin massacres.

The loss of the Old City was not the end of the story for Israel. As the British departed Jerusalem and the Arab Legion entered, the Israelis managed not only to occupy some prime real estate abandoned by the British in the city center but also to consolidate all the previously Jewish areas in the New City. The perimeter of the New City, however, now became the front line. By the end of May, the Israelis had successfully repelled Arab attempts to break into it.

The Jews of Jerusalem, however, were still starving, as food supplies from Tel Aviv were blocked from reaching them. By the end of May 1948, the ration for each person was about two slices of bread per day. Most homes had no additional food whatsoever. People foraged in yards for edible weeds and grasses. The city's infrastructure was seriously damaged. There was no running water. Water trucks delivered a small pail of water per day to each family. There was no electricity and no fuel. Military equipment was also in short supply. Ammunition, like food, was rationed.

The Israelis knew that to save Jerusalem they needed to break the siege. The only obvious way to do so was to wrest the strategic stronghold of Latrun from the legion's control. Several attempts to do so failed. An alternative solution was finally found in June, before the UN-imposed truce went into effect. Hundreds of elderly workers managed to convert a rough stretch of dirt into the "Burma Road," thus reestablishing Jerusalem's link with the coast. The siege of the city had ended.

Neither the breaking of the siege in June nor the imposition of the second UN truce in mid-July, however, eliminated the pressure on the New City. Arab attacks ended only on November 30, 1948, when both sides accepted a "sincere ceasefire." The year's war in Jerusalem was unofficially over.

Although no peace treaties were signed, leaving Israel technically at war, Israel and the individual Arab invaders did sign armistice agreements. As part of the armistice signed in March 1949 with Transjordan (which shortly became known as the Hashemite Kingdom of Jordan), the two Jewish institutions on Mount Scopus—Hebrew University and Hadassah Hospital—were to be permitted to resume operations. Free access was to be permitted to the Old City's Jewish Holy Places. But Jordan's failure to comply with the terms made the agreement meaningless. Periodically the Jordanians would harass Israeli convoys replacing personnel on Mount Scopus.

The armistice agreement left Jordan in control not only of East Jerusalem but also of the hill country called by Israelis "Judea and Samaria" and by the rest of the world "the West Bank."

In December 1949 the United Nations General Assembly voted again to internationalize Jerusalem, as intended in the 1947 partition plan. Although the Zionists, unlike the Arabs, had reluctantly agreed to that part of the 1947 plan, Israel rejected the proposal in 1949. In January 1950 Jerusalem became Israel's

official capital, although most countries have refused to recognize it as such to
this day.

With the elevation of Jerusalem's political status, the prospects for the city's
general future brightened. Its water, electrical, and transportation systems were
all renewed. New homes were found for Hebrew University and Hadassah
Hospital, and the city's cultural life intensified. But for nineteen years, through
the city's heart ran a wall—the border between Israel and Jordan.

91

"OPERATION MAGIC CARPET" AND "OPERATION EZRA AND NEHEMIAH"

Beginning in 1949, Jewish communities in several Muslim countries moved en masse to the new Jewish state. The Jewish Agency organized special "operations" to facilitate the mass immigration. The best known are "Operation Magic Carpet," which brought to Israel some 45,000 Yemenite Jews, and "Operation Ezra and Nehemiah," involving about 122,000 Iraqi Jews.

Israel bashers are always quick to point to the Arab refugee problem that resulted from Israel's victory in the War of Independence. UN statistics indicate that 656,000 Palestinian Arabs fled the country during the hostilities, creating their own Diaspora in the Arab world. Few are as quick to note, however, that in the first years following the creation of Israel, over 320,000 Jews living in Arab lands poured into the Jewish state. Just as the displaced Palestinian Arabs had lived in what was now the Jewish homeland for many generations, so the Jewish refugees from Muslim lands were either encouraged or forced to abandon Jewish communities that had existed for centuries or even millennia. While the Palestinian refugee problem remains unsolved to this day, Israel from the outset made every effort to absorb the Jewish refugees from Arab lands.

The two largest Jewish communities from Muslim countries to migrate as a group to Israel were more than 45,000 Yemenite Jews and nearly 122,000 Iraqi Jews. The Jewish Agency oversaw the evacuation of these two communities, using evocative code names for each project: "Operation Magic Carpet" for the Jews of Yemen and "Operation Ezra and Nehemiah" for the Jews of Iraq. Although the circumstances of each group's departure differed, each contributed to the torrent of immigration that flowed into Israel immediately following statehood.

The Jews of Yemen were the first to arrive en masse after the inmates of the camps for "illegal" immigrants in Cyprus and for displaced persons in Germany and Austria. Jews had lived in Yemen, in the southwest corner of the Arabian peninsula, from pre-Islamic times. The Jews of Yemen were not forced to leave, but were encouraged to do so by the country's ruler, the imam Ahmad, who came to the throne in 1948. Yemenite Jews and Muslims alike saw the hand of God in the establishment of Israel and the subsequent Israeli military victories. For the Jews, steeped in the biblical tradition that God had expelled their ancestors from the land of Israel for their sins, the proclamation of Israel was a sign of God's forgiveness. In the face of such a sign, the only reverent response seemed to be to emigrate to the homeland themselves. For the equally religious Muslims, the idea of impeding the Jews' departure seemed tantamount to challenging God's will.

The imam's only demand of Jews wishing to leave for Israel was that they first sell their property. He forbade government officials from taxing the emigrants, although unscrupulous individuals extorted illegal payments from some Jews. The imam's attitude enabled the Jewish Agency to mount and complete "Operation Magic Carpet" in a year and a half. When the operation was complete, only a few thousand Jews remained in Yemen. (About 250 Jews secretly migrated to Israel from Yemen in 1992–1993.)

Yemenite Jews were used to a medieval lifestyle, and "Operation Magic Carpet" was their first introduction to 20th-century technology. Although they began their journey on foot, traveling south to the departure point in the British colony of Aden, from there they were transported to Israel in a large-scale airlift. Their unfamiliarity with airplanes led the immigrants to conclude that, like their biblical forebears liberated from Egyptian slavery, they were about to be carried "on eagles' wings" (Exodus 19:4). Awaiting air transport in Aden, the Yemenite Jews lived in a camp, called "Redemption," where the Jewish Agency saw to their nutritional, medical, and educational needs.

The circumstances attending the Iraqi Jewish community's decision to move as a whole to Israel were very different. Jews had lived in large numbers in Iraq (formerly Babylonia) since Nebuchadnezzar had exiled them from the land of Israel in 586 B.C.E. (see nutshell #12). Although many returned under the leadership of Ezra and Nehemiah a century later (see nutshell #15), a thriving Jewish community remained, whose achievements included the Babylonian Talmud (see nutshell #33). In more recent times, however, the Jews of Iraq had suffered extensively. The last Turkish governor was a tyrant who tortured Jews accused of illegal commerce. New freedoms available under the British Mandate for Iraq (1917–1932) made possible Zionist activity there, but by 1929 the government began to persecute Zionists.

In 1932 Iraq became independent, and the condition of Iraqi Jews dramatically worsened. From 1935 the government demanded that all Jewish travelers to Palestine leave behind a significant sum of money on deposit until their return. In spring 1941 no secret was made of the government's sympathy with Hitler's cause and objectives vis-à-vis the Jews. During a two-day riot the government did nothing to prevent the torture and murder of hundreds of Jews, the looting of their property, and the desecration of their synagogues. The following year Iraqi Jews organized an underground Zionist movement. Its membership numbered several hundred.

In 1948 Iraq forbade Jews to depart the country. When Israel became a state on May 14, and for the duration of the War of Independence, Jews were rounded up by the hundreds. That summer Zionist affiliation joined communist affiliation as an offense punishable by imprisonment or even death. A Jew accused of selling arms to Israel was hanged, as were two Jewish communists. The government imposed heavy fines on the Jewish population, hoping thus to enrich the government treasury and to destroy the Zionist underground.

In March 1950 the government changed tactics: any Jew willing to renounce Iraqi nationality in writing was permitted to leave the country, but only with a pitifully small amount of cash. A year later, the government froze the assets of all such Jews. Despite the loss in property emigration entailed, nearly the entire Jewish community of Iraq chose to make *aliyah*. The Jewish Agency's "Operation Ezra and Nehemiah"—named for the leaders of the first Jews to return from Babylonian exile—involved flying the immigrants to Cyprus and bringing them from there to Israel by air or sea. Following the completion of "Operation Ezra and Nehemiah," only 8,000 Jews (of 130,000) remained in Iraq. Nearly the entirety of the oldest Jewish community outside Israel had now been "ingathered."

In the first three and a half years following statehood, Israel's population doubled. The Yemenite immigrants of "Operation Magic Carpet" and the Iraqi immigrants of "Operation Ezra and Nehemiah" figured significantly in that achievement.

92

GERMAN RESTITUTION
TO VICTIMS OF NAZISM

In 1952 West Germany passed laws to make restitution to Jewish survivors of the Hitler era through payments to individuals and to the government of Israel. The willingness of the Israeli government to negotiate with Germany caused a domestic political uproar. An additional agreement was made in 1992, following the 1989 collapse of communism in eastern Europe, to compensate some Jews from eastern European countries who had been unable to benefit from the earlier program.

At a time when many American Jews continued to boycott German-made products, as a way of expressing their enduring horror of the country responsible for the Holocaust, visitors to Israel were sometimes surprised to note the number of Mercedes and Volkswagens in the streets. As many readers of this book probably know, the presence of these German cars can be traced to the reparations and compensation agreements Israel entered into with West Germany in 1952.

Fewer readers, however, will be aware that the decision of Ben-Gurion's government to enter into direct restitution negotiations with West Germany led to riots in the streets of Jerusalem. The central figure in the opposition was Menachem Begin, formerly the leader of the right-wing nationalist militant group that had bombed the British offices in the King David Hotel in 1946. Begin was later to emerge as Israel's prime minister.

When Israel first became a state, popular sentiment agreed that official contact with Germany would desecrate the memory of the Jews who had died in the Nazi era and was therefore unthinkable. Within a short period of time, however, it became clear to Ben-Gurion and to others that a boycott was not in the country's best interest. West Germany under Konrad Adenauer (1876–1967) was prepared to offer extensive reparations by way of atonement for the atrocities of the previous regime. As a fledgling state with a mix of burdens, including the need to absorb thousands of immigrants and to maintain a strong defense, Israel was in no position to turn its back on a significant offer of economic help. In Ben-Gurion's estimation, rejecting German restitution would only ensure that "the murderers of our nation" would "also be its heirs," while accepting compensation could help ease the lives of Holocaust survivors.

In December 1951 Ben-Gurion's cabinet agreed to pursue direct negotiations with West Germany, assuming the approval of the Knesset (Israel's parliament) could be won. Right-wing Knesset member Menachem Begin had himself just over a year earlier urged the government to demand restitution from Germany for Jewish property stolen by the Nazis. But seeing a possibility now for discrediting Ben-Gurion's Labor government, Begin began to denounce the proposed negotiations.

On the afternoon of January 7, 1952, during the debate on the issue in the Knesset, Begin presided over a mass demonstration in downtown Jerusalem. The thousands who participated included many out-of-town demonstrators brought in from around the country by chartered bus. Jerusalem police prepared for the demonstration by surrounding the Knesset with barriers and closing streets to all but residents and local shopkeepers.

Begin's address to the crowd was calculated to stir emotion. He not only called all Germans murderers but also implicated Ben-Gurion's government in Nazi-like behavior. Were not the Jerusalem police surrounding the demonstrators carrying German-made tear-gas grenades? Were they not prepared to use German gas on their fellow Jews?

Begin returned to the Knesset following his speech, but the crowd did not disperse. Instead, a riot broke out. Windows of the legislative chamber were broken. The police responded with tear gas. The session had to be interrupted for several hours. Before calm was restored several hundred demonstrators and policemen were wounded and hundreds more arrested.

Although Begin had a lot of support on that day, the demonstration backfired. The riot shifted people's focus from the morality of negotiations with Germany to the viability of democracy in Israel. The threat of mob rule led many to rally round Ben-Gurion. Not only did the Knesset suspend Begin for several months, but Holocaust survivors also showed which side they supported by their willingness to accept the compensation due them.

Six months after negotiations between Israel and Germany began in March 1952, an agreement had been reached. The agreement marked the first time in history that an attempt was made to compensate Jews for the persecution they had endured at the hands of an antisemitic regime. Germany agreed to pay Israel, in annual installments over a period of a dozen years, over $800 million in goods. With the reparations money, Israel built up its merchant fleet and developed its electrical system, water supply, and railways. The German equipment for agriculture and construction improved the quality of life in the young country.

The German restitution agreements were not solely with the state of Israel.

Three men signed the agreements: Israeli foreign minister Moshe Sharett, German chancellor Adenauer, and Dr. Nahum Goldmann, president of the Conference on Jewish Material Claims Against Germany. Thanks to Goldmann's skillful negotiation, over the years more than 250,000 Israelis and about three times as many Jews in other countries received personal compensation from Germany.

Forty years after West Germany entered into the reparations agreements, Chancellor Helmut Kohl's unified Germany signed an additional agreement with the chairman of the Conference on Jewish Material Claims Against Germany. During the cold war, many thousands of Holocaust survivors lived under Communist governments in eastern Europe and the Soviet Union that forbade them from filing claims for compensation. Under the new agreement, many of these survivors of Nazi persecution would qualify for monthly payments beginning in August 1995.

cts in Stalin's grand drama were wrenching enough. He began
by arranging the murder—disguised as an accident—of the
of the two million Soviet Jews to survive the Holocaust. The
n Mikhoels, was a beloved Yiddish actor whose eminence in
munity had been heightened by his appointment as chairman
ment-sponsored Jewish Anti-Fascist Committee.

er was shortly followed by a media campaign condemning the
cosmopolitanism" of foreign elements likely to betray the home-
hand for Jews. Jewish cultural institutions and publications were
and Jewish artists and other cultural figures were arrested and
risons and concentration camps. In August 1952, twenty-six lead-
cultural figures were secretly executed. The allegations against
uded their ties with Western espionage and their intention to create
republic in the Crimea in order to use it as a base for Western impe-
ntures. In addition to the arrests and liquidations of Jewish intellec-
ens of thousands of Jews of all backgrounds were arrested, and mass
ations of Jews from different parts of the Soviet Union to Siberia
ed in 1948–1949.

en, in late 1951, Stalin arranged a dress rehearsal for the "Doctors' Plot"
Soviet satellite state of Czechoslovakia. He ordered the Czech president
prison Rudolph Slansky, the Jewish-born head of the Czech Communist
y. The ensuing Slansky trial of November 1952 also involved thirteen other
Czech Communist leaders; of the fourteen, eleven were Jews. The accusa-
ns against them included their plotting with Zionists to overthrow the govern-
ent and restore capitalism. Slansky was charged with attempting to murder
e Czech president by selecting for him corrupt and corruptible physicians.
lansky "confessed" to having (1) masterminded a Zionist plan to destroy
Czechoslovakia; (2) worked with the American Jewish Joint Distribution Committee ("the Joint"), a philanthropic organization founded in 1914 by anti-
Zionist American Jews, to establish Israel as an American military base; and
(3) selected a physician to "medically murder" the Czech president, thus ensuring Slansky's rise to power. According to the prosecutor, the trial had proven
that all of Czechoslovakia's problems were attributable to Slansky's "Central
Organization for Plotting Against the State," with connections in Israel and
America. The show trial was permeated with the spirit of *The Protocols of the
Elders of Zion* (see nutshell #80).

Six weeks after the Slansky trial, the "Doctors' Plot" was announced to the
Soviet public, although arrests of eminent Jewish physicians had begun earlier.
According to the official announcement, which came five years to the day after
the murder of Solomon Mikhoels, the doctors had murdered two of Stalin's
closest aides and were now involved in a Zionist-imperialist plot to kill other
Soviet political and military leaders. The announcement went on to say that

The opening
in January 1948
de facto leader
victim, Solom
the Jewish co
of the govern
The murd
intellectual
land—shor
shut down
thrown in
ing Jewis
them inc
a Jewish
rialist v
tuals, t
deport
occur
Th
in th
to i
par
to
tic
m

THE "DOC
PRELUDE TO
"FINAL SOLU

In January 1953 Pravda and Radio Moscow ann
eminent physicians for conspiring to murder pro,
The six Jews among them were said to be engaged i,
with the American Jewish Joint Distribution Commi.
organization. Recent evidence suggests that only Stal,
three months later prevented the so-called Doctors' Pl
the prelude to his own version of the Final Solution.

Most people have heard of Stalin's "Five-Year Plans" for the
opment of the Soviet Union. Fewer people are aware of an elab
plan he began to hatch in 1948, with the likely intention of effe
"Final Solution" to the "Jewish problem." The "Doctors' Plot" d
was not only the culmination of Stalin's five-year antisemitic ca
was also intended to justify the dictator's decision to deport most o.
of the Soviet Union to camps east of the Urals. Some of the details of
scenario have only emerged in recent years, when the memoirs of the l,
vivor of the "Doctors' Plot" were published in 1988, thanks to Gorbac
policy of *glasnost*, or openness.

The word *scenario* in the previous sentence is not used casually, for more th,
one historian compares Stalin to a dramaturge, carefully crafting the "Doctor,
Plot," the events leading up to it, and its intended aftermath. The point of view
shaping his cruel artistry was a product of his paranoiac suspicion of Jews, which
worsened as he approached his final years. As a group, Soviet Jews were not to
be trusted because many had family connections in America or Israel, and were
therefore both exposed to foreign attitudes and liable to become turncoats. In
addition, Jewish philanthropic organizations in the West were among the most
vocal objectors to Stalin's policies of social engineering, which, according to some
scholars, had resulted in over 20 million deaths in the 1930s alone.

Mikhoels had initiated the entire plot, including the involvement in it of the Joint Distribution Committee.

The announcement of the "Doctors' Plot" had widespread effects. For weeks afterward, the media in the Soviet Union and its satellite states mounted an unrelenting antisemitic campaign. Jews were identified as a "fifth column." When a Hungarian newspaper alleged that "the Joint" regularly included poison and weapons in its packages of used clothing, every Jew who had ever received an aid package all of a sudden was implicated in treason. Each day brought news of additional arrests of spies and economic criminals with clearly Jewish names. Not only average citizens but also many Russian intellectuals believed the accusations. Yevgeny Yevtushenko (b. 1933), later the philosemitic poet of "Babi Yar" (1962), admits to having been completely swayed by what he read and heard. Throughout the Soviet world Jews in many lines of work lost their jobs. Even in the Gulag, the infamous Soviet forced-labor camp system, authorities and gentile prisoners threatened the Jewish inmates. Holocaust survivors even in western Europe felt threatened; in Holland alone, in the month following the announcement of the "Doctors' Plot," 1,000 Jews applied for U.S. visas, anticipating a Soviet invasion through Berlin.

With what sort of climax did Stalin intend to conclude his grand drama? There is evidence that the doctors, having been found guilty, were to have been hanged publicly in Red Square during Easter season. The trial of these "poisoner doctors" was to have been followed by a trial of the remaining Jewish intellectuals, "poisoners of Soviet culture." The secret police would meantime coordinate a series of antisemitic attacks. In response to these, "The Jewish Statement" would appear. This letter, already being circulated among eminent Soviet Jews for their signatures, was never released by the Soviets, but its text has been recreated by those who were asked to sign it. The Jewish elite's request of Stalin that the Jews be sent to camps in order to protect them was to have served as justification for mass deportations of nearly all Soviet Jews to distant camps. Only some token "good Jews" would remain in the large Russian cities to prove to the world that the authorities had not sent all Jews into exile.

Stalin's scenario did not work out as he had planned, but only because he had a fatal stroke. Different versions of the denouement exist, but according to one, at the final meeting with his associates, Stalin announced the need to respond to the Zionist plot by deporting the Jews en masse. Not only did two Soviet officials object, on the grounds that world opinion would make it impossible to carry out the plan, but a third—married, like others of Stalin's associates, to a Jew—dramatically threw his party card down, saying he would not belong to an organization that could consider such a plan. As the story goes, Stalin, enraged by this boldness, shouted that it was up to him alone to decide when an individual was deprived of his party membership. Immediately thereafter he suffered the stroke.

This story in its various versions was leaked in 1957, perhaps to prove that antisemitism was not an endemic Soviet trait, since three of Stalin's closest colleagues objected to the deportation. Whether or not such reasoning accounted for the leak, it is clear that the official retraction of the "Doctors' Plot" in early April 1953, remarkable though it was, did not acknowledge the antisemitic crux of the plan. The official communiqué stated that the doctors had been unlawfully arrested and their confessions extracted through torture, but it ignored the alleged involvement of "the Joint." Although the doctors were released, they were warned not to talk about their cases.

In 1956 Nikita Khrushchev, who would soon become premier of the USSR (1958–1964), began the process of "de-Stalinization," but though he blamed the "Doctors' Plot" on Stalin, he neither addressed its antisemitic nature nor included among Stalin's crimes his actions against the Jews. In fact, even after the retraction of the accusations against the doctors, few of the masses of Jews throughout the Soviet world who had lost jobs were reinstated.

The "Doctors' Plot" may not have yielded the devastating outcome that Stalin had hoped for, but the damage it caused to individuals was incalculable. As the last survivor of the "Doctors' Plot" told *The New York Times* thirty-five years after the event, "The generations that follow must know about this."

94

THE SINAI CAMPAIGN

The Sinai Campaign was a short war (October 29–November 5, 1956) between Egypt and Israel, which overlapped partly with an unsuccessful attempt by Britain and France to reverse Egypt's nationalization of the Suez Canal. Israel's invasion was a response to several years of provocative Egyptian acts, including the support of terrorist raids into Israel and the blocking of Israeli shipping. Unlike the Anglo-French Suez effort, Israel's Sinai Campaign was a stunning military success, but in March 1957, Israel gave in to world political pressure and withdrew from the Sinai Peninsula and the Gaza Strip, which were then secured by a United Nations peacekeeping force.

Following Israel's swift and stunning military success in the Sinai Campaign, a threatening letter to Israel's prime minister David Ben-Gurion from Russian Premier Bulganin called Egypt a victim of Israel's "unprovoked aggression." The accusation was hardly defensible. The Armistice Agreements that Israel had entered into with the Arab nations in 1949 put an end to the War of Independence but were far from peace treaties. In defiance of the United Nations charter and of a 1951 Security Council resolution, the Arab states continued to claim that they were at war with Israel.

Egypt, under Gamal Abdel Nasser, who took control in 1956, led the way in belligerency. On the economic front, Egypt organized not only an economic boycott of Israel but also a maritime blockade, interfering with Israel's right of free navigation in the Suez Canal and in the Gulf of Aqaba. On the military front, Egypt used bases in the Gaza Strip to train Palestinian commandos, called *fedayeen*, for raids on Israel. On October 24, 1956, Egypt also entered into a three-way military pact with Syria and Jordan, which rendered Israel extremely vulnerable on three sides. To put an end to the terrorist raids and to secure Israel's freedom of navigation, the Israeli government decided to make a preemptive strike against Egypt by undertaking the Sinai Campaign.

Despite the fact that Ben-Gurion was in bed with the flu for the duration of the hostilities, within days after the invasion began Israel controlled the entire Sinai Peninsula and the Gaza Strip. So impressive was the Israeli victory that an American military historian called the Sinai Campaign the most brilliant battle in world history. Great Britain and France had not achieved the same success in their simultaneous attempt to force upon Egypt international control of the Suez Canal.

But the Israeli military victory was not the final chapter in the story of the Sinai Campaign. After engaging in a political struggle for several months, pitted against the joint opposition of the United States and the Soviet Union, Israel was forced to give up the territory it had seized. UN peacekeeping troops were strategically stationed to prevent a renewal of terrorist attacks and to ensure Israeli ships free passage through the Gulf of Aqaba. Some Israelis opposed Ben-Gurion's decision to bow to external political pressure and completely evacuate the conquered territories. To them, the retreat under outside pressure was not only tantamount to capitulation but also bespoke Israel's lack of total control over its destiny. But Ben-Gurion was unwilling to alienate the United States and to court worldwide ostracism. In the event, despite the territorial concession, the Sinai Campaign secured for over a decade Israel's goals of eliminating *fedayeen* training bases and of securing freedom of navigation for Israeli ships.

The Sinai Campaign clearly established the role the Middle East would play in the cold war. Despite the fact that the United States and the Soviet Union united in their insistence that Israel withdraw from the occupied areas, the political struggle surrounding the Sinai Campaign redefined the Arab-Israeli conflict in cold war terms. The failure of Britain and France in their Suez operation left the United States and the USSR as the main contenders for influence in the Arab world. As Ben-Gurion told the Israeli parliament, the forces competing in the Middle East were no longer primarily the local armies but rather "the world blocs of the East and the West." Until the decomposition of the Soviet Union some thirty-five years after the Sinai Campaign, the USSR consistently aligned itself with the Arab cause.

Popular historical accounts of the Sinai Campaign from the Israeli perspective differ in emphasis. For Abba Eban, who as chief Israeli delegate to the UN argued Israel's case for the Sinai Campaign before the world, the operation ushered Israel into a fruitful decade. He focused on the relationships Israel made in those years with the developing nations of Africa and Asia. For some younger Israelis, the Sinai Campaign seems in retrospect to have been a questionable military undertaking, resulting from Israel's alliance with a Britain and a France unwilling to yield gracefully to the end of colonialism.

While assessments of the Sinai Campaign with the advantage of hindsight may differ, all historians consider it the second major episode in the ongoing Arab-Israeli war. Although four decades later the conflict has not yet ended, optimists see progress in several areas. Not only has the cold war itself become history, with the collapse of the Soviet Union, but a "cold peace" between Israel

The opening acts in Stalin's grand drama were wrenching enough. He began in January 1948 by arranging the murder—disguised as an accident—of the de facto leader of the two million Soviet Jews to survive the Holocaust. The victim, Solomon Mikhoels, was a beloved Yiddish actor whose eminence in the Jewish community had been heightened by his appointment as chairman of the government-sponsored Jewish Anti-Fascist Committee.

The murder was shortly followed by a media campaign condemning the intellectual "cosmopolitanism" of foreign elements likely to betray the homeland—shorthand for Jews. Jewish cultural institutions and publications were shut down, and Jewish artists and other cultural figures were arrested and thrown in prisons and concentration camps. In August 1952, twenty-six leading Jewish cultural figures were secretly executed. The allegations against them included their ties with Western espionage and their intention to create a Jewish republic in the Crimea in order to use it as a base for Western imperialist ventures. In addition to the arrests and liquidations of Jewish intellectuals, tens of thousands of Jews of all backgrounds were arrested, and mass deportations of Jews from different parts of the Soviet Union to Siberia occurred in 1948–1949.

Then, in late 1951, Stalin arranged a dress rehearsal for the "Doctors' Plot" in the Soviet satellite state of Czechoslovakia. He ordered the Czech president to imprison Rudolph Slansky, the Jewish-born head of the Czech Communist party. The ensuing Slansky trial of November 1952 also involved thirteen other top Czech Communist leaders; of the fourteen, eleven were Jews. The accusations against them included their plotting with Zionists to overthrow the government and restore capitalism. Slansky was charged with attempting to murder the Czech president by selecting for him corrupt and corruptible physicians. Slansky "confessed" to having (1) masterminded a Zionist plan to destroy Czechoslovakia; (2) worked with the American Jewish Joint Distribution Committee ("the Joint"), a philanthropic organization founded in 1914 by anti-Zionist American Jews, to establish Israel as an American military base; and (3) selected a physician to "medically murder" the Czech president, thus ensuring Slansky's rise to power. According to the prosecutor, the trial had proven that all of Czechoslovakia's problems were attributable to Slansky's "Central Organization for Plotting Against the State," with connections in Israel and America. The show trial was permeated with the spirit of *The Protocols of the Elders of Zion* (see nutshell #80).

Six weeks after the Slansky trial, the "Doctors' Plot" was announced to the Soviet public, although arrests of eminent Jewish physicians had begun earlier. According to the official announcement, which came five years to the day after the murder of Solomon Mikhoels, the doctors had murdered two of Stalin's closest aides and were now involved in a Zionist-imperialist plot to kill other Soviet political and military leaders. The announcement went on to say that

93

THE "DOCTORS' PLOT": PRELUDE TO STALIN'S "FINAL SOLUTION"?

In January 1953 Pravda and Radio Moscow announced the arrest of nine eminent physicians for conspiring to murder prominent Soviet officials. The six Jews among them were said to be engaged in espionage in league with the American Jewish Joint Distribution Committee, a philanthropic organization. Recent evidence suggests that only Stalin's death less than three months later prevented the so-called Doctors' Plot from becoming the prelude to his own version of the Final Solution.

Most people have heard of Stalin's "Five-Year Plans" for the economic development of the Soviet Union. Fewer people are aware of an elaborate five-year plan he began to hatch in 1948, with the likely intention of effecting a Soviet "Final Solution" to the "Jewish problem." The "Doctors' Plot" of early 1953 was not only the culmination of Stalin's five-year antisemitic campaign but was also intended to justify the dictator's decision to deport most of the Jews of the Soviet Union to camps east of the Urals. Some of the details of Stalin's scenario have only emerged in recent years, when the memoirs of the last survivor of the "Doctors' Plot" were published in 1988, thanks to Gorbachev's policy of *glasnost*, or openness.

The word *scenario* in the previous sentence is not used casually, for more than one historian compares Stalin to a dramaturge, carefully crafting the "Doctors' Plot," the events leading up to it, and its intended aftermath. The point of view shaping his cruel artistry was a product of his paranoiac suspicion of Jews, which worsened as he approached his final years. As a group, Soviet Jews were not to be trusted because many had family connections in America or Israel, and were therefore both exposed to foreign attitudes and liable to become turncoats. In addition, Jewish philanthropic organizations in the West were among the most vocal objectors to Stalin's policies of social engineering, which, according to some scholars, had resulted in over 20 million deaths in the 1930s alone.

and Egypt has been in place since they signed a treaty in 1979 (see nutshell #98). In October 1991 peace talks began that brought Israeli delegates face to face with representatives of Syria, Lebanon, and a joint Jordanian-Palestinian delegation. While those peace talks seemed to many to be moving nowhere, the world was galvanized in late summer 1993 by news of an impending agreement between Israel and the Palestinians. On September 13 of that year, Yasir Arafat and Yitzhak Rabin shook hands on the White House lawn, ushering in what many hoped would be a new era of peace and cooperation in the Middle East.

95

THE EICHMANN TRIAL

In May 1960 Israeli intelligence agents kidnapped Adolf Eichmann, the Nazi official responsible for the deportation of Jews to death camps, who was then living in Argentina under an alias. Eichmann was brought to Israel, where he was tried and found guilty for war crimes, despite his claim that he was merely a cog in the Nazi machine. In May 1962 Eichmann was executed, his body cremated, and the ashes scattered in the sea. The Eichmann trial not only stimulated Holocaust research along new lines but also marked a transition in Israel's attitude toward the Holocaust.

Conscientious readers of this book will remember that Adolf Eichmann was not only present at the January 1942 Wannsee Conference, where the bureaucratic details of implementing the "Final Solution" were ironed out, but was also the Nazi official responsible for transporting the Jews of Europe to Hitler's death camps (see nutshell #85). Although at his trial he claimed that he was merely carrying out orders, there are many indicators that he relished his role. Unlike other Nazi functionaries who served in a variety of roles during their careers, Eichmann remained head of the Gestapo's Department for Jewish Affairs from 1939 until the end of the war. His 1944 visit to Auschwitz led him to suggest a variety of ways to maximize results by raising the number of daily deaths from 10,000 to 12,000.

Following the war, Eichmann—his identity unknown—was imprisoned in an American army prison camp, but with the help of fellow Nazis he managed to escape to Argentina, where for ten years he lived as Ricardo Clement. His dramatic kidnapping on May 11, 1960, helped establish the reputation of the Mossad, Israel's premier intelligence agency. Twelve days later, Prime Minister David Ben-Gurion informed the Israeli parliament that Eichmann would soon be tried under Israel's 1950 war crimes statute.

In bringing Eichmann to trial, Ben-Gurion had more than justice in mind. He understood the political and educational impact that such a trial could have, and was careful to craft its various aspects to suit specific didactic purposes. With respect to the nations of the world, Ben-Gurion sought to emphasize that

314

the Holocaust not only justified the existence of the Jewish state but also obligated them to support it. He hoped that the trial would prove that it was incumbent on all those committed to opposing antisemitism to support the only country capable of preventing future Holocausts.

With respect to the citizens of Israel, there seem to have been several items on Ben-Gurion's agenda. First, he wished to change the attitude of young Israelis, who tended to be contemptuous of Holocaust victims, dismissing them as weaklings who had walked meekly to their deaths. Second, he felt the need of a unifying historical experience to meld Israelis of different national origins into a single nation. Israelis from Arab countries had not been personally touched by the Nazis' "Final Solution," but Ben-Gurion hoped the Eichmann trial would underscore the common bond among all Jews in the face of such a threat. Third, he hoped to instill national pride in all Israelis by underscoring that only the state of Israel could guarantee a secure future for Jews. Finally, he wished to prove that although his government engaged in negotiations with the new Germany, it was not prepared to "forgive and forget" the crimes of Germans under the previous regime.

In order to achieve these purposes, not only Eichmann's involvement in the plan to exterminate the Jews but the entire Nazi war against the Jews would also have to be detailed. To this end, more than 100 Holocaust survivors were chosen to testify at the trial. Until the Eichmann trial, survivors had tended to repress memories of their wartime experiences. By encouraging such testimony, the trial served to initiate what has been described as national psychotherapy. But the survivors' testimony, often completely unconnected to Eichmann's role, led the judges on more than one occasion to urge the prosecution to focus on the defendant. In fact, in handing down the verdict in December 1961, some months after the four-month trial (April–August 1961), the judges relied primarily on documents implicating Eichmann rather than on the highly emotional and often irrelevant testimony of the witnesses.

Among the hundreds of foreign correspondents attending the trial, the coverage of one was to assume particular and long-lasting importance. Hannah Arendt, an American philosopher and an émigré from Nazi Germany, covered the trial for *The New Yorker.* Her articles, later published in book form as *Eichmann in Jerusalem: A Report on the Banality of Evil,* became the most significant intellectual product of the trial. Angered by what she saw as the Israeli government's manipulation of the Holocaust to serve its own policy ends, Arendt pursued two lines of thought that would clearly not mesh well with Ben-Gurion's aims. First, she implicated the Nazi-appointed Jewish councils in the deaths of many Jews, claiming that had the Jewish leadership refused to do the Nazis' administrative work for them, the extermination procedure could never have been as effective as it was. Second, as the subtitle of her book indicates, she argued that Eichmann was not an evil monster but rather a typical bureaucrat. Arendt's work not only aroused a great deal of agitated controversy at the time but also encouraged other scholars to pursue research into such issues as the role the Jewish councils played in the Holocaust and the psychology of war criminals. Her work on the councils has since been widely discredited.

Arendt's book demonstrates the limitations on Ben-Gurion's attempt to stage-manage the Eichmann affair, but his goal of using the trial to transform Israeli society certainly succeeded. Just as about a decade later for many Americans the Watergate hearings became a full-time occupation, for Israelis, 1961 was the year of the Eichmann trial. Israelis from all backgrounds and all walks of life became deeply involved in the process of the trial, gluing themselves to their radios. The superiority that young people had tended to feel toward Holocaust victims gave way not only to empathy but also to identification, even among Israelis whose roots were not in Europe.

But some modern analysts feel that the identification with the Holocaust that the Eichmann trial accelerated has become too complete, with damaging results. In May 1983, two decades after Eichmann's execution, the results of an Israeli poll indicated that 87 percent of the country's citizens agreed with the statement: "From the Holocaust we learn that Jews cannot rely on non-Jews."

A decade later, as Israeli identification with the Holocaust seems to intensify rather than diminish over time, a number of critical voices both in Israel and in the Diaspora have suggested that Israelis are being taught to draw the wrong lessons from the searing event. Some argue that the lesson Israelis should learn from the Holocaust is not that the outside world is forever suspect but rather that Jews everywhere must work to strengthen democracy, fight racism, and support human rights.

96

THE SIX-DAY WAR

Israel's war with Egypt, Jordan, Syria, and Iraq, fought from June 5 to June 10, 1967, came to be known as the Six-Day War. The war left Israel in control of the Sinai Peninsula, the Gaza Strip, the West Bank, East Jerusalem, and the Golan Heights. The Six-Day War marked a watershed in relations between Israel and Jews in the Diaspora. By making Israel into an occupying power, it also led to the Intifada, *or Palestinian uprising, that began in December 1987.*

The war Israel fought with Egypt, Jordan, Syria, and Iraq in June 1967 was an extraordinary event in many ways. More than a quarter of a century after the war, people around the world still remember Israel's military victories. It is the rare non-Israeli, however, who remembers one of the war's unique features: what Israelis referred to as the "waiting period" that preceded it.

For everyone knew that a war was in the works. Beginning in April, the Syrians increased their pressure on Israeli villages along the northern frontier. In May, emissaries from the Soviet Union fed Egypt's Nasser disinformation about a supposed major Israeli military buildup along the Syrian border. Nasser responded by mobilizing about 100,000 troops in the Sinai along the border with Israel and demanding the withdrawal of the UN Emergency Force that had patrolled that region since the end of the Sinai Campaign. The UN meekly acceded to Nasser's demand. Within days, Nasser announced that Egypt would once again block all shipping to and from Israel—an act that Israel had on many occasions declared would be tantamount to a declaration of war. At the end of the month Nasser signed military agreements with Jordan and Iraq, who thereby placed their troops under Egyptian command. Israel was surrounded by troops not only from its own hostile neighbors but also from other Arab countries, including Kuwait and Algeria.

The "waiting period" before the outbreak of war was, in fact, a period of frenzied activity on several fronts. On the diplomatic front, Israeli prime minister Levi Eshkol, David Ben-Gurion's much less charismatic successor, sent foreign minister Abba Eban on a tour of foreign capitals to try to drum up support. His mission was unsuccessful. Despite the assurances of the maritime powers following the Sinai Campaign that Israel's right of free navigation would be protected, no action was taken to impede Nasser's plans.

On the Israeli political front, Eshkol acceded to pressure to reorganize his government by including opposition figures. The national unity government that resulted was fateful in two ways. By replacing himself as defense minister with Moshe Dayan, the commander of Israel's forces during the Sinai Campaign, Eshkol bolstered the country's eroding confidence that it could fight and win the war. By including as minister without portfolio right-wing political leader Menachem Begin, Eshkol conferred upon Begin for the first time a mantle of legitimacy. Begin's ability to claim partial credit for Israel's success in the Six-Day War played no small part in his becoming prime minister a decade later.

On the Israeli military front, the reserves were called up to active duty. Their rigorous training in the field contributed to Israel's success in the days to follow. On the civilian front, anxiety grew as Israelis glued to their radios listened to incessant Arab threats that this time they would truly succeed in exterminating the Zionists. While a stream of Israelis did leave the country (many of whom later returned), many more displayed quiet heroism by filling the jobs normally performed by those in the reserves. Macabre notes were sounded, too, as the elderly and schoolchildren worked side by side preparing bomb shelters, and as delegates of the Tel Aviv Religious Council consecrated parks and vacant lots for use as cemeteries.

When Israel finally decided to make a preemptive strike on June 5, the tension dissipated as success followed success. Within three hours on the first day, Israel succeeded in destroying the air forces of Egypt, Jordan, and Syria, ensuring Israel's air superiority for the remainder of the war, and enabling the Israel air force to support all ground operations. In lightning succession, Israel crippled its foes. On the southern front, Israel not only seized the Gaza Strip and reached Suez, but also decimated the Egyptian forces and captured Egyptian troops and tanks. On the northern front, Israel not only took the Golan Heights, from which Syrians had been shelling Israeli villages, but also established a military presence on the main highway to Damascus. On the Jordanian front, Israel not only took the West Bank but also captured the Old City of Jerusalem. By the end of June, Israel had removed the barriers that had run through the heart of Jerusalem for nineteen years, reuniting the city.

The Six-Day War had a dramatic effect on the map of Israel as well as on its relations with Jews in the Diaspora. As tensions rose in the weeks before the war, Jews in the United States and other Western countries—even those who had hitherto considered themselves only vestigially Jewish—found themselves deeply empathizing with the embattled Israelis. Many young people rushed to volunteer to serve Israel in whatever capacity they could. Other Jews indicated their concern by contributing record amounts of money. Following the war,

97

THE YOM KIPPUR WAR

The Yom Kippur War began with a surprise Egyptian-Syrian attack on Israel on Yom Kippur day of 1973 (October 6) and ended when a ceasefire came into force on October 24. After suffering significant initial setbacks, the Israelis pushed back the Arab forces with the aid of arms airlifted by the United States. Although Israeli forces triumphed militarily, stopping only 101 kilometers from Cairo, the war's effects included a loss of diplomatic support for Israel, a political shakeup in Israel, damage to the Israeli self-concept, and an increase in the prestige of Egyptian president Sadat.

Although the fourth Arab-Israeli war is called by the name Yom Kippur—the fast marking the most holy day on the Jewish religious calendar—it would be just as appropriate to call it "the 10th of Ramadan War." When Egyptian leaders settled on a day to open hostilities, they chose the 10th day of Ramadan, the Muslim month of fasting. On that day in 624, Mohammed began to prepare for the battle of Badr, which culminated in his victorious arrival in Mecca in 630 and led to the expansion of Islam (see nutshell #34). Egypt's Anwar el-Sadat (who had become president upon Nasser's death on September 28, 1970) had both religions in mind when confirming the date. On the one hand, he believed the Israelis would never suspect Arab soldiers would begin a full-scale war during Ramadan. On the other hand, the majority of Israelis themselves would be observing the Yom Kippur fast and would hardly be at their highest level of military preparedness. The outbreak of war did take the Israelis by surprise, but the Arabs' choice of date worked in the Israelis' favor in at least one way: since people were either at home or in synagogue, mobilization of forces was able to proceed very efficiently.

The roots of the Yom Kippur War lay in Israel's victory in the Six-Day War. The Arabs felt their loss of honor very keenly and vowed to learn from their mistakes, while the Israelis, overconfidently basking in the fruits of their victory, disregarded military weaknesses and occasionally threw caution to the winds. For example, in crooning about their successes in the 1967 war, Israel's military commanders broadcast full details of their operations. Nasser had these the number of tourists from the West, as well as the number of those seeking to make *aliyah*, increased dramatically.

Even more startlingly, the war had a galvanizing effect on the Jews of the Soviet Union. Soviet government denunciations of "Israeli aggression" may have succeeded in inciting antisemitism in some quarters, but they also intensified national feelings and Jewish identity among large numbers of even highly assimilated Soviet Jews. The Six-Day War thus reinvigorated Zionism in the land from which so many early Zionists had hailed. Within a few years, that movement added the new word *refusenik* to the lexicon, referring to those Soviet citizens, usually Jewish, who had been denied permission to emigrate.

The euphoria that followed the Six-Day War, particularly with the return to the Western Wall and other ancient sites in the West Bank, led to some hyperbolic comparisons. Some likened the war's six days to the six days of creation. But even in the heady days immediately after the war, there were those who expressed concern about what some aspects of the victory might entail. How would playing the new role of occupying power affect the morality of the state? While most Israelis believed that a united Jerusalem must remain forever Israel's, deep differences emerged within the country as to what its map should ultimately look like. On the right and within some religious parties, the feeling was that Israel must retain control of the territories. On the left, many felt that Israel should be prepared to cede most of the territories in exchange for peace.

Following the defeat of the regular Arab armies in the Six-Day War, Arab states began to increase their support of the Palestine Liberation Organization. The PLO had been founded a few years earlier to coordinate Palestinian efforts to establish an Arab state in the former Palestine. Twenty years after the Six-Day War, a large-scale Palestinian uprising, soon to be known as the *Intifada* (Arabic for "shaking off"), broke out in the territories won by Israel during that war. The lingering failure to resolve what had become a war within Israel's borders threatened to turn at least a part of the Six-Day War's triumphs into a Pyrrhic victory.

More than twenty-six years after the Six-Day War, Israelis and Palestinians finally showed serious signs of willingness to make peace. In September 1993, Israel and the PLO signed a "Declaration of Principles" in Washington, outlining a process meant to culminate in Palestinian self-rule in the Israeli-occupied West Bank and Gaza Strip. In May 1994, Israeli troops withdrew from the Gaza Strip and the West Bank town of Jericho. Israel also yielded to some of the PLO's requests that it be permitted to use Palestinian flags and other "symbols of statehood" in the areas newly under Palestinian control.

97

THE YOM KIPPUR WAR

The Yom Kippur War began with a surprise Egyptian-Syrian attack on Israel on Yom Kippur day of 1973 (October 6) and ended when a ceasefire came into force on October 24. After suffering significant initial setbacks, the Israelis pushed back the Arab forces with the aid of arms airlifted by the United States. Although Israeli forces triumphed militarily, stopping only 101 kilometers from Cairo, the war's effects included a loss of diplomatic support for Israel, a political shakeup in Israel, damage to the Israeli self-concept, and an increase in the prestige of Egyptian president Sadat.

Although the fourth Arab-Israeli war is called by the name Yom Kippur—the fast marking the most holy day on the Jewish religious calendar—it would be just as appropriate to call it "the 10th of Ramadan War." When Egyptian leaders settled on a day to open hostilities, they chose the 10th day of Ramadan, the Muslim month of fasting. On that day in 624, Mohammed began to prepare for the battle of Badr, which culminated in his victorious arrival in Mecca in 630 and led to the expansion of Islam (see nutshell #34). Egypt's Anwar el-Sadat (who had become president upon Nasser's death on September 28, 1970) had both religions in mind when confirming the date. On the one hand, he believed the Israelis would never suspect Arab soldiers would begin a full-scale war during Ramadan. On the other hand, the majority of Israelis themselves would be observing the Yom Kippur fast and would hardly be at their highest level of military preparedness. The outbreak of war did take the Israelis by surprise, but the Arabs' choice of date worked in the Israelis' favor in at least one way: since people were either at home or in synagogue, mobilization of forces was able to proceed very efficiently.

The roots of the Yom Kippur War lay in Israel's victory in the Six-Day War. The Arabs felt their loss of honor very keenly and vowed to learn from their mistakes, while the Israelis, overconfidently basking in the fruits of their victory, disregarded military weaknesses and occasionally threw caution to the winds. For example, in crooning about their successes in the 1967 war, Israel's military commanders broadcast full details of their operations. Nasser had these the number of tourists from the West, as well as the number of those seeking to make *aliyah*, increased dramatically.

Even more startlingly, the war had a galvanizing effect on the Jews of the Soviet Union. Soviet government denunciations of "Israeli aggression" may have succeeded in inciting antisemitism in some quarters, but they also intensified national feelings and Jewish identity among large numbers of even highly assimilated Soviet Jews. The Six-Day War thus reinvigorated Zionism in the land from which so many early Zionists had hailed. Within a few years, that movement added the new word *refusenik* to the lexicon, referring to those Soviet citizens, usually Jewish, who had been denied permission to emigrate.

The euphoria that followed the Six-Day War, particularly with the return to the Western Wall and other ancient sites in the West Bank, led to some hyperbolic comparisons. Some likened the war's six days to the six days of creation. But even in the heady days immediately after the war, there were those who expressed concern about what some aspects of the victory might entail. How would playing the new role of occupying power affect the morality of the state? While most Israelis believed that a united Jerusalem must remain forever Israel's, deep differences emerged within the country as to what its map should ultimately look like. On the right and within some religious parties, the feeling was that Israel must retain control of the territories. On the left, many felt that Israel should be prepared to cede most of the territories in exchange for peace.

Following the defeat of the regular Arab armies in the Six-Day War, Arab states began to increase their support of the Palestine Liberation Organization. The PLO had been founded a few years earlier to coordinate Palestinian efforts to establish an Arab state in the former Palestine. Twenty years after the Six-Day War, a large-scale Palestinian uprising, soon to be known as the *Intifada* (Arabic for "shaking off"), broke out in the territories won by Israel during that war. The lingering failure to resolve what had become a war within Israel's borders threatened to turn at least a part of the Six-Day War's triumphs into a Pyrrhic victory.

More than twenty-six years after the Six-Day War, Israelis and Palestinians finally showed serious signs of willingness to make peace. In September 1993, Israel and the PLO signed a "Declaration of Principles" in Washington, outlining a process meant to culminate in Palestinian self-rule in the Israeli-occupied West Bank and Gaza Strip. In May 1994, Israeli troops withdrew from the Gaza Strip and the West Bank town of Jericho. Israel also yielded to some of the PLO's requests that it be permitted to use Palestinian flags and other "symbols of statehood" in the areas newly under Palestinian control.

broadcasts recorded, which enabled him to study them carefully, to figure out exactly what made the Israeli army tick. Nasser also wanted his officers to understand their adversaries, so he had skilled university graduates sent to officers' school, where they were encouraged to learn Hebrew. In addition, first Nasser and then Sadat had the army study the daily Israeli routines along the Suez Canal so that they could anticipate their reactions. In brief, Egypt's loss of face in the Six-Day War led it to modernize its army, while Israel's triumph led it to rest on its laurels.

One of the lessons the Arabs learned from studying the details of the Six-Day War was that the advantage lay in the court of the server: rather than let the Israelis initiate the next war, they would do so themselves. To prevent a preemptive Israeli strike, the Arabs set about to deceive the Israelis about their military intentions. The Egyptians leaked false stories to the press to mislead the Israelis. When Sadat expelled 20,000 Soviet advisers from Egypt in 1972, the Israelis were encouraged to believe that the Egyptians would now be unable to use effectively all the arms the Soviets had supplied them. The Egyptian military leaders also took care to disguise their preparations for war. During the summer before its outbreak, the Egyptians dug trenches near the Suez Canal, where they hid equipment under cover of night. As troops were moved in, the Israelis were fooled into thinking that the Egyptians were only carrying out exercises. The Israelis also misread the relative calm along the Syrian front as proof that the threat there had been neutralized for the time being, whereas in fact the Syrians were busy preparing for all-out war.

It has never been determined whether a Palestinian hostage-taking operation carried out in Europe a week to the day before the war was a part of the overall Arab deception plan. Whether or not it was, it also helped focus Israeli concerns away from the Egyptian and Syrian fronts at a crucial time.

Although it has been argued that the war was ultimately a military success for Israel, its effects on Israel at home and abroad were devastating. The war intensified Israel's isolation in the world. The Arab oil-producing states decided to use their resource as a diplomatic tool. They imposed a five-month oil embargo on countries aiding Israel to make governments carefully weigh the price of friendship with Israel. Most African nations broke diplomatic ties with Israel, while European governments published pro-Arab statements. Israel became more dependent on the United States, which had airlifted it supplies without which it could not have repelled the Arab forces. But the United States also committed itself to support of Sadat's Egypt. The human and economic costs of the Yom Kippur War were staggering in a small country with a fragile economy: the war resulted in 2,500 deaths—one out of every thousand Israeli Jews—and cost Israel a year's GNP. Dissatisfaction with the Labor government, which had led Israel from the time of statehood, intensified. An investigation into the causes of Israel's ill-preparedness for the war resulted in a shakeup in the military but exculpated Defense Minister Moshe Dayan. Public discontent with the inquiry's findings ultimately led Prime Minister Golda Meir to resign her office in April 1974. Meanwhile, the right-wing opposition of the newly formed Likud party grew stronger.

On a level deeper than the diplomatic or the political, the Yom Kippur War began to erode Israel's self-definition. To be sure, Israelis had begun to identify with Holocaust victims since the time of the Eichmann trial twelve years earlier (see nutshell #95), but never before had the nation as a whole felt so vulnerable. Israelis had been reared to believe that a Jewish state was not only the solution to antisemitism but also a guarantee that future Holocausts could not take place. The Yom Kippur War seemed to give the lie to these basic concepts that underlay the national identity.

As Israeli morale plummeted, so Arab morale soared. In fact, an unexpected consequence of the war lay in its redemption of Arab honor. Although by the war's end Israel controlled 325 square miles of Syrian and about 1,600 square miles of Egyptian territory, had taken thousands of enemy tanks, and destroyed the greater part of the enemy's air forces and fleets, the Yom Kippur War restored the Arabs' self-respect and repaired its bruised military reputation. In particular, Sadat's prestige rose. Now that he had succeeded in assuaging Arab pride, he could become the first Arab leader to openly discuss peace with Israel.

98

PEACE WITH EGYPT

In November 1977, Egyptian President Anwar el-Sadat made a historic visit to Jerusalem in search of a "permanent peace based on justice" for the entire Middle East. In September 1978, Sadat and Israeli Prime Minister Menachem Begin signed the Camp David Accords, hammered out under the guidance of President Jimmy Carter of the United States, which led to the signing of a formal peace treaty in March 1979.

People around the world sat glued to their television sets on November 20, 1977, when President Anwar el-Sadat of Egypt traveled to Jerusalem to address the Parliament of Israel, a country with which Egypt had been technically at war for nearly thirty years. So unprecedented was the undertaking that there were those who feared an Egyptian ruse, along the lines of the Trojan Horse: when Sadat's plane landed in Israel, would the diplomats inside turn out to be soldiers intent on assassinating Israel's leaders?

In the event, Sadat's intentions were entirely honorable. He unambiguously announced his acceptance of the existence of Israel. But he made it crystal clear from the outset that what he was after was not a separate peace between Israel and Egypt but rather a "permanent peace based on justice" (a phrase he repeated several times in the course of his address to the Knesset) for the entire region. Although peace with Israel would be to Egypt's advantage, enabling the country to concentrate its energy on development rather than defense, Sadat emphasized that at the root of the Mideast problem lay the aspirations of the Palestinian people for a state. He emphasized that true peace would require Israel to withdraw from all the occupied Arab lands, including East Jerusalem.

Sadat's visit enabled Israeli and Egyptian political figures to interact socially for the first time. Former prime minister Golda Meir had the chance to meet with the man whose surprise attack on Israel four years earlier had cost her her office. In honor of the recent birth of Sadat's first grandchild, Mrs. Meir gave him a baby gift, "as a grandmother to a grandfather."

Not surprisingly, however, the official talks that followed the historic visit did not progress smoothly. When they reached a deadlock, President Jimmy Carter performed yeoman service in overcoming obstacles. (Begin later joked that Carter had "worked harder than our forefathers did in Egypt building the pyramids.") Under Carter's direction, Sadat and Begin met in September 1978 at the presidential retreat at Camp David, Maryland. After twelve days of intense negotiations, they were able to agree on the wording of the two documents known as the Camp David Accords. One set out the terms for a peace treaty between Egypt and Israel, while the other set up a framework for granting self-government to the Palestinians in the Israeli-occupied territories. When additional obstacles threatened to prevent the accords from culminating in an actual peace treaty, Carter again intervened. As a result, Israel and Egypt signed a treaty of peace on March 26, 1979.

In the six months between the signings of the Camp David Accords and the formal peace treaty, the 1978 Nobel Peace Prize was awarded to Sadat and Begin. Soviet Foreign Minister Andrei Gromyko called the award "something of a joke," a reaction that should not be entirely dismissed as standard Soviet propaganda. Sadat did not attend the awards ceremony, because he was meeting instead in Egypt with Carter's secretary of state Cyrus Vance, who was desperately trying to keep the accords from dying. Sadat's spokesman at the ceremony avoided mentioning Begin by name and stressed that Egypt and Israel were still far from agreement on many issues, notably that of the Palestinians. As for Begin, in accepting his award, he underscored one of the differences separating the two sides by speaking of Jerusalem as "the eternal capital of Israel."

The opposition Begin faced with regard to specific provisions of the Camp David Accords and the subsequent treaty came not only from Sadat. While an overwhelming majority of the Knesset approved the terms of the peace treaty, it is worth noting that one of the two abstentions came from Yitzhak Shamir, who would become prime minister in 1986. Shamir and other Israelis opposed the concessions Israel had to make according to the treaty's terms. In exchange for a formal end to the state of war and the establishment of diplomatic, economic, and cultural relations, Israel had to yield to Egypt the whole of Sinai (which it had occupied since 1967). That meant giving up oilfields, airbases, military installations, and some twenty settlements. The settlers of one Sinai community, Yamit, resisted evacuation, affixing yellow Stars of David on their clothes like the ones Jews had been forced to wear in Nazi-occupied Europe, and threatening to commit collective suicide rather than yield their town. In the end, the town was not only evacuated but also bulldozed to discourage the return of Israeli settlers.

The response of the world to the peace treaty was not what any of the signatories had hoped. The Palestinians in the occupied territories refused to become involved in the negotiations leading to their autonomy according to the treaty's terms. The hope that other Arab states would follow Egypt's path was immediately dashed when, within days of the treaty's signing, eighteen Arab countries and the PLO agreed in Baghdad to cut off diplomatic and economic relations with Egypt. The peace treaty increased not only Egypt's but also Israel's isolation in the world. None of the African countries that had broken off diplomatic relations with Israel in 1973 made efforts to restore them. Relations between Israel and Europe also worsened, as the nine members of the Common Market issued the Venice Declaration in June 1980, calling for total Israeli withdrawal to the pre-1967 borders, the establishment of a Palestinian state, and the creation of a European military force to protect Israel's borders. The anti-Israel stance of the United Nations also hardened in the years directly following the signing of the peace treaty.

The most tragic victim of the Israel–Egypt peace treaty was its initiator, Anwar el-Sadat. At a military procession in Cairo on October 6, 1981—the 8th anniversary of the Yom Kippur War—Sadat was assassinated when a group of men in Egyptian army uniforms broke out of the parade and opened fire on the reviewing stand. The assassins were Muslim fundamentalist extremists. Ironically, in his address to the Knesset in November 1977, Sadat had praised the Egyptian people, "who do not know fanaticism," for their ability to live together "in a state of cordiality, love, and tolerance." Although Sadat's successor, Hosni Mubarak, implemented the Egyptian terms of the treaty, the peace with Israel has been at best a cold one.

Over a dozen years have now passed since the signing of the Israel–Egypt peace treaty, and Egypt remains the only Arab state to have normalized relations with Israel. In October 1991, however, Israel entered into direct, if rocky, peace talks with Syria, Lebanon, and a joint Jordanian-Palestinian delegation. More excitingly, in September 1993 Prime Minister Yitzhak Rabin and the PLO chairman Yasir Arafat shook hands on the White House lawn and signed accords aimed at leading to Palestinian autonomy within the occupied territories. Following that historic handshake, other Arab nations began to make peaceful overtures to Israel. Even Syria began to suggest that if Israel withdrew from the Golan Heights it, too, might be willing to live in true peace with its neighbor. Perhaps President Sadat's dream of a "permanent peace based on justice" in the Middle East will still become a reality.

99

THE ORDINATION
OF FEMALE RABBIS

The feminist movement has profoundly altered American Jewish life. The Reform movement ordained its first female rabbi in 1972. The decision of the Conservative Jewish Theological Seminary of America to admit women to its rabbinical school in 1984 followed years of internal struggle and led to a schism in the movement. By the early 1990s, over 300 American women had been ordained.

Possibly one of the most significant turning points in modern American Jewish history came on October 24, 1983, when the faculty of the Conservative movement's Jewish Theological Seminary of America (JTS) ended nearly a decade of tumultuous debate by voting in favor of the ordination of women.

Interestingly enough, some of the tension that surrounded the decision can be found suppressed in a ruling of the JTS in its earliest years. In 1903 Henrietta Szold, who would become the founder of the Zionist woman's organization Hadassah, was permitted to study at the seminary, but only if she renounced all intentions to seek ordination.

Forceful pressure on the seminary to admit women to the rabbinical school began to be exerted almost seventy years after any aspirations Szold might have had toward that end were squelched. In March 1972 a determined group of uninvited guests appeared at the annual convention of the Conservative movement's Rabbinical Assembly. A group of Jewish feminists, well educated both secularly and Jewishly, had formed the previous year. Their intellectual incisiveness was apparent in the very name they had chosen for themselves, "*Ezrat Nashim*," which not only refers to the area to which women are relegated in Orthodox synagogues but also means, literally, "the help of women." The women presented a petition to the rabbis, demanding religious equality with men within Conservative Judaism.

The women of Ezrat Nashim were aware that later that year, the Reform movement's Hebrew Union College would ordain its first female rabbi. (It had taken only fifty years to reach that milestone following the Reform movement's

Central Conference of American Rabbis' 1922 statement that women "cannot justly be denied the privilege of ordination.") They also knew that the Reconstructionist Rabbinical College had accepted women candidates for ordination since its opening in 1968. But the women of Ezrat Nashim wanted parity with men within Conservative Judaism. They knew how significant their inclusion within that movement would be. Reform Judaism never claimed to accept the authority of Jewish law, and Reconstructionist Judaism remained a small, if influential, movement. Conservative Judaism, by contrast, was not only the largest American Jewish denomination but also claimed to be the most genuine contemporary embodiment of Jewish tradition by keeping Jewish law responsive to contemporary needs.

Although the women of Ezrat Nashim were not exactly welcomed at the Rabbinical Assembly, being told it was "not convenient" to deal with their agenda at the moment, they had the delayed pleasure of seeing some of their demands implemented over the next few years. The very next year a majority of the Rabbinical Assembly Committee on Jewish Law and Standards declared that Conservative congregations may count women as part of the *minyan*, the religious quorum needed for public prayer. And in 1974 a minority of six committee members ruled that women should be allowed to serve as witnesses in Jewish legal matters. (Conservative congregations are free to adopt as a legitimate option a minority position held by more than three of the committee's members.)

But the major struggle, to have women admitted as candidates for ordination to the seminary's rabbinical school, was yet to come. In its own way, that struggle marked as painful a period in the Conservative movement's history as the Civil War was in American history.

At the 1977 convention of the Rabbinical Assembly, a majority voted in favor of forming a commission to examine the issue of ordaining women from all aspects. The commission's report in January 1979 concluded that "there is no cogent argument" based on Jewish law "for denying a sincere, committed woman the opportunity to study for and achieve the office of rabbi." That being the case, the commission expressed its conviction that it would be "ethically indefensible" as well as destructive to the future of the Conservative movement to reject women as future spiritual leaders.

The commission's recommendation, however, was passionately rejected by some of the movement's most respected talmudists as well as by some pulpit rabbis. Since the Rabbinical Assembly had left it to the faculty of the JTS to cast the decisive vote, faculty meetings turned passionate and often vituperative. An example of how heated the debate became can be found in the words of a professor of rabbinics, who accused proponents of the ordination of women of "violating the rabbinic prohibition to assist transgressors."

In December 1979 some of the dissidents called a conference on the Jewish legal process, at which they singled out the handling of the issue of women's ordination as an example of the Conservative movement's veering from "serious commitment" to Jewish law. Also that month, a group of women who had been studying at the seminary wrote to the faculty, beseeching them to consider with all deliberate speed the Jewish legal ramifications of ordaining women.

To defuse the issue, in 1980 the seminary began a "separate but equal" program for women, to run parallel with the men's rabbinic program. Not satisfied with this halfway measure, the Rabbinical Assembly voted that year in favor of women's ordination. In the fall of 1983, despite the opposition of all the senior members of the seminary's Talmud department, the seminary faculty voted to admit women to the regular rabbinical program by a vote of 34 to 8. The seminary's chancellor expressed his belief that the decision to ordain women, far from breaking Jewish law, exemplified its adaptation, in time-honored fashion, in order to accommodate "the religious and ethical norms of a new generation." The students entering the seminary's rabbinical school in September 1984 included eighteen women and twenty-one men.

The division within the movement that the controversy surrounding the issue had uncovered, however, could not be patched up so quickly. A small but eminent group of Conservative rabbis, scholars, and laypeople felt betrayed by the decision. How, they wondered, could Conservative Judaism claim to be the authentic transmitter of Jewish tradition if it played fast and loose with Jewish law in order to harmonize religious life with modern secular culture? This group broke from the movement to form the Union for Traditional Conservative Judaism. Founded in 1984, the Union (which has since removed the word "Conservative" from its name) opened its own rabbinical school five years later, to train only male rabbis in the traditionalist way. Although the Union's existence represents both a schism in the Conservative movement and the defection of some of its most highly respected scholars, it has not attracted significant membership.

While many people acknowledge that the presence of women rabbis has done much to energize American Jewish religious life, feminists do not feel that the battle is over. Although women have a growing voice in the Conservative, Reform, and Reconstructionist movements, the religious needs of Orthodox Jewish women are yet to be met in many significant ways. Some women rabbis express dissatisfaction with lingering signs of paternalism, ranging from lower salaries to congregational distrust of their fiduciary skills to hostility from some male congregants. And while women are being admitted to rabbinical training on an equal basis with men, they are significantly underrepresented on the faculties of the rabbinical schools. More fundamentally, sheer numbers of women rabbis and of women professors at rabbinical seminaries cannot by themselves address what many feminists see as the basic need: to transform the self-concept of the Jewish community. These Jewish feminists hope to change that self-concept, which has until now been defined exclusively by men, by incorporating into it in a truly meaningful way the experience and sensibility of Jewish women.

100

THE FALASHAS ARRIVE IN ISRAEL

*From 1975 to 1985, thousands of Falashas—the black Jews of Ethiopia—
went on foot to Sudan, from which they were secretly airlifted to Israel.
Thousands more were airlifted directly from Ethiopia in 1991, and immigration has continued. Although the 45,000 Falashas in Israel have experienced some absorption problems as a community, they continue to find
hope in their new land.*

In January 1985 news leaks of the secret airlift of Ethiopian Jews to Israel via
Sudan abruptly terminated the aptly named "Operation Moses." In evaluating
the story, *The New York Times* noted that, for the first time in history, thousands
of blacks were being transported from one country to another not as slaves but
as free citizens. Who were these black newcomers to Israel and under what
circumstances had they been transported?

Known by Ethiopian non-Jews as "Falashas," or exiles, the Ethiopian Jews call
themselves "*Beta Yisrael*," or the House of Israel. According to their own tradition, they are the descendants of the Jewish retinue who left Jerusalem to accom-
pany Menelik, son of King Solomon and the queen of Sheba, on his return to his
country. Others over the course of Jewish history have called them the remnants
of the ten tribes exiled by the Assyrians in 721 B.C.E. But in the view of ethnolo-
gists, in all likelihood they are not Semites at all, but rather descendants of a local
people who, in the centuries before and after the development of Christianity,
adopted Judaism under the influence of Jews living in southern Arabia.

After the ruling dynasty of Ethiopia converted to Christianity in the 4th
century C.E., persecution led the Jews of Ethiopia to migrate northward into
the mountains near the source of the Blue Nile. There the Ethiopian Jews lived
isolated from mainstream Judaism for over a thousand years, developing their
own form of Judaism in complete ignorance of the Talmud, upon which normative Judaism elsewhere developed. But memories of and longing for Zion
permeated the prayers and dreams of the Jews of Ethiopia just as they did those
of Diaspora Jews elsewhere.

Rumors of the existence of Beta Yisrael circulated among Jews for centuries, but it was not until the mid-19th century, when Protestant missionaries

publicized the success they were finding among the Falashas, that Jews else-where began to feel responsible for preserving their existence as Jews. In 1921 the Ashkenazic chief rabbi of Palestine announced that it was the duty of world Jewry to save them from extinction. Some fifty years later, the Sephardic chief rabbi of Israel reissued that call, adding that the time had come to expedite their immigration to Israel. In April 1975 Israel passed a law clarifying the right of Beta Yisrael, like all other Jews, to Israeli citizenship.

By that time, world Jewry's concerns for Beta Yisrael had intensified as a result of developments in Ethiopia. Following the Yom Kippur War of October 1973, Ethiopia broke off diplomatic relations with Israel. Relations were not renewed in 1974, when a Marxist regime took over. The new government sanc-tioned Coptic Christianity and Islam as official religions, but outlawed all other religions. Not only the practice of Judaism but also the teaching of Hebrew was banned, because of that language's connection to the "Zionist enemy." When severe famine struck the country, many Ethiopians blamed the Jews.

From 1977 Falashas began to cross the border from Ethiopia to Sudan, where they settled in refugee camps. Secret negotiations among the Israelis, the Ameri-cans, and the Sudanese made possible the airlift of thousands of these refugees to Israel. The promise of American aid made President Numeiri of Islamic Sudan receptive to the plan, but he insisted on secrecy, particularly after Anwar el-Sadat's assassination in 1981 intensified his feelings of vulnerability.

While the airlifts succeeded in bringing many Falasha refugees to Israel, the rigors of the trek from Ethiopia, coupled with overcrowding and inadequate food and water, left many more ill and dying in the refugee camps. Persecu-tion of the Falashas also continued in the camps, where Christian Ethiopians—likewise fleeing conditions in Ethiopia—blamed them for the famine at home and disease in the camps. By 1984 the situation had developed into a crisis.

Fearing that delay would result in thousands of Jewish deaths, Israel real-ized it had to undertake an immediate, massive rescue effort. Enlisting the aid of an Orthodox Jew who ran a Belgian air charter company, it embarked on "Operation Moses." Just as Moses had brought the Israelites out of Egypt, Israel hoped to rescue all the Falashas in the refugee camps of Sudan. From late November 1984 through the first week of January 1985, thirty-five flights brought thousands of Falashas from Sudan's Khartoum International Airport to Israel. When word of the operation leaked out to the press, however, and was later confirmed by Israel, Operation Moses was brought to a sudden halt, its mission not yet complete.

Again, promises of American aid induced Numeiri to allow the remaining Falasha refugees to leave Sudan. This time, however, he insisted that Israel play no part in the effort. Thus, "Operation Sheba," which brought over 1,000 Jews to Israel in late March 1975, was strictly an American undertaking.

There were still thousands of Jews anxious to leave Ethiopia itself, however. In November 1989, diplomatic ties between Israel and Ethiopia were restored. When Israel opened an embassy in the Ethiopian capital, Addis Ababa, Jews left their homes in the mountains and congregated in the city, in what they hoped would be the first stage of their journey to Jerusalem. The Marxist government permitted nearly 5,000 Falashas to emigrate in order to join family members already in Israel. Then, in mid-May 1991, the president of Ethiopia fled the country. With the agreement of the various forces in control, "Operation Solomon" was launched. Over a twenty-five-hour period in late May, more than 14,000 Ethiopian Jews were flown from Addis Ababa to Israel on forty-two flights.

In the years since the two massive airlifts of 1984 and 1991, many Ethiopian Jews have adapted successfully to life in their new home. Two issues in particular, however, have angered not only Falashas but also many of their supporters in Israel and abroad. One relates to doubts as to the authenticity of their religion. Although they feel their Jewishness should be above suspicion— it is, after all, what kept them a distinctive group and caused their persecution in Ethiopia—the Orthodox rabbinate in Israel requires them to "renew the covenant" by undergoing ritual immersion and formally agreeing to accept the yoke of the commandments. In addition, the legitimacy of their traditional religious leaders, or *kessim*, has been called into question, with the rabbinate demanding that the *kessim* study rabbinic law to bring them into the mainstream of normative Judaism. A second issue relates to what they see as Israel's responsibility to welcome members of their families, still in Ethiopia, who have left the Jewish fold under duress. While agreeing to consider requests for reunification with these *Falash Mura* on a case by case basis, Israel has thus far refused to admit them as a group.

Problems may remain in the absorption of Ethiopian Jewry into the fabric of Israeli life, but there is no question that in Israel their contribution to society will be nurtured and valued as it had never been in Ethiopia.

SELECTED BIBLIOGRAPHY

General Works

Ben-Sasson, H. H., ed. *A History of the Jewish People*. Cambridge, 1976.
Encyclopaedia Judaica. Jerusalem, 1970.
Finkelstein, Louis, ed. *The Jews: Their History, Culture and Religion*. Philadelphia, 1960.
Hallo, William, et al. *Heritage: Civilization and the Jews*. New York, 1984.
Johnson, Paul. *A History of the Jews*. New York, 1987.
Margolis, M., and Marx, A. *A History of the Jewish People*. Philadelphia, 1927.
Seltzer, Robert M. *Jewish People, Jewish Thought: The Jewish Experience in History*. New York, 1980.

Early Israel and Biblical History

Albright, William F. *Archaeology and the Religion of Israel*, 3rd ed. Baltimore, 1953.
———. *Samuel and the Beginning of the Prophetic Movement*. Cincinnati, 1961.
Bickerman, Elias. *From Ezra to the Last of the Maccabees*. New York, 1962.
———. *The Jews in the Greek Age*. Cambridge, 1988.
The Cambridge Ancient History, 2 vols. 3rd ed. Cambridge, 1970–1975.
Childs, B. S. *Isaiah and the Assyrian Crisis*. Naperville, IL, 1967.
Cornfeld, Gaalyah, and Freedman, David N. *Archaeology of the Bible Book by Book*. New York, 1976.
Gardiner, A. *Egypt of the Pharaohs*. Oxford, 1961.
Gordon, Cyrus H. *The World of the Old Testament*. Garden City, NY, 1958.
Hermann, S. *A History of Israel in Old Testament Times*. Philadelphia, 1975.
Noth, M. *The History of Israel*. London, 1960.
Olmstead, A. T. *History of the Persian Empire*. Chicago, 1948.
Pritchard, James B., ed. *Ancient Near Eastern Texts Relating to the Old Testament*, 3rd ed. Princeton, NJ, 1969.
Rostovtzeff, Michael. *The Social and Economic History of the Hellenistic World*, 3 vols. Oxford, 1953.

Schürer, E. *The History of the Jewish People in the Age of Jesus Christ*. Revised by G. Vermes and F. Millar. Edinburgh, 1973.

Smith, Morton. *Palestinian Parties and Politics That Shaped the Old Testament*. New York, 1971.

Tarn, W. W. *Hellenistic Civilization*. London, 1952.

Tcherikover, Victor. *Hellenistic Civilization and the Jews*. Philadelphia, 1959.

de Vaux, Roland. *Ancient Israel*. New York, 1961.

Wright, G. E. *Biblical Archaeology*. Philadelphia, 1962.

The Roman Period

Allon, G. *The History of the Jews of Palestine in the Period of the Mishna and the Talmud*, 2 vols. Jerusalem, 1976.

Cohen, Shaye J. *From the Maccabees to the Mishnah*. Louisville, KY, 1987.

Finkelstein, Louis. *Akiba, Scholar, Saint and Martyr*. Northvale, NJ, 1990.

———. *The Pharisees*, 2 vols. Philadelphia, 1962.

Goodman, Martin. *The Ruling Class of Judaea*. Cambridge, 1993.

———. *State and Society in Roman Galilee, A.D. 132–212*. Totowa, NJ, 1983.

Johnson, Paul. *A History of Christianity*. New York, 1976.

Leon, H. J. *The Jews of Ancient Rome*. Philadelphia, 1960.

Littman, Robert J. "Anti-semitism in the Greco-Roman Pagan World." In *Remembering for the Future*, vol. 1. Ed. Yehuda Bauer et al., pp. 825–835. Oxford, 1989.

Moore, G. F. *Judaism in the First Centuries of the Christian Era*, 3 vols. Cambridge, MA, 1971.

Neusner, Jacob. *A History of the Jews in Babylonia*, 4 vols. Leiden, 1965–1970.

———. *A Life of Rabban Yochanan Ben Sakkai*. Leiden, 1962.

Vermes, Geza. *Jesus and the World of Judaism*. London, 1983.

———. *The Religion of Jesus the Jew*. London, 1993.

Yadin, Yigael. *Masada: Herod's Fortress and the Zealots' Last Stand*. New York, 1966.

The Medieval Period

Baer, Y. *A History of the Jews in Christian Spain*, 2 vols. Philadelphia, 1961–1966.

Baron, Salo W. *A Social and Religious History of the Jews*, 15 vols. New York, 1957–1973.

Chasan, R. *Medieval Jewry in Northern France*. Baltimore, 1973.

Goitein, S. D. *A Mediterranean Society*. Berkeley, CA, 1967.

Hailperin, H. *Rashi and the Christian Scholars*. Pittsburgh, 1963.

Kamen, H. *The Spanish Inquisition*. New York, 1968.

Kisch, G. *The Jews in Medieval Germany*. Chicago, 1949.

Nemoy, L., ed. *Karaite Anthology*. New Haven, CT, 1952.

Roth, Cecil. *Doña Gracia*. Philadelphia, 1947.

———. *Gleanings*. New York, 1967.

———. *History of the Jews of Italy*. Philadelphia, 1946.

———. *History of the Jews in Venice*. Philadelphia, 1930.

———. *History of the Marranos*. New York, 1974.

———. *House of Nasi: the Duke of Naxos*. Philadelphia, 1948.

———. *Jews in the Renaissance*. Philadelphia, 1959.

Roth, Cecil, ed. *The World History of the Jewish People*, vol. 2. Tel Aviv, 1960.

Modern Period

Baron, Salo W. *The Russian Jew under Tsars and Soviets*. New York, 1976.

Bauer, Yehuda. *From Diplomacy to Resistance: A History of Jewish Palestine, 1939–1945*. Philadelphia, 1970.

Bauer, Yehuda, and Keren, Nili. *A History of the Holocaust*. New York, 1982.

Ben-Gurion, David. *Israel: A Personal History*. New York, 1971.

———. *Israel: Years of Challenge*. New York, 1963.

Berenbaum, Michael. *The World Must Know: The History of the Holocaust as Told in the United States Holocaust Memorial Museum*. Boston, 1993.

Daniel, Clifton, ed. *Chronicle of the 20th Century*. New York, 1987.

Dawidowicz, Lucy S. *The War Against the Jews, 1933–1945*. New York, 1975.

Eban, Abba. *My People: The Story of the Jews*. New York, 1968.

Elon, Amos. *Herzl*. New York, 1975.

Faber, Eli. *A Time for Planting: The First Migration, 1654–1820*. Baltimore, 1992.

Feingold, Henry L. *A Time for Searching: Entering the Mainstream, 1920–1945*. Baltimore, 1992.

Fishman, Sylvia B. *A Breath of Life: Feminism in the American Jewish Community*. New York, 1993.

Gilbert, Martin. *The Holocaust: The Jewish Tragedy*. New York, 1986.

Gittelman, Zvi Y. *Jewish Nationality and Soviet Politics: The Jewish Sections of the CPSU, 1917–1930*. Princeton, NJ, 1972.

Goldscheider, Calvin, and Zuckerman, Alan S. *The Transformation of the Jews*. Chicago, 1986.

Goldsmith, Emanuel S., et al., eds. *The American Judaism of Mordecai M. Kaplan*. New York, 1990.

Greenberg, Simon, ed. *The Ordination of Women as Rabbis: Studies and Responsa*. New York, 1988.

Hertzberg, Arthur, ed. *The Zionist Idea: A Historical Analysis and Reader*. Westport, CT, 1970.

Herzog, Chaim. *The War of Atonement, October 1973*. Boston, 1975.

Hyman, Paula. *From Dreyfus to Vichy: The Transformation of French Jewry, 1906–1939*. New York, 1979.

———. *The Emancipation of the Jews of Alsace: Acculturation and Tradition in the Nineteenth Century*. New Haven, CT, 1991.

Karp, Abraham J. *Haven and Home: A History of the Jews in America*. New York, 1985.

Kimche, Jon, and Kimche, David. *Both Sides of the Hill: Britain and the Palestine War*. London, 1960.

Kleebatt, Norman L., ed. *The Dreyfus Affair: Art, Truth and Justice*. Berkeley, CA, 1987.

Kochan, Lionel, ed. *The Jews in Soviet Russia Since 1917*. Oxford, 1978.

Levin, Nora. *The Jews in the Soviet Union Since 1917: Paradox of Survival*. New York, 1978.

Marcus, Jacob R. *The American Jewish Woman: 1654–1980*. Cincinnati, 1981.

Meyer, Michael A. *Response to Modernity: A History of the Reform Movement in Judaism*. Oxford, 1988.

Morais, Vamberto. *A Short History of Anti-Semitism*. New York, 1976.

Morton, Frederic. *The Rothschilds: A Family Portrait*. New York, 1962.

Noveck, Simon, ed. *Great Jewish Personalities in Modern Times*. Washington, DC, 1960.

Parfitt, Tudor. *Operation Moses: The Untold Story of the Secret Exodus of the Falasha Jews from Ethiopia*. London, 1985.

Pasachoff, Naomi. *Great Jewish Thinkers: Their Lives and Work*. West Orange, NJ, 1992.

Pawel, Ernst. *The Labyrinth of Exile: A Life of Theodor Herzl*. New York, 1989.

Plaskow, Judith. *Standing Again at Sinai: Judaism from a Feminist Perspective*. New York, 1990.

Quandt, William B. *Camp David: Peacemaking and Politics*. Washington, DC, 1986.

Rapoport, Louis. *Stalin's War Against the Jews: The Doctors' Plot and the Soviet Solution*. New York, 1990.

Samuel, Maurice. *Blood Accusation: The Strange History of the Beiliss Case*. London, 1966.

Segev, Tom. *The Seventh Million: The Israelis and the Holocaust*. New York, 1993.

Shapiro, Edward S. *A Time for Healing: American Jewry since World War II*. Baltimore, 1992.

Silberman, Charles E. *A Certain People: American Jews and Their Lives Today*. New York, 1985.

Sorin, Gerald. *A Time for Building: The Third Migration, 1880–1920*. Baltimore, 1992.

Stein, Leonard J. *The Balfour Declaration.* New York, 1961.

Yovel, Yirmiyahu. *Spinoza and Other Heretics: The Marrano of Reason.* Princeton, NJ, 1989.

Articles from *The New York Times*

"About 250 Jews Are Said to Have Immigrated to Israel from Yemen," July 15, 1993.

Binder, David. "Germany to Pay Jewish Victims of Nazis," November 7, 1992.

———. "Jews of Nazi Era Get Claims Details," December 22, 1992.

Erlanger, Steven. "Russian Court Calls 'Protocols' Anti-Semitic Forgery," November 27, 1993.

Haberman, Clyde. "Cry of the Ancient Kin: Don't Doubt Our Judaism!" September 29, 1992.

———. "Israel Cool to Admitting a New Ethiopian Group," January 25, 1993.

Holmes, Steven A. "Nazi Victims Face Deadline on Claims," December 31, 1992.

Kinzer, Stephen. "Germany Marks Place Where Horror Began," January 20, 1992.

"One in Five Polled Voices Doubt on Holocaust," April 20, 1993.

Perlez, Jane. "At Warsaw Ghetto, Poles and Jews Bound by Hope," April 20, 1993.

Riding, Alan. "100 Years Later, Dreyfus Affair Still Festers," February 9, 1994.

INDEX

About the Authors

Naomi Pasachoff is the author of *Basic Judaism for Young People* (3 volumes, 1986, 1987) and *Great Jewish Thinkers: Their Lives and Work* (1992). Her science textbooks are widely used in elementary and junior-high schools throughout the country. A graduate of Ramaz School in New York and of Radcliffe College, she has a master's degree in English literature from Columbia University and a doctorate from Brandeis University. She has lived and worked in Jerusalem. Dr. Pasachoff has taught at Skidmore College, Rensselaer Polytechnic University, Williams College, and Berkshire Community College. She lives in Williamstown, Massachusetts, with her husband, Jay. They are the parents of two daughters at Harvard College.

Robert J. Littman is a professor of classics at the University of Hawaii. He holds an M.Litt. in Litterae Humaniores from Oxford University and a Ph.D. in classical philology from Columbia University. He is the author of books and numerous articles on Greek history, the history of medicine, and the ancient Near East, including *The Greek Experiment* (1974) and *Kinship and Politics in Athens 600–400 B.C.* (1990). He held the Herodotus Fellowship at the Institute for Advanced Study at Princeton and has been a visiting scholar at the Oxford Centre for Postgraduate Hebrew Studies. He lives in Honolulu with his wife, Bernice, and three children.

I ♡ STATIONERY

First published in the United States
of America in 2012 by

UNIVERSE PUBLISHING

A Division of Rizzoli International Publications, Inc.

300 Park Avenue South

New York, NY 10010

www.rizzoliusa.com

Copyright © RotoVision SA 2012

Sales and Editorial Office

Sheridan House, 114 Western Road

Hove BN3 1DD, UK

Tel: +44 (0)1273 72 72 68

Fax: +44 (0)1273 72 72 69

2012 2013 2014 2015 / 10 9 8 7 6 5 4 3 2 1

ISBN: 978-0-7893-2488-7

Library of Congress Control Number: 2011933609

Printed in China by 1010 Printing International Ltd.

I ♡ STATIONERY

  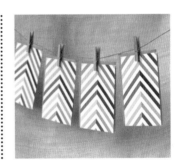

CHARLOTTE RIVERS

UNIVERSE

CONTENTS

INTRODUCTION

Despite digital technology dominating the way we communicate and record information—from e-mailing to texting to blogging—the stationery industry today is thriving and is home to some of the most interesting examples of illustration and design, and creative artisan processes. It seems that despite the onslaught of digital media there are those who still like to indulge in the slower, more tactile medium of the handwritten letter or card, and they are matched by an abundance of designers, printers, and crafters creating stationery. As Jen Shaffer of Minnesota-based Painted Fish Studio explains: "I would like to think that people who buy my paper goods are those who value aspects of a slower way of life: instead of texting or sending an e-mail, they prefer to send a letter. They're writing their thoughts in a journal, not in a blog."

It is a testament to the many designers and crafters out there that the stationery industry is so strong. The market is huge, with a number of fairs and shows held worldwide, such as the National Stationery Show in New York. Recent years have also seen an increase in the popularity of craft and design markets, many of which incorporate stationery, such as the Finders Keepers markets in Australia. Of course the continued success of online market-places such as Etsy and Folksy, where much of the work shown on the pages of this book can be found, is further proof that the demand for handmade products from smaller practitioners is growing.

Throughout this book you will find work by designers from around the world, showcasing a number of different artisan processes. From screen printing,

block printing, illustration, letterpress, and more, the way in which each stationery item is made is as important as its actual design. For the purposes of this book, stationery includes greeting cards, notecards, writing paper, envelopes, wrapping paper, gift tags, calendars, journals, notebooks, diaries, and stamps. It has all been organized according to the technique or process used to create it.

Hand-Drawn Illustration celebrates the abundance of stationery featuring original illustrations created by hand. Styles vary hugely, from simple pen-and-ink drawings to more complex works using gouache paint or digitally colored imagery. What they all have in common, however, is that any given illustrative style is unique to its creator—instantly recognizable as theirs.

Screen Printing explores the ways and means by which designers and printers use this technique to design stationery. Like other artisan printing processes, screen printing has seen a huge rise in popularity in recent years. It offers creatives an economical, hands-on way to print onto many different surfaces and materials. The Japanese Gocco printing system has also gained a huge following in recent times. Its manageable size and high-quality output make it an appealing choice for designers and printers, alongside traditional screen-printing methods.

4

5

6

7

8

It's hard to have missed the revival in the fortunes of *Letterpress Printing* in recent years. Presses that were once destined for the scrap heap have been restored and brought into designers' studios, and are now used to print the vast quantities of beautiful letterpress-printed stationery available today. From small runs printed on Adana tabletop presses to larger runs printed on Golding Jobber platen presses, this resurgence in popularity shows no sign of abating.

Block Printing is a lesser-used artisan craft, but it is slowly on the rise, and as the work in this chapter shows, there is a real skill in carving and creating blocks for printing. Although most artists today use linoleum for their blocks rather than wood, the method of carving, which has existed for hundreds of years, remains unchanged.

Digital Illustration takes us away from traditional artisan crafts and into a world that has transformed the way in which designers and artists are able to create imagery. Software such as Adobe Photoshop and Illustrator offers huge scope for image creation and manipulation—either solely or together with hand-drawn or scanned elements. This chapter includes work featuring both vector-based illustrations and "hand-drawn" digital illustrations, created freehand using either a mouse or a graphics tablet.

Firmly back within the world of the handmade, *Calligraphy* showcases the work of some of today's best-known contemporary calligraphic practitioners. Inspired by traditional calligraphic styles, or "hands," this chapter explores the ways in which today's artists are experimenting with those long-established styles to create innovative new work for today's design-conscious market. Calligraphy is no longer consigned to just wedding stationery. In its modern, contemporary forms, its uses are far more versatile.

Another ancient craft that has seen a huge increase in popularity in recent years is *Papercutting*. With roots as far back as the sixth century, this method of creating delicate, hand-cut imagery is fast being adopted by many of today's young creatives. Techniques differ but, as the work in this chapter shows, the results remain the same— quite simply, beautiful.

The final chapter covers work that includes *Collage, 3-D, and Sewn* elements. This is where that ever-popular term "handmade" really comes into its own. Some pieces feature the ancient Japanese art of origami, while others use mixed media ranging from fabrics to card to embroidery floss to buttons, and more, to create a truly eclectic mix of work.

Together these chapters cover a wide range of skills and techniques. I hope that the work presented in them serves to inspire and delight as well as to inform. The overwhelming quantity of work received and selected for inclusion in this book really goes to show how, even in this age of digital media, beautiful handcrafted paper goods still have their place.

Charlotte Rivers

1	PAPERCUTTING
2	BLOCKPRINTING
3	PAPERCUTTING
4	SCREENPRINTING
5	HAND-DRAWN ILLUSTRATION
6	CALLIGRAPHY
7	BLOCKPRINTING
8	SEWING

TECHNIQUES &
PRACTITIONERS

CHAPTER 1

HAND-DRAWN ILLUSTRATION

Hand-drawn illustrations add something of a personal touch to a design, giving a piece that ever-popular handmade aesthetic. Styles vary considerably, but each artist will have their own unique approach, resulting, over time, in a signature style that can be recognized instantly.

Hand-drawn illustrations feature heavily in stationery design, and the techniques used to create them are many and varied. Most start with a pencil, or pen and ink, on paper. Some are left as simple line drawings; others are colored. Coloring may be done using dry media (such as crayons, colored pencils, chalks, or oil pastels), wet media (inks, watercolors, or gouache paints), or digitally, using Adobe Photoshop or Illustrator. Whether this last method is used or not, the process of taking a hand-drawn illustration to print will generally involve the use of digital technology at some point. In some cases an illustration will simply be scanned and imported into Adobe Photoshop, Illustrator, or similar software, "cleaned up," and then saved as a high-resolution image ready for printing. In other cases an image will be digitally enhanced. This could involve coloring, adding in other elements, incorporating this image into a wider design layout, or adding in lettering or type.

Hand-drawn illustrations are also printed using other methods, such as block printing, screen printing, and letterpress printing, each with its own process for creating print-ready imagery.

HAND-DRAWN ILLUSTRATION TOOLS

PAPER

The choice of stock will depend on the drawing implements being used. Standard sketchbooks containing 100lb (150gsm) white acid-free cartridge paper serve well for both pencil and pen-and-ink drawings, as well as paint. However, some illustrators like to use heavier specialist paper, with a variety of flat or textured surfaces, when working with watercolors, acrylics, gouache, or other paints to create color. Vellum paper and Bristol paper give different results with pens. Layout paper allows for the tracing and redrawing of images.

PENS

Brush or fiber tips, fine liners, roller balls, nib pens, markers, or Sharpies; the range of pens available is huge and the choice is personal. Illustrators tend to settle on the pen that they find most comfortable to hold and that gives them the application they desire.

PAINT

Typically, watercolor, acrylic, or gouache paints.

BRUSHES

Artists' paintbrushes come in a number of different shapes, sizes, and hairs (natural or synthetic). The ultimate brush is made using sable hair, although many synthetic brushes compare well.

PENCILS

Graphite or colored—again, the choice is wide and varied and illustrators tend to use pencils that are comfortable to hold and suited to their particular drawing technique.

SCANNER

Used to import hand-drawn imagery onto a computer in order to make it print ready.

AMYMARCELLA

MILWAUKEE,
WISCONSIN, USA

Amy M. Soczka is a designer and illustrator working under the name of amymarcella. This calendar features her hand-drawn illustrations in a format that is an ode to her "obsessive list-making habit" and was printed on 100lb bright white cardstock. "I like to collect plant matter and flowers, always paying attention to the repetitive patterns and variegated lines in the details," she explains. "My botanical illustrations are a combination of any of these elements."

The cards are part of a series called Compliments and feature an exaggerated version of Amy's own handwriting. The goal of the series was simply to design cards that could be sent to "brighten up someone's day." The hand-drawn lettering was imported into Illustrator to be digitized and colored before being printed on 80lb recycled French Paper cardstock.

SUKIE

·····································

BRIGHTON, UK

Sukie was founded by Darrell and Julia Gibbs. They design and produce a variety of notebooks, accessories, and home furnishings for their own brand as well as working with other brands on design projects. "We focus on design that is conceptual as well as decorative, functional, and fun—and high quality, but affordable at the same time," explains Darrell.

Shown here are their notebooks, My First Novel and Note Book for Winners. Both feature hand-drawn illustrations and artwork. "We use various methods for our artwork," Darrell says. "They always start off as drawings. Then we make them into lino prints or give them texture by copying them on a fax machine. The final image is then put together on the Mac."

The notebooks were printed on recycled paperback card and paper stock.

SWISS COTTAGE DESIGNS

NEW YORK, NEW YORK, USA

Swiss Cottage Designs is run by Courtney Jentzen and is a custom design studio, specializing in stationery, invitations, and personal and corporate branding. "I have a strong background in illustration and like to incorporate hand-drawn elements in my work wherever I can," Jentzen explains. "I have an affinity with whimsical illustration and great typography."

Both of these greeting cards feature Jentzen's illustrations. For the Love Is in the Air card she drew the letters by hand in pencil before painting in the color using watercolors on a 130lb cold-press surface. For the Day in Fort Greene card she drew the illustration and then colored it in digitally using Photoshop.

DRAWCITY

·············

CAPE TOWN,
SOUTH AFRICA

South African graphic designer and
illustrator Fayrooz Abader trades
under the name of Drawcity.

All of Abader's illustrations are
drawn by hand using black felt-tip
pen. They are then imported into
Adobe Photoshop so that color can
be added; otherwise the original
images are not digitally altered at all.

MAI AUTUMN
. . . .
ASBURY PARK,
NEW JERSEY, USA

Christine Lindstrom is an artist and
designer who works under the name
of Mai Autumn.

"I wanted to capture a lovely sense
of nostalgia in an item that could be
used as an everyday luxury," she
says of these vintage-style cards.
"I think that stationery is a perfect
vehicle for little daily reminders of
our own memories and daydreams.
These folk-art notecards were inspired
by my childhood memories of the
decorative art in my grandmother's
home. Each design is a compilation
of traditional floral motifs from the
1950s, '60s, and '70s."

The illustrations for the cards
were created by Lindstrom using
Italian watercolor paints on heavy
watercolor paper.

HEIDI BURTON

LONDON, UK

Heidi Burton is a freelance illustrator whose work is inspired by folktales, nature, music, literature, and poetry. Her output varies, from original illustrations, prints, handpainted ceramics, and altered Moleskine journals to greeting cards.

"My ethos is to create a positive and unique personal experience for each customer, with a handmade touch. My ongoing self-initiated brief is to create a series of altered journals with the theme of literature from around the nineteenth century. I read a lot of old poetry and folktales and my instinct as an illustrator is to respond to the text with drawings."

Burton works with Tombow double-ended pens or Rotring or Pilot fineliner ink pens. She also uses 2B or 3B pencils for her sketches and drawings. She applies color directly onto the paper using brush pens or watercolor paints.

PAPER & TYPE

LOS ANGELES,
CALIFORNIA, USA

Both of these products from paper & type (see also pages 136 and 168) feature Victoria Vu's hand-drawn illustrations.

The sketches for the This Year's Flowers writing set span four panels (or sheets), so a four-page letter will yield a complete print. Vu also added bright berry-colored lines to the paper and included a supply of aqua blue envelopes to counter the grayness of the pencil sketches.

The Perpetual Planner features the same hand-drawn flower illustrations on both the kraft paper cover and the white inner pages.

ENORMOUSCHAMPION

NEW YORK, NEW YORK, USA

This company is run by photographer and letterpress printer Jordan Provost and graphic designer and illustrator Jason Wong. "We use recycled paper in our stationery, sustainably harvested wood in our animal silhouettes, and unbleached linen in our dishcloths. Everything is produced in the United States, and we use minimal cardboard and paper packaging for our goods," the husband-and-wife team explain.

Shown here are their Whale card box set and Fite-Cycles notecards. The whale illustrations are by Wong, while the Fite-Cycles are the work of Tim Fite.

The hand-drawn illustrations were imported into Adobe Illustrator and redrawn, ready to be made into photopolymer plates for printing on 110lb recycled cover stock.

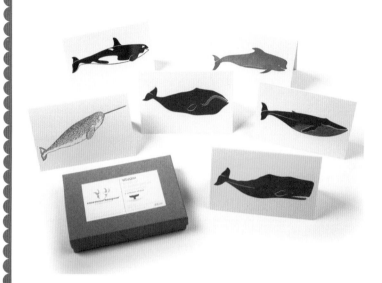

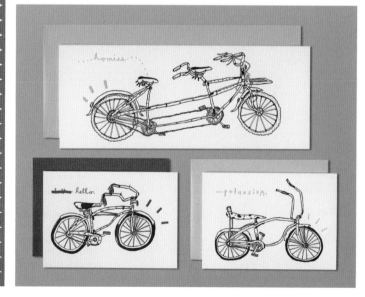

OH MY DEER HANDMADES

NASHVILLE, TENNESSEE, USA

Oh My Deer Handmades is run by artist and illustrator Chelsea Petaja.

Petaja's love of wreaths led to her designing this *Seasons of the Wreath* calendar, featuring her hand-drawn illustration and lettering.

The wreath in the center of the calendar mimics each of the seasons, going from spring to summer to fall to winter, and was handpainted using watercolors on smooth Bristol bright white cardstock. The illustration was complemented by the addition of handpainted lettering for the year and names of the months.

SUNLIGHT ON CLOSED LIDS

WEST YORKSHIRE, UK

This is the work of Kate Holliday, founder and designer at Sunlight on Closed Lids. "I merge textiles, design, hand-drawn illustration, vintage patterns, and nostalgic imagery in order to form an original, colorful, energetic, and playful world within my stationery," she explains. "I offer heartfelt greetings, wise words, a story, personal message, words of love, or just a simple hello."

The illustrations shown on these greeting cards were created by hand, employing a variety of methods. "I like to use superfine black gel pens for the initial illustrations and enjoy using collage, colored pencils, gouache paints, and screen printing to create patterns and textures," she adds.

All cards were printed on Accent Antique white textured stock.

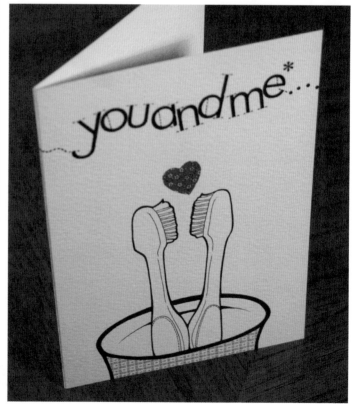

ANDY PRATT

NEW YORK, NEW YORK, USA

Andy Pratt uses a variety of techniques to produce his cards. These are a few of his Location Collection cards—Queens (New York), Seattle, Washington, and Vancouver; created during and after visits to each city.

The illustrations were sketched by hand before being scanned and inked in Flash and then colored in Illustrator using a tablet monitor. "Thus far all the cards in this series are of places I've been; in fact the Queens card was inspired by my commute on the subway from my old apartment," explains Pratt. "Recently I've been getting requests to illustrate cities I haven't yet had a chance to visit so for those cards I'll rely on photos taken by family and friends."

The cards were letterpress-printed on Crane's 110lb Pearl White Lettra cover stock.

JILL BLISS

PORTLAND, OREGON, USA

Jill Bliss is a freelance illustrator and designer. These are her hand-illustrated Sea Flowers postcard set and Succulent journals and stationery set.

"Before I begin each drawing I do lots of research—studying guidebooks, searching online, talking to naturalists, and making visits to a specific place with sketchbook and camera in hand," Bliss explains. "Everything is drawn by hand with pen and ink, then scanned into the computer to be put on various items, such as cards and journals. I add in the background colors digitally."

Each item in Bliss's line is printed with vegetable- or soy-based inks on 100 percent postconsumer recycled paper stock.

JO CLARK DESIGN

CAMBRIDGE, UK

Jo Clark is an illustrator and designer.
This is a selection of cards from her
collection, which aims to celebrate
the beauty of nature. "My designs
emerge from organic shapes,
with a sensitive use of line and a
sophisticated color palette," she
explains. "Inspiration for my flower
designs comes from gardens and
from train journeys to Norfolk,
passing through countryside
abundant in wild flora."

Clark works with graphite and
pencils, pencil crayons, and marker
pens. "I love to use marker pens
for their versatility; they create an
instant flat color and can also be
layered to create depth and texture."

Final images are then scanned into
Adobe Photoshop so that a card
template can be created and sent
to the printers.

KAROLIN SCHNOOR

LONDON, UK

Originally from Berlin but now settled in London, freelance designer and illustrator Karolin Schnoor creates the drawings for her card lines by hand before coloring and finishing them digitally.

Schnoor uses both digital printing and screen-printing for her cards. Shown here are her Folk Wolf, Folk Owl, Valentine, Thank You, and Cloak designs, all featuring her hand-drawn illustrations and type. Each card was printed on thick Fine Art Trade Guild (UK)–approved textured paper stock using archival inks.

LUCY KING DESIGN
....

MELBOURNE, AUSTRALIA

Lucy King is a freelance illustrator and designer, originally from the United Kingdom but now living in Melbourne.

King has a background in textile and surface pattern design, having designed tableware for Wedgwood. She is now known for her muted watercolor florals and loose painterly style, although her artwork still often reflects her appreciation of vintage tableware: "I love to draw brightly painted florals, delicious cupcakes, and vintage china," she says.

Her mix-and-match line of cards incorporates all of these things. Each original artwork was created using Winsor & Newton watercolors and Arches watercolor paper, and then scanned and imported into Adobe Photoshop, where King created the final design. The cards were then digitally printed.

GEMMA CORRELL

BERLIN,
GERMANY

Gemma Correll is a freelance illustrator and designer who creates stationery items, T-shirts, and tote bags. Her quirky hand-drawn illustrations are created simply using pen and ink. "I specialize in the fun side of the illustration spectrum, where the concept and use of words and humor are just as important as the image, if not more so," Correll says. "My work always has a narrative basis."

Both of these cards were created for a collaborative group project called "Love to Print" and were produced and sold for Valentine's Day. The original hand-drawn images were scanned and imported into Adobe Photoshop to be prepared for printing on a Gocco printer.

MELANIE LINDER / SPREAD THE LOVE

FLEETWOOD, PENNSYLVANIA, USA

Spread the Love is run by Melanie Linder, who designs and prints various stationery goods. "Love is my theme and happiness is my goal," she says. "I work in a spontaneous, whimsical way, dreaming up ideas or being inspired by music. This calendar was created as, after a few difficult years, I wanted to believe the next year would be 'my year' so I proclaimed this on the calendar I designed."

Linder drew the illustrations for the calendar by hand before importing them into Adobe Illustrator and adding typography to create the layout. The font used is called Folk and the calendar was printed on 80lb Wassau cardstock.

O-CHECK DESIGN GRAPHICS (SPRING COME, RAIN FALL)

SEOUL,
SOUTH KOREA

O-Check Design Graphics produces a wide variety of stationery goods. "The name O-Check comes from the Korean word *gongcheck*, meaning 'notebook,'" explains designer Cho Su-Jung. "The aim of our brand is to evoke strong emotions and feelings of nostalgia. Our products are mainly printed with soy ink and made with eco-friendly materials, including recycled paper and linen."

The notebooks shown here all feature hand-drawn illustrations. Also shown are some of O-Check's Christmas decoration cards. These are designed to be sent as holiday cards that can then be made into decorations and hung up by the recipient.

ALLISON COLE ILLUSTRATION

PROVIDENCE,
RHODE ISLAND, USA

Allison Cole is an illustrator who works out of a former candy factory. She creates products ranging from paper products to soft goods and accessories such as tote bags and pillows.

The cards in the Bonjour card set feature Cole's ink drawings. These were scanned into Adobe Photoshop where they were colored and arranged ready for printing onto thick coated cardstock. The imagery for the hand-printed notebooks was created and arranged in the same way, but was screen printed by hand onto recycled cardstock.

KRISTIN CARLSON

MOSCOW, IDAHO,
USA

Kristin Carlson is a printmaker working primarily in screen printing and mixed media. "Much of my work is inspired by the look of written correspondence and letterforms," she explains. "Some of my printmaking work also uses imagery based on maps and architecture from places I have lived."

This postcard set features past and present iconic buildings in the city of Providence. The image of each building was first created on board using drawing, watercolors, and collage. The text for the reverse side was hand-lettered on a separate sheet. Then the sheets were scanned and manipulated in Adobe Photoshop to achieve the appropriate contrast and color before being digitally printed as double-sided cards using soy-based inks.

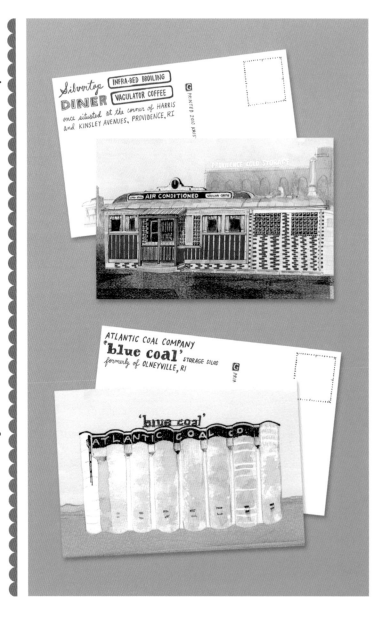

CHAPTER 2

SCREEN PRINTING

A screen print is created by passing ink through a screen containing a stencil onto a given substrate. The process can be used to apply artwork to many different surfaces, from paper and card to cotton, wood, or canvas.

Like letterpress printing and other artisan crafts, screen printing is currently enjoying a revival. It hails originally from Asia—particularly China and Japan, where it has been widely used from as far back as the tenth century. Despite its popularity in Asia, it wasn't widely adopted in Western Europe until the early twentieth century, when it began to be used to print wallpaper, linens, and silks.

Screens are created by stretching a piece of finely woven mesh material within a solid frame. Stencils are usually made using the photo-emulsion technique. A copy of the original image is created on a transparent overlay such as acetate, ensuring that the areas to be inked are opaque. The printer then selects a mesh screen, coats it in photo emulsion, and allows it to dry in the dark. Once dry, the overlay holding the artwork is placed over the screen and exposed to ultraviolet light, which passes through the clear areas of the overlay and hardens the emulsion on the mesh screen. The screen is then washed so that the unexposed areas of emulsion dissolve and wash away, leaving the stencil in place. To print, ink is pulled down over the screen and pressed through the threads of the mesh onto the substrate.

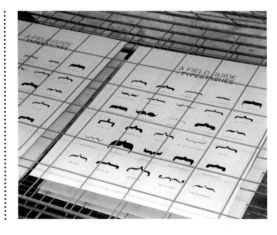

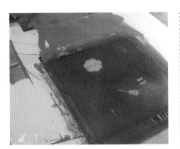

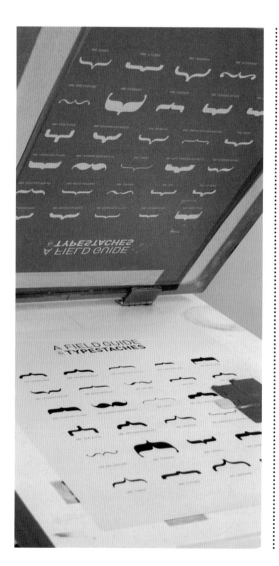

Print-ready stencils can also be created using the block-out method or the original cut-stencil method. For the first, the printer draws around the negative areas of the artwork with a glue-based solution, thus blocking the ink flow to these areas when printed. The second method sees the positive area of the image cut out of paper, leaving only the negative area. This is then secured to the screen so that the ink flows only through the areas of the screen not covered by the stencil, i.e., the intended image.

In addition to traditional screen-printing methods, the Japanese Gocco printing system is often used. It serves more as a craft method than an industry standard, but it has gained an avid cult following within the design and printmaking community. A Gocco press provides a superfine level of detail within images, produces great results with metallic and fluorescent inks, and allows complex multicolor split-fountain designs, which means several ink colors can be used at the same time. Gocco's parent company, Riso Japan, no longer produces the machines; however, its fans are now experimenting with other more readily available alternatives.

SCREEN-PRINTING TOOLS

PRESS
There are three common types of screen-printing press: flatbed, cylinder, and rotary.

INK
Solvent-, plastisol-, and water-based inks are the most commonly used.

FRAME
A wooden frame is used to hold the screen in place over the substrate. It is held high when the ink is applied and lowered when ready to print. Aluminum frames are also available; these are more resistant but also more expensive.

STENCIL
An image of the artwork, today created most commonly using acetate.

SQUEEGEE
This rubber-bladed tool is used to press the ink evenly through the mesh screen.

PHOTO-SENSITIVE EMULSION
A liquid that is applied to the mesh screen, enabling the creation of a stencil when it is exposed to ultraviolet light.

CORRUPIOLA

SÃO JOSÉ, BRAZIL

Corrupiola creates *experiências manuais,* or "handmade experiences," and is run by artist and designer Leila Lampe and writer and web designer Aleph Ozuas (see also page 50 and page 95). Everything they create is carefully made by hand.

This selection of recycled mininotebooks was made from paper that was left over from the creation of other notebooks for their line. The mininotebooks feature a series of screen-printed, open-source dingbat images. Colored Fabriano Tiziano paper was used for the covers, and 80gsm Pollen Paper from Suzano for the signatures. Both papers are acid free.

Also shown here is their Golden Box, which features notebooks with fabric covers and silk-screen-printed covers, all housed together in a papercut recycled-cardboard sleeve.

HEART ZEENA

LONDON, UK

Zeena Shah, who makes handmade goods using locally sourced materials, founded and runs this stationery and home accessories company (see also page 152). To reduce the impact of her business on the environment, she uses organic and recycled materials, and water-based dyes.

Shah specializes in hand silk-screen printing, but will often work by turning her drawings into papercuts and then using these to create new designs. These are her A Birdie Called Bob greeting cards, Birdie gift tags, Wonderous wrapping paper, and Nigel notebooks. The notebooks and wrapping papers have screen-printed covers, which were inspired by Shah's love of sewing and cross-stitch.

All items were screen printed and the Nigel notebooks feature hand-stitched binding.

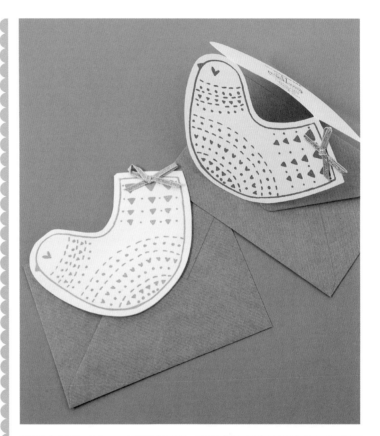

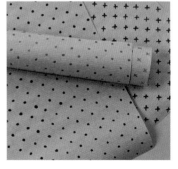

CORRUPIOLA AND THEREZA ROWE

··

SÃO JOSÉ, BRAZIL /
LONDON, UK

This illustrated notebook is the result
of a collaboration between Brazilian
designers and printers Corrupiola
(see also page 46 and 95) and
the London-based designer and
illustrator Thereza Rowe (see also
page 133). It was inspired by
a love of cats, shared by both
Rowe and the Corrupiola duo.

The illustrations were created first
as rough pencil sketches and then
drawn in more detail using a graphic
tablet and Adobe Illustrator.
"I like the flexibility of working with
vectors," explains Rowe. "You can
draw freely without worrying so
much about size or dimensions,
since vectors can be blown to any
size without loss of quality."

The notebook was screen printed
by hand on acid-free Pollen 90gsm
stock for the body and Duo 300gsm
design paper for the cover.

LA RARA

SYDNEY, AUSTRALIA

This limited-edition, screen-printed stationery company is run by Lara Raymond.

Raymond creates her designs in Adobe Photoshop and/or Illustrator, using a mix of vintage and modern illustrations and typography. Each of her stationery items is then thermally imprinted on a screen before being hand-printed using a Gocco printer and original Japanese Gocco inks in limited runs.

"The cards are made from start to finish in the same room. It is a very immediate process—reassuringly time-consuming but with beautiful results," she explains. "Each item is truly unique and slightly different from the others, which I love."

ME AND AMBER

SYDNEY, AUSTRALIA

Karen Enis and Amber Molnar are the duo who run this company, producing a variety of handmade items, from housewares to stationery. Their designs feature simple, bold silhouette graphics, illustrations, and typography.

"We love everything to do with greeting cards—not just their design or their physicality, but also the meaning associated with them. The act of giving and receiving a card is really special, particularly in this age of e-mail and digital technology. As we've always loved notebooks, they were a natural progression when we wanted to expand our line of greeting cards."

All of these cards and notebooks were printed on recycled paper using the old-fashioned stencil screen-printing technique.

NORA WHYNOT
PAPER GOODS
....
BRISBANE, AUSTRALIA

This Australian company produces a variety of paper goods using environmentally responsible materials and 100 percent recycled card and paper. Much of their work features hand-drawn or digital illustrations, and all their products are silk-screen printed except, as shown here, the bookplates and garden journal, which were printed by offset lithography.

The design of the perpetual calendar was inspired by old wives' tales and features specially created illustrations. The cooking folders, decorated with silhouette illustrations, were created using heavy box card and are part of the "Nora says... File it!" collection of boxboard folders, as is the ruler folder.

HELLO JENUINE

....

DUNDEE, UK

Hello Jenuine is Jen Collins, an illustrator who often employs screen printing to complement her illustration work.

Collins created the illustrations for these notebooks by hand using brushes and inks. She then screen printed each cover before hand binding the cover and inner pages together.

Both the cover and paper inside are made from recycled stock.

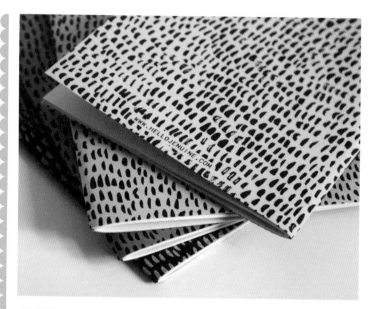

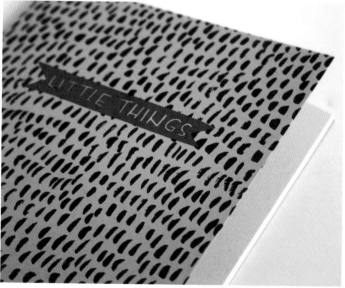

MORRIS & ESSEX

LIMINGTON, MAINE, USA

Morris & Essex is a stationery company run by designer and printmaker Eliza Jane Curtis (see also page 87).

Curtis printed these greeting cards in her home studio using the traditional (large-format) silk-screen process. She used hand-cut stencils and a combination of Rubylith film and thick black construction paper to make the design and burn the silk screen.

"I have a very hands-on aesthetic that comes from a love of tactile crafts; I seldom use the computer," she explains. "Designs combine my love of historic ornament and decorative ephemera and memories of childhood daydreams in the fields and forests of Maine to create motifs of geometry, fantasy, and nature."

ANJA JANE

LONDON, UK

This print company, run by Anja Jane Sheriden, specializes in printed textiles and screen prints as well as greeting cards. "I love color and pattern and try to incorporate as much as possible into my products," Sheriden explains. "I screen print all my paper products in my London studio. It is so wonderful in a digital age to step away from the computer and mix real paints and work physically to create images."

This Owl card was created from a limited-edition screen print. The image was first drawn in pen and ink and then scanned and tidied up to be made into a screen. It was then screen printed using two layers.

W+K STUDIO GOODNESS

•••••••••••••••••••••••••••••••

PORTLAND, OREGON, USA

Goodness (see also page 82) is a side project of the Wieden + Kennedy graphic design studio. When not making ads, the creatives there design T-shirts, calendars, greeting cards, posters, and more.

This calendar features the work of twelve different designers and was created with the aim of showcasing a wide range of talent from the studio within a functional object. Each designer was asked to create artwork for a given month, the results of which see a mix of hand-drawn illustrations, vector art, and type.

The calendar was screen printed in black and white on French Paper kraft stock.

AKIMBO

ADELAIDE, AUSTRALIA

Akimbo is run by graphic designer Alicia Parsons, who designs invitations, cards, and other stationery items. This is her Woodland collection, which features a fill-in invitation, Christmas card, gift tag, and food flag. The collection was commissioned by Mary & Gabrielle Events and Poppies Flowers.

"The theme was a rustic Christmas with oak leaf details and a palette of berry and natural materials," explains Parsons. "The natural woodsy details inspired the oak leaf, acorn, and squirrel motifs that I then screen printed by hand in white onto kraft paper. I just love the solid color that can be achieved against a dark paper."

ACUTE & OBTUSE
....

SEATTLE, WASHINGTON, USA

Acute & Obtuse is husband-and-wife team Heidi and Jose Rodriguez. They enjoy working with recycled materials and exploring multiple printing techniques and processes.

This series of cards was created with the intention of making interactive products that could also be shared. "We wanted to create something that both the giver and the receiver could keep a piece of. We brainstormed and out popped the wishbone and popsicle," explains Heidi.

The cards were silk-screen printed and then perforated so that they can be torn and shared.

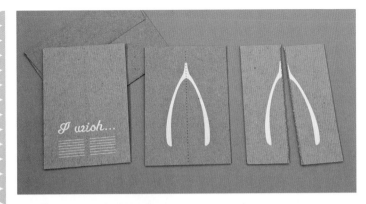

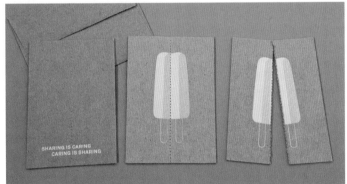

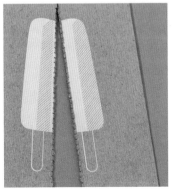

SAKURA SNOW

·····································

AMSTERDAM, THE NETHERLANDS

Suzanne Norris (see also page 151) is an artist and designer. In addition to working on client-based design projects, she creates a line of stationery and paper goods for her Sakura Snow store.

These are her A Wolf and Bear in a Winter Wood greeting cards. "I wanted to make a card design that would exude a sense of peace and equilibrium as an antidote to all the 'festive craziness,'" she explains. "A forest after a heavy snowfall is a magical place—still and tranquil—and I hoped to convey something of this peacefulness in this simple design."

The cards were screen printed in two colors on off-white 220gsm Hahnemühle acid-free card. The designs wrap around both the front and back of the cards.

CABIN + CUB

VANCOUVER,
CANADA

Cabin + Cub is run by Valerie Thai and specializes in art direction, print design, and illustration for nonprofit, socially conscious, and sustainable companies. Thai also designs and prints a stationery line.

The artwork for these notebooks was inspired by vintage children's book illustrations from the 1950s, '60s, and '70s. The illustrations were drawn by hand before being imported into Adobe Illustrator and then burned onto Print Gocco screens. These were then screen printed onto the notebooks using the Gocco printing machine.

CHAPTER 3

LETTERPRESS PRINTING

This form of relief printing was, for many years, the primary method of printing for the masses. During the 1960s, however, it was somewhat superseded by offset lithography printing, save for a small number of specialist printers who continued to champion it.

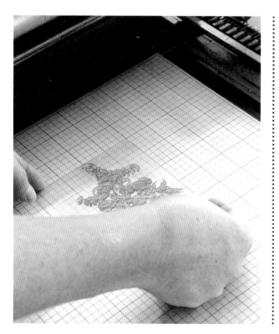

In recent years, though, this unique and much-loved printing method has seen something of a resurgence in popularity as an increasing number of individuals and small companies are setting up shop and producing letterpress materials and goods.

Letterpress printing works by setting type, plates, or blocks in a chase and placing them on a printing bed. They are then inked and a relief print is made on paper or card. How this happens depends on the printing press itself. Presses range from small tabletop models to larger hand-fed models, such as the Chandler & Price or Golding Jobber platen presses, and presses with automatic feeds, such as the Heidelberg Windmill and the motorized Heidelberg KSBA flatbed cylinder press.

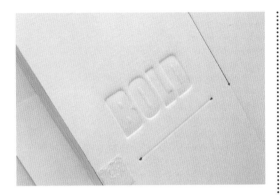

There are a number of ways to create artwork for letterpress printing. Designs can be created by hand using metal or wood type and blocks; lead type is hand set using a composing stick whereas wood type, which tends to be larger, is set in a chase directly on the printing bed. Alternatively, artwork can be created digitally and transferred onto a plate ready for printing. Hand-carved linoleum blocks can also be used on some presses.

LETTERPRESS-PRINTING TOOLS

PRESSES

There are various kinds of printing presses available. For the smaller printer a tabletop model such as the Adana 8x5 and/or a foot-operated platen press such as a Chandler & Price will suffice. For those wanting to produce a larger volume or size of work a Heidelberg Windmill or Vandercook flatbed press will serve better.

METAL TYPE

The individual letters and punctuation marks used in traditional letterpress printing. The main material used is lead.

WOOD TYPE

Wood type can be used together with, or instead of, metal type. It is often used on a large scale and has today become a highly collectable item.

PLATES

Printing plates, or blocks, are created from digital or hand-carved artwork and are typically created using zinc, magnesium, copper, photopolymer, or hand-carved linoleum blocks. A different plate will be created for each pass of color required for a particular design. All can be used on printing presses as long as they are "type high" (as high as the standard height of type, which is $^{15}/_{16}$in [23.3mm]).

INK

Water-soluble rubber-based or soy-based inks are the most popular inks today. Inks can be either used straight from the can or mixed to produce a particular shade or color. Use ink sparingly—one spoonful will go a very long way.

COMPOSING STICK

A metal instrument used to assemble individual pieces of metal type into words, lines, and sentences in preparation for printing.

QUOINS

These are small locks that are used within the printing chase to lock and secure it ready for printing.

KEY

A T-shaped tool used by a printer to tighten up quoins in the printing chase.

ROLLERS

Rollers come in all shapes and sizes and are found on all presses. They take the ink and pass it on to the type or block ready for printing.

EGG PRESS

....

PORTLAND, OREGON,
USA

Egg Press is known for producing inspiring handcrafted letterpress greeting cards and other paper goods. They were one of the pioneers in driving the current resurgence in the popularity of letterpress printing. Egg Press create stationery both for their own lines as well as taking on commissions.

Shown here is a calendar, plus a selection of cards from their Valentine line. All feature hand-drawn illustrations created using brush pens and typeset messages and dates. The cards and calendars were printed either on a Vandercook or Chandler & Price press using Mohawk Superfine Ultra White stock with Van Son Rubber Base inks.

THESE ARE THINGS

COLUMBUS, OHIO,
USA

These Are Things—run by designers Jen Adrion and Omar Noory—were famed initially for their simple, modern, letterpressed world maps. They now produce other paper items, including the *This Year's Adventures* calendar and Fill in the Blank card sets shown here.

"Our design process is super collaborative," Noory explains. "We pass the piece back and forth digitally until we're happy with the final product, then it's off to the print shop."

They work with Allison Chapman of Igloo Letterpress, translating each of their digitally designed pieces to beautiful letterpress-printed items using a Vandercook no.4 proof press and Johnson Peerless platen press with Van Son Rubber Base inks.

SEESAW DESIGNS

••••••••••••••••••••••••••••••••••

SCOTTSDALE, ARIZONA,
USA

This creative studio, run by Angela
Hardison, Raquel Raney, and
Lindsay Tingstrom, works on brand
identity and other graphic design
projects for various clients. They also
produce a letterpress stationery line.

The illustrations for the calendar
and cards were all created by hand
before being scanned and traced
digitally for letterpress printing.

The calendar features both
letterpressed elements and foil
stamping in rose gold. Both were
printed on Crane's Lettra 110lb
(300gsm) stock using Van Son
Rubber Base inks and a Kluge
platen press.

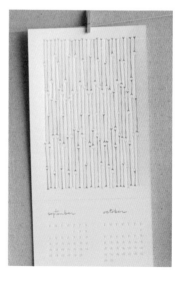

PAPERSHEEP PRESS

NEW YORK, NEW YORK, USA

Papersheep Press is run by Gina Houseman, who combines photography and graphic design to create letterpress stationery.

Houseman's projects often begin with a photograph or drawing that is then inputted into design software and layered with design elements before being made into a polymer plate ready for printing. She uses Crane's Lettra 110lb (300gsm) stock when wanting to make impressions, or Ecru colored paper. "I love the tactile quality of letterpress printing and strive to let the impression shine as much as possible," she explains. "I do this by often utilizing the blind impression technique."

The designs for these notecards were inspired by her surroundings, and each was hand printed.

1CANOE2

COLOMBIA, MISSOURI,
USA

This stationery company is run by
Beth Snyder and Carrie Shryock,
who print their designs using two
antique Chandler & Price letterpresses.
"We try and concentrate on creating
happy, fun work with a focus on
hand-drawn illustrations as opposed
to computer-generated artwork,"
they explain.

These letterpressed recipe and
address cards were printed on
French Paper 140lb cardstock
and come with homemade wooden
boxes. The Thank You cards feature
hand-drawn illustrations created
using pencil, paper, and ink. The cards
were printed on Crane's Lettra 110lb
(300gsm) stock in Fluorescent White
using Van Son Rubber Base inks.

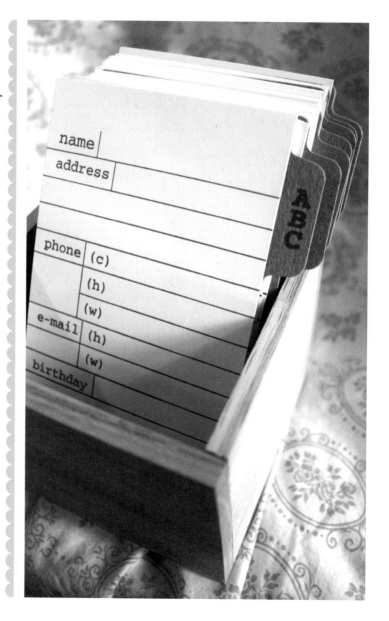

INK+WIT

FAYETTEVILLE,
NEW YORK, USA

INK+WIT is run by designer and illustrator Tara Hogan.

Every year Hogan designs a limited-edition calendar. Her 2010 *Beings and Places* calendar was inspired by trips to Iceland, England, and France. Bold shapes, lines, and vintage colors form the overall aesthetic.

The 2011 *Totem Animals at Play (Pulling the Weeds, Planting Good Seeds)* calendar was inspired both by her research on totem animals and by the yogic phrase "Pull your weeds, plant good seeds." "This phrase captures how we need to weed our mental garden and manifest goodness in order to be truly happy," she explains.

All designs were sketched in pencil and then drawn in Adobe Illustrator before being sent to a letterpress printer and printed on Crane Lettra stock using a Vandercook press.

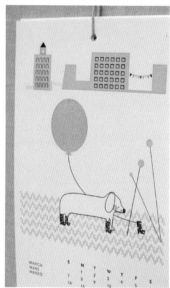

OLD TOM FOOLERY

MINNEAPOLIS,
MINNESOTA, USA

Old Tom Foolery was founded by Lauren Weinblatt and Joel Gryniewski, based on their appreciation for letterpressed goods and their desire to produce a series of cards that expressed their dry sense of humor.

"Our tagline is 'Unsappy, uncrappy greetings and more,' which pretty much sums up our philosophy," explains Weinblatt. "We want to make premium-quality products that are surprisingly witty."

These cards are from the Footnotes collection and were created with the aim of appealing to both men and women. The idea was for them to be witty cards with a clean, simple design.

The cards were printed on a cylinder press by San Francisco–based Dependable Letterpress using Van Son Rubber Base ink and Reich Paper 118lb (320gsm) Savoy Natural White stock.

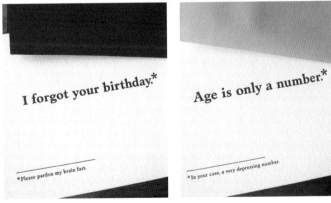

SESAME LETTERPRESS
....
NEW YORK, NEW YORK, USA

Sesame Letterpress is a Brooklyn-based print shop. Their work is influenced by the Victorian era, the period from which their presses date. They are inspired by etchings of nineteenth-century advertising cuts and botanical and animal illustrations. "We share the Victorian fascination with nature, etiquette, taxidermy, and other curiosities," explains founder Breck Hostetter, "and we've found a niche by pairing this vintage imagery with contemporary design and bright colors."

Each of these pieces was printed by hand on their circa 1890 Golding Jobber press. The stock used is either 110lb Strathmore or Manila cardstock.

"We love the idea that, in this digital age, we create something beautiful that passes from our hands to a client's hands, to their friend or loved one's hands, sometimes traveling around the world to do so."

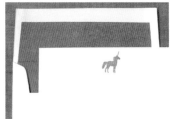

HAPPY BIRTHDAY

I LOVE YOU

HAPPY BIRTHDAY

CHEERS

THE HUNGARY WORKSHOP

BRISBANE, AUSTRALIA

This collaborative letterpress and design project was set up by Simon and Jenna Hipgrave. "What excites us about letterpress is controlling the entire process from concept to execution," says Jenna. "We believe there is a little more to letterpress than a smart typeface with a rich color and a deep impression."

All of their cards have a unique twist. Their Bye Bye Beard is a quirky Valentine's Day card for (real) men. No printed "love" or hearts, but plenty of love in the gesture and heart in the sentiment.

All the cards were printed on a Heidelberg Windmill platen press using hand-mixed Van Son Rubber Base inks and Stephen Smart White 330gsm Australian-made, 50 percent recycled stock.

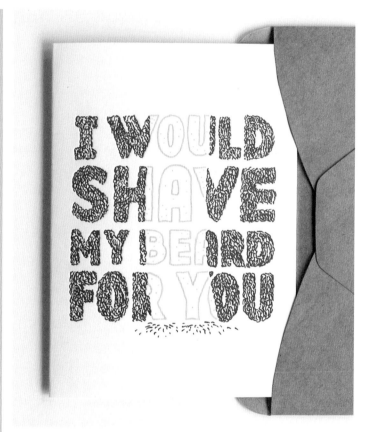

MAY DAY STUDIO

MONTPELIER, VERMONT, USA

May Day Studio is a bookbinding and letterpress studio whose roots are in traditional letterpress techniques, including hand-set metal, wood type, and hand-carved linoleum. They also ensure that they use the most eco-friendly papers and inks in their studio.

Shown here are a number of their greeting cards, all of which were printed using linseed-oil inks on 100 percent cotton Stonehenge paper on the studio's Chandler & Price 8x12 or Vandercook SP15 printing presses.

Also shown is their Square Journal. The decorative cover papers are original May Day designs and were printed on the Vandercook SP15 using hand-carved linoleum blocks and linseed-oil inks.

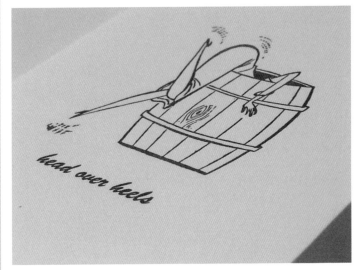

JESSE BREYTENBACH

CAPE TOWN, SOUTH AFRICA

These cards by printmaker Jesse Breytenbach (see also page 108) were designed in collaboration with Cape Town letterpress printers Planet Press.

"With these cards I wanted to design something that I wouldn't be able to carve and print myself so as to exploit the letterpress's ability to reproduce fine lines," Breytenbach explains. Her original pen-and-ink drawings were scanned and vectorized ready for printing on a Heidelberg platen press using Van Son Rubber Base inks.

CODY HALTOM

AUSTIN, TEXAS,
USA

Cody Haltom is a designer working in art direction, visual identity, print and interactive design, and illustration. He is also a founding member of Public School, a creative collective composed of designers, illustrators, and photographers.

This is his business card design for Crimson & Whipped Cream, a bakery and coffee bar located near the University of Oklahoma. Old recipe cards served as rough inspiration and Haltom took the design in a more modern direction. The cards were letterpressed by Vertallee Press on Neenah Classic Crest Natural 130lb cover stock in order to give them a stronger tactile feel. The shape was then created using a custom die-cut. Hand-drawn type for the cards was created by Will Bryant.

W+K STUDIO
GOODNESS

······································

PORTLAND, OREGON,
USA

Goodness is a side project of the
Wieden + Kennedy graphic design
studio (see also page 59).

Their Warm Fuzzies and Embroidered
card series were both letterpress-
printed on Crane's 110lb Pearl White
Lettra stock using a Chandler &
Price 10x15 press. The Warm Fuzzies
collection was inspired by vintage
crochet and knitting patterns,
while the Embroidered series takes
its inspiration from cross-stitch
patterns and charts.

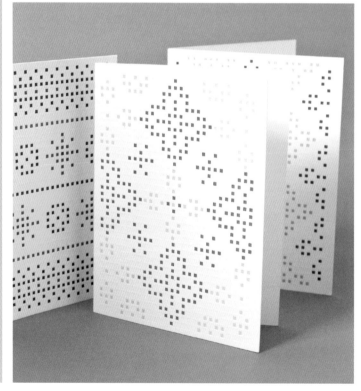

HAMMERPRESS

KANSAS CITY, MISSOURI, USA

This U.S. letterpress and design company runs three Vandercook Universal I presses, a Heidelberg Windmill, and a number of Chandler & Price presses. These greeting cards were created using their substantial letterpress type and ornament collection.

"We have grown to a store of four full-time people and we work collaboratively, bouncing our ideas off one another," explains designer and founder Brady Vest. "Our design process begins with doodles and sketches, then some of our designs are created directly on the press, while others will be created digitally prior to printing."

All of their cards are printed by hand on 30 percent or 100 percent recycled stock.

SPRING OLIVE

·····································

CHICAGO, ILLINOIS,
USA

Spring Olive is owned and run by
graphic designer, illustrator, and
letterpress printer Olivia Samson.
"I've always had a passion for
creating with paper and ink, from
Crayolas and paint-by-numbers to
ballpoint pens and printer ink," she
explains. "Spring Olive bloomed from
this passion, and my mission is to
create cheery, optimistic pieces that
bring a smile and warm the heart."

These greeting cards feature Samson's
hand-drawn illustrations and were
letterpress printed on an antique
Vandercook no.4 proof press using
Van Son Rubber Base inks. Samson
used various paper stocks, including
Crane's Lettra 100 percent fluorescent
white and 100 percent cotton pearl
white, and French Paper's super
thick Whip Cream and Mod-Tone
Taupe paper.

KIRTLAND HOUSE PRESS

CHICAGO, ILLINOIS, USA

Kirtland House Press produces vintage-style greeting cards, note-cards, ready-to-write invitations and announcements, calendars, prints, and gifts—all letterpressed by hand on an antique Vandercook press.

"Kirtland House Press began out of a passion for design, paper, and all things vintage, especially antique Vandercook presses!" explains designer and principal Kerrie Kirtland. "We find delight in mixing ink by hand to create the perfect hue, cranking a freshly kissed design off the press, and feeling the crisp, deep impression on a luxurious cotton sheet."

They digitize vintage printer cuts by scanning them and using Adobe Illustrator and InDesign to create fresh designs. They then make polymer plates of these designs to print with. All products are printed on 100 percent tree-free paper made from recycled fibers.

MORRIS & ESSEX

LIMINGTON, MAINE,
USA

These letterpress-printed greeting
cards are the work of Eliza Jane Curtis
(see also page 57).

"I work with an old-fashioned master
printer near my hometown in Maine,
who prints on an impressive collection
of beautiful antique letterpress
machines," she explains. "I design
with pencil and paper, then have
metal plates engraved for printing."

The cards were printed on French
Paper's Whip Cream 100lb paper
stock, using custom-mixed Patriot
oil-based inks.

JOIE STUDIO

....

PASADENA, CALIFORNIA,
USA

Joie Studio is a boutique artisan design
and letterpress studio producing
custom and ready-made letterpress
products on a Golding Pearl Improved
platen press and a Vandercook no. 4
Old Style precision proof press.

These Cheeky Faces cards were
produced in collaboration with Shop
Toast, a Hawaii-based custom favor
company that is heavily influenced
by J-pop and Asian-style animation.

Also shown here is Joie Studio's 2011
Exotic calendar, which was inspired
by classic Asian design, art, and
textiles. It has been printed on
eco-friendly bamboo paper to
complement the Asian designs.

DWRI LETTERPRESS

PROVIDENCE, RHODE ISLAND, USA

Shown here is a collaborative calendar project between Dan Wood of DWRI Letterpress and Alec Thibodeau. "Tiny Showcase asked Alec to come up with a design for a lunar calendar (now four years running) and decided to print it on a letterpress," explains Wood. "Alec creates amazing ink portraits of people, places, and things, which were the inspiration for this piece."

The calendar was printed using a mix of polymer plates, and hand-set lead type for the blind debossed titling and numbering. To create moons that would glow on the yellow paper, the moon plate was run through the press three times and then overprinted with a glow-in-the-dark varnish. The stock used was Smart Papers Passport Marigold 80lb cover.

WINGED WHEEL

TOKYO, JAPAN

Winged Wheel is a Japanese stationery company specializing in cards, letter sheets, and envelopes, with stores in both Tokyo and Osaka.

Shown here are two of their notecard lines, each of which has been printed on 100 percent pure cotton paper that is exclusively produced at the foot of Mount Fuji. The illustrations for the cards were created by hand and then letterpress printed.

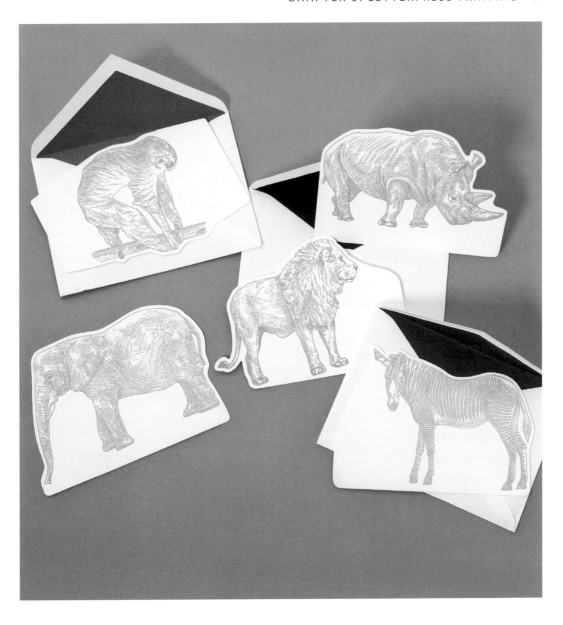

SNAP + TUMBLE

································

TORONTO, CANADA

Snap + Tumble is run by Tanya Roberts out of her home studio in Toronto. Her specialty is printing original, small-sized letterpress goods in short runs. These are her Homemade Journals and Lined Envelopes.

The journals feature letterpress-printed type and were made with a simple binding technique, using a cover-weight cardstock, bond paper, waxed thread, an awl, and bookbinding tape. The envelope liners were created using paper from rolls of vintage wallpaper that Roberts found in thrift stores. The notecards within the envelopes feature handset 12pt Franklin Gothic metal type and were blind printed.

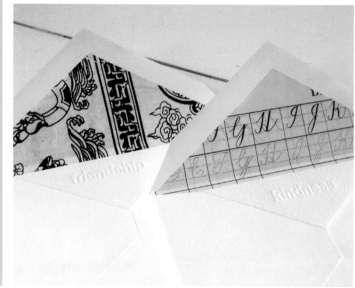

NATASHA
MILESHINA / BUBBO
....
NEW YORK, NEW YORK,
USA

As well as working as a designer, Natasha Mileshina runs a company called bubbo, producing stationery, organizers, and notebooks. Products feature custom-made calligraphy and mostly use recycled materials. "My clients tend to be creative people who appreciate a clean, simple aesthetic and custom-made products, and love to keep their notes and thoughts in the 'old school' way—on paper rather than digitally," she explains. "They often come by looking for a special gift for their friends or significant others."

Shown here is her Valentine's Day gift wrapping set, which was inspired by cross-stitch embroidery, and her Etsy shop identity, which was inspired by old wax seals. Both items were letterpress printed using soy-based inks.

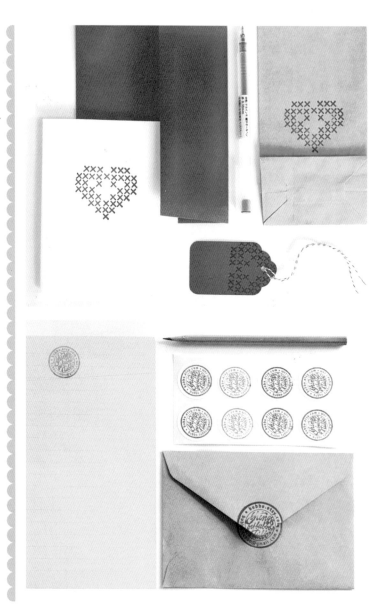

CORRUPIOLA

SÃO JOSÉ, BRAZIL

These letterpressed notebooks were inspired purely by the letters and numbers that Corrupiola (see also pages 46 and 50) bought with a letterpress printing machine. The designs for the covers were all created directly in the letterpress galley.

Once the covers were designed and printed, the signature pages were added and the books were then hand-sewn together. The types used were Grotesca Reforma Preta Estreita and Grotesca Larga Meia Preta and the press was a restored Minerva machine. The cover stock is kraft paper while the signature pages are Pollen Paper from Suzano.

CHAPTER 4

BLOCK PRINTING

Block printing is a form of relief printing that involves carving designs directly into a chosen surface—wood, linoleum, cork, rubber, vinyl, or even foam. It originated in China and India, where it has been used for centuries to print images and patterns onto fabric.

A printer will carve a design into a solid block using tools such as a veiner, awl, chisel, or carving knife. Designs can include text or be purely visual. A predetermined design or pattern can be drawn onto the block prior to carving, or the artist can carve freehand into the block.

Once the design is completed, the surface of the block is inked ready for printing by hand onto the chosen substrate. Alternatively, the block can be mounted so that it is type high (see page 67) and then locked up and printed using a letterpress. Blocks can also be attached to acrylic or wood for better stability and control when stamping.

Since wood can be quite challenging to work with, linoleum is often the preferred choice for creating a block. It is far softer then wood and thus easier to carve. However, it provides enough resistance to allow precise cuts, which results in crisp details, and produces a block that is better for registering multiple stampings. Rubber is less popular, but its softness and flexibility make it very easy to carve.

Water- or oil-based inks can be used, but traditional block printing is done with natural dyes. In order to print a design with multiple colors the printer will need to carve a separate block for each color, making sure they fit together exactly. Most traditional textile prints have three or four colors, so these would have required a block for the background, outline, and fill color of each design. A block that is well cared for can be used repeatedly for different projects.

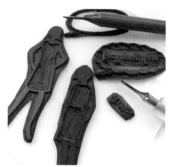

BLOCK-PRINTING TERMS AND TOOLS

BLOCK
Block printers carve patterns and designs in a range of different materials, with linoleum tending to be the most popular.

VEINER
A gouging tool, usually with a U- or a V-shaped cutter. A veiner cuts thick, deep lines or "veins" that create larger relief spaces when the cuts are overlapped. Veiners also produce tapered lines.

CHISEL
This is a carving tool with a small, usually flat, metal tip and a narrow handle. Some chisels have blades; others have gouge tips.

KNIVES
Both fine-edged carving knives and utility knives are used to create intricate detail on blocks. Knives used for block printing can have rounded edges, flat edges, or sharp pointed tips, and are often small, with a cutting edge of an inch or less.

REGISTRATION
Ensuring multiple blocks line up on one print.

AWL
An awl has a mushroom-shaped narrow handle and a sharp, pointed tip that can be used to mark a block without cutting it. Awls are used to create tiny dots in a design.

ROLLER
An important tool for block printing, the roller—also called a brayer—is used to apply ink to the finished block for printing.

BARREN
A barren is used to transfer the ink from the block onto the paper. It has a wide, flat surface and a handle. The artist places the paper against the back of the block and applies pressure while moving the barren in a circular motion.

PALETTE
Used to hold paint or ink while working. Glass sheets are popular for this purpose.

ANNA FEWSTER / LAMPYRIDAE PRESS

BRIGHTON, UK

Anna Fewster runs a small block-printing and letterpress studio on the south coast of England, producing custom-made and ready-made stationery under the imprint Lampyridae Press. Her work is greatly inspired by the decorative interiors and printed designs of the Bloomsbury Group. The designs for these cards were hand cut into linoleum blocks. The blocks were then mounted and printed layer by layer using an Adana 8x5 platen press with linseed oil printing inks from T. N. Lawrence. "I like the painterly quality you can achieve with linoleum blocks; something that is difficult to get with more 'perfect' materials such as photopolymer plates," Fewster says.

The corresponding envelopes were lined by hand with acid-free tissue paper in complementary colors.

KATHARINE WATSON

· ·

WASHINGTON, D.C.,
USA

Katharine Watson specializes in block printing by hand on both fabric and paper using a hand-carved linoleum block.

"After studying printmaking I went to India and did an apprenticeship at a block-printing factory, spending hours sitting cross-legged on the floor learning to chisel tiny wood blocks," she explains. "Now I combine the two techniques—linoleum printing and Indian block printing—to create my own style of work."

The greeting cards and notebooks here feature designs that have been inspired by the patterns found in textiles, architecture, and nature. "I'm drawn to floral and geometric patterns, and I love the way block printing enables you to take a very delicate pattern and make it bright and bold."

TUESDAY DESIGNS

MELBOURNE, AUSTRALIA

Tuesday Designs is a collaboration between sisters Taryn and Elise Eales. "Elise and I have always made little bits and pieces together since we were tiny, so it seemed completely natural to build on our childhood games and make-believe and start Tuesday Design," says Taryn. "We also share a love of birds, which continues to be a thread in our work."

The sisters created these block-printed bird cards by first sketching out some ideas, then transferring them to linoleum and chiseling out the design. The blocks were then blind embossed. "I soaked a heavy art paper and blind embossed the image on the block under heavy pressure and blankets using an etching press," Taryn explains. The stock used was Hahnemühle 380gsm, a heavy German etching paper.

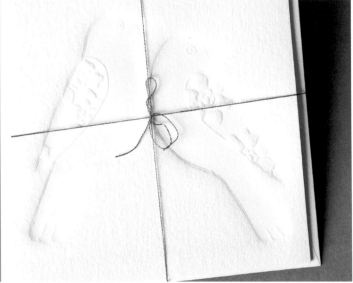

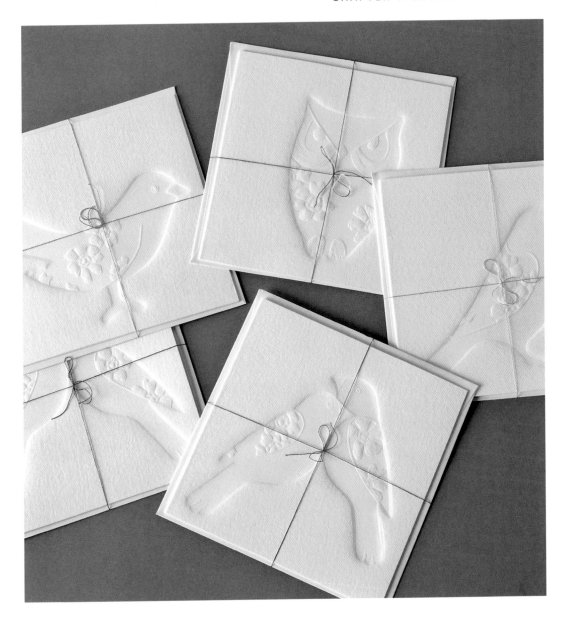

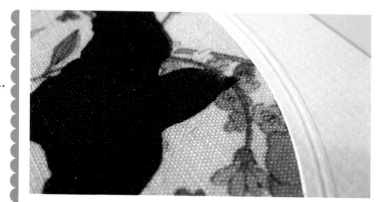

HAVE & HOLD DESIGN
∙∙∙∙∙∙∙∙∙∙∙∙∙∙∙∙∙∙∙∙∙∙∙∙∙∙∙∙∙
TORONTO, CANADA

Have & Hold Design was founded and is run by Samantha Dubeau (see also page 175). "My business began with one simple idea: life should be celebrated," she explains. "When holidays and momentous occasions occur it's an opportunity to celebrate. My pieces honor this and are meant to be cherished and held on to."

Shown here is her Treasures of Yesterday collection of cards. Each one was block printed by hand. "I designed this line of cards for anyone who appreciates the antique aesthetic," Dubeau says. She began by making digital mock-ups of her designs before carving them into rubber blocks. The designs were then printed onto found vintage fabrics and, finally, glued inside the framed cards. "As with many of my other works, I wanted something that incorporated the sense of touch," Dubeau adds.

FIELD GUIDE DESIGN

KINGSTON, NEW YORK, USA

Field Guide Design is run by artist and designer Darbie Nowatka from her home in upstate New York. This is a sample of her hand-printed wrapping paper. "I had picked up some old Indian hand-carved wooden printing blocks at a yard sale because I loved the patterns and wanted to make something beautiful with them," she explains. "I took them home where I made hundreds of individual prints with black printing ink on plain white paper before scanning the best of the bunch into Photoshop to create my patterns."

Nowatka had a large silk screen made to print the final pieces with opaque water-based fluorescent inks on 100 percent recycled brown paper. "I was able to make something that had the beauty and imperfections of hand printing with a much higher level of consistency than I would have been able to achieve using the blocks as they were originally intended."

PINE STREET MAKERY
....
NASHVILLE, TENNESSEE, USA

Pine Street Makery is run by Jessica Maloan, a native Tennessean. Following an internship at letterpress print shop Hatch Show Print, where she learned how to incorporate her linocut illustrations with wood and metal type, Maloan started selling her linocut greeting cards and prints on Etsy and in small stores.

Shown here are her Valentine Teepee cards, Microscope card, and Travel Camper card. The artwork for each started life as a sketch, before Maloan carved it into a linoleum block ready for printing. Each was printed on Paper Source A2 cardstock.

RUBY VICTORIA LETTERPRESS & PRINTMAKING

HOBART, AUSTRALIA

Ruby Victoria is run by Narelle Badalassi, who specializes in linocut and letterpress printing. Her designs are drawn by hand, then carved out of linoleum blocks or hand set using letterpress type before being printed on an Adana 8x5 tabletop press.

"I make prints because I enjoy the process. I find carving an image in lino very calming and I can get lost in the process for hours. The only other thing I like as much as carving is seeing the first print pulled from the block."

For her Merry Christmas notecards and gift tags, Badalassi wanted to create something clean and classic. The heart design was hand-carved and the cards and tags created using 36-point Bodoni bold lead type.

JESSE BREYTENBACH

CAPE TOWN, SOUTH AFRICA

Jesse Breytenbach (see also page 80) uses carved linoleum blocks to produce both fabrics and papers, and prints on her kitchen table using a rolling pin and sometimes an old bookbinding press.

"I try to work as simply as possible, producing small runs at a time," she explains. "My primary aim is not to waste; I try to use every scrap of fabric or paper. For instance, my gift tags are printed on leftover pieces from my greeting cards."

The illustrations for these gift tags were first drawn in pencil, then carved into a linoleum block ready for printing using Van Son Rubber Base inks. The illustration for the block-printed fabric portfolio case was first hand drawn, scanned, and then finalized digitally. This too was carved into a linoleum block, then printed using water-based inks on leftover scraps of fabric.

CHAPTER 5

DIGITAL ILLUSTRATION

Digital technology has transformed the way designers and illustrators create artwork. Most creatives tend to work using Adobe Illustrator or Photoshop, as these programs are the most comprehensive on offer, with seemingly endless features and options, while InDesign can be used for multipage designs.

Artwork can be created in a variety of ways—the most popular is to draw freehand or to draw using vector graphics. The latter involves using geometrical shapes, lines, and curves to create images and patterns. Vector graphics are created using mathematical formulae, as opposed to pixels, which means that any given image can be scaled to any size and detail without pixelating, and that you can move, rotate, and align objects easily to achieve your desired look. However, if you require more freedom, or a more hand-drawn aesthetic, you can use a mouse or graphics tablet. These digitally mimic traditional hand-drawn methods. In addition to Adobe Illustrator and Photoshop, programs such as Studio Artist contain freehand drawing–based tools that allow artists to replicate pastel, watercolor, or chalk drawings. Digital technology is also used to add color or manipulate hand-drawn imagery.

DIGITAL ILLUSTRATION TERMS AND TOOLS

ILLUSTRATOR
A vector-based drawing program popular with digital illustrators for images and layouts.

PHOTOSHOP
A graphics-editing program used to manipulate photographs and imagery and assemble layouts.

INDESIGN
Software used for creating page layouts.

STUDIO ARTIST
A painting and graphics application with a huge range of brushes.

GRAPHICS TABLET
This allows freehand drawing digitally, using a graphics tablet pen and, in some cases, your finger.

DIGITAL PRINTING
Photo printers that use archival inks print well and on many types of paper, even up to thick chipboard stock. Since they use up to eight different inks, good color range and increased vibrancy can easily be achieved.

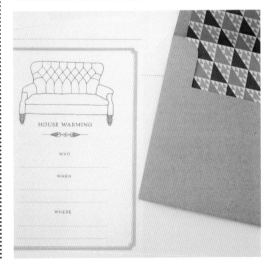

BRIE HARRISON

SUFFOLK, UK

This is textile designer and illustrator Brie Harrison's Berry Field Collection for New York–based stationers Galison. Inspired by gardens and nature in general, her repeated pattern format is reminiscent of fabric and textile design.

Harrison starts by sketching out her ideas with a fine liner. She then scans her drawings and continues to work on them in Adobe Photoshop, experimenting with colors, details, and patterns to create her final designs. She uses a Wacom pen and tablet and various digital brushes.

(Photos courtesy of Galison)

DARLING CLEMENTINE

OSLO, NORWAY

Darling Clementine is a Norwegian stationery company run by designers Tonje Holand and Ingrid Reithaug. As well as creating designs for their own stationery line, they work on commissions.

Shown here is their Folk and Flora line of cards, the illustrations for which were drawn in Adobe Illustrator. "This line was inspired by the aesthetics of our Scandinavian upbringing," Reithaug explains. "We wanted to create a series of cards that had a cozy atmosphere and depicted life here."

The cards were digitally printed on 300gsm paper.

ALYSSA NASSNER

·······································

PHILADELPHIA,
PENNSYLVANIA, USA

Alyssa Nassner works as an illustrator and, together with screen printer and graphic designer Christopher Muccioli, also runs Small Talk Studio. The studio creates paper goods and simple home accessories, including screen prints, art prints, card sets, notebooks, notepads, and throw pillows.

As an illustrator, Nassner has worked with clients such as Chronicle Books and DwellStudio, as well as *UPPERCASE* and *Canadian Family* magazines. Some of her digital illustrations are shown on these pieces. The artwork for the Garden To Do pad was inspired by her houseplant collection. This, and the artwork for the Pencil notebook and Christmas card set, was created using Adobe Illustrator.

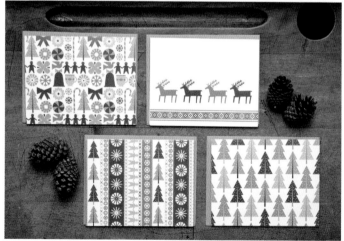

GIGI GALLERY

SAN FRANCISCO,
CALIFORNIA, USA

Gigi Gallery is a paper goods, design, and illustration store run by designer Gabriela Silva. Silva specializes in pattern and typography, and she is inspired by different cultures and by the handmade.

Silva's Monogram letter set and Native blue and red cards were inspired by Navajo culture and pattern; the Gracias card reflects her interest in typography, and the Weave cards display her love of color and pattern.

The designs were all created using pen and ink before being scanned and finished in Photoshop and Illustrator.

Each card was printed on French Paper's 140lb Speckletone in Starch White and comes with a Speckletone kraft envelope. Both of these are postconsumer, recycled materials.

WIT & WHISTLE

CARY, NORTH CAROLINA, USA

Wit & Whistle is run by designer and maker Amanda Rae Wright, who produces illustrated greeting cards and paper goods. "I illustrate all my products—sometimes by hand and sometimes digitally," she explains. "It is very important to me that only the products I love and am proud of bear the Wit & Whistle name."

The digital imagery for these cards and notebooks was created in Adobe Illustrator using a Wacom tablet. Each item was digitally printed on recycled speckled paper or brown kraft cardstock that was milled using clean, renewable hydroelectric energy.

Wright prints her cards herself, which gives her complete control over the production process. She uses archival-quality, pigment-based inks that resist fading and are very water resistant.

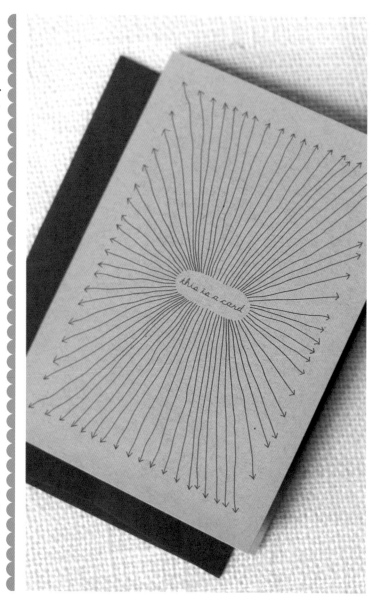

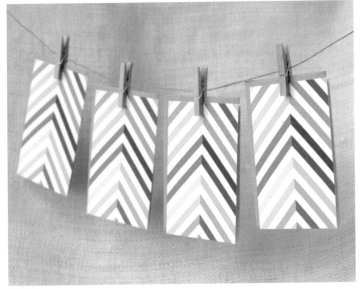

CRICICIS DESIGN

BOSTON,
MASSACHUSETTS, USA

This paper goods and illustration
company is run by Leah Ammerman.
Her work has a minimal aesthetic,
with an emphasis on clean, bright
digital illustrations. "Many of my
illustrations are of actual objects that
you might find in my workspace, like
cats or airport chairs," she explains.

Ammerman mostly uses Adobe
Illustrator to create the drawings
for her notecards and notebooks,
although some illustrations begin life
as hand-drawn sketches. All of the
items shown here were printed on
Neenah Paper cardstock.

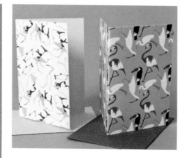

THE INDIGO BUNTING
....
NEW YORK, NEW YORK,
USA

The Indigo Bunting is run by Erin Jang who creates unique, one-of-a-kind designs with modern illustrations and details. This is one of her calendar designs.

"I wanted to make something that I would want to hang in my home and something I could share with friends and family," she explains. "I aimed for a design that would feel timeless yet modern and brainstormed different icons that could work for each month. I then illustrated each month accordingly."

The clean, bold illustrations were created digitally and then type was added in Merriam and Futura. The calendar was four-color printed with a matte finish.

NANCY & BETTY STUDIO
....
CANTERBURY, UK

Nancy & Betty Studio is run by husband-and-wife team Andy and Hannah Bidmead. "Our designs are whimsical with bright colors and have a 'pretty tomboy,' retro feel to them," Hannah explains. "We like putting a bit of British in there too, as well as a good pun. Photography is a key part of our designs. They are then manipulated in Photoshop and applied to a product or design."

All artwork for the goods they produce is created digitally. All cards are printed on 300gsm white matte Forest Stewardship Council (FSC)–certified card using vegetable-based inks. The wrapping paper is printed on 90gsm FSC-certified recycled matte paper and postcards are printed on 280gsm matte cardstock—both also using vegetable-based inks.

ONE FINE DAE
....
SEATTLE, WASHINGTON, USA

One Fine Dae (see also page 177) is run by Linda-Thuan Pham, a designer, crafter, photographer, and traveler. "Paper is my main medium. Sometimes, I will also throw in thread or fabric to complement what I'm doing with the paper," she says, "but paper comes first."

Her Bon Voyage postcards were inspired by primary colors and her love of traveling. "I first sketched the designs on the computer, then printed them on cardstock," explains Pham. "I used an X-Acto knife to carefully hand cut the shapes of each design, then placed these cutout templates on brown paper chipboard and painted over them with acrylic paint. The process is a bit cumbersome, but it allows each card to have its own, unique, and subtle differences. These postcards have a very nostalgic quality, and they remind me of summers when I was young."

PRESENT & CORRECT

LONDON, UK

"We love anything stationery/office-based so the Present & Correct brand is an extension of that—an excuse to hunt for new and vintage wares as well as design our own products," explains Neal Whittington of Present & Correct. "Inspiration comes from old ephemera we have collected—anything to do with education, midcentury children's books and pamphlets, mail and stamp-based articles."

The illustrations, geometric patterns, and designs for their Geometry Set notebooks and Crown card were created using Adobe Illustrator. The Crown card can be folded up and worn as a crown.

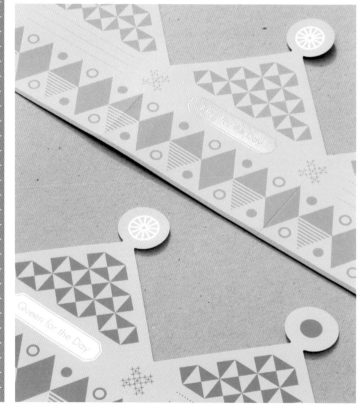

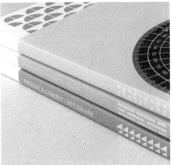

SMOCK PAPER

SYRACUSE, NEW YORK,
USA

Smock Paper is a stationery and
letterpress company that prints on
sustainable bamboo and 100 percent
postconsumer recycled papers. It is
a member of Green America's Green
Business Network and also takes part
in a number of other green initiatives.
All printing is entirely wind powered.

This selection of wrapping paper,
printed with digital illustrations
designed by Amy Graham Stigler,
was inspired by a combination
of things—vintage fabrics, 1940s
poster art, vintage sheet music,
Henri Matisse, and Milton Avery.

MERRY DAY

BANGKOK, THAILAND

Merry Day is run by freelance designer and illustrator Pavinee Sripaisal. "I produce cute and whimsical illustrated paper goods," she says. "All items originate from my daily doodles, which are scanned and digitally finished using Adobe Illustrator. I print the goods myself using my own inkjet printer. That way I can control the color quality and more easily experiment with different kinds of paper."

This is Sripaisal's Simplicity Flower Greeting card set. "I want to make a set of flower greeting cards that look fresh and bright yet modern and cute at the same time," she explains. "Something that makes one feel good just looking at it."

FLOWERMILL

CAPE TOWN,
SOUTH AFRICA

This stationery company is run by its founders Robyn van der Toorn, Deborah Inkson, and Ingrid Blohm. "We saw a gap in the market for a locally designed and produced stationery line and decided to take the plunge," van der Toorn explains. "Now Flowermill has become something of a design escape for us."

These wrapping paper samples feature bold shapes and patterns, all created digitally, inspired by tumbleweed, wild flowers, and gypsy damask. "The design challenge was to create continuous patterns that would work on a cylinder, as we printed sheets flexographically," she adds. "Flexographic printing creates a stamp so the outlines are not sharp but appear a bit wobbly, which adds to the feel of the paper." Each was printed on Sappi Platinum 85gsm.

REDSTAR INK

SAN DIEGO, CALIFORNIA,
USA

REDSTAR ink is a handmade paper goods company started by designer Marcie Hicks. The design emphasis is on a clean aesthetic and personal organization, producing products that are simple, bold, and modern. "In an age of computers and hand-held technology, we celebrate the tactile quality of paper," explains Hicks. "There is something satisfying about checking items off a list or opening a piece of mail from a friend."

Featured here are Hicks's Honey Do, Left Brain/Right Brain, and Bills notebooks, and her *One* calendar, all of which combine clean digital typography with the company's handmade aesthetic. All were printed and produced using 100 percent recycled paper stock and chipboard covers.

SCOUT BOOKS

PORTLAND, OREGON,
USA

Scout Books is a publishing platform that allows users to create custom notebooks and book projects. Researching new ideas back in 2009, Pinball Publishing had spotted a gap in the market for a notebook that their customers could design themselves.

Each book is offset printed using one or two spot colors on uncoated and recycled board and paper stock. All the typography and illustrations are created digitally, and all the inks used are made from plant oils such as soy, canola, safflower, and corn.

"The scout book is a customizable print format that has an endless number of uses," explains designer Nicole Lavelle. "It has become much more than a notebook as our clients devise innovative ways to use it."

JHILL DESIGN

BOSTON,
MASSACHUSETTS, USA

This graphic design studio is owned by Jennifer Hill. She creates patterned prints based on imaginary vacations that she then uses to create greeting cards and calendars. "Each initial pattern I create is initiated by a simple detail—for example, tiled mosaics in Isfahan," she explains. "I then research a city for more inspiration, with the aim of capturing the essence of a place within my illustrations."

Hill first sketches out ideas before moving to the computer, where she designs her final patterns using Adobe Illustrator.

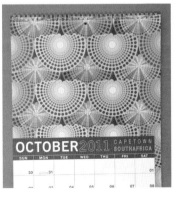

LOX+SAVVY

SYDNEY, AUSTRALIA

Lox+Savvy is a Sydney-based stationery and paper goods maker. Founded by Lisa Loxley, the company produces a whole array of items, including wrapping paper, notecards, pencil blocks, paper pockets, and gift tags.

"After running my own design studio and freelancing for years I had a yearning to start up my own stationery business," Loxley explains. "While creating scribbles and designs over a couple of years of some ideas I had, Lox+Savvy was conceived."

With a love for bold, pastel, and fluorescent colors, much of the Lox+Savvy line has a strong, colorful, graphic look. Each product was printed digitally on recycled or carbon-neutral paper, and all envelopes were folded, glued, and finished by hand.

THEREZA ROWE

LONDON, UK

Illustrator and graphic designer
Thereza Rowe (see also page 50)
uses a variety of media to create her
illustrations—from Adobe Illustrator
to collage to papercuts and ink.

The illustrations on Rowe's Gatos
card are of her own cats. The
illustrations were created using ink
on paper and were then imported
into Adobe Illustrator to be finished
and rendered. "Black ink and paper
is how my ideas usually come about,"
she says. "It's always a starting point.
Then I scan images and play with
them in Photoshop."

The Hello cards were created using
illustrations and cutouts from found
paper. The type on the postcards was
also hand drawn and edited in both
Adobe Photoshop and Illustrator.

CHAPTER 6

CALLIGRAPHY

Calligraphy is an ancient form of handwriting and lettering that has existed for thousands of years. It is still popular today—both in its traditional forms and in more modern, adapted styles, as contemporary practitioners experiment and innovate with those long-established traditions.

Different calligraphic styles are described as "hands," and these hands are categorized according to the type of pen or nib used to create them. Broad-edge pen alphabets, for instance, include hands such as Foundational, Unical, Gothic, Versals, Neuland, and Bone, to name a few. Pointed-pen alphabets include Copperplate and Spencerian, as well as a number of contemporary pointed-pen styles. Brush alphabets use scripts created with flat and pointed brushes.

In addition to the traditional pens and nibs, some practitioners work with felt or ballpoint pens to create a more modern aesthetic. Nevertheless, they still tend to draw inspiration from the traditional hands. The choice of stock to write on is an important and highly personal one. Calligraphers either experiment with different varieties to achieve a range of results or settle on a preferred favorite.

CALLIGRAPHY TOOLS

PENS

A calligrapher can choose between traditional nib pens, which are dipped in inks; or pens that have built-in ink cartridges.

DIP PENHOLDERS

Used to hold calligraphy and drawing nibs.

NIBS

Nibs are attached to penholders and come in a range of shapes, including round hand, tape, italic, copperplate, poster, ornamental and drawing, and mapping.

INKS

Water- or acrylic-based inks are used. Chinese sumi inks are the most popular.

PAPER

This can be anything from simple photocopier paper to heavier stock. Layout paper is good to have on hand for tracing purposes.

SLOPING BOARD

It is advisable to work on a sloping board (tilted at an angle) when writing calligraphy.

PAPER & TYPE

LOS ANGELES,
CALIFORNIA, USA

Paper & type is run by graphic designer Victoria Vu (see also pages 24 and 168). She works with clients to create one-of-a-kind designs as well as a stationery line consisting of greeting cards and notebooks. Inspired by florals, calligraphy, and simple typography, Vu likes to make products that encourage correspondence for both everyday and significant occasions.

Her Thanks So Much card combines calligraphy with hand-drawn illustrations, while her How Are You card takes advantage of the loopy nature of calligraphy. The calligraphy for both cards was done using India ink and a medium-sized writing nib.

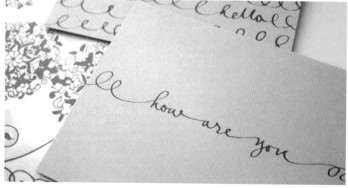

PAPERFINGER

BROOKLYN, NEW YORK, USA

Bryn Chernoff of Paperfinger specializes in modern calligraphy, unique hand lettering, and illustration to produce anything from invitations to logos and branding, rubber stamps, tattoos, and stationery. Chernoff always works with a pen on paper, employing traditional calligraphy tools such as nibs and dip pens for different effects. She then scans her work for reproduction as needed.

Shown here are her Choose Your Greeting holiday card and Thank You card, alongside some of her ready-made and customized stamp sets.

K IS FOR CALLIGRAPHY

MORAGA, CALIFORNIA, USA

Designer and calligrapher Katy Jamison runs this calligraphy and handmade craft business, producing greeting cards, gift tags, envelope seals, and other calligraphic art objects. She creates her unique lettering using Brause 361 Steno pointed nibs with vintage nib-holders, together with either black Moon Palace sumi ink, acrylic ink, or Winsor and Newton gouache.

Jamison has developed nineteen different lettering styles, and the items shown here feature lettering derived from two of these—her Bend it like Bickham and Con Tiempo.

MEANT TO BE CALLIGRAPHY AND FIG 2 DESIGN

....

WASHINGTON, D.C. / BETHESDA, MARYLAND, USA

This series of cards is the result of a collaboration between Michele Hatty Fritz of Meant To Be Calligraphy and stationery designer Claudia Smith of Fig 2 Design. The cards feature a combination of type set in Chalet Comprime and Fritz's hand-drawn calligraphy.

"Claudia asked me to use my signature style to put my own spin on three phrases: Thanks for Bringing Sexy Back, Get Your Groove On, and You Rock My World," explains Fritz. "I looked at each phrase separately and then tried to make each flow together in a cohesive way."

Fritz used a Brause EF 66 nib to create the lettering. The cards were then letterpress printed using fluorescent inks on 100 percent Crane's Lettra Fluorescent White cardstock.

FAWNSBERG

LYNDONVILLE,
VERMONT, USA

Fawnsberg is the stationery side of the already established modern, whimsical calligraphy company, Primele. It is run by sisters Patricia and Rachel Mumau. "We love letter writing and have devoted the launch of Fawnsberg to letter sheets," explains Patricia. "Our vision is that others will use our papers to write to loved ones without occasion—merely to say hello, reflect on the day, perhaps express thoughts that they've had. We hope to encourage people to celebrate the 'everyday.'"

Their I Often Think of You and For You I Pine cards both feature contemporary calligraphy. The lettering for the Often card was created using pointed pen, while the For You I Pine lettering was created using pencil before being scanned and redrawn using a graphics tablet.

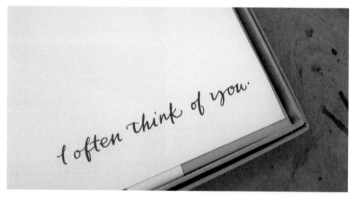

THE LEFT HANDED CALLIGRAPHER

DALLAS, TEXAS, USA

The Left Handed Calligrapher is Nicole Black. Almost everything she makes is created by hand using ink on paper, and she specializes in pointed-pen calligraphy.

These two greeting cards combine calligraphy with Black's hand-drawn illustrations. The holiday card was created using sumi ink and a Gillott 303 nib; it was printed on Strathmore Writing 80lb Cover Bristol paper. The design for the Thank You card was made using Prismacolor watercolor pencils and was printed on the same paper.

PLURABELLE CALLIGRAPHY

LOS ANGELES,
CALIFORNIA, USA

Plurabelle Calligraphy is run by
Molly Suber Thorpe. Thorpe uses
a number of vintage calligraphic
styles and modern styles of her own
creation. Many of her letterforms are
based on traditional styles—such
as Copperplate and Spencerian—but
these are then combined with modern
layouts and color palettes to create
a contemporary feel.

Thorpe created the lettering for
these stamps using a pointed pen
with black ink on white paper.
This was then scanned and cleaned
up in Photoshop.

The gift tags feature Thorpe's own
lettering creation, Tigerlily, a
Copperplate-inspired contemporary
alphabet, written using a Brause
66EF pointed steel nib.

(Photography by Lilian Day)

CHAPTER 7

PAPERCUTTING

The art of papercutting and paper crafting as a whole has seen a considerable rise in popularity in recent years, but it has been in existence since as far back as the sixth century.

Papercutting is an ancient form of folk art and its history lies in China, where the art is known as *jian zhi*. Long traditions in papercutting exist in other countries too, including *kirie* in Japan, *sanjhi* in India, and the famous *papel picados* in Mexico.

Creatives working in this medium use a number of different techniques. Some cut straight into a chosen paper, essentially drawing with their cutting tool. Others first sketch or print out their design and then cut around its marked-out lines. Tools may include scissors, scalpels, X-Acto knives, or other forms of blade.

Most papercutters tend to start each new piece by cutting out the most difficult parts first, before moving on to the rest of the artwork. Curved areas are best cut with a swift, confident movement; angular areas with shorter stabbing motions. Another good tip is to cut toward yourself and rotate the artwork on a table to make that possible. This is not practical when working on large pieces but works well for smaller pieces.

Once a papercut is complete it is advisable to mount it. This can be as simple as mounting it onto another piece of paper, either plain or colored, or onto a heavier stock. In cases where a design has been cut directly into a greeting card or notebook cover, a sheet of paper can be inserted behind the cut to add depth and color. Laser cutting is also an option if an original papercut design is to be produced in large numbers.

PAPERCUTTING TOOLS

PAPER

It is best to use a light- to medium-weight paper when cutting more intricate, detailed designs, but for simpler designs a heavier stock can be used. As a general rule, try not to use a highly textured stock as the fibers in the paper will drag when you cut it.

X-ACTO KNIFE

A brand of scalpel popular among papercutters.

SCALPEL

Also known as a lancet, a scalpel is a sharp, steel-bladed instrument used for cutting. Scalpels are either disposable or have replaceable blades.

CRAFT MAT

Otherwise known as a self-healing mat, this is important as it protects both the work surface and your blade and provides a solid base on which to work.

ASHLEY PAHL DESIGN

NAPERVILLE, ILLINOIS,
USA

Crafter and maker Ashley Pahl used papercutting to create this selection of cards. "I love creating simple designs in clean silhouettes," she explains. "Patterns from nature, such as woodgrain, topography, or even animal forms are most common in my line, often with a little lace or ruffle to bring back that element of celebration. I prefer to work with kraft paper, kraft cardstock, and twine, since they have a very natural look, and are usually made from recycled materials."

Pahl first sketches out her designs in pencil before using an X-Acto blade to cut along her penciled lines. She then uses a vinyl eraser to get rid of any lingering pencil marks.

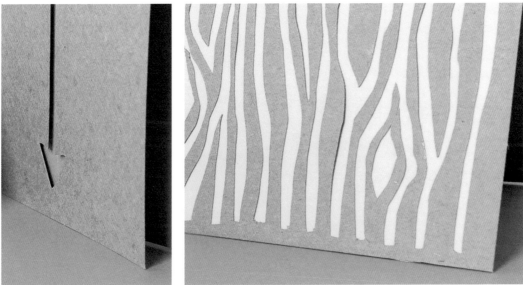

RUBY WREN DESIGNS

KETTERING, UK

This small business is based in a small town in Northamptonshire. "We work to create products as greenly and as ethically as possible, while aiming to be stylish and unique," explains founder Hayley Mitchell. "Our main line consists of designs hand cut into Ellie Poo paper, which is made from 100 percent postconsumer waste and elephant poo. I love working with this stock—the natural texture gives a beautiful rustic effect and the off-white color of the recycled paper looks stunning in contrast to the bright colors that show through the hand-cut shapes on our cards."

These greeting cards were inspired by birds, animals, wildlife, and nature in general. Each was hand cut using a scalpel and colored paper was then glued to the inside.

HELLO JENUINE
....

DUNDEE, UK

Illustrator Jen Collins of Hello Jenuine (see also page 56) works mainly in pencil, ink, and watercolors. Shown here is her papercut Thank You card.

"I wanted to try a new tool for making a card design. Since I print a lot of my work, I wanted to try my hand at laser cutting to create a simple but effective design," she explains. "After creating the hand-drawn lettering design, the card was then laser cut at my local print studio, where visitors are allowed to use the machine themselves to work on personal projects. Once the design was cut, a layer of paper was applied inside the card, adding color and emphasizing the papercut design."

The card was created using 100 percent recycled card and Murano paper.

SAKURA SNOW

AMSTERDAM, THE NETHERLANDS

Shown here are a series of papercut cards designed by Suzanne Norris of Sakura Snow (see also page 62).

Created as seasonal greeting cards, these were inspired by Japanese kirigami as well as other folk-art papercutting traditions. "I began by doodling ideas in my sketchbook, then made a couple of prototypes to figure out sizing, positioning, and color combinations," Norris explains. "Once these initial decisions were made, and the card and paper were selected and purchased, I began the process of cutting and constructing the cards."

Each card was made from 220gsm card from Rössler Papier's Paperado line.

HEART ZEENA

·····································

LONDON, UK

These papercut letter cards are by Zeena Shah of heart zeena (see also page 48). "I wanted to create something really special, personal, and unique using papercutting," she says. "I first created a series of drawings, chose one to work from, then cut into it. Things often change as I cut—what I really love about papercutting is that no two items are ever the same."

Shah then likes to finish her cards with extra details; these ones have stitched spines.

SKINNY LAMINX

CAPE TOWN,
SOUTH AFRICA

Heather Moore is the textile-designing
creative behind Skinny laMinx, a
company that produces screen-printed
pillows, dishcloths, and aprons, as well
as a line of fabrics.

Moore also creates a number of
paper items, examples of which are
these papercut gift tags and card.
These were created by first drawing
the bird images onto white paper,
taping them to double-sided card,
and then cutting out the images
using an NT cutter blade.

The images were scanned and traced
in Adobe Illustrator. Moore then gave
the digital files to a laser cutter who
could produce the cards and tags in
larger numbers.

The stock used is a firm brown card
known as Cape Liner.

MRYEN

LEEDS, UK

Designer and papercutter Jonathan Chapman, otherwise known as MrYen, creates both personal and commissioned works, from artworks to notebooks to cards. This is a selection of some of his hand-cut paper notebooks. The vintage map notebooks feature his typography and are made from found vintage maps. Each was hand bound.

The geometric series of notebooks, also hand bound, were cut with a scalpel. Each page was also rounded using a corner-cutting tool.

The notes series, again, features Chapman's hand-cut typography, set in Lobster with the braces in Baskerville.

Each of the four notepads features either crossed, lined, dotted, or gridded paper.

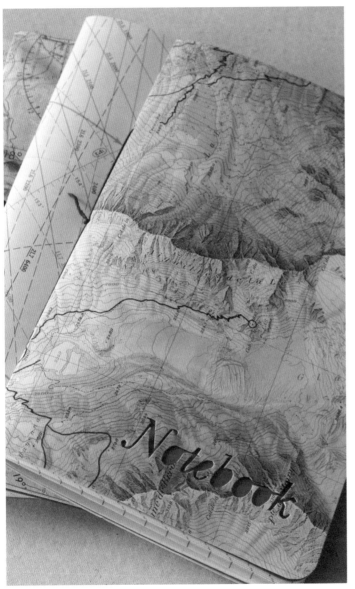

PAINTED FISH STUDIO

MINNEAPOLIS,
MINNESOTA, USA

Painted Fish Studio is run by Jen Shaffer, who makes stationery goods and gifts. These are some of her punched cards and notebooks.

Each card is designed digitally before a template is printed out and then used for guiding the punching. Shaffer uses a Japanese bookbinding drill to create the holes that make up the letters and words on both cards and notebooks.

"I would like to think that people who buy my paper goods are those who value aspects of a slower way of life: instead of texting or sending an e-mail, they prefer to send a letter," she says. "Rather than uploading all their photos online, they're having them printed and stored in a handmade photo album. They're writing their thoughts in a journal, not in a blog."

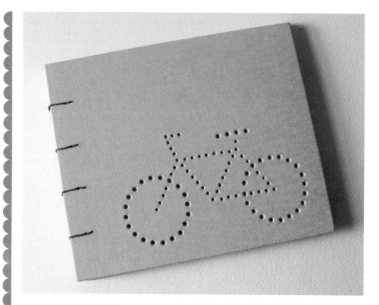

MADE BY JULENE

SUSSEX, UK

Made by Julene is papercutting artist Julene Harrison's company. She makes handmade papercuts to order—from invitations to cards to letterheads—in her distinctive illustrative and typographic style.

"Originally a constructed textile designer, I have now started papercutting. It's a medium I have quickly grown to love," she explains. "I get a lot of pleasure turning a single sheet of paper into something people seem to enjoy."

Harrison starts her designs in rough in Adobe Photoshop, working out a layout and sketching details of more specific elements. She then prints out her rough design ready for the cutting process, for which she uses a scalpel.

CHAPTER 8

COLLAGE / 3-D / SEWN

Creating artwork for stationery goods using mixed media is becoming increasingly widespread. From collage to origami to stitching and sewing, there are many ways to bring greeting cards, journals, or other stationery items to life.

Collage in all its forms—from paper and card only, to paper, beads, stamps, and more—is a great way to create a journal or greeting card with a handmade aesthetic. Using found ephemera to create collage has the additional benefit of using materials that would otherwise be discarded.

Origami is the traditional Japanese art of paper folding. Steeped in history, it remains popular and is increasingly used by crafters and designers. Using it in its flatter form—modular origami—allows stationery designers to add a 3-D element to a piece while keeping it practical and usable.

Sewing or stitching imagery, lettering, or patterns directly onto paper or card is often used to distinguish an otherwise simple design, and offers opportunities for experimentation. Some designers sew or stitch freehand, while others draw out a design and follow it; some even punch holes in the paper or card through which to pass their thread.

The best thread is embroidery floss, which is of good quality, comes in a huge variety of colors, and is strong enough to withstand being pulled through cardstock. A sewing machine can also be used to create patterns or imagery or to secure other materials to a card or journal cover.

COLLAGE / 3-D / SEWN TOOLS

PAPER AND CARD
Paper choice is dependent on the type of project. It can be anything from lightweight tissue to heavy cardstock.

FABRIC
As with paper, the use and choice of fabric is dependent on the project.

NEEDLES
Needles must be sharp enough to be able to push through whatever stock is being used.

PUNCHES
Not just hole punches but also hearts, flowers, larger circles, and more—punches are crafters' essential tools.

THREAD
Embroidery floss is the most popular thread due to its quality and versatility.

GLUE
Crafters tend to work with water-based PVA glue, as it is nontoxic, dries clear, and works with many different materials.

MOD PODGE
An all-in-one glue, sealer, and finisher beloved by crafters.

DOUBLE-SIDED TAPE
Popular with crafters as it is easy, quick, and secure.

PAPER PATH

WALLA WALLA,
WASHINGTON, USA

Rachel Smith works under the name
of Paper Path, creating unique
stationery goods using paper, string,
colored thread, 3-D objects, and a
typewriter. Her cards are made out
of heavy watercolor paper or Bristol
board. Smith then either adds text,
using a 1950s Royal Quiet De Luxe
typewriter, or fastens on 3-D
elements, such as buttons, poker
chips, or letters.

Smith's Cute as a Button new baby
card and Love, Hello, Hi, and Happy
cards use buttons and Scrabble tiles
to spell out their messages. "I love
using 3-D objects to add a little more
dimensionality to a flat card," she
explains. "Finding fun geometric
papers and cardstock then adds
a flourish of color and helps the
letters stand out."

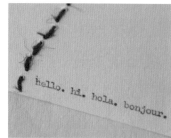

CURIOUS DOODLES

....

PORTLAND, OREGON,
USA

Curious Doodles is run by designer
Laura Trimmell, who produces a
hand-stitched stationery line and
Do It Yourself Stitchies packs. "I am
trying to promote nondigital, slow
communication with my embroidery
card kits. Each kit requires my
customer to add a bit of themselves
with their stitches and the words
they write inside. The finished
product is oh-so-tactile and will be
treasured far longer than a mass-
produced card."

Each card and card pack is made up
of recycled paper and high-quality
embroidery floss. "I originally started
creating hand-stitched cards for my
loved ones, and they were so well
received I decided to expand the line
to make them available for my
customers," says Trimmell.

A QUICK STUDY

··

PHILADELPHIA,
PENNSYLVANIA, USA

Zoe Rooney is the designer behind
A Quick Study, and produces paper
goods dedicated to the tradition of
handwritten communication. "While
I love blogging and the Internet, I don't
think there's any comparison with
writing down messages, thoughts,
and ideas longhand on paper," she
explains. "I've been creating paper
goods for a while but recently I've
been focusing on embroidered paper.
I love the tactile aspects of perforating
the paper using an awl, then pulling
the needle and thread through to
create designs."

Rooney drew these designs in pencil
before using an awl to perforate the
cardstock with evenly spaced holes
along the lines of the letters. She then
stitched two strands of embroidery
floss through the holes. The stitches
Rooney uses most often are back
stitch and chain stitch.

BUNNYFUZZ DESIGNS

KANSAS CITY,
MISSOURI, USA

Bunnyfuzz Designs is run by Molly
Ralston, who creates her stationery
goods using mainly felt, paper, and
thread, and sometimes buttons.
"I am inspired by nature, and
particularly love clouds. My best ideas
are often pretty random ones and
I tend to create spontaneously when
just the right idea strikes me," she
explains. "My clients are those who
still appreciate 'snail mail' and are
looking for something unique to send."

Each of these cards was created by
hand. Ralston used textured card
and then lined each with a smoother
stock more suitable for writing on.
"Hand-stitching adds a quality that
can't be replicated by a machine,"
she adds. "It also allows me to stitch
in greater detail."

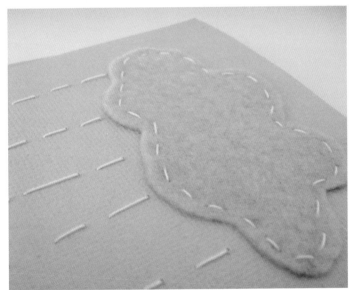

POLKADOTSHOP

TAMPA, FLORIDA,
USA

Tammy Lombardi is the crafter
and maker behind polkadotshop.
She creates greeting cards, gift tags,
and other paper goods by sewing
on paper or fabric and mixing in
hand-drawn details. "I enjoy using
different colors and textures in my
work," she explains. " I love drawing
and my special sketchbook—full
of drawings and sketches of all the
places I have visited—is my main
source of inspiration."

Shown here are her stitched Owl
and Tasty Cupcake cards and
Bunting Banner gift tags. Each one
features the use of collage using
paper, card, or fabric with additional
features added in either ribbon,
chalk, or cotton thread stitches.

MR.PS

....

MANCHESTER, UK

Mr.PS was set up and is run by designer and illustrator Megan Price. As well as paper goods she produces housewares and artworks. All goods in her lines have a distinctive handmade aesthetic, with the use of bright colors and bold text, which take inspiration from vintage signage and British traditions.

Her card line was developed with old-fashioned communication methods in mind. "Today our friendships tend to be scattered around the country and the world. We stay in touch digitally and remotely; by e-mail, Facebook, Twitter," says Price. "While these methods are to be embraced there is something quite joyous about receiving a printed card with a handwritten message."

The letters for each of these cards were screen printed and then cut out and fixed to the cards with glue dots.

COOKIE CUTTER

SINGAPORE

Cookie Cutter is run by Sandy Ng, who loves working with her hands. "Most of the time you'll find me hanging out with my sewing machine in the little work area in my apartment," she explains. "I am deeply in love with Japanese cotton linen but my love for textures extends to paper as well."

Intrigued by the idea of sewing on paper, Ng created this series of notecards. She started by creating the digital artwork and printing the writing lines before machine-sewing each card's border. She then embroidered "Hello" and finished each one off by sewing on two buttons. Ng used a thick, white, textured paper stock that would hold the weight of the buttons and would not tear when sewn.

REWORK STUDIO

ROCHESTER, NEW YORK,
USA

Rework Studio is run by graphic designer Dezirae Moore and came about after many years of playing with paper. "As a graphic designer with an itch for the insanely detailed and handmade, I've maintained a variety of hobbies, most of which incorporate hand lettering, calligraphy, and bookbinding. Most recently, these hobbies have meshed together and resulted in the hand-stitched letters and designs on paper that I make for Rework Studio."

Shown here are Moore's hand-stitched greeting cards. The design for each originated with hand-drawn lettering or artwork that was then transferred onto precut and scored paper. Sewing holes were punched and then each card was individually sewn by hand. "I love the idea of marrying paper and string together to help bring the design off the paper. The texture of the string on paper is surprising yet pleasing," says Moore.

PAPER & TYPE

LOS ANGELES,
CALIFORNIA, USA

This greeting card was made by
graphic designer Victoria Vu of
paper & type (see also pages 24 and
136). It was created for Valentine's
Day but it can be used at any time
of year and for any reason.

"I'd been getting into sewing at the
time I created this card so had an array
of red patterned fabrics. These inspired
the eclectic mix of sewn hearts," explains
Vu. "My plan was to keep the design
simple and the message subtle enough
for it to be used at any time."

LIZZIMARIE

APPLETON, WISCONSIN, USA

Lizzimarie is run by creative crafter Liz Tubman, who enjoys lots of different art forms, including hand-printed and stitched artwork, stationery, and paper goods. "I strive to create unique, handmade, and inspiring pieces that you wouldn't be able to find in a large store," she explains. "I love to create and my goal is to impart that love and inspiration to anyone who comes through my shop."

Shown here are her handcrafted, recycled yellow and blue Bunting notebooks, Japanese-bound Notes notebook, stitched Pinwheel card, and stitched Hello cards.

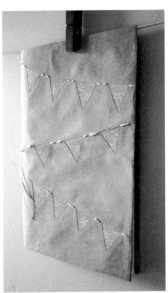

TOKYO CRAFTS
....

SEATTLE, WASHINGTON,
USA

Miki Bloch is the designer and artist behind stationery company Tokyo Crafts. Originally from Tokyo, she now lives in Seattle, where she both runs her company and teaches Japanese art.

"The traditional Japanese technique of origami is my lifelong passion," she explains. "I love to make unique and lovely items. I fold any type of origami you can imagine—including 'modular origami' (also known as 3-D origami)—and make everything with high-quality paper from Japan."

These greeting cards feature her handcrafted origami shapes and characters, including a dachshund and a bulldog.

SARA BALCOMBE

EDMONTON, CANADA

Sara Balcombe is a designer by day and a paper crafter by night. "I like making pretty things and I like doing it in a different way," she explains. "I like taking ordinary tools and, rather than using them for what they were originally intended, I like to use them to make something completely unexpected."

These greeting cards were created using a number of different materials and techniques, including stamps, punches, glue, and chalk pastels mixed with water. "I love stamps and punches because they give you a lovely uniformity to work with," she says. "I also use chalk pastel for color. I use it like paint—you can get really excellent shades and opacities simply by adding less or more water."

CAMPBELL RAW PRESS
NEW YORK, NEW YORK,
USA

Shown here is the work of bookbinder and letterpress printer Maggie Campbell of Campbell Raw Press. She specializes in decorative, exposed bindings and uses a variety of materials, including silk, linen, and cotton cloths, Japanese silk-screened and stenciled papers, acid-free papers, linen thread, ribbons, and vintage stamps.

These journals and albums are made using the "coptic stitch" structure, which is both elegant and sturdy. They feature acid-free materials, including *chiyogami* (Japanese silk-screened papers), bookboard, printmaking papers, and waxed linen thread.

"It's very important to me to create beautiful, unique work that is also functional, lasting, and elegant," explains Campbell. "I want people to enjoy my books for many generations to come."

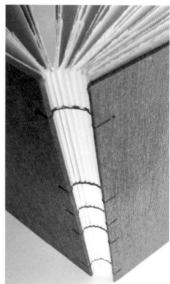

BY BELINDA
....

LOS ANGELES,
CALIFORNIA, USA

By Belinda is owned and run by Belinda Vong. She specializes in hand-embroidered paper art and greeting cards. "I value celebrating the everyday and sharing with people just how special they are to you," she explains. "I create cards that aren't going to be lost in a sea of other cards, get shoved into a box and put away, or tossed into the trash. Instead, they are to be treasured as a piece of art."

Each card she creates starts with an image or a phrase. Vong then hand draws the image onto the card before stitching it. She uses only white thread on colored card. The text is typed out on an electronic typewriter, cut out, and then glued in place.

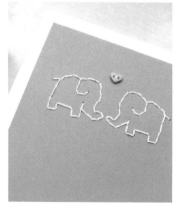

HAVE & HOLD DESIGN

TORONTO, CANADA

These cards are from the Celebrate! collection by designer Samantha Dubeau (see also page 104). Each one was handcrafted and is truly unique.

The cards feature crepe streamers, ribbons, cupcake liners, thread, and various bits of colored paper. "I collaged, punched the confetti, and cut the fringe by hand. I jumped on the sewing machine a few times too," Dubeau explains. "I like to mix things up by incorporating unexpected techniques and elements. It makes the pieces all the more dynamic."

DOGSRULE

VERNON, NEW JERSEY, USA

Janice Lagard of dogsrule is a designer and crafter who specializes in paper goods using the Japanese art of origami. "I like the crispness of the paper folds and the intricate designs that are created from the precise folding and layering," she explains.

The card and gift tags shown here feature origami medallions that were created using a technique sometimes known as "tea bag" folding. They were made using eight hand-cut pieces of French paper that were folded to create a 3-D effect. Lagard then affixed them to the card and tags and gently "lifted" them to add to the effect.

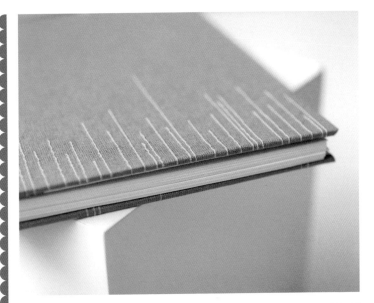

ONE FINE DAE

SEATTLE, WASHINGTON, USA

Shown here are the Remember This album and The City Sleeps notebook by Linda-Thuan Pham (see also page 121). "I've always loved a good notebook and carry one with me everywhere, so it's what I specialize in," she explains. "I'm drawn to simple and modern aesthetics with a dash of vintage charm. I like feeling nostalgic and I hope that my pieces will provoke that same feeling in my customers."

The artwork for these two pieces was created digitally and then printed onto the back of a sheet of book cloth. Pham then used a sewing machine to stitch over the printed design; what you see on the finished product is the front of the book cloth. "I always like to add a bit of texture to my books, to have some sort of tactile feedback," Pham says. "The threaded lines are subtle, yet add detail to the overall design and respond to you when you run your fingers over them."

RESOURCES

SUPPLIERS

PAPER

Alexander Paper Supplies
www.alexanderpapersupplies.co.uk

Antalis
www.antalis.co.uk

California Paper Goods
www.californiapapergoods.com

Crane & Co.
www.crane.com

eco-craft
www.eco-craft.co.uk

The Exotic Paper Company
www.elliepoopaper.co.uk

Finch Paper
www.finchpaper.com

French Paper Company
www.frenchpaper.com

Green Paper Company
www.greenpapercompany.com

Hahnemühle Fine Art
www.hahnemuhledirect.com

JPP (John Purcell Paper)
www.johnpurcell.net

K.W.Doggett Fine Paper
www.kwdoggett.com.au

Kate's Paperie
www.katespaperie.com

Keldon Paper
www.keldonpaper.com

Kelly Paper
www.kellypaper.com

Legion Paper
www.legionpaper.com

Letterpress Paper
www.letterpresspaper.com

The Paper Mill Store
www.thepapermillstore.com

Paper Presentation
www.paperpresentation.com

Paper Source
www.paper-source.com

Vlieger
www.vliegerpapier.nl

LETTERPRESS

Bison Bookbinding & Letterpress
www.bisonbookbinding.com

Box Car Press
www.boxcarpress.com

Briar Press
www.briarpress.org

British Letterpress
www.britishletterpress.co.uk

Elum Letterpress Plates
www.letterpressplates.com

Five Roses
www.fiveroses.org

Hamilton Wood Type
& Printing Museum
www.woodtype.org

I Love Letterpress
www.iloveletterpress.com

Ladies of Letterpress
www.ladiesofletterpress.ning.com

Letterpress Alive
www.letterpressalive.co.uk

NA Graphics
www.nagraph.com

SCREEN PRINTING

Adelco
www.adelco.co.uk

Art 2 Screenprint.com
www.art2screenprint.com

D. Roper Ltd
screenprintsupplies.co.uk

London Screen Service
www.londonscreenservice.co.uk

Nehoc Australia
www.nehoc.com.au

Renaissance Graphic Arts, Inc.
www.printmaking-materials.com

Screen Stretch
www.screenstretch.co.uk

SilkScreeningSupplies.com
www.silkscreeningsupplies.com

Standard Screen
www.standardscreen.com

Victory Factory
www.victoryfactory.com

Wicked Printing Stuff
www.wickedprintingstuff.com

GENERAL ARTS AND CRAFTS

A.I. Friedman
www.aifriedman.com

Clear Bags
www.clearbags.com

Deans Art
www.deansart.com.au

Dick Blick
www.dickblick.com

Eckersley's Art & Craft
www.eckersleys.com.au

eco-craft
www.eco-craft.co.uk

Envelopper Inc
www.envelopperinc.com

Merrypak
www.merrypak.co.za

Mountain Cow
www.mountaincow.com

NA Graphics
www.nagraph.com

Neil's Art Store
www.e-artstore.net

New York Central Art Supply
www.nycentralart.com

Oxford Art Supplies
www.oxfordart.com.au

Paper Convention
www.paperconvention.com

Peter van Ginkel
www.petervanginkel.nl

Simon's Stamps
www.simonstamp.com

Speedball Art
www.speedballart.com

The Square Envelope Company
www.squareenvelope.com.au

Vlieger
www.vliegerpapier.nl

Waste Not Paper
www.wastenotpaper.com

BLOGS AND ONLINE COMMUNITIES

Craftster
www.craftster.org

The Daily Smudge
thedailysmudge.blogspot.com

Design*Sponge
www.designsponge.com

Designers Toolbox
www.designerstoolbox.com

Etsy
www.etsy.com

FPO: For Print Only
www.underconsideration.com/fpo

Lottie Loves
charlotterivers.blogspot.com

Oh Joy!
ohjoy.blogs.com

Oh So Beautiful Paper
www.ohsobeautifulpaper.com

Origami Club
www.en.origami-club.com

Paper Craft Planet
www.papercraftplanet.com

Paper Crave
www.papercrave.com

Poppytalk
poppytalk.blogspot.com

Print & Pattern
printpattern.blogspot.com

Printeresting
www.printeresting.org

Printspecs
print-specs.blogspot.com

Pushing Papers
www.pushing-papers.com

Save Gocco
www.savegocco.com

Snap + Tumble
snapandtumble.blogspot.com

Uppercase
uppercase.squarespace.com

TRADE SHOWS

Autumn Fair International
www.autumnfair.com

Brooklyn Flea
www.brooklynflea.com

The Finders Keepers
www.thefinderskeepers.com

Hong Kong International Stationery Fair
www.hktdc.com/fair/hkstationeryfair-en

Life Instyle
www.lifeinstyle.com.au

National Stationery Show
www.nationalstationeryshow.com

New York International Gift Fair
www.nyigf.com

Printsource New York
www.printsourcenewyork.com

Progressive Greetings Live:
The London International Card Show
www.progressivegreetingslive.co.uk

Pulse
www.pulse-london.com

Reed Gift Fairs
www.reedgiftfairs.com.au

Renegade Craft Fair
www.renegadecraft.com

Spring Fair International
www.springfair.com

Stationery Show
www.stationeryshow.co.uk

Surtex
www.surtex.com

Top Drawer London
www.topdrawer.co.uk

CONTRIBUTOR DETAILS

1canoe2
www.1canoe2.com

Acute & Obtuse
acuteandobtuse.com

Akimbo
www.akimbo.com.au

Allison Cole Illustration
www.allisoncoleillustration.com

Alyssa Nassner
www.alyssanassner.com

amymarcella
www.amymarcella.etsy.com

Andy Pratt
www.andypratt.net

Anja Jane
www.anjajane.com

Anna Fewster / Lampyridae Press
www.annafewster.co.uk

Ashley Pahl Design
www.ashleypahl.com

Brie Harrison
www.briedee.com

Bunnyfuzz Designs
www.bunnyfuzz.etsy.com

By Belinda
bybelinda.etsy.com

Cabin + Cub
www.cabinandcub.com

Campbell Raw Press
www.brooklynbookbinder.com

Cody Haltom
codyhaltom.com

Cookie Cutter
cookiecutteretsy.etsy.com

Corrupiola
corrupiola.com.br

cricicis design
www.cricicisdesign.com

Curious Doodles
www.curiousdoodles.etsy.com

Darling Clementine
www.darlingclementine.no

Dependable Letterpress
www.dependableletterpress.com

dogsrule
www.dogsrule.etsy.com

Drawcity
www.drawcity.etsy.com

DWRI Letterpress
dwriletterpress.net

Egg Press
www.eggpress.com

enormouschampion
enormouschampion.com

Fawnsberg
fawnsberg.myshopify.com

Field Guide Design
fieldguide35.blogspot.com

Fig 2 Design
www.fig2design.com

Flowermill
www.flowermill.co.za

Galison
www.galison.com

Gemma Correll
www.gemmacorrell.com

Gigi Gallery
www.gigigallery.etsy.com

Good On Paper Design
www.goodonpaperdesign.com

Hammerpress
hammerpress.net

Have & Hold Design
www.haveandholddesign.com

heart zeena
zeenashah.com

Heidi Burton
heidiburton.co.uk

Hello Jenuine
www.hellojenuine.com

The Hungary Workshop
thehungryworkshop.com.au

Igloo Letterpress
iglooletterpress.com

The Indigo Bunting
indigobuntingshop.bigcartel.com

INK + WIT
www.inkandwit.com

Jesse Breytenbach
www.jessebreytenbach.co.za

JHill Design
www.jhilldesign.co.uk

Jill Bliss
jillbliss.com

Jo Clark Design
www.joclarkdesign.co.uk

Joie Studio
www.joiestudio.com

K is for Calligraphy
www.kisforcalligraphy.etsy.com

Karolin Schnoor
www.karolinschnoor.com

Katharine Watson
www.katharinewatson.com

Kirtland House Press
www.kirtlandhouse.com

Kristin Carlson
www.kristincarlson.net

la rara
www.la-rara.com

The Left Handed Calligrapher
www.thelefthandedcalligrapher.com

Lizzimarie
www.lizzimarie.etsy.com

Lox+Savvy
www.loxsavvy.com.au

Lucy King
www.lucykingdesign.com

Made by Julene
madebyjulene.com

Mai Autumn
maiautumn.com

Mary & Gabrielle Events
maryandgabrielle.com

May Day Studio
www.maydaystudio.com

me and amber
www.meandamber.com

Meant To Be Calligraphy
www.meanttobecalligraphy.com

Melanie Linder
www.melanielinderillustration.com

Merry Day
merryday.etsy.com

Morris & Essex
www.morrisessex.com

Mr.PS
www.mr-ps.co.uk

MrYen
www.mr-yen.com

Nancy & Betty Studio
www.nancyandbetty.com

Natasha Mileshina / bubbo
www.bubbo.etsy.com

Nora Whynot Paper Goods
www.norawhynot.com.au

O-Check Design Graphics
(Spring come, rain fall)
www.o-check.net

Oh My Deer Handmades
www.ohmydeer.etsy.com

Old Tom Foolery
www.oldtomfoolery.com

One Fine Dae
onefinedae.etsy.com

Painted Fish Studio
paintedfishstudio.com

paper & type
www.paperandtype.com

Paper Path
www.etsy.com/shop/paperpath

Paperfinger
www.paperfinger.com

Papersheep Press
www.papersheeponline.com

Pine Street Makery
www.etsy.com/shop/
pinestreetmakery

Planet Press
www.planetpress.biz

Plurabelle Calligraphy
plurabellecalligraphy.com

polkadotshop
www.etsy.com/shop/polkadotshop

Poppies Flowers
poppiesflowers.com.au

Present & Correct
www.presentandcorrect.com

Primele
primele.com

Publique Living
www.publiqueliving.com

A Quick Study
aquickstudyonline.com

REDSTAR ink
www.redstarink.com

Rework Studio
www.etsy.com/shop/reworkstudio

Ruby Victoria Letterpress
& Printmaking
www.rubyvictoria.etsy.com

Ruby Wren Designs
www.rubywren.com

Sakura Snow
www.sakurasnow.com

Sara Balcombe
sarabalcombe.com

Satsuma Press
www.satsumapress.com

Scout Books
www.scoutbooks.com

Seesaw Designs
www.seesawdesigns.com

Sesame Letterpress
www.sesameletterpress.com

Shanna Murray
shannamurray.com

Shop Toast
www.toast-ed.com

Skinny laMinx
www.skinnylaminx.com

Smock Paper
smockpaper.com

Snap + Tumble
snapandtumble.com

Spring Olive
springolive.com

Sukie
www.sukie.co.uk

Sunlight on Closed Lids
www.sunlightonclosedlids.co.uk

Swiss Cottage Designs
www.swisscottagecustomdesign.com

Thereza Rowe
www.therezarowe.com

These Are Things
thesearethings.com

Tokyo Crafts
www.tokyocrafts.etsy.com

Tuesday Designs
www.tuesdaydesigns.com.au

Vertallee Letterpress
www.vertallee.com

W+K Studio Goodness
wkstudio.bigcartel.com

Will Bryant
willbryant.com

Winged Wheel
www.winged-wheel.co.jp/en/store.html

Wit & Whistle
www.witandwhistle.etsy.com

INDEX